FEDERAL CIVIL PROCEDURE LOGIC MAPS

A COLLECTION OF LOGIC MAPS DESIGNED TO ASSIST IN
THE UNDERSTANDING OF FEDERAL CIVIL PROCEDURE

2ND EDITION

BY

WILLIAM M. JANSSEN
Associate Professor of Law
CHARLESTON SCHOOL OF LAW
Charleston, South Carolina

SERIES EDITOR
SYDNEY A. BECKMAN
Vice President, Dean, and Professor of Law
DUNCAN SCHOOL OF LAW AT LINCOLN MEMORIAL UNIVERSITY
Knoxville, Tennessee

© 2012 by THOMSON REUTERS
    1 New York Plaza, 34th Floor
    New York, NY 10004
    Phone Toll Free (877) 888-1330
    Fax (646) 424-5201
    foundation-press.com
Printed in the United States of America

ISBN: 978-0-314-28511-9

Mat #41331044

How to Use Your *LOGIC MAPS*

Like any study guide for law students, FEDERAL CIVIL PROCEDURE LOGIC MAPS is just a supplement. It will not displace your casebook or your rules book. It will not eliminate your need to study before class, or your pre-examination outlining of your civil procedure course. But what these LOGIC MAPS will do is orient you to the material of the course, its organizing structure (and flow), and the relationships and connections between topics. In this way, these LOGIC MAPS will help you identify the "big picture" of your various civil procedure topics, and then will visually guide you to see the schematic structure within those topics. More simply stated, these LOGIC MAPS ought to help you better see the forest, but without obscuring where all the individual trees are planted. You may find these LOGIC MAPS especially useful for very dense or complicated topics, to help you disassemble those topics into their component parts. However you use these LOGIC MAPS, we hope you find them helpful in mastering the sometimes confusing, and often nuanced, subject of federal civil procedure. Thank you for adding LOGIC MAPS to your study library!

What's New In This SECOND EDITION:

This second edition of FEDERAL CIVIL PROCEDURE LOGIC MAPS is current through Summer 2012. It now includes coverage of (as well as the inserted text of) the *Federal Courts Jurisdiction and Venue Clarification Act*, which took effect in January 2012. This Second Edition also modifies nearly all Maps to incorporate helpful suggestions and recommendations from students, researchers, and scholars.

❧ ❦

More Comments or Suggestions?

The author welcomes your comments, recommendations, and suggestions for improving FEDERAL CIVIL PROCEDURE LOGIC MAPS. Federal civil procedure continues to evolve at a torrid pace, and the author endeavors to keep LOGIC MAPS as useful and reader-friendly as possible. Please send along those suggestions to:

Professor William M. Janssen
CHARLESTON SCHOOL OF LAW
81 Mary Street – Charleston, South Carolina 29403
wjanssen@charlestonlaw.edu

This page left intentionally blank

Author's & Creator's Notes

About the Author of FEDERAL CIVIL PROCEDURE LOGIC MAPS

Professor William M. Janssen is an associate professor of law at the Charleston School of Law in Charleston, South Carolina, where he teaches civil procedure, products liability, and first amendment law. In addition to FEDERAL CIVIL PROCEDURE LOGIC MAPS, he is a co-author of three nationally distributed texts on federal civil procedure – *Federal Civil Rules Handbook* (West); *A Student's Guide to the Federal Rules of Civil Procedure* (West); and *Wright & Miller's Federal Practice and Procedure* (Vol. 12B) (West) – and also an author of numerous articles and book chapters on civil procedure and pharmaceutical/medical device law. He has been honored three times by the Charleston students as their "professor-of-the-year". He joined the Charleston faculty after a lengthy career with an AmLaw-200 law firm in Philadelphia, where he was a litigation partner, chair of the interdisciplinary life sciences practice group, and a member of the firm's executive committee. He received his law degree from the American University – Washington College of Law, and his undergraduate degree in international relations from Saint Joseph's University.

Author Acknowledgements

The author is indebted to Dean Sydney Beckman for his ingenuity and farsightedness in developing the LOGIC MAPS concept. The author acknowledges the memorable "up-sloping" and "down-sloping" terminology used by Professors Richard D. Freer and Wendy Collins Perdue to describe Rule 14(a) claims by and against impleaded parties in CIVIL PROCEDURE: CASES, MATERIALS, AND QUESTIONS (5th ed. 2008); as well as their reference to the "cogent nexus" explanation of "relevance" in discovery offered by Christopher G. Frost in Note, *The Sound and the Fury and the Sound of Silence*, 37 GA. L. REV. 1039, 1067 (Spring 2003). The author thanks Jessica N. Eubanks and Robert P. Varner for their fine editorial assistance with this project.

About the Creator & Editor

Dean Sydney Beckman is the founding Dean and Vice President of the Lincoln Memorial University Duncan School of Law in Knoxville, Tennessee. He had formerly been a faculty member at the Charleston School of Law, an adjunct professor at Texas Wesleyan University School of Law, and in active law practice in Fort Worth, Texas. Dean Beckman received his law degree from Baylor University School of Law and his Bachelor of Arts in Psychology from Stephen F. Austin State University. He has lectured throughout the United States and in Canada on using technology effectively in the classroom and has spoken throughout the years at various law-related functions and CLE activities. Dean Beckman remains committed to using cutting-edge technology in the classroom to maximize student learning.

This page left intentionally blank

TABLE OF CONTENTS

This page left intentionally blank

Legend

The symbols used in the *Federal Civil Procedure Logic Maps* follow the familiar format used generally throughout the *Logic Maps* series, with a few adjustments to accommodate the nature of civil procedure. All symbols should be read carefully, as the results and logic may differ from map to map (i.e., rule to rule).

Blue Indicator This symbol identifies a decision point on the *Logic Map*, a question that, when answered, leads to an outcome or decision.

Green Indicator This symbol identifies a positive or affirmative result that will follow from the decision point discussed.

Red Indicator This symbol identifies a negative result that will follow from the decision point discussed.

Yellow Indicator This symbol identifies a pertinent legal principle or concept derived from the U.S. Constitution, the highest source of federal law.

White Indicator This symbol identifies a pertinent legal principle or concept emanating from the RULES, statutory law, case law, or elsewhere.

Go to Map x.x This symbol directs the reader to a different map. At times, additional logic is required to be able to continue following a particular map. At other times, the resulting logic simply takes the reader to another map for final disposition.

OFFICIAL FORM No. x This symbol refers the reader to the Official Forms that accompany the Federal Rules of Civil Procedure. The significance of the Official Forms is explained in Map 2.4, and the complete set of the Official Forms is reprinted at the end of *Federal Civil Procedure Logic Maps* .

  This symbol points out pitfalls that students commonly make, to assist the reader in avoiding those same mistakes.

 This symbol is designed to warn the reader about the consequences of a certain choice, or to guide away from what may be an incorrect map.

 This symbol is used to direct the student's attention to information that may not be readily apparent, or to provide other relevant information that may be found elsewhere.

  This symbol supplements information with language from the rule

Notes

The Master Map:
The Architecture of a
Federal Civil Lawsuit
Map 1.0

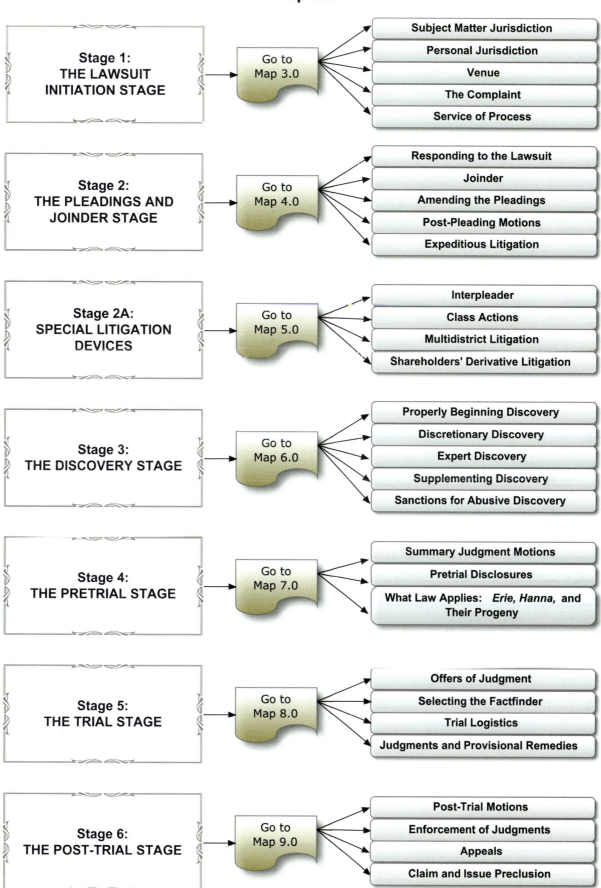

Stage 1:
THE LAWSUIT INITIATION STAGE → Go to Map 3.0 →
- Subject Matter Jurisdiction
- Personal Jurisdiction
- Venue
- The Complaint
- Service of Process

Stage 2:
THE PLEADINGS AND JOINDER STAGE → Go to Map 4.0 →
- Responding to the Lawsuit
- Joinder
- Amending the Pleadings
- Post-Pleading Motions
- Expeditious Litigation

Stage 2A:
SPECIAL LITIGATION DEVICES → Go to Map 5.0 →
- Interpleader
- Class Actions
- Multidistrict Litigation
- Shareholders' Derivative Litigation

Stage 3:
THE DISCOVERY STAGE → Go to Map 6.0 →
- Properly Beginning Discovery
- Discretionary Discovery
- Expert Discovery
- Supplementing Discovery
- Sanctions for Abusive Discovery

Stage 4:
THE PRETRIAL STAGE → Go to Map 7.0 →
- Summary Judgment Motions
- Pretrial Disclosures
- What Law Applies: *Erie, Hanna,* and Their Progeny

Stage 5:
THE TRIAL STAGE → Go to Map 8.0 →
- Offers of Judgment
- Selecting the Factfinder
- Trial Logistics
- Judgments and Provisional Remedies

Stage 6:
THE POST-TRIAL STAGE → Go to Map 9.0 →
- Post-Trial Motions
- Enforcement of Judgments
- Appeals
- Claim and Issue Preclusion

Notes

Preliminaries:
Starting Cautions and Notices
Map 2.0

⚠ CAUTION

Not Legal Advice.

This publication is a study aid for law students. It is not rendering legal or other professional advice, and is not a substitute for the advice of an attorney. If you require legal advice, consult a competent, licensed attorney.

⚠ CAUTION

Not A Substitute For Consulting the Rules.

This publication is designed to assist in understanding how the Federal Rules of Civil Procedure interact and flow. The treatment here is necessarily broad and conceptual. Use this publication as an orientation only. The actual text of the Rules should be consulted when reviewing these *Logic Maps*. Additional, in-depth guidance on the Rules may be found in the official Advisory Committee notes for the Rules, your Civil Procedure casebook, and a hornbook or other sound textual study aid.

⚠ CAUTION

Current as of Summer 2012 (and Dec. 2010 RULES amendments).

The Federal Rules of Civil Procedure are regularly amended. Be sure to consult the most current version of the Rules. This edition of *Federal Civil Procedure Logic Maps* is current through Summer 2012 (including the December 1, 2010 RULES amendments and the January 2012 Venue act).

NOTICE

The Term "RULES".

This publication uses the term **RULES** to refer to the Federal Rules of Civil Procedure.

Notes

Preliminaries:
How the RULES Come to Be
Map 2.1: *U.S. Constitution & 28 U.S.C. § 2072*

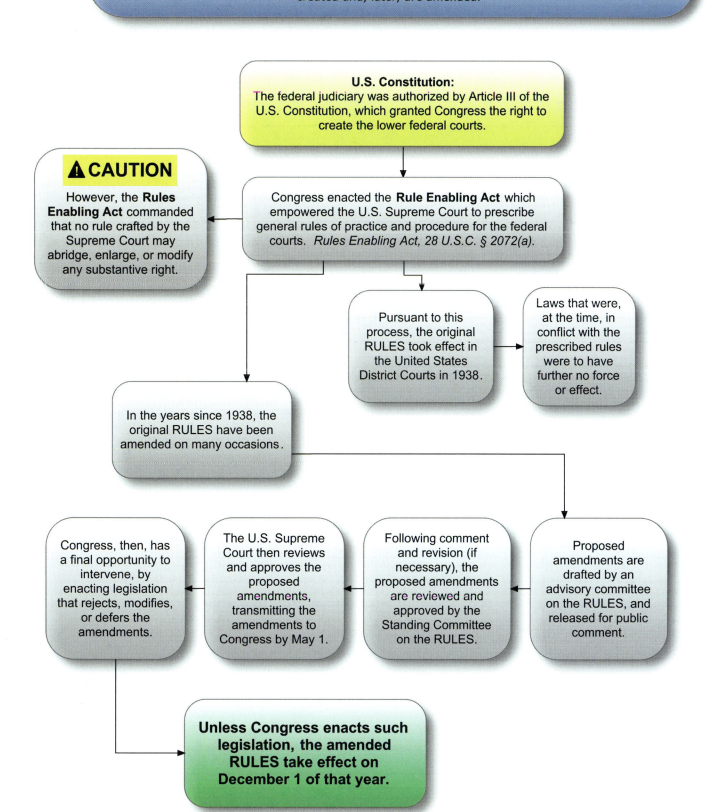

Premise
This Map explains the authority under which the Federal Rules of Civil Procedure (the "RULES") were created and, later, are amended.

U.S. Constitution:
The federal judiciary was authorized by Article III of the U.S. Constitution, which granted Congress the right to create the lower federal courts.

⚠ CAUTION
However, the **Rules Enabling Act** commanded that no rule crafted by the Supreme Court may abridge, enlarge, or modify any substantive right.

Congress enacted the **Rule Enabling Act** which empowered the U.S. Supreme Court to prescribe general rules of practice and procedure for the federal courts. *Rules Enabling Act, 28 U.S.C. § 2072(a).*

Pursuant to this process, the original RULES took effect in the United States District Courts in 1938.

Laws that were, at the time, in conflict with the prescribed rules were to have further no force or effect.

In the years since 1938, the original RULES have been amended on many occasions.

Congress, then, has a final opportunity to intervene, by enacting legislation that rejects, modifies, or defers the amendments.

The U.S. Supreme Court then reviews and approves the proposed amendments, transmitting the amendments to Congress by May 1.

Following comment and revision (if necessary), the proposed amendments are reviewed and approved by the Standing Committee on the RULES.

Proposed amendments are drafted by an advisory committee on the RULES, and released for public comment.

Unless Congress enacts such legislation, the amended RULES take effect on December 1 of that year.

Notes

Preliminaries:
Purpose and Scope of the RULES
Map 2.2: *Fed. R. Civ. P. 1 & 2*

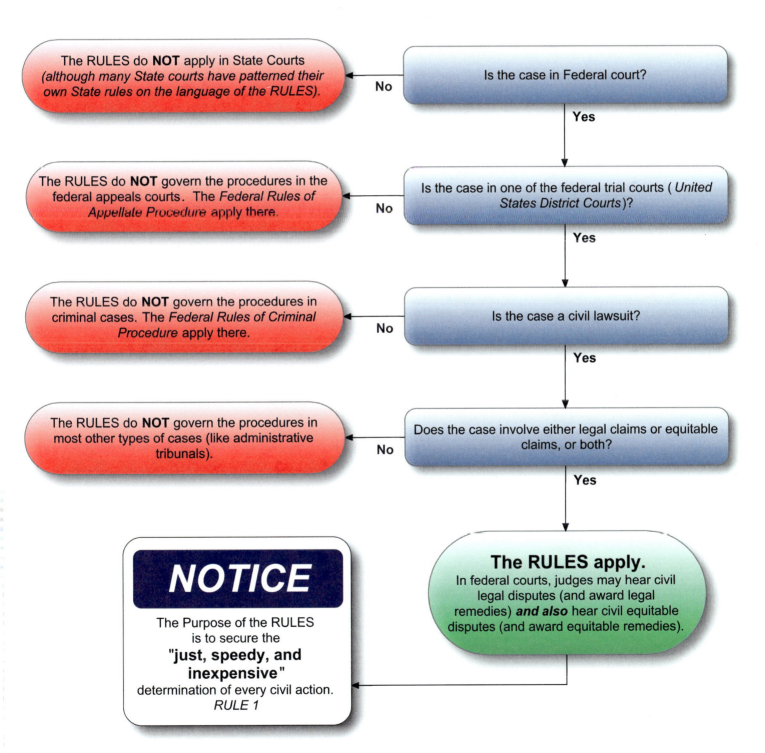

Premise
This Map identifies when the RULES apply, and explains their purpose in civil litigation.

Is the case in Federal court?

No → The RULES do **NOT** apply in State Courts *(although many State courts have patterned their own State rules on the language of the RULES).*

Yes ↓

Is the case in one of the federal trial courts (*United States District Courts*)?

No → The RULES do **NOT** govern the procedures in the federal appeals courts. The *Federal Rules of Appellate Procedure* apply there.

Yes ↓

Is the case a civil lawsuit?

No → The RULES do **NOT** govern the procedures in criminal cases. The *Federal Rules of Criminal Procedure* apply there.

Yes ↓

Does the case involve either legal claims or equitable claims, or both?

No → The RULES do **NOT** govern the procedures in most other types of cases (like administrative tribunals).

Yes ↓

The RULES apply.
In federal courts, judges may hear civil legal disputes (and award legal remedies) ***and also*** hear civil equitable disputes (and award equitable remedies).

NOTICE
The Purpose of the RULES is to secure the
"just, speedy, and inexpensive"
determination of every civil action.
RULE 1

Notes

Preliminaries:
Local Procedures Can Supplement the RULES
Map 2.3: *Fed. R. Civ. P. 83*

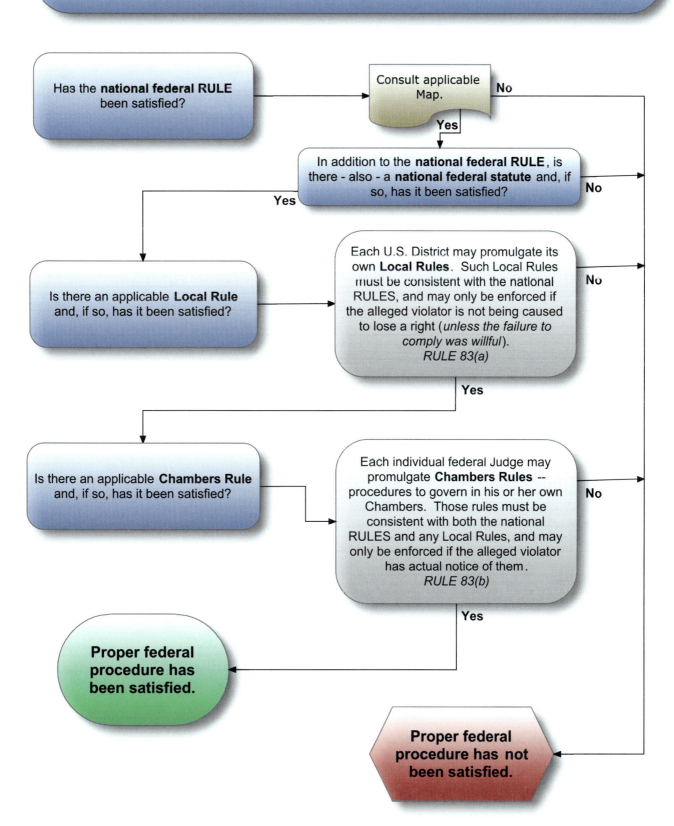

Premise

This Map explains that the RULES are not the only requirements of proper federal procedure. Local Rules and Chambers Rules may supplement the national RULES.

Has the **national federal RULE** been satisfied?

Consult applicable Map.

No

Yes

In addition to the **national federal RULE**, is there - also - a **national federal statute** and, if so, has it been satisfied?

No

Yes

Is there an applicable **Local Rule** and, if so, has it been satisfied?

Each U.S. District may promulgate its own **Local Rules**. Such Local Rules must be consistent with the national RULES, and may only be enforced if the alleged violator is not being caused to lose a right (*unless the failure to comply was willful*).
RULE 83(a)

No

Yes

Is there an applicable **Chambers Rule** and, if so, has it been satisfied?

Each individual federal Judge may promulgate **Chambers Rules** -- procedures to govern in his or her own Chambers. Those rules must be consistent with both the national RULES and any Local Rules, and may only be enforced if the alleged violator has actual notice of them.
RULE 83(b)

No

Yes

Proper federal procedure has been satisfied.

Proper federal procedure has not been satisfied.

Notes

Preliminaries:
Official Forms for the RULES
Map 2.4: *Fed. R. Civ. P. 84*

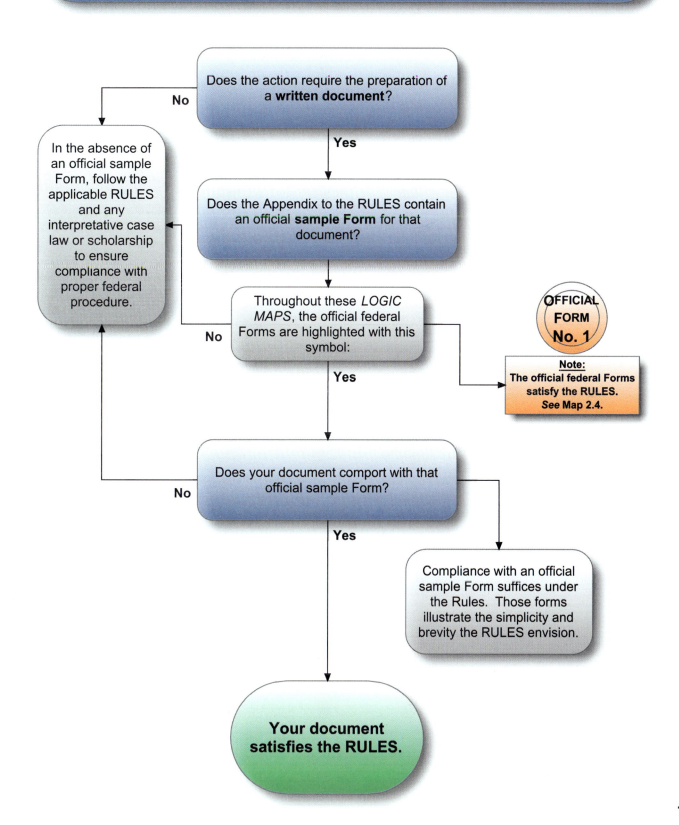

Premise

This Map identifies the official Forms prepared by the drafters of the RULES, and reminds that a compliance with those Forms satisfies the RULES.

Does the action require the preparation of a **written document**?

No

Yes

In the absence of an official sample Form, follow the applicable RULES and any interpretative case law or scholarship to ensure compliance with proper federal procedure.

Does the Appendix to the RULES contain an official **sample Form** for that document?

Throughout these *LOGIC MAPS*, the official federal Forms are highlighted with this symbol:

No

Yes

OFFICIAL FORM No. 1

Note:
The official federal Forms satisfy the RULES.
See Map 2.4.

Does your document comport with that official sample Form?

No

Yes

Compliance with an official sample Form suffices under the Rules. Those forms illustrate the simplicity and brevity the RULES envision.

Your document satisfies the RULES.

Notes

Preliminaries:
Computing Time Under the RULES
Map 2.5: *Fed. R. Civ. P. 6*

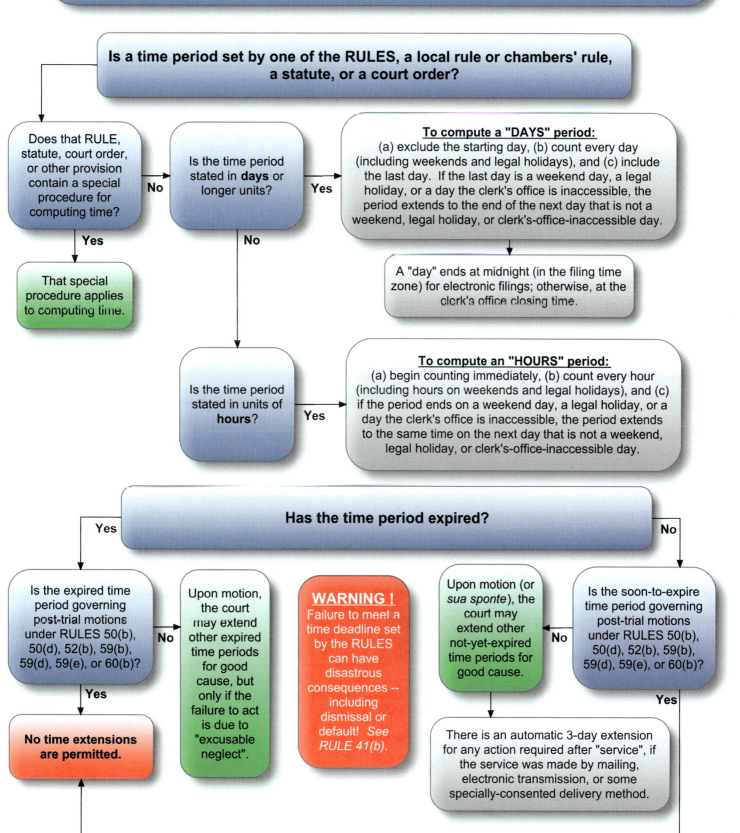

Premise
This Map explains how the time periods set by the RULES are to be counted and, if appropriate, extended.

Is a time period set by one of the RULES, a local rule or chambers' rule, a statute, or a court order?

Does that RULE, statute, court order, or other provision contain a special procedure for computing time?

No →

Is the time period stated in **days** or longer units?

Yes →

To compute a "DAYS" period:
(a) exclude the starting day, (b) count every day (including weekends and legal holidays), and (c) include the last day. If the last day is a weekend day, a legal holiday, or a day the clerk's office is inaccessible, the period extends to the end of the next day that is not a weekend, legal holiday, or clerk's-office-inaccessible day.

A "day" ends at midnight (in the filing time zone) for electronic filings; otherwise, at the clerk's office closing time.

Yes (below "Does that RULE...")

That special procedure applies to computing time.

No (below "Is the time period stated in days...")

Is the time period stated in units of **hours**?

Yes →

To compute an "HOURS" period:
(a) begin counting immediately, (b) count every hour (including hours on weekends and legal holidays), and (c) if the period ends on a weekend day, a legal holiday, or a day the clerk's office is inaccessible, the period extends to the same time on the next day that is not a weekend, legal holiday, or clerk's-office-inaccessible day.

Has the time period expired?

Yes (left) / **No** (right)

Is the expired time period governing post-trial motions under RULES 50(b), 50(d), 52(b), 59(b), 59(d), 59(e), or 60(b)?

No →

Upon motion, the court may extend other expired time periods for good cause, but only if the failure to act is due to "excusable neglect".

WARNING !
Failure to meet a time deadline set by the RULES can have disastrous consequences -- including dismissal or default! *See RULE 41(b).*

Upon motion (or *sua sponte*), the court may extend other not-yet-expired time periods for good cause.

No →

Is the soon-to-expire time period governing post-trial motions under RULES 50(b), 50(d), 52(b), 59(b), 59(d), 59(e), or 60(b)?

Yes (below "Is the expired time period...")

No time extensions are permitted.

Yes (below "Is the soon-to-expire...")

There is an automatic 3-day extension for any action required after "service", if the service was made by mailing, electronic transmission, or some specially-consented delivery method.

Notes

Preliminaries:
Ethics in Federal Civil Litigation, Generally
Map 2.6: *Fed. R. Civ. P. 11 & 28 U.S.C. § 1927*

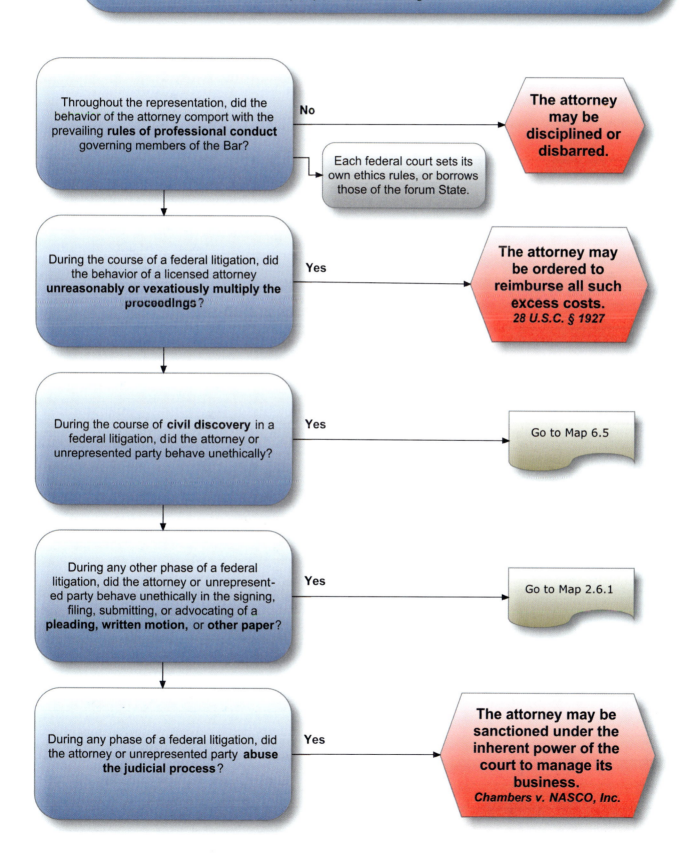

Premise
This Map explains some of the ethical obligations required of every attorney and unrepresented party in federal civil litigation.

Throughout the representation, did the behavior of the attorney comport with the prevailing **rules of professional conduct** governing members of the Bar?

No → **The attorney may be disciplined or disbarred.**

Each federal court sets its own ethics rules, or borrows those of the forum State.

During the course of a federal litigation, did the behavior of a licensed attorney **unreasonably or vexatiously multiply the proceedings**?

Yes → **The attorney may be ordered to reimburse all such excess costs.** *28 U.S.C. § 1927*

During the course of **civil discovery** in a federal litigation, did the attorney or unrepresented party behave unethically?

Yes → Go to Map 6.5

During any other phase of a federal litigation, did the attorney or unrepresented party behave unethically in the signing, filing, submitting, or advocating of a **pleading, written motion,** or **other paper**?

Yes → Go to Map 2.6.1

During any phase of a federal litigation, did the attorney or unrepresented party **abuse the judicial process**?

Yes → **The attorney may be sanctioned under the inherent power of the court to manage its business.** *Chambers v. NASCO, Inc.*

Notes

Preliminaries:
Ethics in Federal Civil Litigation, RULE 11
Map 2.6.1: *Fed. R. Civ. P. 11*

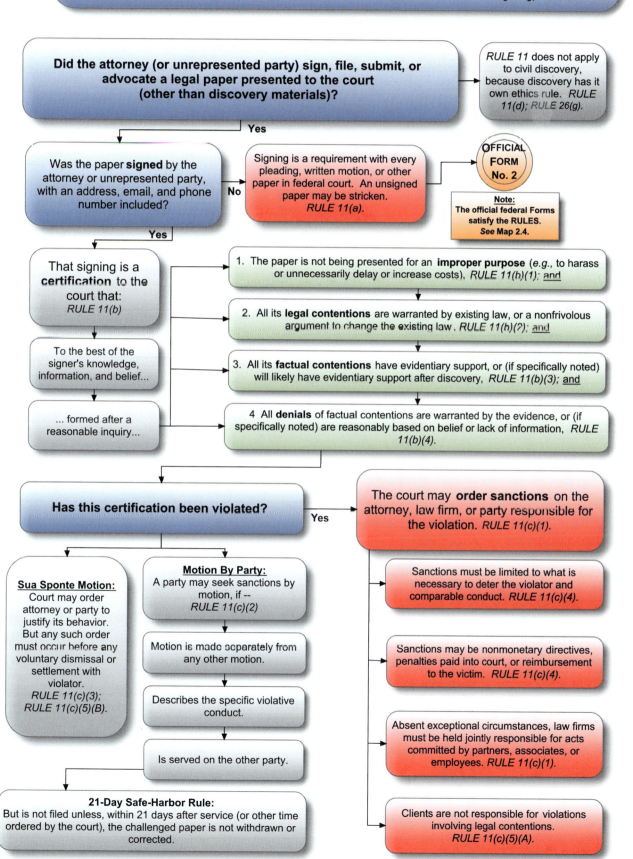

Premise
This Map explains the operation of one of the federal court's core tools to ensure ethical litigating, RULE 11.

Did the attorney (or unrepresented party) sign, file, submit, or advocate a legal paper presented to the court (other than discovery materials)?

RULE 11 does not apply to civil discovery, because discovery has it own ethics rule. *RULE 11(d); RULE 26(g).*

Yes

Was the paper **signed** by the attorney or unrepresented party, with an address, email, and phone number included?

No

Signing is a requirement with every pleading, written motion, or other paper in federal court. An unsigned paper may be stricken. *RULE 11(a).*

OFFICIAL FORM No. 2

Note:
The official federal Forms satisfy the RULES. *See* Map 2.4.

Yes

That signing is a **certification** to the court that: *RULE 11(b)*

1. The paper is not being presented for an **improper purpose** (*e.g.*, to harass or unnecessarily delay or increase costs), *RULE 11(b)(1);* <u>and</u>

To the best of the signer's knowledge, information, and belief...

2. All its **legal contentions** are warranted by existing law, or a nonfrivolous argument to change the existing law, *RULE 11(b)(2);* <u>and</u>

3. All its **factual contentions** have evidentiary support, or (if specifically noted) will likely have evidentiary support after discovery, *RULE 11(b)(3);* <u>and</u>

... formed after a reasonable inquiry...

4 All **denials** of factual contentions are warranted by the evidence, or (if specifically noted) are reasonably based on belief or lack of information, *RULE 11(b)(4).*

Has this certification been violated?

Yes

The court may **order sanctions** on the attorney, law firm, or party responsible for the violation. *RULE 11(c)(1).*

Sua Sponte Motion:
Court may order attorney or party to justify its behavior. But any such order must occur before any voluntary dismissal or settlement with violator. *RULE 11(c)(3); RULE 11(c)(5)(B).*

Motion By Party:
A party may seek sanctions by motion, if -- *RULE 11(c)(2)*

Sanctions must be limited to what is necessary to deter the violator and comparable conduct. *RULE 11(c)(4).*

Motion is made separately from any other motion.

Sanctions may be nonmonetary directives, penalties paid into court, or reimbursement to the victim. *RULE 11(c)(4).*

Describes the specific violative conduct.

Absent exceptional circumstances, law firms must be held jointly responsible for acts committed by partners, associates, or employees. *RULE 11(c)(1).*

Is served on the other party.

21-Day Safe-Harbor Rule:
But is not filed unless, within 21 days after service (or other time ordered by the court), the challenged paper is not withdrawn or corrected.

Clients are not responsible for violations involving legal contentions. *RULE 11(c)(5)(A).*

Notes

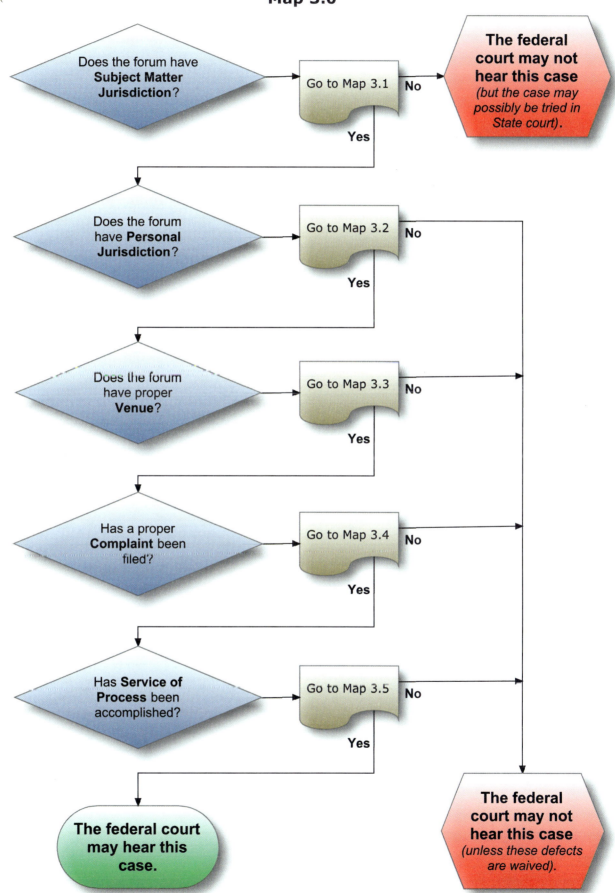

Does the forum have Subject Matter Jurisdiction?

Go to Map 3.1 — No → **The federal court may not hear this case** *(but the case may possibly be tried in State court).*

Yes ↓

Does the forum have Personal Jurisdiction?

Go to Map 3.2 — No →

Yes ↓

Does the forum have proper Venue?

Go to Map 3.3 — No →

Yes ↓

Has a proper Complaint been filed?

Go to Map 3.4 — No →

Yes ↓

Has Service of Process been accomplished?

Go to Map 3.5 — No →

Yes ↓

The federal court may hear this case.

The federal court may not hear this case *(unless these defects are waived).*

Notes

Federal Subject Matter Jurisdiction, Generally
Map 3.1: *U.S. Constitution; 28 U.S.C. §§ 1331-1367*

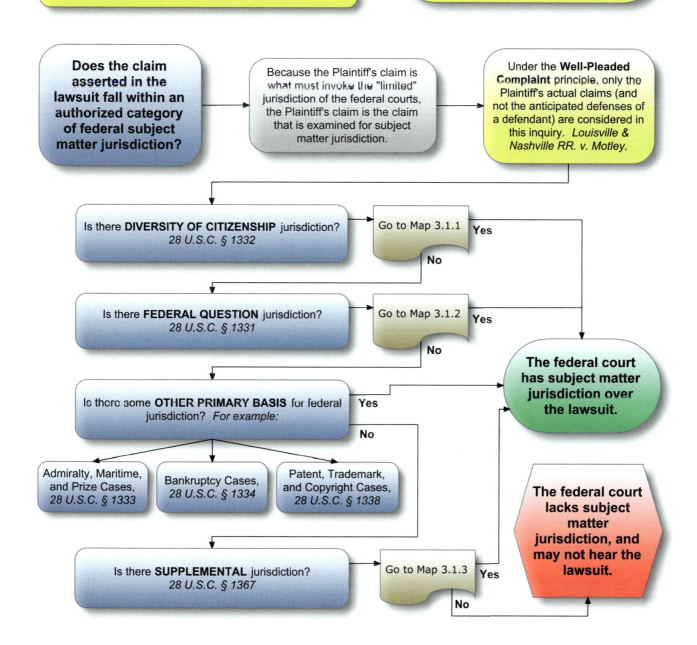

Premise
This Map answers the question from Map 3.0: *Does the Forum Have Subject Matter Jurisdiction?*

U.S. Constitution:
The U.S. Constitution authorizes the federal courts to hear only nine categories of disputes. (Thus, the federal courts are considered courts of "limited" subject matter jurisdiction.

Subject matter jurisdiction is a **structural** limitation. It cannot be consented to, waived, or excused. If this type of jurisdiction is missing, a judgment entered by the federal court would be void.

Although the Nine Heads are constitutional, they are not self-executing. Instead, Congress must enact a statute that invests the federal courts with each type of jurisdiction.

The Nine "Heads" of Federal Jurisdiction
(1) cases arising under the Constitution, federal law, or treaties; (2) case affecting ambassadors; (3) admiralty and maritime cases; (4) controversies where the United States is a party; (5) controversies between States; (6) controversies between a State and citizens of another State; (7) controversies between citizens of different States; (8) certain land-grant controversies; and (9) controversies between a State or its citizens and foreign nations or their citizens.
U.S. Const. art. III, § 2.

Does the claim asserted in the lawsuit fall within an authorized category of federal subject matter jurisdiction?

Because the Plaintiff's claim is what must invoke the "limited" jurisdiction of the federal courts, the Plaintiff's claim is the claim that is examined for subject matter jurisdiction.

Under the **Well-Pleaded Complaint** principle, only the Plaintiff's actual claims (and not the anticipated defenses of a defendant) are considered in this inquiry. *Louisville & Nashville RR. v. Motley.*

Is there **DIVERSITY OF CITIZENSHIP** jurisdiction? *28 U.S.C. § 1332* → Go to Map 3.1.1 — **Yes**
No

Is there **FEDERAL QUESTION** jurisdiction? *28 U.S.C. § 1331* → Go to Map 3.1.2 — **Yes**
No

Is there some **OTHER PRIMARY BASIS** for federal jurisdiction? *For example:* — **Yes**
No

- Admiralty, Maritime, and Prize Cases, *28 U.S.C. § 1333*
- Bankruptcy Cases, *28 U.S.C. § 1334*
- Patent, Trademark, and Copyright Cases, *28 U.S.C. § 1338*

Is there **SUPPLEMENTAL** jurisdiction? *28 U.S.C. § 1367* → Go to Map 3.1.3 — **Yes**
No

The federal court has subject matter jurisdiction over the lawsuit.

The federal court lacks subject matter jurisdiction, and may not hear the lawsuit.

Notes

Diversity of Citizenship Jurisdiction
Map 3.1.1: *28 U.S.C. § 1332; U.S. Constitution*

Premise
This Map answers the question from Map 3.1: *Is there Diversity of Citizenship Jurisdiction?*

Jurisdiction based on **diversity of citizenship** was intended to authorize a neutral federal forum for lawsuits that might be vulnerable to local State court bias against (a) foreign nations and their citizens or (b) citizens of other States.

No

Yes

Requirement #1:
Are the litigants completely diverse?
(Any permutation below is sufficient.)

Diversity must be **COMPLETE:** all parties on one side of the "versus" line must have different citizenships from all parties on the other side. *Strawbridge v. Curtiss.*

Between citizens of different U.S. States?

Between citizens of a U.S. State and citizens or subjects of a foreign Nation?

Between citizens of different U.S. States, with citizens or subjects of a foreign Nation as parties?

Between a plaintiff foreign Nation and citizens of a U.S. State?

INDIVIDUALS are citizens of their place of domicile. (*Aliens having permanent residence are deemed citizens of their State of domicile.*)

LEGAL REPRESENTATIVES are citizens only of the States where their decedent, minor, or incompetent is domiciled.

CORPORATIONS are citizens of *both* their (a) place of incorporation *and* (b) principal place of business (*where officers direct, control, and coordinate company activities*). *28 U.S.C. § 1332(a); Hertz Corp. v. Friend.*

UNINCORPORATED BUSINESSES are citizens of each State where any partner or member is domiciled.

Citizenship is measured at the time the lawsuit is filed. So long as it is not collusive or fraudulent, a post-filing change in citizenship does not affect jurisdiction.

Requirement #2:
Is the Amount-In-Controversy met?

In testing for Amount-in-Controversy, the sum the Plaintiff claims will be accepted, unless it is not made in **apparent good faith** or the court finds, to a legal certainty, that it is **overstated**. *St. Paul Mercury Indemn. Co. v. Red Cab Co.*

Does the claim *exceed $75,000, exclusive of interest and costs?*

No

Yes

A single plaintiff suing a single defendant (or several joint-tortfeasors) may **aggregate** multiple claims to reach the Amount-in-Controversy threshold.

There is no diversity of citizenship jurisdiction.

Diversity of citizenship jurisdiction exists.

Notes

Federal Question Jurisdiction
Map 3.1.2: *28 U.S.C. § 1331; U.S. Constitution*

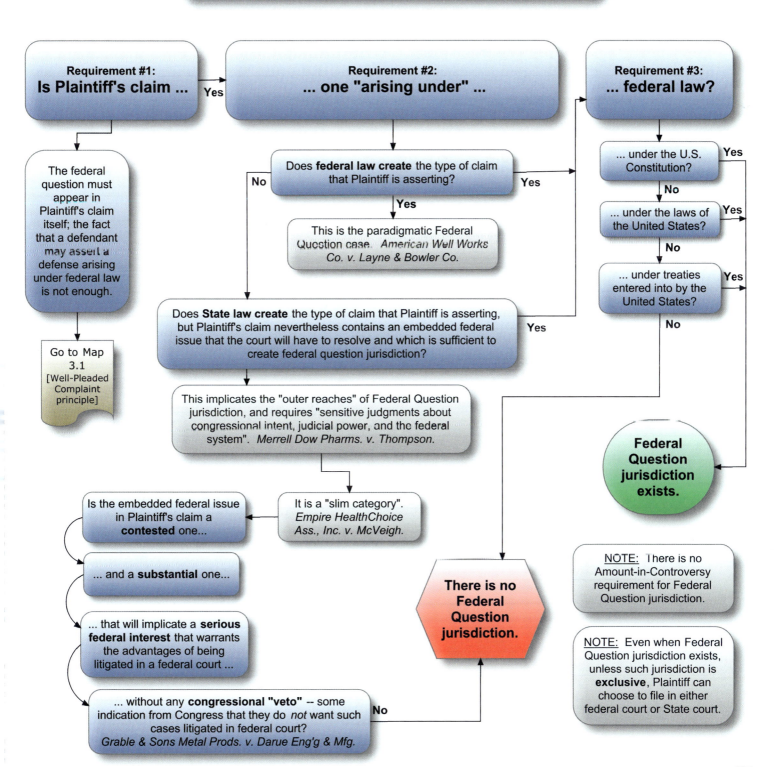

Premise
This Map answers the question from Map 3.1: *Is there Federal Question Jurisdiction?*

Jurisdiction over cases "arising under" federal law is the first of the "Nine Heads" of constitutional jurisdiction. It was intended to ensure the presence of a forum familiar with and expert in federal law, with a judiciary envisioned to be more inclined to apply fully and faithfully those federal laws.

Requirement #1:
Is Plaintiff's claim ...
Yes →

Requirement #2:
... one "arising under" ...

Requirement #3:
... federal law?

The federal question must appear in Plaintiff's claim itself; the fact that a defendant may assert a defense arising under federal law is not enough.

Go to Map 3.1 [Well-Pleaded Complaint principle]

Does **federal law create** the type of claim that Plaintiff is asserting?
No / Yes

This is the paradigmatic Federal Question case. *American Well Works Co. v. Layne & Bowler Co.*

Does **State law create** the type of claim that Plaintiff is asserting, but Plaintiff's claim nevertheless contains an embedded federal issue that the court will have to resolve and which is sufficient to create federal question jurisdiction?
Yes

This implicates the "outer reaches" of Federal Question jurisdiction, and requires "sensitive judgments about congressional intent, judicial power, and the federal system". *Merrell Dow Pharms. v. Thompson.*

... under the U.S. Constitution? — Yes
No
... under the laws of the United States? — Yes
No
... under treaties entered into by the United States? — Yes
No

Federal Question jurisdiction exists.

Is the embedded federal issue in Plaintiff's claim a **contested** one...

... and a **substantial** one...

... that will implicate a **serious federal interest** that warrants the advantages of being litigated in a federal court ...

... without any **congressional "veto"** -- some indication from Congress that they do *not* want such cases litigated in federal court?
Grable & Sons Metal Prods. v. Darue Eng'g & Mfg.
No

It is a "slim category". *Empire HealthChoice Ass., Inc. v. McVeigh.*

There is no Federal Question jurisdiction.

NOTE: There is no Amount-in-Controversy requirement for Federal Question jurisdiction.

NOTE: Even when Federal Question jurisdiction exists, unless such jurisdiction is **exclusive**, Plaintiff can choose to file in either federal court or State court.

Notes

Supplemental Jurisdiction
Map 3.1.3: *28 U.S.C. § 1367; U.S. Constitution*

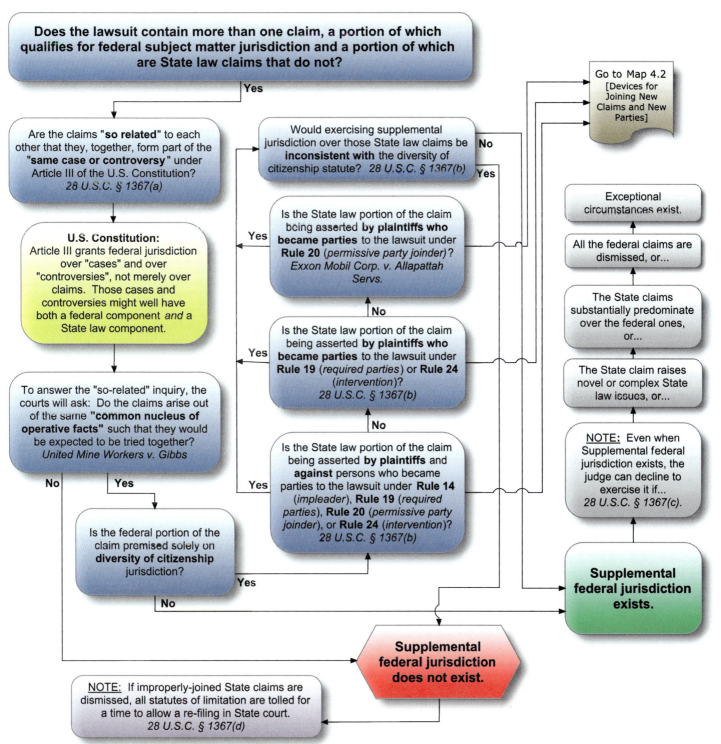

Premise

This Map answers the question from Map 3.1: *Is there Supplemental Jurisdiction?*

When a State law claim (over which there would not be subject matter jurisdiction in federal court) is sufficiently related to a claim that qualifies for federal subject matter jurisdiction, the federal court may accept jurisdiction over the entire dispute and hear both claims. The purpose for this "**supplemental**" jurisdiction is efficiency, convenience, and (in many instances) fairness.

Does the lawsuit contain more than one claim, a portion of which qualifies for federal subject matter jurisdiction and a portion of which are State law claims that do not?

Yes

Go to Map 4.2
[Devices for Joining New Claims and New Parties]

Are the claims "**so related**" to each other that they, together, form part of the "**same case or controversy**" under Article III of the U.S. Constitution? *28 U.S.C. § 1367(a)*

Would exercising supplemental jurisdiction over those State law claims be **inconsistent with** the diversity of citizenship statute? *28 U.S.C. § 1367(b)*

No

Yes

U.S. Constitution:
Article III grants federal jurisdiction over "cases" and over "controversies", not merely over claims. Those cases and controversies might well have both a federal component *and* a State law component.

Is the State law portion of the claim being asserted **by plaintiffs who became parties** to the lawsuit under **Rule 20** (*permissive party joinder*)? *Exxon Mobil Corp. v. Allapattah Servs.*

Yes

No

Exceptional circumstances exist.

All the federal claims are dismissed, or...

To answer the "so-related" inquiry, the courts will ask: Do the claims arise out of the same "**common nucleus of operative facts**" such that they would be expected to be tried together? *United Mine Workers v. Gibbs*

Is the State law portion of the claim being asserted **by plaintiffs who became parties** to the lawsuit under **Rule 19** (*required parties*) or **Rule 24** (*intervention*)? *28 U.S.C. § 1367(b)*

Yes

No

The State claims substantially predominate over the federal ones, or...

The State claim raises novel or complex State law issues, or...

No

Yes

Is the federal portion of the claim premised solely on **diversity of citizenship** jurisdiction?

Is the State law portion of the claim being asserted **by plaintiffs** and **against** persons who became parties to the lawsuit under **Rule 14** (*impleader*), **Rule 19** (*required parties*), **Rule 20** (*permissive party joinder*), or **Rule 24** (*intervention*)? *28 U.S.C. § 1367(b)*

Yes

<u>NOTE:</u> Even when Supplemental federal jurisdiction exists, the judge can decline to exercise it if... *28 U.S.C. § 1367(c).*

Yes

No

Supplemental federal jurisdiction exists.

Supplemental federal jurisdiction does not exist.

<u>NOTE:</u> If improperly-joined State claims are dismissed, all statutes of limitation are tolled for a time to allow a re-filing in State court. *28 U.S.C. § 1367(d)*

Notes

Making the Federal/State Court Choice (+ Removal)

Map 3.1.4: *28 U.S.C. §§ 1441, 1446, & 1447*

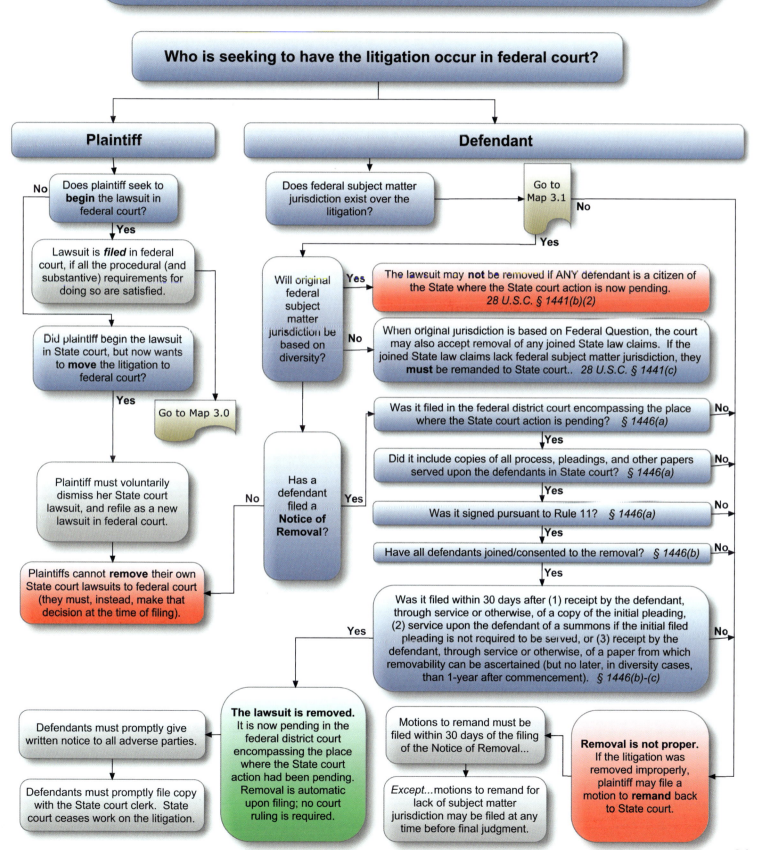

Premise

This Map closes the question from Map 3.1 (*Is There Federal Question Jurisdiction?*), by explaining how the federal court *versus* state court decisions are made.

Who is seeking to have the litigation occur in federal court?

Plaintiff

No — Does plaintiff seek to **begin** the lawsuit in federal court?

Yes

Lawsuit is *filed* in federal court, if all the procedural (and substantive) requirements for doing so are satisfied.

Did plaintiff begin the lawsuit in State court, but now wants to **move** the litigation to federal court?

Yes

Go to Map 3.0

Plaintiff must voluntarily dismiss her State court lawsuit, and refile as a new lawsuit in federal court.

Plaintiffs cannot **remove** their own State court lawsuits to federal court (they must, instead, make that decision at the time of filing).

Defendant

Does federal subject matter jurisdiction exist over the litigation?

Go to Map 3.1 — **No**

Yes

Will original federal subject matter jurisdiction be based on diversity?

Yes — The lawsuit may **not** be removed if ANY defendant is a citizen of the State where the State court action is now pending. *28 U.S.C. § 1441(b)(2)*

No — When original jurisdiction is based on Federal Question, the court may also accept removal of any joined State law claims. If the joined State law claims lack federal subject matter jurisdiction, they **must** be remanded to State court.. *28 U.S.C. § 1441(c)*

Has a defendant filed a **Notice of Removal**?

No

Yes — Was it filed in the federal district court encompassing the place where the State court action is pending? *§ 1446(a)* — **No**

Yes

Did it include copies of all process, pleadings, and other papers served upon the defendants in State court? *§ 1446(a)* — **No**

Yes

Was it signed pursuant to Rule 11? *§ 1446(a)* — **No**

Yes

Have all defendants joined/consented to the removal? *§ 1446(b)* — **No**

Yes

Was it filed within 30 days after (1) receipt by the defendant, through service or otherwise, of a copy of the initial pleading, (2) service upon the defendant of a summons if the initial filed pleading is not required to be served, or (3) receipt by the defendant, through service or otherwise, of a paper from which removability can be ascertained (but no later, in diversity cases, than 1-year after commencement). *§ 1446(b)-(c)*

Yes / **No**

Defendants must promptly give written notice to all adverse parties.

Defendants must promptly file copy with the State court clerk. State court ceases work on the litigation.

The lawsuit is removed. It is now pending in the federal district court encompassing the place where the State court action had been pending. Removal is automatic upon filing; no court ruling is required.

Motions to remand must be filed within 30 days of the filing of the Notice of Removal...

Except... motions to remand for lack of subject matter jurisdiction may be filed at any time before final judgment.

Removal is not proper. If the litigation was removed improperly, plaintiff may file a motion to **remand** back to State court.

Notes

Personal Jurisdiction, Generally
Map 3.2: *U.S. Constitution*

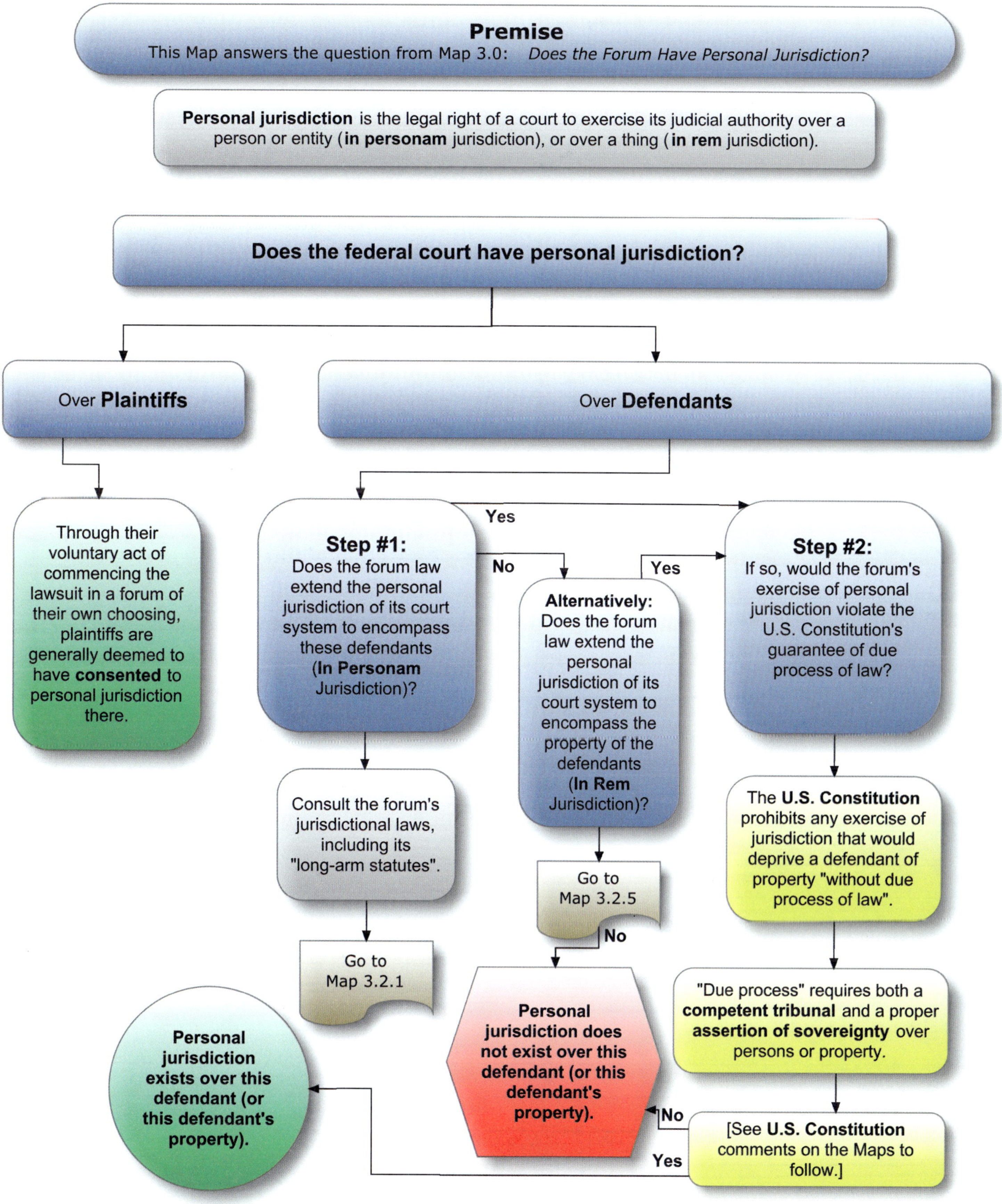

Premise

This Map answers the question from Map 3.0: *Does the Forum Have Personal Jurisdiction?*

Personal jurisdiction is the legal right of a court to exercise its judicial authority over a person or entity (**in personam** jurisdiction), or over a thing (**in rem** jurisdiction).

Does the federal court have personal jurisdiction?

Over **Plaintiffs**

Over **Defendants**

Through their voluntary act of commencing the lawsuit in a forum of their own choosing, plaintiffs are generally deemed to have **consented** to personal jurisdiction there.

Step #1:
Does the forum law extend the personal jurisdiction of its court system to encompass these defendants (**In Personam** Jurisdiction)?

Yes

No

Alternatively:
Does the forum law extend the personal jurisdiction of its court system to encompass the property of the defendants (**In Rem** Jurisdiction)?

Yes

Step #2:
If so, would the forum's exercise of personal jurisdiction violate the U.S. Constitution's guarantee of due process of law?

Consult the forum's jurisdictional laws, including its "long-arm statutes".

Go to Map 3.2.5

The **U.S. Constitution** prohibits any exercise of jurisdiction that would deprive a defendant of property "without due process of law".

Go to Map 3.2.1

No

"Due process" requires both a **competent tribunal** and a proper **assertion of sovereignty** over persons or property.

Personal jurisdiction does not exist over this defendant (or this defendant's property).

Personal jurisdiction exists over this defendant (or this defendant's property).

No

[See **U.S. Constitution** comments on the Maps to follow.]

Yes

Notes

In Personam Jurisdiction
Map 3.2.1: *Fed. R. Civ. P. 4(k)*

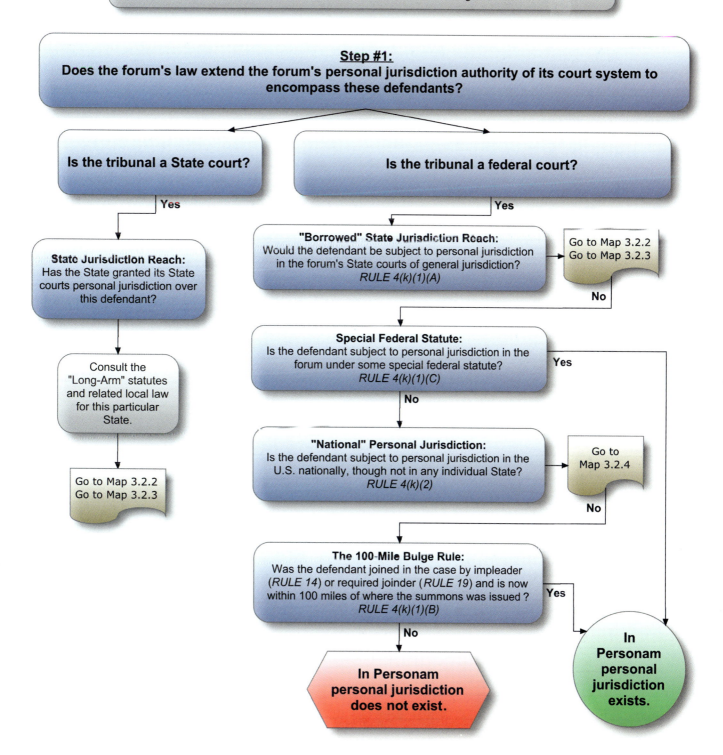

Premise
This Map explains the first step from Map 3.2, the laws by which the U.S. Congress has extended the **In Personam** personal jurisdiction of the federal court system.

In Personam jurisdiction is jurisdiction over the person. Once validly entered, a judgment In Personam follows the defendant throughout the U.S., and can be enforced anywhere in the U.S. pursuant to the Constitution's "Full Faith and Credit" guarantee.

Step #1:
Does the forum's law extend the forum's personal jurisdiction authority of its court system to encompass these defendants?

Is the tribunal a State court?

Yes

State Jurisdiction Reach:
Has the State granted its State courts personal jurisdiction over this defendant?

Consult the "Long-Arm" statutes and related local law for this particular State.

Go to Map 3.2.2
Go to Map 3.2.3

Is the tribunal a federal court?

Yes

"Borrowed" State Jurisdiction Reach:
Would the defendant be subject to personal jurisdiction in the forum's State courts of general jurisdiction?
RULE 4(k)(1)(A)

Go to Map 3.2.2
Go to Map 3.2.3

No

Special Federal Statute:
Is the defendant subject to personal jurisdiction in the forum under some special federal statute?
RULE 4(k)(1)(C)

Yes

No

"National" Personal Jurisdiction:
Is the defendant subject to personal jurisdiction in the U.S. nationally, though not in any individual State?
RULE 4(k)(2)

Go to Map 3.2.4

No

The 100-Mile Bulge Rule:
Was the defendant joined in the case by impleader (*RULE 14*) or required joinder (*RULE 19*) and is now within 100 miles of where the summons was issued?
RULE 4(k)(1)(B)

Yes

No

In Personam personal jurisdiction does not exist.

In Personam personal jurisdiction exists.

Notes

In Personam Jurisdiction - Reach of State Jurisdiction

Map 3.2.2: *U.S. Constitution; Rule 4(k)*

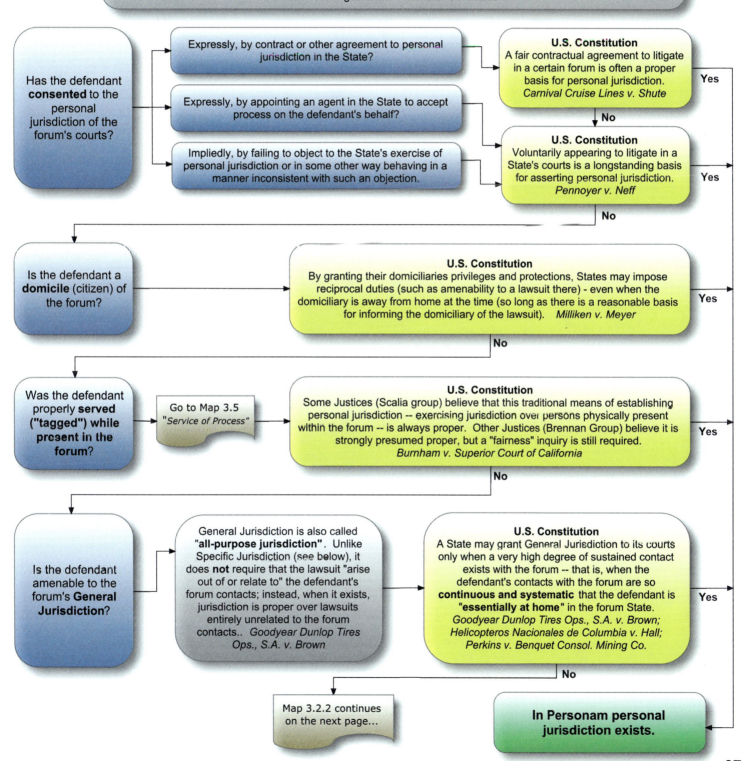

Premise

This Map expands upon the first of the four ways in which a federal court may acquire In Personam personal jurisdiction over a defendant - namely, by "borrowing" the State personal jurisdiction law of the forum. *RULE 4(k)(1)(A).*

The "reach" of each State's personal jurisdiction varies -- because the government of each State is entitled to set that reach (most often by State statute) to align with that State's internal policy choices. This Map highlights five common approaches States have used to define the **in personam** jurisdictional reach of their court systems. Because the actual particular approaches vary widely, State to State, this Map charts only the general contours of these five approaches, but also notes the outer limits (that is, the maximum permitted reach) of such State judicial power, as constrained by the Due Process guarantee in the U.S. Constitution.

Has the defendant consented to the personal jurisdiction of the forum's courts?

- Expressly, by contract or other agreement to personal jurisdiction in the State?
- Expressly, by appointing an agent in the State to accept process on the defendant's behalf?
- Impliedly, by failing to object to the State's exercise of personal jurisdiction or in some other way behaving in a manner inconsistent with such an objection.

U.S. Constitution
A fair contractual agreement to litigate in a certain forum is often a proper basis for personal jurisdiction. *Carnival Cruise Lines v. Shute* — **Yes**

No

U.S. Constitution
Voluntarily appearing to litigate in a State's courts is a longstanding basis for asserting personal jurisdiction. *Pennoyer v. Neff* — **Yes**

No

Is the defendant a domicile (citizen) of the forum?

U.S. Constitution
By granting their domiciliaries privileges and protections, States may impose reciprocal duties (such as amenability to a lawsuit there) - even when the domiciliary is away from home at the time (so long as there is a reasonable basis for informing the domiciliary of the lawsuit). *Milliken v. Meyer* — **Yes**

No

Was the defendant properly served ("tagged") while present in the forum?

Go to Map 3.5 *"Service of Process"*

U.S. Constitution
Some Justices (Scalia group) believe that this traditional means of establishing personal jurisdiction -- exercising jurisdiction over persons physically present within the forum -- is always proper. Other Justices (Brennan Group) believe it is strongly presumed proper, but a "fairness" inquiry is still required. *Burnham v. Superior Court of California* — **Yes**

No

Is the defendant amenable to the forum's General Jurisdiction?

General Jurisdiction is also called **"all-purpose jurisdiction"**. Unlike Specific Jurisdiction (see below), it does **not** require that the lawsuit "arise out of or relate to" the defendant's forum contacts; instead, when it exists, jurisdiction is proper over lawsuits entirely unrelated to the forum contacts.. *Goodyear Dunlop Tires Ops., S.A. v. Brown*

U.S. Constitution
A State may grant General Jurisdiction to its courts only when a very high degree of sustained contact exists with the forum -- that is, when the defendant's contacts with the forum are so **continuous and systematic** that the defendant is **"essentially at home"** in the forum State. *Goodyear Dunlop Tires Ops., S.A. v. Brown; Helicopteros Nacionales de Columbia v. Hall; Perkins v. Benquet Consol. Mining Co.* — **Yes**

No

Map 3.2.2 continues on the next page...

In Personam personal jurisdiction exists.

Notes

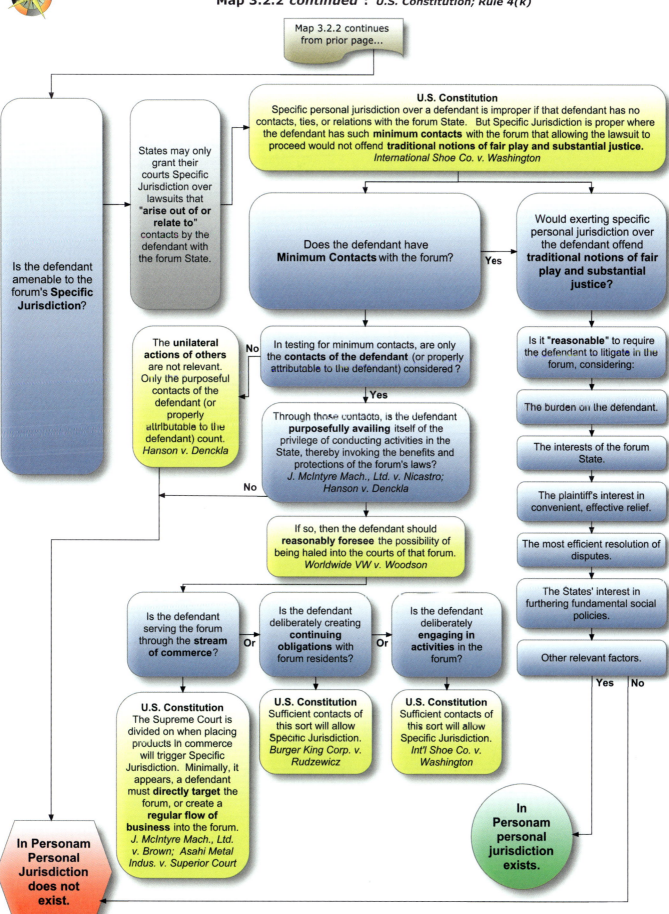

Map 3.2.2 continues from prior page...

U.S. Constitution
Specific personal jurisdiction over a defendant is improper if that defendant has no contacts, ties, or relations with the forum State. But Specific Jurisdiction is proper where the defendant has such **minimum contacts** with the forum that allowing the lawsuit to proceed would not offend **traditional notions of fair play and substantial justice.** *International Shoe Co. v. Washington*

Is the defendant amenable to the forum's **Specific Jurisdiction**?

States may only grant their courts Specific Jurisdiction over lawsuits that **"arise out of or relate to"** contacts by the defendant with the forum State.

Does the defendant have **Minimum Contacts** with the forum?

Would exerting specific personal jurisdiction over the defendant offend **traditional notions of fair play and substantial justice?**

The **unilateral actions of others** are not relevant. Only the purposeful contacts of the defendant (or properly attributable to the defendant) count. *Hanson v. Denckla*

No — In testing for minimum contacts, are only the **contacts of the defendant** (or properly attributable to the defendant) considered?

Yes — Is it **"reasonable"** to require the defendant to litigate in the forum, considering:

Yes

Through those contacts, is the defendant **purposefully availing** itself of the privilege of conducting activities in the State, thereby invoking the benefits and protections of the forum's laws? *J. McIntyre Mach., Ltd. v. Nicastro; Hanson v. Denckla*

No

The burden on the defendant.

The interests of the forum State.

The plaintiff's interest in convenient, effective relief.

If so, then the defendant should **reasonably foresee** the possibility of being haled into the courts of that forum. *Worldwide VW v. Woodson*

The most efficient resolution of disputes.

The States' interest in furthering fundamental social policies.

Is the defendant serving the forum through the **stream of commerce**?

Or

Is the defendant deliberately creating **continuing obligations** with forum residents?

Or

Is the defendant deliberately **engaging in activities** in the forum?

Other relevant factors.

Yes | **No**

U.S. Constitution
The Supreme Court is divided on when placing products in commerce will trigger Specific Jurisdiction. Minimally, it appears, a defendant must **directly target** the forum, or create a **regular flow of business** into the forum. *J. McIntyre Mach., Ltd. v. Brown; Asahi Metal Indus. v. Superior Court*

U.S. Constitution
Sufficient contacts of this sort will allow Specific Jurisdiction. *Burger King Corp. v. Rudzewicz*

U.S. Constitution
Sufficient contacts of this sort will allow Specific Jurisdiction. *Int'l Shoe Co. v. Washington*

In Personam personal jurisdiction exists.

In Personam Personal Jurisdiction does not exist.

Notes

Internet-Based Personal Jurisdiction

Map 3.2.3: *U.S. Constitution; Rule 4(k)*

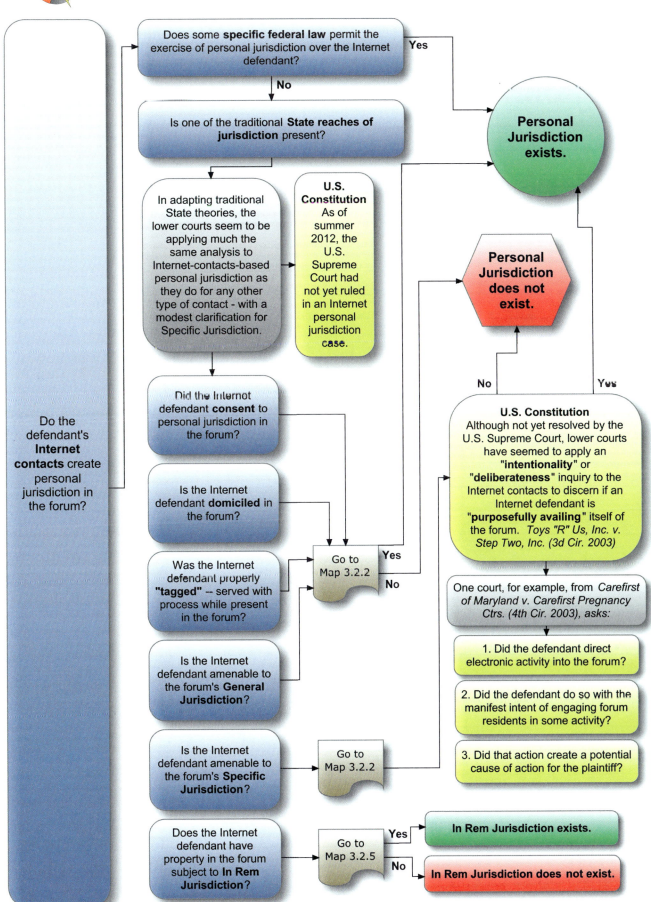

Do the defendant's Internet contacts create personal jurisdiction in the forum?

Does some **specific federal law** permit the exercise of personal jurisdiction over the Internet defendant?

— Yes → **Personal Jurisdiction exists.**

↓ No

Is one of the traditional **State reaches of jurisdiction** present?

In adapting traditional State theories, the lower courts seem to be applying much the same analysis to Internet-contacts-based personal jurisdiction as they do for any other type of contact - with a modest clarification for Specific Jurisdiction.

U.S. Constitution As of summer 2012, the U.S. Supreme Court had not yet ruled in an Internet personal jurisdiction case.

Did the Internet defendant **consent** to personal jurisdiction in the forum?

Is the Internet defendant **domiciled** in the forum?

Was the Internet defendant properly **"tagged"** -- served with process while present in the forum?

Is the Internet defendant amenable to the forum's **General Jurisdiction**?

Go to Map 3.2.2 — Yes → **Personal Jurisdiction exists.**

No →

U.S. Constitution Although not yet resolved by the U.S. Supreme Court, lower courts have seemed to apply an **"intentionality"** or **"deliberateness"** inquiry to the Internet contacts to discern if an Internet defendant is **"purposefully availing"** itself of the forum. *Toys "R" Us, Inc. v. Step Two, Inc. (3d Cir. 2003)*

No → **Personal Jurisdiction does not exist.**

Yes →

Is the Internet defendant amenable to the forum's **Specific Jurisdiction**?

Go to Map 3.2.2

One court, for example, from *Carefirst of Maryland v. Carefirst Pregnancy Ctrs. (4th Cir. 2003), asks:*

1. Did the defendant direct electronic activity into the forum?

2. Did the defendant do so with the manifest intent of engaging forum residents in some activity?

3. Did that action create a potential cause of action for the plaintiff?

Does the Internet defendant have property in the forum subject to **In Rem Jurisdiction**?

Go to Map 3.2.5 — Yes → **In Rem Jurisdiction exists.**

No → **In Rem Jurisdiction does not exist.**

Notes

"National" Personal Jurisdiction
Map 3.2.4: *U.S. Constitution; Rule 4(k)(2)*

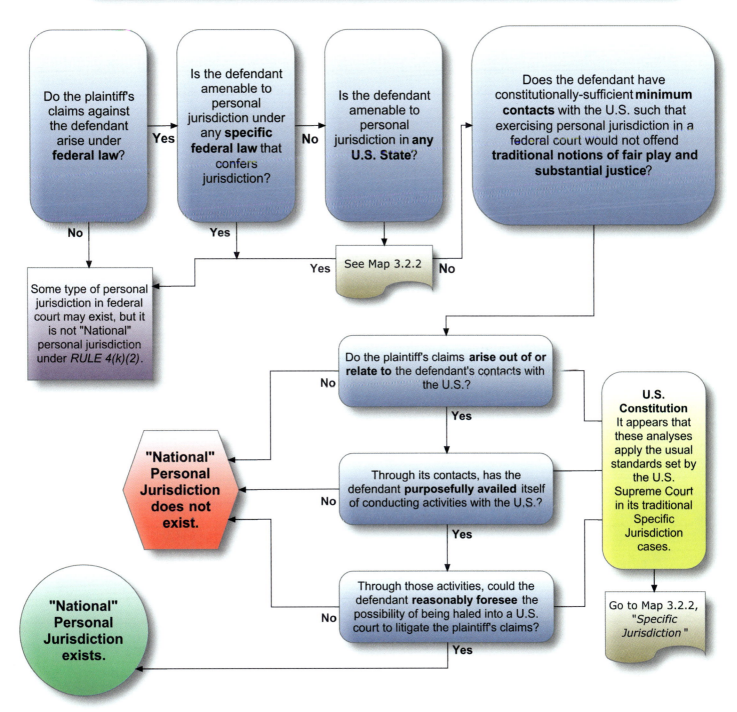

Premise

This Map expands upon the third of the four ways in which a federal court may acquire In Personam personal jurisdiction over a defendant - namely, by asserting "national" personal jurisdiction over a defendant.   *RULE 4(k)(2).*

It is possible that a defendant may have constitutionally-sufficient contacts with the United States generally, but lack adequate contacts to confer personal jurisdiction on any particular State. (For example, an Internet merchant from China may be deliberately, purposefully attempting to exploit the U.S. market to sell its goods, yet have no intent to "aim" its efforts at any one State.) "National" person jurisdiction fills a part of this gap.

Do the plaintiff's claims against the defendant arise under **federal law**?

Yes → Is the defendant amenable to personal jurisdiction under any **specific federal law** that confers jurisdiction?

No → Is the defendant amenable to personal jurisdiction in **any U.S. State**?

No → Does the defendant have constitutionally-sufficient **minimum contacts** with the U.S. such that exercising personal jurisdiction in a federal court would not offend **traditional notions of fair play and substantial justice**?

No (from first box)

Yes (from second box)

Yes → See Map 3.2.2 ← **No** (from third box)

Some type of personal jurisdiction in federal court may exist, but it is not "National" personal jurisdiction under *RULE 4(k)(2)*.

Do the plaintiff's claims **arise out of or relate to** the defendant's contacts with the U.S.?

No → "National" Personal Jurisdiction does not exist.

Yes ↓

Through its contacts, has the defendant **purposefully availed** itself of conducting activities with the U.S.?

No → "National" Personal Jurisdiction does not exist.

Yes ↓

Through those activities, could the defendant **reasonably foresee** the possibility of being haled into a U.S. court to litigate the plaintiff's claims?

No → "National" Personal Jurisdiction does not exist.

Yes → "National" Personal Jurisdiction exists.

U.S. Constitution
It appears that these analyses apply the usual standards set by the U.S. Supreme Court in its traditional Specific Jurisdiction cases.

Go to Map 3.2.2, "*Specific Jurisdiction*"

Notes

In Rem Jurisdiction
Map 3.2.5: *U.S. Constitution & 4(n)*

Premise

This Map explains the "alternative" part of the first step from Map 3.2, the laws by which the U.S. Congress has extended the **In Rem** jurisdiction of the federal court system . *RULE 4(n).*

In Rem jurisdiction is jurisdiction over a particular thing (or asset). Once validly entered, an In Rem judgment may only be executed against that particular thing (or asset). If that does not completely compensate the plaintiff for the claim, the plaintiff must sue again. There are three types of In Rem jurisdiction:

True In Rem: a title-based litigation, to determine who, throughout the world, is the lawful owner of the particular thing.

Quasi In Rem #1: also a title-based litigation, to determine who, among the litigants in court, has the strongest claim to the particular thing.

Quasi In Rem #2: not a title-based litigation (in fact, title to the thing is not contested - it belongs to the defendant), where the court asserts jurisdiction over defendant in an unrelated claim because it has seized defendant's thing.

Alternative Step #1:
Is the defendant subject to the In Rem personal jurisdiction of the federal court?

Does a **special federal statute** authorize the use of in rem jurisdiction? *RULE 4(n)(1)*

No →

Through "reasonable efforts", could In Personam personal jurisdiction be established over this defendant under some **traditional reach of State law**? *RULE 4(n)(2)*

Yes
Go to Map 3.2.2
Go to Map 3.2.3

No

Has the defendant's property (or asset) been **seized** under circumstances and in a manner authorized by the forum State's law? *RULE 4(n)(2)*

U.S. Constitution:
The defendant's property must be seized at the outset of the litigation. *Pennoyer v. Neff*

In Rem Jurisdiction does not exist.

No

Yes

Does the defendant have such **minimum contacts** with the forum that allowing the court to exert jurisdiction over the seized thing would not offend **traditional notions of fair play and substantial justice**? *Shaffer v. Heitner*

Go to Map 3.2.2
"Specific Jurisdiction"

No

In Rem Jurisdiction exists.

Yes

U.S. Constitution:
In Rem jurisdiction will typically satisfy this standard if the lawsuit (a) is a title battle to the property; (b) involves a claim of injury occurring on the property; and (c) executes against the property based on a foreign judgment. *Shaffer v. Heitner*

45

Notes

Venue

Map 3.3: *28 U.S.C. §§ 1390 & 1391*

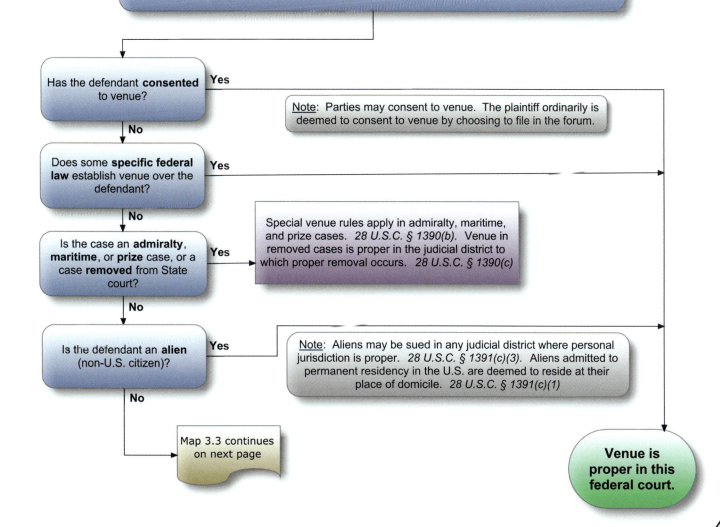

Premise

This Map answers the question from Map 3.0: *Does the Forum Have Proper Venue?*

In addition to proper subject matter and personal jurisdiction, the forum must also be a proper **venue** for the lawsuit. Venue implicates another "fairness" inquiry -- in which particular courthouses (within a court system) may this civil case be litigated. The locations for proper venue are set by the applicable forum's government (here, the U.S. Congress). *28 U.S.C. § 1390*

For purposes of federal venue law, venue is set by "**residence**", and, for that statute, the term "residence" means:

For Individuals: Place of domicile (including for aliens permanently residing in the U.S.) *28 U.S.C. § 1391(c)(1)*

For Corporations, Partnerships, and Associations: As defendants - in any judicial district where personal jurisdiction would be proper at filing; As plaintiffs - in the judicial district of its principal place of business. *28 U.S.C. § 1391(c)(2)*

Note: A party's residence is generally determined as of the time the lawsuit is filed.

Is venue proper in this particular federal court?

Has the defendant **consented** to venue? — **Yes**

Note: Parties may consent to venue. The plaintiff ordinarily is deemed to consent to venue by choosing to file in the forum.

No

Does some **specific federal law** establish venue over the defendant? — **Yes**

No

Is the case an **admiralty**, **maritime**, or **prize** case, or a case **removed** from State court? — **Yes**

Special venue rules apply in admiralty, maritime, and prize cases. *28 U.S.C. § 1390(b)*. Venue in removed cases is proper in the judicial district to which proper removal occurs. *28 U.S.C. § 1390(c)*

No

Is the defendant an **alien** (non-U.S. citizen)? — **Yes**

Note: Aliens may be sued in any judicial district where personal jurisdiction is proper. *28 U.S.C. § 1391(c)(3)*. Aliens admitted to permanent residency in the U.S. are deemed to reside at their place of domicile. *28 U.S.C. § 1391(c)(1)*

No

Map 3.3 continues on next page

Venue is proper in this federal court.

Notes

Venue
Map 3.3 *continued*: *28 U.S.C. §§ 1391 & 1392*

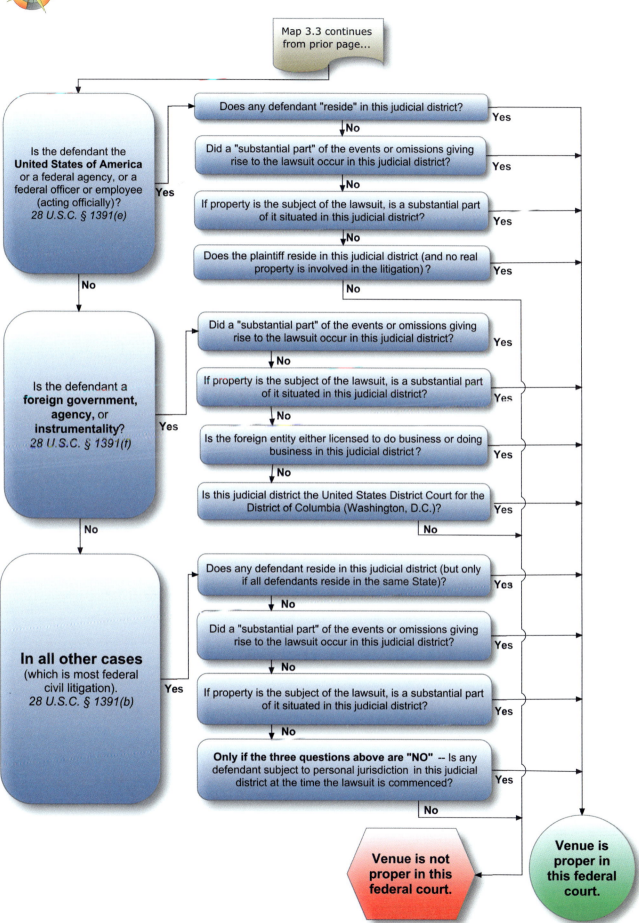

Map 3.3 continues from prior page...

Is the defendant the United States of America or a federal agency, or a federal officer or employee (acting officially)? *28 U.S.C. § 1391(e)*

Yes →

Does any defendant "reside" in this judicial district? — Yes

↓ No

Did a "substantial part" of the events or omissions giving rise to the lawsuit occur in this judicial district? — Yes

↓ No

If property is the subject of the lawsuit, is a substantial part of it situated in this judicial district? — Yes

↓ No

Does the plaintiff reside in this judicial district (and no real property is involved in the litigation)? — Yes

↓ No

No ↓

Is the defendant a foreign government, agency, or instrumentality? *28 U.S.C. § 1391(f)*

Yes →

Did a "substantial part" of the events or omissions giving rise to the lawsuit occur in this judicial district? — Yes

↓ No

If property is the subject of the lawsuit, is a substantial part of it situated in this judicial district? — Yes

↓ No

Is the foreign entity either licensed to do business or doing business in this judicial district? — Yes

↓ No

Is this judicial district the United States District Court for the District of Columbia (Washington, D.C.)? — Yes

↓ No

No ↓

In all other cases (which is most federal civil litigation). *28 U.S.C. § 1391(b)*

Yes →

Does any defendant reside in this judicial district (but only if all defendants reside in the same State)? — Yes

↓ No

Did a "substantial part" of the events or omissions giving rise to the lawsuit occur in this judicial district? — Yes

↓ No

If property is the subject of the lawsuit, is a substantial part of it situated in this judicial district? — Yes

↓ No

Only if the three questions above are "NO" -- Is any defendant subject to personal jurisdiction in this judicial district at the time the lawsuit is commenced? — Yes

↓ No

Venue is not proper in this federal court.

Venue is proper in this federal court.

Notes

The Complaint - Generally
Map 3.4: *Fed. R. Civ. P. 3, 7, 8, 9, 10, & 38*

Premise
This Map answers the question from Map 3.0: *Has a Proper Complaint Been Filed?*

The **Complaint** is the first of the seven "pleadings" permitted in federal court. It is the document that commences a federal civil lawsuit. *RULE 3*. It also places all other parties (and the court) on notice of the lawsuit and of the claims the plaintiff proposes to assert in the litigation.

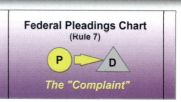

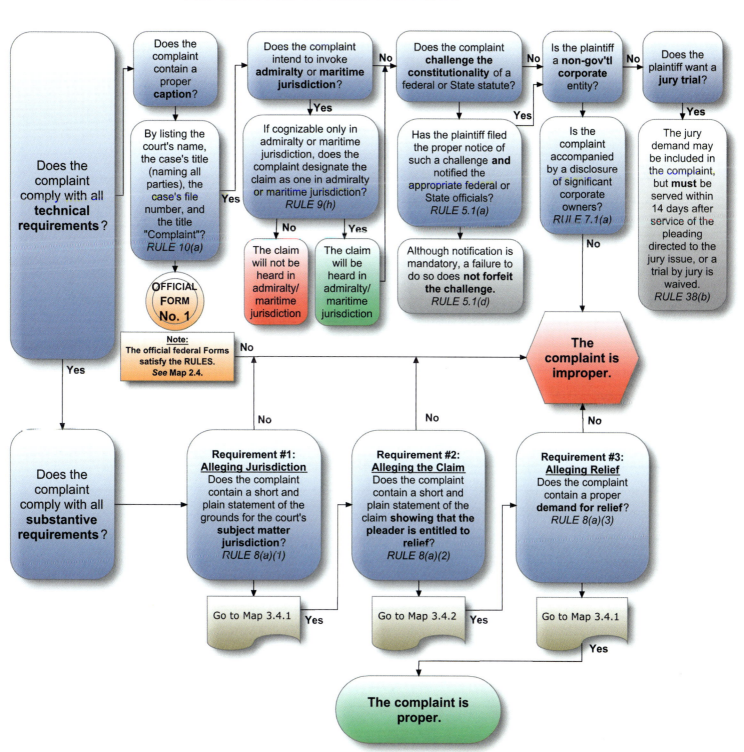

Does the complaint comply with all technical requirements?

Does the complaint contain a proper **caption**?

By listing the court's name, the case's title (naming all parties), the case's file number, and the title "Complaint"? *RULE 10(a)*

OFFICIAL FORM No. 1

Note: The official federal Forms satisfy the RULES. *See Map 2.4.*

Does the complaint intend to invoke **admiralty** or **maritime jurisdiction**?

If cognizable only in admiralty or maritime jurisdiction, does the complaint designate the claim as one in admiralty or maritime jurisdiction? *RULE 9(h)*

The claim will not be heard in admiralty/ maritime jurisdiction

The claim will be heard in admiralty/ maritime jurisdiction

Does the complaint **challenge the constitutionality** of a federal or State statute?

Has the plaintiff filed the proper notice of such a challenge **and** notified the appropriate federal or State officials? *RULE 5.1(a)*

Although notification is mandatory, a failure to do so does **not forfeit the challenge.** *RULE 5.1(d)*

Is the plaintiff a **non-gov'tl corporate** entity?

Is the complaint accompanied by a disclosure of significant corporate owners? *RULE 7.1(a)*

Does the plaintiff want a **jury trial**?

The jury demand may be included in the complaint, but **must** be served within 14 days after service of the pleading directed to the jury issue, or a trial by jury is waived. *RULE 38(b)*

The complaint is improper.

Does the complaint comply with all substantive requirements?

Requirement #1: Alleging Jurisdiction
Does the complaint contain a short and plain statement of the grounds for the court's **subject matter jurisdiction**? *RULE 8(a)(1)*

Go to Map 3.4.1

Requirement #2: Alleging the Claim
Does the complaint contain a short and plain statement of the claim **showing that the pleader is entitled to relief**? *RULE 8(a)(2)*

Go to Map 3.4.2

Requirement #3: Alleging Relief
Does the complaint contain a proper **demand for relief**? *RULE 8(a)(3)*

Go to Map 3.4.1

The complaint is proper.

Notes

Alleging Jurisdiction and Relief
Map 3.4.1: *Fed. R. Civ. P. 8 & 9*

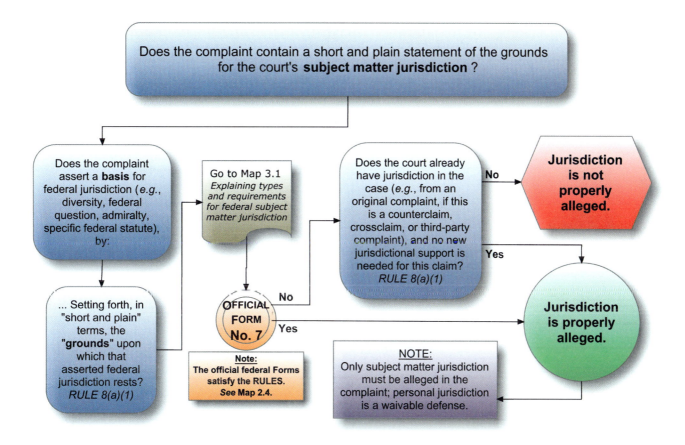

Premise
This Map expands upon the first and last of the RULE 8(a) requirements for a proper complaint -- alleging subject matter jurisdiction and alleging damages. *RULE 8(a)(1) & (a)(3).*

Does the complaint contain a short and plain statement of the grounds for the court's **subject matter jurisdiction** ?

Does the complaint assert a **basis** for federal jurisdiction (*e.g.*, diversity, federal question, admiralty, specific federal statute), by:

... Setting forth, in "short and plain" terms, the **"grounds"** upon which that asserted federal jurisdiction rests? *RULE 8(a)(1)*

Go to Map 3.1
Explaining types and requirements for federal subject matter jurisdiction

OFFICIAL FORM No. 7

Note:
The official federal Forms satisfy the RULES. *See* Map 2.4.

No / Yes

Does the court already have jurisdiction in the case (*e.g.*, from an original complaint, if this is a counterclaim, crossclaim, or third-party complaint), and no new jurisdictional support is needed for this claim? *RULE 8(a)(1)*

No → **Jurisdiction is not properly alleged.**

Yes → **Jurisdiction is properly alleged.**

NOTE:
Only subject matter jurisdiction must be alleged in the complaint; personal jurisdiction is a waivable defense.

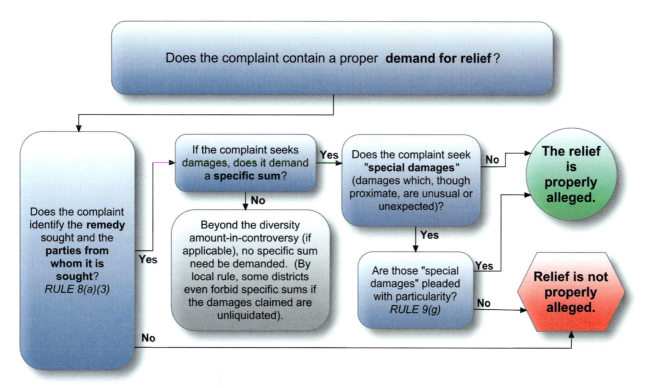

Does the complaint contain a proper **demand for relief** ?

Does the complaint identify the **remedy** sought and the **parties from whom it is sought**? *RULE 8(a)(3)*

Yes →

If the complaint seeks damages, does it demand a **specific sum**?

No ↓

Beyond the diversity amount-in-controversy (if applicable), no specific sum need be demanded. (By local rule, some districts even forbid specific sums if the damages claimed are unliquidated).

Yes → Does the complaint seek **"special damages"** (damages which, though proximate, are unusual or unexpected)?

No → **The relief is properly alleged.**

Yes ↓

Are those "special damages" pleaded with particularity? *RULE 9(g)*

Yes → (up to relief properly alleged)

No → **Relief is not properly alleged.**

No → **Relief is not properly alleged.**

Notes

Alleging the Claim
Map 3.4.2: *Fed. R. Civ. P. 8, 9, & 10*

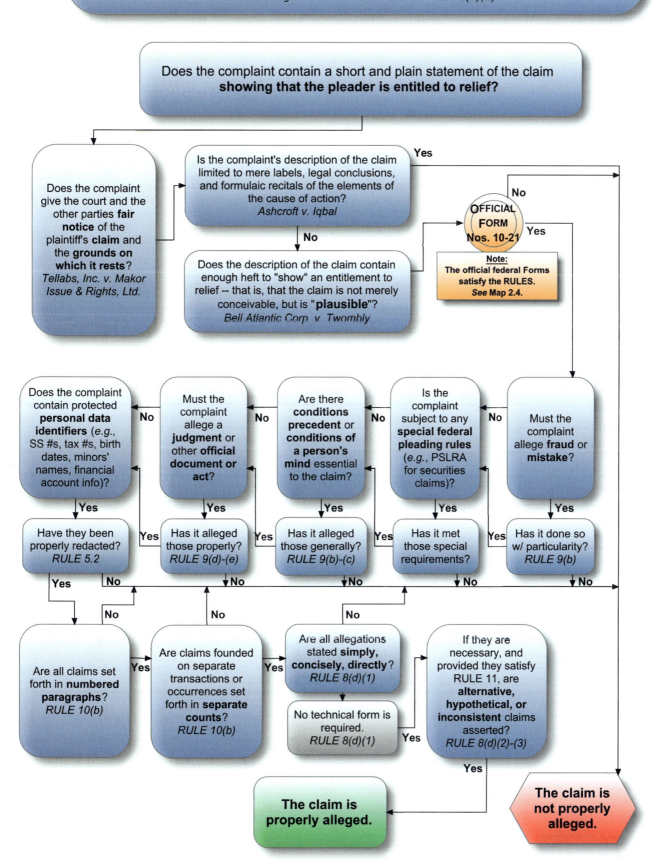

Premise
This Map expands upon the second of the RULE 8(a) requirements for a proper complaint -- alleging a claim "showing an entitlement to relief". *RULE 8(a)(2)*

Does the complaint contain a short and plain statement of the claim **showing that the pleader is entitled to relief?**

Does the complaint give the court and the other parties **fair notice** of the plaintiff's **claim** and the **grounds on which it rests**? *Tellabs, Inc. v. Makor Issue & Rights, Ltd.*

Is the complaint's description of the claim limited to mere labels, legal conclusions, and formulaic recitals of the elements of the cause of action? *Ashcroft v. Iqbal* — **Yes**

No

Does the description of the claim contain enough heft to "show" an entitlement to relief -- that is, that the claim is not merely conceivable, but is "**plausible**"? *Bell Atlantic Corp. v. Twombly*

OFFICIAL FORM Nos. 10-21 — **No**

Yes

Note:
The official federal Forms satisfy the RULES.
See **Map 2.4.**

Does the complaint contain protected **personal data identifiers** (*e.g.*, SS #s, tax #s, birth dates, minors' names, financial account info)? — **No** ←

Must the complaint allege a **judgment** or other **official document or act**? — **No** ←

Are there **conditions precedent** or **conditions of a person's mind** essential to the claim? — **No** ←

Is the complaint subject to any **special federal pleading rules** (*e.g.*, PSLRA for securities claims)? — **No** ←

Must the complaint allege **fraud** or **mistake**?

Yes ↓ (personal data) — Have they been properly redacted? *RULE 5.2*

Yes ↓ — Has it alleged those properly? *RULE 9(d)-(e)*

Yes ↓ — Has it alleged those generally? *RULE 9(b)-(c)*

Yes ↓ — Has it met those special requirements?

Yes ↓ — Has it done so w/ particularity? *RULE 9(b)*

Have they been properly redacted? *RULE 5.2* — **Yes** →

Has it alleged those properly? *RULE 9(d)-(e)* — **Yes** →

Has it alleged those generally? *RULE 9(b)-(c)* — **Yes** →

Has it met those special requirements? — **Yes** →

Has it done so w/ particularity? *RULE 9(b)* — **No** →

Yes ↓ (redacted)
No (redacted)
No
No
No
No

Are all claims set forth in **numbered paragraphs**? *RULE 10(b)* — **Yes** →

Are claims founded on separate transactions or occurrences set forth in **separate counts**? *RULE 10(b)* — **Yes** →

Are all allegations stated **simply, concisely, directly**? *RULE 8(d)(1)* —

No technical form is required. *RULE 8(d)(1)*

If they are necessary, and provided they satisfy RULE 11, are **alternative, hypothetical, or inconsistent** claims asserted? *RULE 8(d)(2)-(3)* — **Yes** →

Yes →

No (numbered)
No (separate counts)
No (allegations)

Yes ↓

The claim is properly alleged.

The claim is not properly alleged.

Notes

Service of Process, Generally

Map 3.5: *U.S. Constitution & Fed. R. Civ. P. 4*

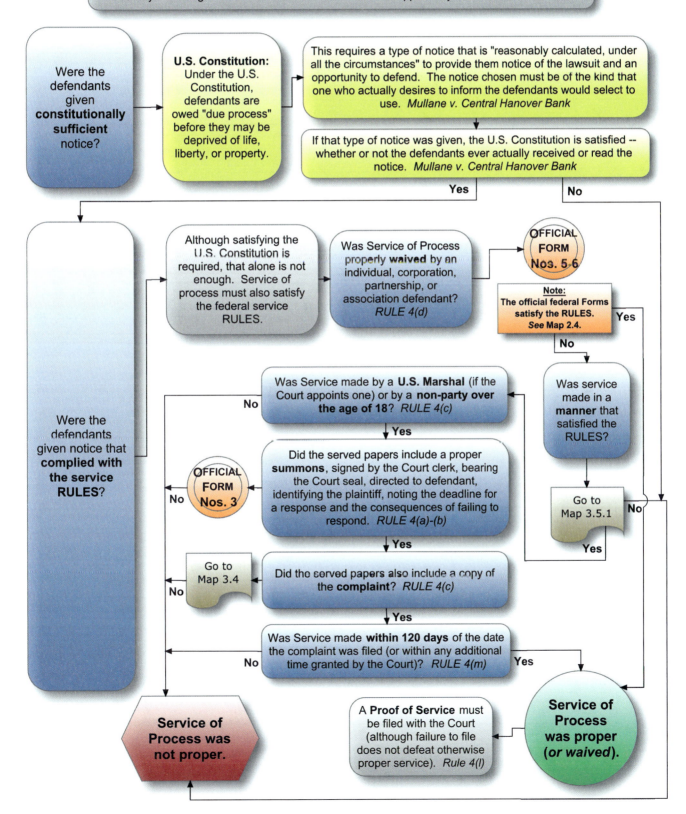

Premise

This Map answers the question from Map 3.0: *Has Service of Process been accomplished?*

Service of Process (or "Original Process") is the formal delivery -- or consensual waiver of formal delivery -- of notice of a pending lawsuit. It is designed to ensure that the defendants are aware that they are being sued and to afford them a reasonable opportunity to be heard in defense.

Were the defendants given **constitutionally sufficient** notice?

U.S. Constitution: Under the U.S. Constitution, defendants are owed "due process" before they may be deprived of life, liberty, or property.

This requires a type of notice that is "reasonably calculated, under all the circumstances" to provide them notice of the lawsuit and an opportunity to defend. The notice chosen must be of the kind that one who actually desires to inform the defendants would select to use. *Mullane v. Central Hanover Bank*

If that type of notice was given, the U.S. Constitution is satisfied -- whether or not the defendants ever actually received or read the notice. *Mullane v. Central Hanover Bank*

Yes / **No**

Were the defendants given notice that **complied with the service RULES**?

Although satisfying the U.S. Constitution is required, that alone is not enough. Service of process must also satisfy the federal service RULES.

Was Service of Process properly **waived** by an individual, corporation, partnership, or association defendant? *RULE 4(d)*

OFFICIAL FORM Nos. 5-6

Note: The official federal Forms satisfy the RULES. *See Map 2.4.*

Yes

No

Was service made in a **manner** that satisfied the RULES?

Was Service made by a **U.S. Marshal** (if the Court appoints one) or by a **non-party over the age of 18**? *RULE 4(c)* — **No**

Yes

Did the served papers include a proper **summons**, signed by the Court clerk, bearing the Court seal, directed to defendant, identifying the plaintiff, noting the deadline for a response and the consequences of failing to respond. *RULE 4(a)-(b)*

OFFICIAL FORM Nos. 3 — **No**

Go to Map 3.5.1 — **No**

Yes

Yes

Did the served papers also include a copy of the **complaint**? *RULE 4(c)*

Go to Map 3.4 — **No**

Yes

Was Service made **within 120 days** of the date the complaint was filed (or within any additional time granted by the Court)? *RULE 4(m)*

No

Yes

Service of Process was not proper.

A **Proof of Service** must be filed with the Court (although failure to file does not defeat otherwise proper service). *Rule 4(l)*

Service of Process was proper (*or waived*).

Notes

Manner of Service of Process

Map 3.5.1: *Fed. R. Civ. P. 4*

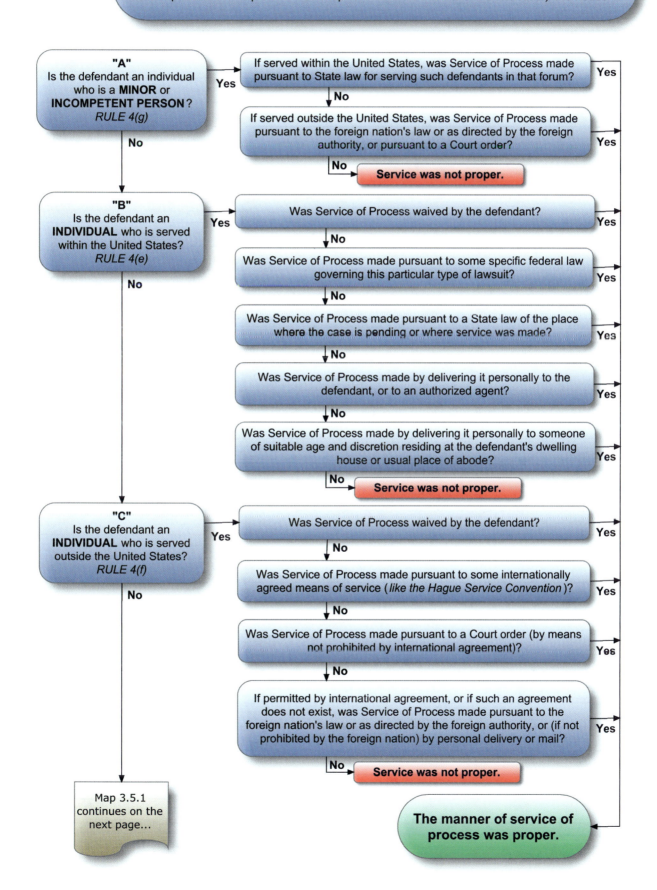

Premise

This Map answers the question from Map 3.5: *Did the Manner of Service satisfy the RULES* ?

"A"
Is the defendant an individual who is a **MINOR** or **INCOMPETENT PERSON**?
RULE 4(g)

— Yes → If served within the United States, was Service of Process made pursuant to State law for serving such defendants in that forum? — Yes →

No ↓

If served outside the United States, was Service of Process made pursuant to the foreign nation's law or as directed by the foreign authority, or pursuant to a Court order? — Yes →

No ↓ **Service was not proper.**

No ↓

"B"
Is the defendant an **INDIVIDUAL** who is served within the United States?
RULE 4(e)

— Yes → Was Service of Process waived by the defendant? — Yes →

No ↓

Was Service of Process made pursuant to some specific federal law governing this particular type of lawsuit? — Yes →

No ↓

Was Service of Process made pursuant to a State law of the place where the case is pending or where service was made? — Yes →

No ↓

Was Service of Process made by delivering it personally to the defendant, or to an authorized agent? — Yes →

No ↓

Was Service of Process made by delivering it personally to someone of suitable age and discretion residing at the defendant's dwelling house or usual place of abode? — Yes →

No ↓ **Service was not proper.**

No ↓

"C"
Is the defendant an **INDIVIDUAL** who is served outside the United States?
RULE 4(f)

— Yes → Was Service of Process waived by the defendant? — Yes →

No ↓

Was Service of Process made pursuant to some internationally agreed means of service (*like the Hague Service Convention*)? — Yes →

No ↓

Was Service of Process made pursuant to a Court order (by means not prohibited by international agreement)? — Yes →

No ↓

If permitted by international agreement, or if such an agreement does not exist, was Service of Process made pursuant to the foreign nation's law or as directed by the foreign authority, or (if not prohibited by the foreign nation) by personal delivery or mail? — Yes →

No ↓ **Service was not proper.**

No ↓

Map 3.5.1 continues on the next page...

The manner of service of process was proper.

Notes

Manner of Service of Process

Map 3.5.1 *continued*: *Fed. R. Civ. P. 4*

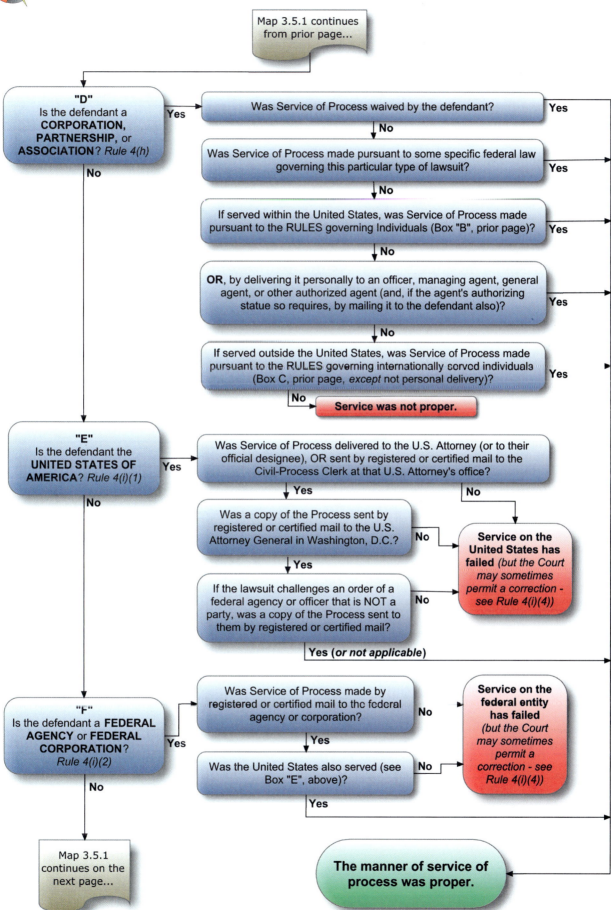

Map 3.5.1 continues from prior page...

"D"
Is the defendant a **CORPORATION, PARTNERSHIP,** or **ASSOCIATION**? *Rule 4(h)*

Yes → Was Service of Process waived by the defendant? → Yes

No → Was Service of Process made pursuant to some specific federal law governing this particular type of lawsuit? → Yes

No → If served within the United States, was Service of Process made pursuant to the RULES governing Individuals (Box "B", prior page)? → Yes

No → **OR**, by delivering it personally to an officer, managing agent, general agent, or other authorized agent (and, if the agent's authorizing statue so requires, by mailing it to the defendant also)? → Yes

No → If served outside the United States, was Service of Process made pursuant to the RULES governing internationally served individuals (Box C, prior page, *except* not personal delivery)? → Yes

No → **Service was not proper.**

"E"
Is the defendant the **UNITED STATES OF AMERICA**? *Rule 4(i)(1)*

Yes → Was Service of Process delivered to the U.S. Attorney (or to their official designee), OR sent by registered or certified mail to the Civil-Process Clerk at that U.S. Attorney's office?

Yes → Was a copy of the Process sent by registered or certified mail to the U.S. Attorney General in Washington, D.C.?

No → **Service on the United States has failed** *(but the Court may sometimes permit a correction - see Rule 4(i)(4))*

Yes → If the lawsuit challenges an order of a federal agency or officer that is NOT a party, was a copy of the Process sent to them by registered or certified mail?

No → **Service on the United States has failed** *(but the Court may sometimes permit a correction - see Rule 4(i)(4))*

Yes (*or not applicable*) →

"F"
Is the defendant a **FEDERAL AGENCY** or **FEDERAL CORPORATION**? *Rule 4(i)(2)*

Yes → Was Service of Process made by registered or certified mail to the federal agency or corporation?

No → **Service on the federal entity has failed** *(but the Court may sometimes permit a correction - see Rule 4(i)(4))*

Yes → Was the United States also served (see Box "E", above)?

No → **Service on the federal entity has failed** *(but the Court may sometimes permit a correction - see Rule 4(i)(4))*

Yes →

No → Map 3.5.1 continues on the next page...

The manner of service of process was proper.

Notes

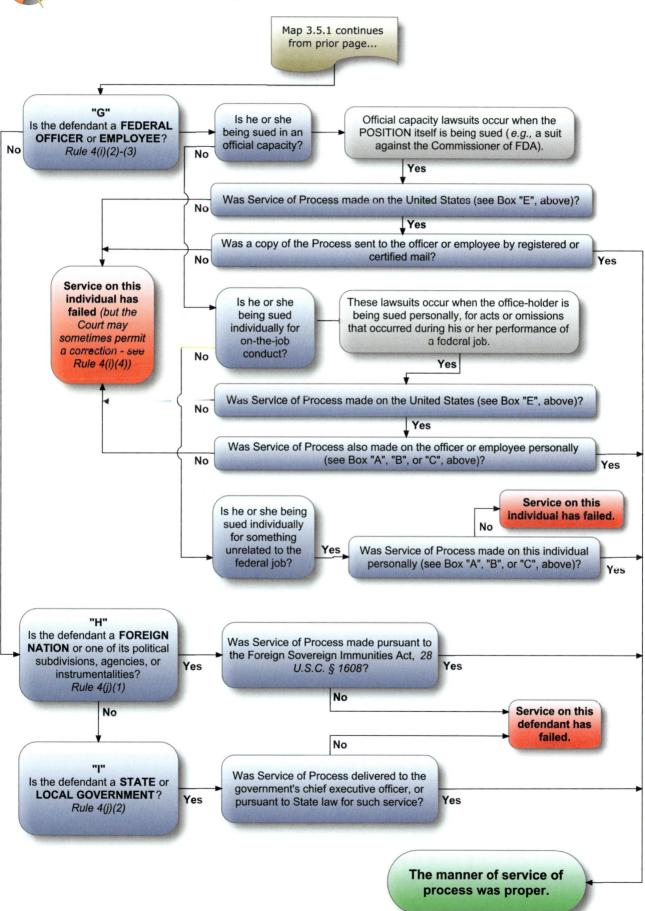

Map 3.5.1 continues from prior page...

"G" Is the defendant a **FEDERAL OFFICER** or **EMPLOYEE**? *Rule 4(i)(2)-(3)*

No

Is he or she being sued in an official capacity?

No

Official capacity lawsuits occur when the POSITION itself is being sued (*e.g.,* a suit against the Commissioner of FDA).

Yes

Was Service of Process made on the United States (see Box "E", above)?

No

Yes

Was a copy of the Process sent to the officer or employee by registered or certified mail?

No

Yes

Service on this individual has failed *(but the Court may sometimes permit a correction - see Rule 4(i)(4))*

Is he or she being sued individually for on-the-job conduct?

No

These lawsuits occur when the office-holder is being sued personally, for acts or omissions that occurred during his or her performance of a federal job.

Yes

Was Service of Process made on the United States (see Box "E", above)?

No

Yes

Was Service of Process also made on the officer or employee personally (see Box "A", "B", or "C", above)?

No

Yes

Is he or she being sued individually for something unrelated to the federal job?

Yes

Was Service of Process made on this individual personally (see Box "A", "B", or "C", above)?

No

Service on this individual has failed.

Yes

"H" Is the defendant a **FOREIGN NATION** or one of its political subdivisions, agencies, or instrumentalities? *Rule 4(j)(1)*

Yes

Was Service of Process made pursuant to the Foreign Sovereign Immunities Act, *28 U.S.C. § 1608*?

Yes

No

No

Service on this defendant has failed.

No

"I" Is the defendant a **STATE** or **LOCAL GOVERNMENT**? *Rule 4(j)(2)*

Yes

Was Service of Process delivered to the government's chief executive officer, or pursuant to State law for such service?

Yes

The manner of service of process was proper.

Notes

Service of All Other Documents
Map 3.5.2: *Fed. R. Civ. P. 5*

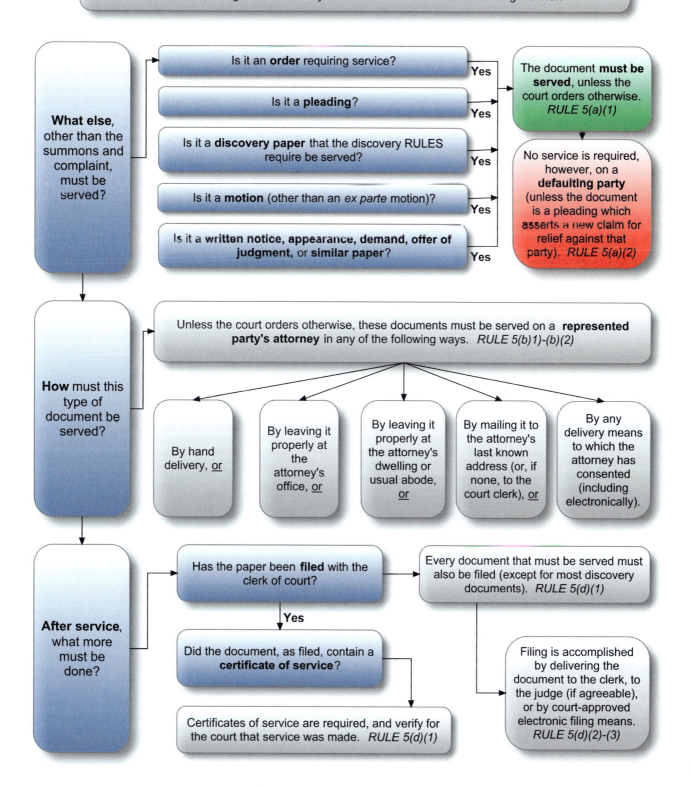

Premise

This Map completes the answer to the question from Map 3.0: *Has Service of Process Been Accomplished?*

Service of process has a unique, one-time objective -- to notify the defendants that they are being sued and to caution them about the need to timely respond. Once that notification has been made, all other documents during the lawsuit may be served in a much less demanding manner.

What else, other than the summons and complaint, must be served?

Is it an **order** requiring service? — Yes

Is it a **pleading**? — Yes

Is it a **discovery paper** that the discovery RULES require be served? — Yes

Is it a **motion** (other than an *ex parte* motion)? — Yes

Is it a **written notice, appearance, demand, offer of judgment,** or **similar paper**? — Yes

The document **must be served**, unless the court orders otherwise. *RULE 5(a)(1)*

No service is required, however, on a **defaulting party** (unless the document is a pleading which asserts a new claim for relief against that party). *RULE 5(a)(2)*

How must this type of document be served?

Unless the court orders otherwise, these documents must be served on a **represented party's attorney** in any of the following ways. *RULE 5(b)1)-(b)(2)*

By hand delivery, <u>or</u>

By leaving it properly at the attorney's office, <u>or</u>

By leaving it properly at the attorney's dwelling or usual abode, <u>or</u>

By mailing it to the attorney's last known address (or, if none, to the court clerk), <u>or</u>

By any delivery means to which the attorney has consented (including electronically).

After service, what more must be done?

Has the paper been **filed** with the clerk of court? — **Yes**

Did the document, as filed, contain a **certificate of service**?

Certificates of service are required, and verify for the court that service was made. *RULE 5(d)(1)*

Every document that must be served must also be filed (except for most discovery documents). *RULE 5(d)(1)*

Filing is accomplished by delivering the document to the clerk, to the judge (if agreeable), or by court-approved electronic filing means. *RULE 5(d)(2)-(3)*

Notes

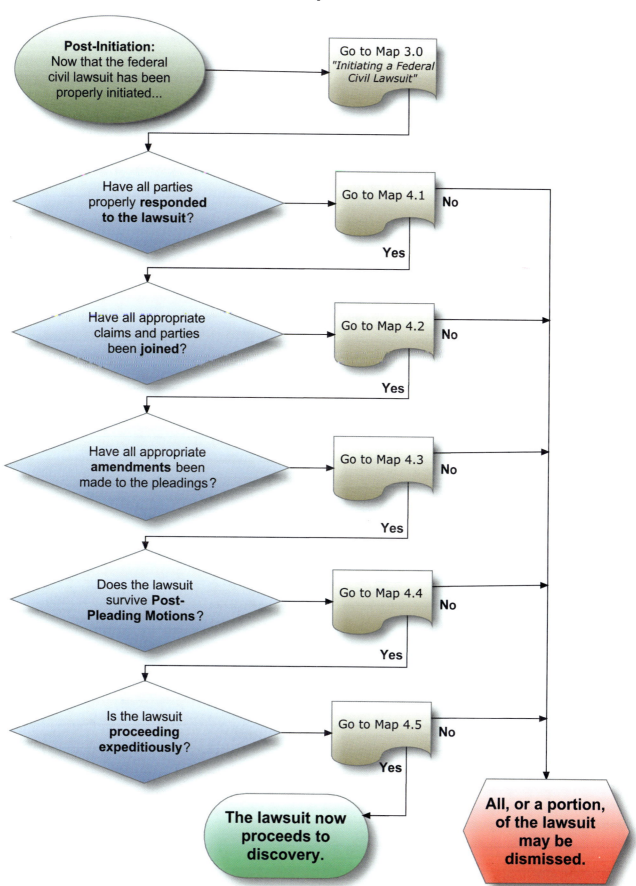

Post-Initiation: Now that the federal civil lawsuit has been properly initiated...

Go to Map 3.0 *"Initiating a Federal Civil Lawsuit"*

Have all parties properly **responded to the lawsuit**?

Go to Map 4.1 — No

Yes

Have all appropriate claims and parties been **joined**?

Go to Map 4.2 — No

Yes

Have all appropriate **amendments** been made to the pleadings?

Go to Map 4.3 — No

Yes

Does the lawsuit survive **Post-Pleading Motions**?

Go to Map 4.4 — No

Yes

Is the lawsuit **proceeding expeditiously**?

Go to Map 4.5 — No

Yes

The lawsuit now proceeds to discovery.

All, or a portion, of the lawsuit may be dismissed.

Notes

Responding to the Lawsuit, Generally
Map 4.1: *Fed. R. Civ. P. 7, 8, 12, 38, & 55*

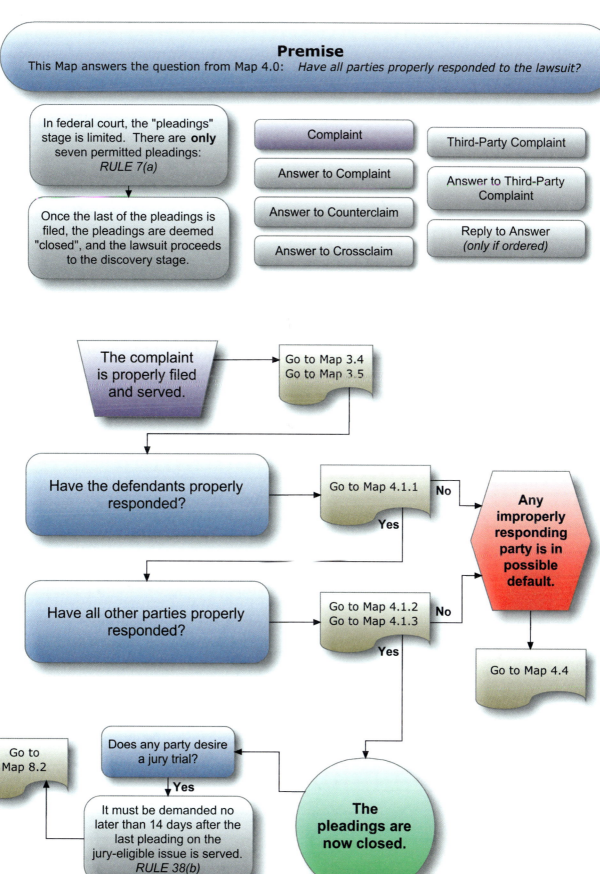

Premise
This Map answers the question from Map 4.0: *Have all parties properly responded to the lawsuit?*

In federal court, the "pleadings" stage is limited. There are **only** seven permitted pleadings: *RULE 7(a)*

Once the last of the pleadings is filed, the pleadings are deemed "closed", and the lawsuit proceeds to the discovery stage.

- Complaint
- Answer to Complaint
- Answer to Counterclaim
- Answer to Crossclaim
- Third-Party Complaint
- Answer to Third-Party Complaint
- Reply to Answer *(only if ordered)*

The complaint is properly filed and served.

Go to Map 3.4
Go to Map 3.5

Have the defendants properly responded?

Go to Map 4.1.1 — **No**

Yes

Have all other parties properly responded?

Go to Map 4.1.2
Go to Map 4.1.3 — **No**

Yes

Any improperly responding party is in possible default.

Go to Map 4.4

The pleadings are now closed.

Does any party desire a jury trial?

Yes

It must be demanded no later than 14 days after the last pleading on the jury-eligible issue is served. *RULE 38(b)*

Go to Map 8.2

Notes

Defender's Response
Map 4.1.1: *Fed. R. Civ. P. 8, 12, & 55*

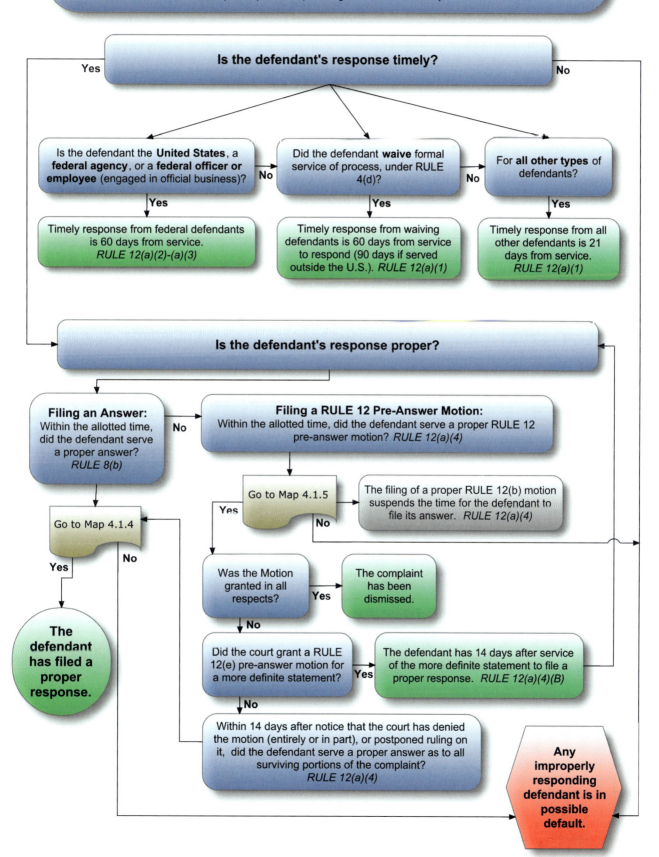

Premise
This Map expands upon the question asked in Map 4.1 by explaining a proper response to a federal complaint (or other pleading that states a claim).

Is the defendant's response timely?

Yes   No

Is the defendant the **United States**, a **federal agency**, or a **federal officer or employee** (engaged in official business)?

No →

Did the defendant **waive** formal service of process, under RULE 4(d)?

No →

For **all other types** of defendants?

↓ Yes

Timely response from federal defendants is 60 days from service. *RULE 12(a)(2)-(a)(3)*

↓ Yes

Timely response from waiving defendants is 60 days from service to respond (90 days if served outside the U.S.). *RULE 12(a)(1)*

↓ Yes

Timely response from all other defendants is 21 days from service. *RULE 12(a)(1)*

Is the defendant's response proper?

Filing an Answer: Within the allotted time, did the defendant serve a proper answer? *RULE 8(b)*

No →

Filing a RULE 12 Pre-Answer Motion: Within the allotted time, did the defendant serve a proper RULE 12 pre-answer motion? *RULE 12(a)(4)*

↓

Go to Map 4.1.5

Yes ↓   No →

The filing of a proper RULE 12(b) motion suspends the time for the defendant to file its answer. *RULE 12(a)(4)*

↓

Go to Map 4.1.4

Yes ↓   No →

The defendant has filed a proper response.

Was the Motion granted in all respects?

Yes → The complaint has been dismissed.

↓ No

Did the court grant a RULE 12(e) pre-answer motion for a more definite statement?

Yes → The defendant has 14 days after service of the more definite statement to file a proper response. *RULE 12(a)(4)(B)*

↓ No

Within 14 days after notice that the court has denied the motion (entirely or in part), or postponed ruling on it, did the defendant serve a proper answer as to all surviving portions of the complaint? *RULE 12(a)(4)*

Any improperly responding defendant is in possible default.

Notes

Responses By Other Parties

Map 4.1.2: *Fed. R. Civ. P. 7, 8, 12, & 55*

Premise

This Map expands upon the question asked in Map 4.1 by explaining a proper response to federal pleadings <u>other</u> <u>than</u> the complaint.

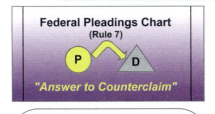

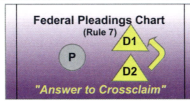

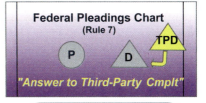

Federal Pleadings Chart (Rule 7)	**Federal Pleadings Chart** (Rule 7)	**Federal Pleadings Chart** (Rule 7)
"Answer to Counterclaim"	*"Answer to Crossclaim"*	*"Answer to Third-Party Cmplt"*

An **Answer to a Counterclaim** is the third of the seven "pleadings" permitted in federal court. The plaintiff (or any other party) defending against a counterclaim uses this to respond to the counterclaim allegations and to assert other claims (as appropriate).

An **Answer to a Crossclaim** is the fourth of the seven "pleadings" permitted in federal court. A defendant defending against a crossclaim uses this to respond to the crossclaim allegations.

An **Answer to a Third-Party Complaint** is the sixth of the seven "pleadings" permitted in federal court. A new party to the lawsuit (a "third-party") uses this to respond to the third-party complaint allegations and to assert other claims (as appropriate).

Has a **counterclaim** been asserted against the party?

Has a **crossclaim** been asserted against the defendant?

Has a **third-party complaint** been asserted against a new party to the lawsuit?

Go to Map 4.2.4 *"Counterclaims"* — **Yes**

Go to Map 4.2.4 *"Crossclaims"* — **Yes**

Go to Map 4.2.5 *"Third-Party Complaints"* — **Yes**

Has that party properly responded to the counterclaim within 21 days of service? *RULE 12(a)(1)(B)*

Has that party properly responded to the crossclaim within 21 days of service? *RULE 12(a)(1)(B)*

Has that party properly responded to the third-party within the time permitted for any original defendant? *RULE 14(a)*

Go to Map 4.1.1 *"Defender's Response"* — **No**

Go to Map 4.1.1 *"Defender's Response"* — **No**

Go to Map 4.1.1 *"Defender's Response"* — **No**

Yes — The answer to the counterclaim is proper.

Yes — The answer to the crossclaim is proper.

Yes — The answer to the third-party complaint is proper.

Go To Map 4.5.3

If the answer is untimely, the responding party may be in default.

If the answer is otherwise improper, it may be dismissed.

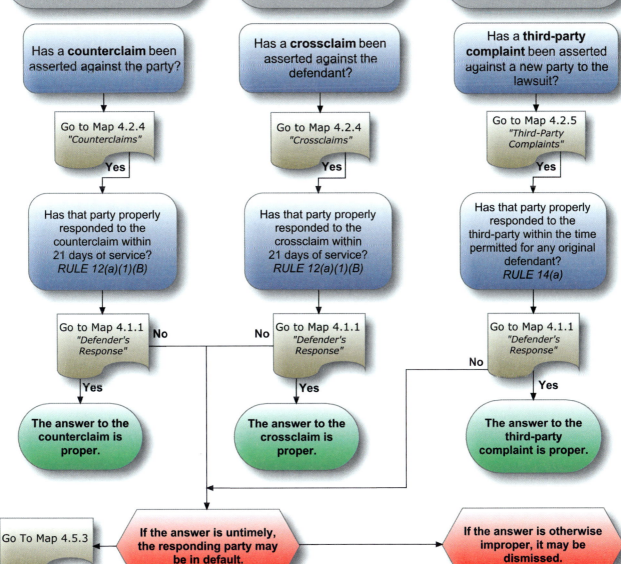

Notes

Replies
Map 4.1.3: *Fed. R. Civ. P. 7 & 8*

Premise
This Map continues to expand upon the question asked in Map 4.1 by explaining the proper use of a "reply" in federal pleadings.

REMINDER:
In federal court, the "pleadings" stage is limited. There are **only** seven permitted pleadings (and this list is exhaustive) :
RULE 7(a).

Complaint

Third-Party Complaint

Answer to Complaint

Answer to Third-Party Complaint

Answer to Counterclaim

Answer to Crossclaim

Reply to Answer
(only if ordered)

Unless they assert counterclaims or crossclaims, answers will contain allegations or defenses that are unresponded to.

Are those unresponded to allegations and defenses considered to be **admitted**?

No.
If a responsive pleading is not required to an allegation, none is permitted. Instead, that unanswered allegation is considered to have been denied.
RULE 8(b)(6)

The federal pleadings stage intentionally ends quickly, with the work of fleshing out the details of the lawsuit left to the discovery stage.

Replies to an answer may be ordered by the court ... but generally are ordered only after a convincing showing of a substantial need.

Notes

The Answer
Map 4.1.4: *Fed. R. Civ. P. 7, 9, 10, & 38*

Premise
This Map answers the question from Map 4.1.1, whether a proper answer has been filed.

The **Answer** is the second of the seven "pleadings" permitted in federal court. A defendant uses its answer to respond to the plaintiff's allegations, to assert counterclaims against the plaintiff, and to assert crossclaims against fellow defendants. (An answer is also used to respond to counterclaims, crossclaims, and third-party claims.)

OFFICIAL FORM Nos. 30-31

Note: The official federal Forms satisfy the RULES. *See* Map 2.4.

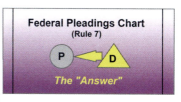

Federal Pleadings Chart (Rule 7)

P ← D

The "Answer"

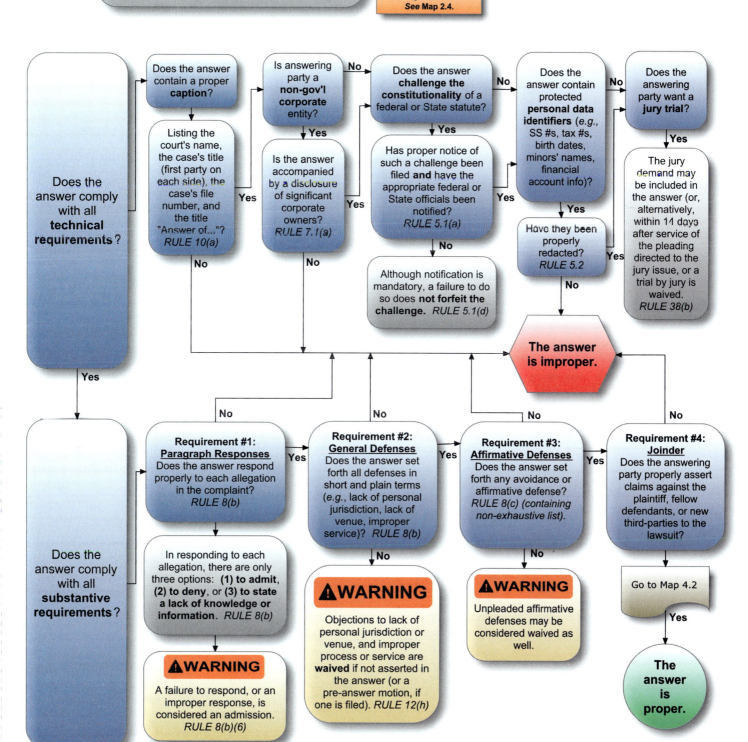

Does the answer comply with all technical requirements?

Does the answer contain a proper **caption**?

— Yes → Listing the court's name, the case's title (first party on each side), the case's file number, and the title "Answer of...."? *RULE 10(a)*

Is answering party a **non-gov'l corporate** entity?

— **No** →

— **Yes** → Is the answer accompanied by a disclosure of significant corporate owners? *RULE 7.1(a)*

Does the answer **challenge the constitutionality** of a federal or State statute?

— **No** →

— **Yes** → Has proper notice of such a challenge been filed **and** have the appropriate federal or State officials been notified? *RULE 5.1(a)*
  — **No** → Although notification is mandatory, a failure to do so does **not forfeit the challenge.** *RULE 5.1(d)*

Does the answer contain protected **personal data identifiers** (*e.g.,* SS #s, tax #s, birth dates, minors' names, financial account info)?

— **No** →

— **Yes** → Have they been properly redacted? *RULE 5.2*
  — **No** →

Does the answering party want a **jury trial**?

— **Yes** → The jury demand may be included in the answer (or, alternatively, within 14 days after service of the pleading directed to the jury issue, or a trial by jury is waived. *RULE 38(b)*

The answer is improper.

Does the answer comply with all substantive requirements?

— Yes →

Requirement #1: Paragraph Responses
Does the answer respond properly to each allegation in the complaint? *RULE 8(b)*

— **No** →

— **Yes** → In responding to each allegation, there are only three options: **(1) to admit, (2) to deny,** or **(3) to state a lack of knowledge or information.** *RULE 8(b)*

⚠ **WARNING**
A failure to respond, or an improper response, is considered an admission. *RULE 8(b)(6)*

Requirement #2: General Defenses
Does the answer set forth all defenses in short and plain terms (*e.g.,* lack of personal jurisdiction, lack of venue, improper service)? *RULE 8(b)*

— **No** →

— **Yes** →

⚠ **WARNING**
Objections to lack of personal jurisdiction or venue, and improper process or service are **waived** if not asserted in the answer (or a pre-answer motion, if one is filed). *RULE 12(h)*

Requirement #3: Affirmative Defenses
Does the answer set forth any avoidance or affirmative defense? *RULE 8(c) (containing non-exhaustive list).*

— **No** →

— **Yes** →

⚠ **WARNING**
Unpleaded affirmative defenses may be considered waived as well.

Requirement #4: Joinder
Does the answering party properly assert claims against the plaintiff, fellow defendants, or new third-parties to the lawsuit?

— **No** →

Go to Map 4.2

— **Yes** →

The answer is proper.

Notes

Pre-Answer Motions, Generally
Map 4.1.5: *Fed. R. Civ. P. 7 & 12*

Premise
This Map expands upon the question from Map 4.1.1, whether a proper RULE 12 pre-answer motion was filed.

As the term denotes, **Pre-Answer Motions** are motions filed <u>before</u> an Answer. Their typical purpose is to seek an early dismissal (or other culling) of the pleading to which they are directed.

→ A **"Motion"** is a request to the court seeking a ruling. *RULE 7(b)(1)*

OFFICIAL FORM No. 40

Note:
The official federal Forms satisfy the RULES. *See* Map 2.4.

← **Yes** — In responding to a pleading, did the party choose to file a **pre-answer motion**? — **No** → Pre-Answer Motions are not required by the RULES. A party can, instead, respond to a prior pleading by filing an Answer.

Motion to Dismiss for...
- Lack of Subject Matter Jurisdiction, *RULE 12(b)(1)*
- Lack of Personal Jurisdiction, *RULE 12(b)(2)*
- Improper Venue, *RULE 12(b)(3)*
- Insufficient Process, *RULE 12(b)(4)*
- Insufficient Service of Process, *RULE 12(b)(5)*
- Failure to State a Claim Upon Which Relief Can Be Granted, *RULE 12(b)(6)*
- Failure to Join a RULE 19 Party, *RULE 12(b)(7)*

Motion for a More Definite Statement, *RULE 12(e)*

Motion to Strike, *RULE 12(f)*

Go to Map 4.1.6

Did the party add to the **pre-answer motion** every other RULE 12 defense or objection then available?

Yes → The party has the right to add to a Pre-Answer Motion any other RULE 12 defense or objection then available. *RULE 12(g)(1)*

No → No subsequent Pre-Answer Motion may be made to raise other RULE 12 defenses or objections. *RULE 12(g)(2)*

⚠**WARNING**
The 4 defenses of lack of **personal jurisdiction**, **venue**, **proper process**, or **proper service** are <u>WAIVED</u> if not included in a Pre-Answer Motion (if one is filed) or the Answer (if the motion is not filed). *RULE 12(h)(1)*

The 2 defenses of lack of a **required party** and **failure to state a claim** are not <u>WAIVED</u> so long as they are made no later than trial. The defense of lack of **subject matter jurisdiction** is never waived. *RULE 12(h)(2)-(3)*

Notes

Pre-Answer Motions In Detail

Map 4.1.6: *Fed. R. Civ. P. 12*

What Motion does the party want to make?	If the court grants the Motion, what happens?	When must the Motion be filed?	What must be shown to win the Motion?
Motion to Dismiss - No Subject Matter Jurisdiction, *RULE 12(b)(1)*	The federal court dismisses the lawsuit. The plaintiff may file in State court.	Anytime. A lack of subject matter jurisdiction can never be waived.	The party invoking the federal court's subject matter jurisdiction has the burden - must show a proper basis for federal jurisdiction (*e.g.,* that the parties are completely diverse and satisfy the amount-in-controversy requirement), that the claim "arises under" federal law, etc.).
Motion to Dismiss - No Personal Jurisdiction, *RULE 12(b)(2)*	The federal court dismisses the lawsuit. The plaintiff may file in another location.	Waived, unless raised in Pre-Answer Motion (if any is filed) or in the Answer.	The party invoking the federal court's personal jurisdiction has the burden - must show that all defendants are amendable to the court's personal jurisdiction under RULE 4(k) and that the exercise of that jurisdiction would be constitutional under the due process guarantee.
Motion to Dismiss - Improper Venue, *RULE 12(b)(3)*	The federal court dismisses the lawsuit (or transfers it to a proper venue).	Waived, unless raised in Pre-Answer Motion (if any is filed) or in the Answer.	The courts are divided on who has the burden to show venue (or lack of venue) - most courts impose that burden on the plaintiff - must show that the federal court has venue under 28 U.S.C. § 1391 or some special federal venue statute.
Motion to Dismiss - Insufficient Process or Service, *RULE 12(b)(4) - (5)*	Typically, service is just quashed. The plaintiff may try to serve again.	Waived, unless raised in Pre-Answer Motion (if any is filed) or in the Answer.	The party attempting to serve has the burden - must show that all defendants (a) were served with a proper summons and complaint, <u>and</u> (b) that service was accomplished upon them properly pursuant to RULE 4, or that they waived formal service under RULE 4(d).
Motion to Dismiss - Failure to State a Claim, *RULE 12(b)(6)*	The federal court may dismiss all or part of the lawsuit, or permit the plaintiff to re-plead.	Not waived, unless the motion is delayed until the trial ends.	The movant has the burden - must show that the pleading is <u>legally insufficient</u> (*e.g.,* the law does not recognize the type of claim or defense being asserted) or <u>factually insufficient</u> (*e.g.,* the allegations fail to meet the *Twombly* test of a "plausible" claim, or otherwise fail to place the defendants on proper notice of the basis for the claim).
Motion to Dismiss - Unjoined Required Party, *RULE 12(b)(7)*	Under RULE 19(b), the court must determine whether it is fair to proceed without the party, or to dismiss.	Not waived, unless the motion is delayed until the trial ends.	The movant has the burden - must show that an absent unjoined party is "required" under RULE 19(a) and further, under RULE 19(b), that "in equity and good conscience" the trial cannot proceed in that party's absence. (The plaintiff may re-file in a jurisdiction where all parties -- including the absent party -- can be joined.)
Motion for a More Definite Statement, *RULE 12(e)*	The federal court may order the pleader to enhance the pleaded allegations.	Waived, if not asserted prior to filing a responsive pleading.	The movant has the burden - must show that the pleading is so utterly unintelligible that attempting to answer it would be impossible.
Motion to Strike, *RULE 12(f)*	The federal court may strike the offending portion of the pleading.	Waived, if not asserted prior to filing a responsive pleading.	The movant has the burden. **[1]** The motion can be used as a plaintiff's equivalent of a RULE 12(b)(6) motion, to strike off an insufficient defense (those standards apply). **[2]** Or it can be used to strike off "redundant, immaterial, impertinent, or scandalous" pleaded allegations (to prevail, must show a complete lack of relevance <u>and</u> prejudice).

Notes

Some Nuances About Pre-Answer Motions
Map 4.1.7: *Fed. R. Civ. P. 12 & 83; 28 U.S.C. §§ 1404 & 1406*

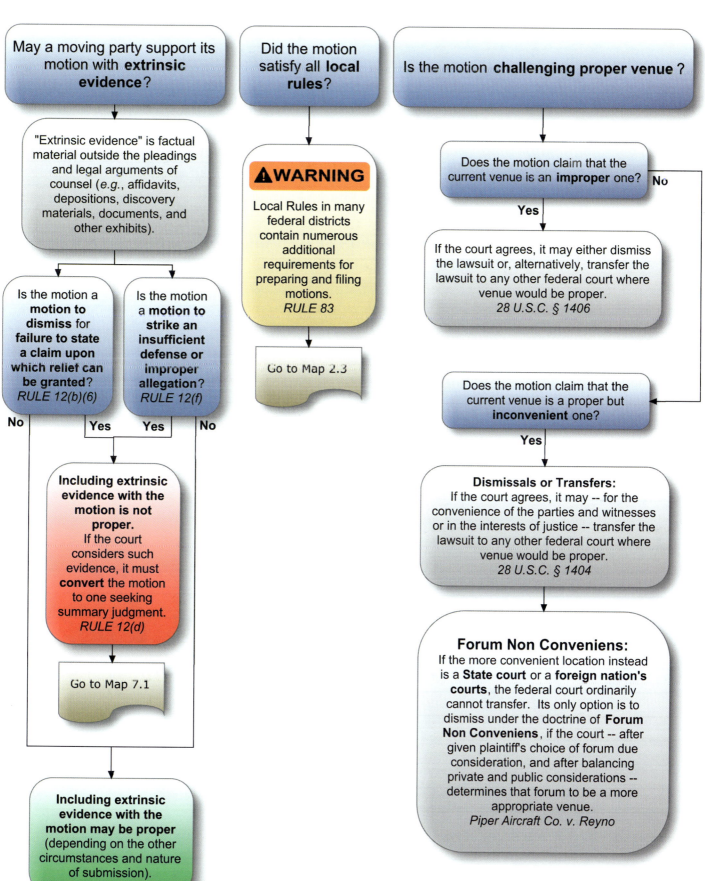

May a moving party support its motion with extrinsic evidence?

"Extrinsic evidence" is factual material outside the pleadings and legal arguments of counsel (*e.g.*, affidavits, depositions, discovery materials, documents, and other exhibits).

Is the motion a motion to dismiss for failure to state a claim upon which relief can be granted? *RULE 12(b)(6)*

Is the motion a motion to strike an insufficient defense or improper allegation? *RULE 12(f)*

No — Yes — Yes — No

Including extrinsic evidence with the motion is not proper. If the court considers such evidence, it must **convert** the motion to one seeking summary judgment. *RULE 12(d)*

Go to Map 7.1

Including extrinsic evidence with the motion may be proper (depending on the other circumstances and nature of submission).

Did the motion satisfy all local rules?

⚠ **WARNING**

Local Rules in many federal districts contain numerous additional requirements for preparing and filing motions. *RULE 83*

Go to Map 2.3

Is the motion challenging proper venue?

Does the motion claim that the current venue is an improper one? — No

Yes

If the court agrees, it may either dismiss the lawsuit or, alternatively, transfer the lawsuit to any other federal court where venue would be proper. *28 U.S.C. § 1406*

Does the motion claim that the current venue is a proper but inconvenient one?

Yes

Dismissals or Transfers:
If the court agrees, it may -- for the convenience of the parties and witnesses or in the interests of justice -- transfer the lawsuit to any other federal court where venue would be proper. *28 U.S.C. § 1404*

Forum Non Conveniens:
If the more convenient location instead is a **State court** or a **foreign nation's courts**, the federal court ordinarily cannot transfer. Its only option is to dismiss under the doctrine of **Forum Non Conveniens**, if the court -- after given plaintiff's choice of forum due consideration, and after balancing private and public considerations -- determines that forum to be a more appropriate venue. *Piper Aircraft Co. v. Reyno*

Notes

Joinder, Generally

Map 4.2: *Fed. R. Civ. P. 13, 14, 17, 18, 19, 20, 21, 22, 24, 25, & 42*

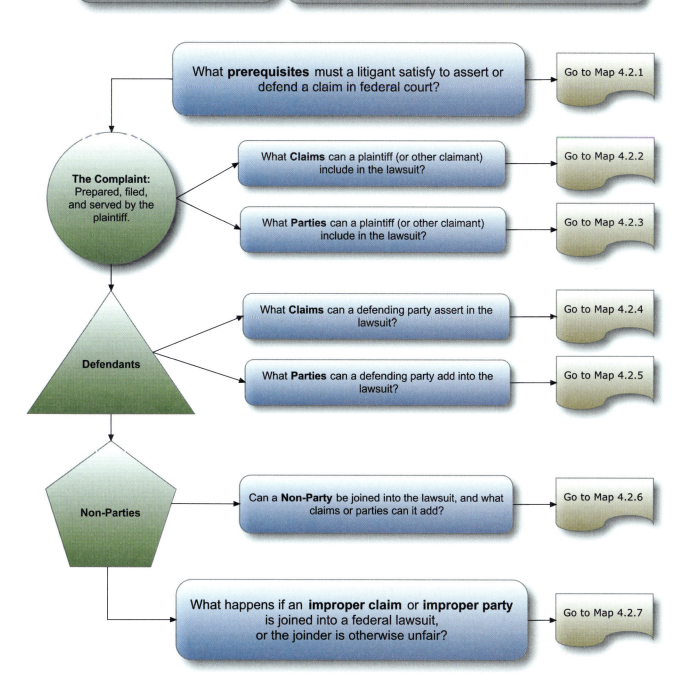

Premise

This Map answers the question from Map 4.0: *Have all appropriate claims and parties been joined into the lawsuit?*

The plaintiff begins the lawsuit by filing a complaint. The **Joinder** procedures address four general questions: (1) what claims and parties can the plaintiff include in the lawsuit? (2) what claims and parties can the defendant insert into the lawsuit? (3) what claims by unjoined strangers can enter the lawsuit? (4) what happens if a claim or party that should not be in the lawsuit is added?

Joinder brings with it both benefits and disadvantages.

Beneficially, it aids efficiency and economy by disposing of similar disputes together in one, single litigation, and it aids fairness by diminishing the risk that the absence of claims or parties could be used strategically to injure another party or defeat justice.

Disadvantageously, it may deprive parties of their litigation strategy, lengthen the litigation and add to its expense, introduce cluttering (and distracting) side-shows, and confuse the factfinder.

What **prerequisites** must a litigant satisfy to assert or defend a claim in federal court? → Go to Map 4.2.1

The Complaint: Prepared, filed, and served by the plaintiff.

What **Claims** can a plaintiff (or other claimant) include in the lawsuit? → Go to Map 4.2.2

What **Parties** can a plaintiff (or other claimant) include in the lawsuit? → Go to Map 4.2.3

Defendants

What **Claims** can a defending party assert in the lawsuit? → Go to Map 4.2.4

What **Parties** can a defending party add into the lawsuit? → Go to Map 4.2.5

Non-Parties

Can a **Non-Party** be joined into the lawsuit, and what claims or parties can it add? → Go to Map 4.2.6

What happens if an **improper claim** or **improper party** is joined into a federal lawsuit, or the joinder is otherwise unfair? → Go to Map 4.2.7

Notes

Prerequisites To Be A Litigant

Map 4.2.1: *U.S. Constitution & Fed. R. Civ. P. 17*

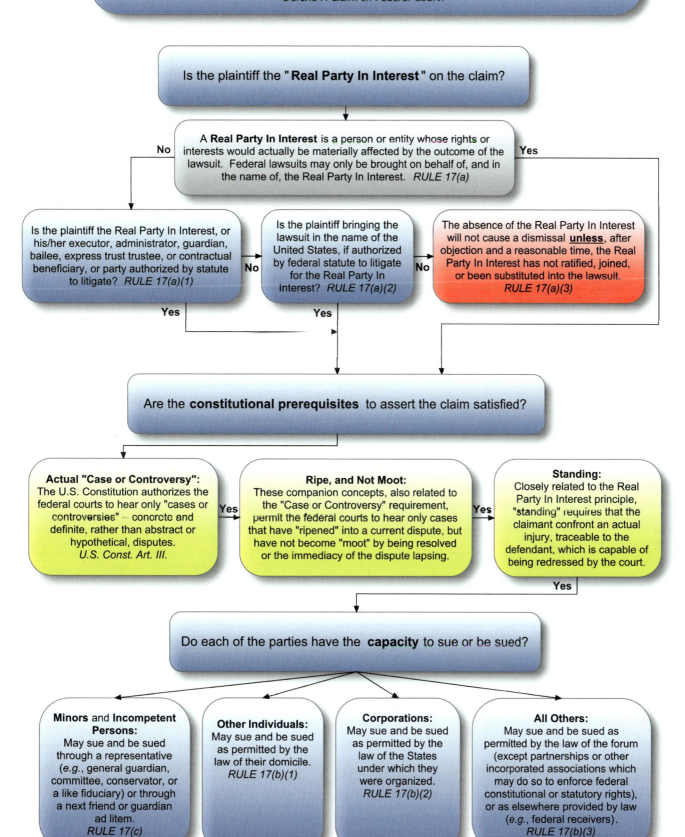

Premise
This Map answers the question posed in Map 4.2: *What Prerequisites Must A Litigant Satisfy To Assert Or Defend A Claim In Federal Court?*

Is the plaintiff the "**Real Party In Interest**" on the claim?

A **Real Party In Interest** is a person or entity whose rights or interests would actually be materially affected by the outcome of the lawsuit. Federal lawsuits may only be brought on behalf of, and in the name of, the Real Party In Interest. *RULE 17(a)*

No

Yes

Is the plaintiff the Real Party In Interest, or his/her executor, administrator, guardian, bailee, express trust trustee, or contractual beneficiary, or party authorized by statute to litigate? *RULE 17(a)(1)*

No

Is the plaintiff bringing the lawsuit in the name of the United States, if authorized by federal statute to litigate for the Real Party In Interest? *RULE 17(a)(2)*

No

The absence of the Real Party In Interest will not cause a dismissal **unless**, after objection and a reasonable time, the Real Party In Interest has not ratified, joined, or been substituted into the lawsuit. *RULE 17(a)(3)*

Yes

Yes

Are the **constitutional prerequisites** to assert the claim satisfied?

Actual "Case or Controversy":
The U.S. Constitution authorizes the federal courts to hear only "cases or controversies" — concrete and definite, rather than abstract or hypothetical, disputes. *U.S. Const. Art. III.*

Yes

Ripe, and Not Moot:
These companion concepts, also related to the "Case or Controversy" requirement, permit the federal courts to hear only cases that have "ripened" into a current dispute, but have not become "moot" by being resolved or the immediacy of the dispute lapsing.

Yes

Standing:
Closely related to the Real Party In Interest principle, "standing" requires that the claimant confront an actual injury, traceable to the defendant, which is capable of being redressed by the court.

Yes

Do each of the parties have the **capacity** to sue or be sued?

Minors and Incompetent Persons:
May sue and be sued through a representative (*e.g.*, general guardian, committee, conservator, or a like fiduciary) or through a next friend or guardian ad litem. *RULE 17(c)*

Other Individuals:
May sue and be sued as permitted by the law of their domicile. *RULE 17(b)(1)*

Corporations:
May sue and be sued as permitted by the law of the States under which they were organized. *RULE 17(b)(2)*

All Others:
May sue and be sued as permitted by the law of the forum (except partnerships or other incorporated associations which may do so to enforce federal constitutional or statutory rights), or as elsewhere provided by law (*e.g.*, federal receivers). *RULE 17(b)(3)*

Notes

Claim Joinder By Claimants
Map 4.2.2: *Fed. R. Civ. P. 14 & 18*

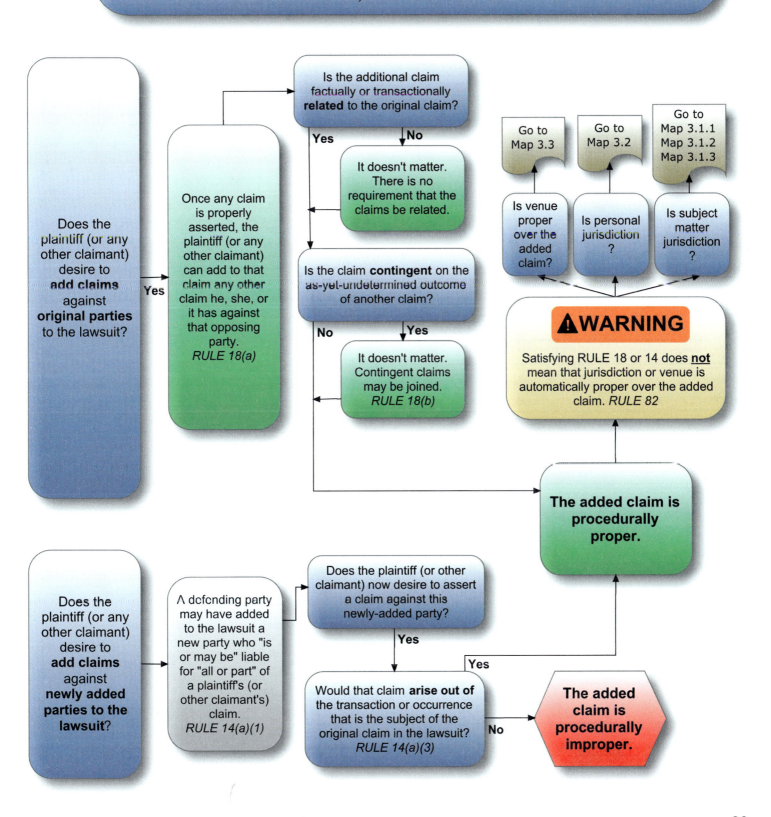

Premise

This Map answers the question asked in Map 4.2: *What CLAIMS and PARTIES Can A Plaintiff (Or Other Claimant) Include In The Lawsuit?*

Does the **plaintiff (or any other claimant) desire to add claims against original parties** to the lawsuit?

Yes →

Once any claim is properly asserted, the plaintiff (or any other claimant) can add to that claim any other claim he, she, or it has against that opposing party. *RULE 18(a)*

Is the additional claim factually or transactionally **related** to the original claim?

Yes / **No**

It doesn't matter. There is no requirement that the claims be related.

Is the claim **contingent** on the as-yet-undetermined outcome of another claim?

No / **Yes**

It doesn't matter. Contingent claims may be joined. *RULE 18(b)*

Go to Map 3.3

Go to Map 3.2

Go to Map 3.1.1 Map 3.1.2 Map 3.1.3

Is venue proper over the added claim?

Is personal jurisdiction?

Is subject matter jurisdiction?

⚠ WARNING

Satisfying RULE 18 or 14 does **not** mean that jurisdiction or venue is automatically proper over the added claim. *RULE 82*

The added claim is procedurally proper.

Does the **plaintiff (or any other claimant) desire to add claims against newly added parties to the lawsuit**?

A defending party may have added to the lawsuit a new party who "is or may be" liable for "all or part" of a plaintiff's (or other claimant's) claim. *RULE 14(a)(1)*

Does the plaintiff (or other claimant) now desire to assert a claim against this newly-added party?

Yes

Would that claim **arise out of** the transaction or occurrence that is the subject of the original claim in the lawsuit? *RULE 14(a)(3)*

Yes →

No →

The added claim is procedurally improper.

Notes

Party Joinder By Claimants

Map 4.2.3: *Fed. R. Civ. P. 13, 14, & 20*

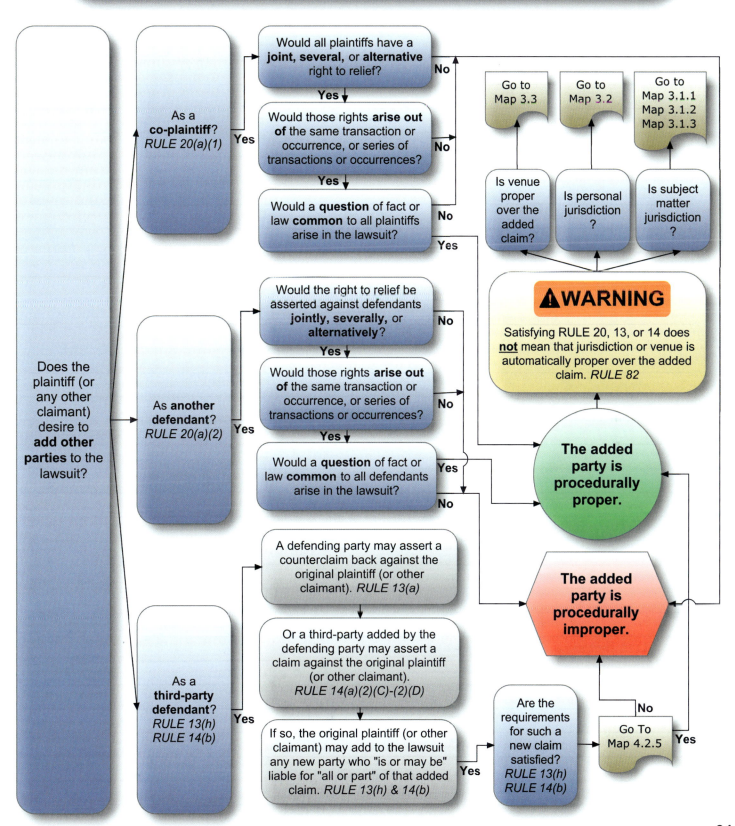

Premise

This Map continues to answer the question asked in Map 4.2: *What CLAIMS and PARTIES Can A Plaintiff (Or Other Claimants) Include In The Lawsuit?*

Does the plaintiff (or any other claimant) desire to **add other parties** to the lawsuit?

As a **co-plaintiff**? *RULE 20(a)(1)*

Would all plaintiffs have a **joint**, **several**, or **alternative** right to relief? **No**

Yes

Would those rights **arise out of** the same transaction or occurrence, or series of transactions or occurrences? **No**

Yes

Would a **question** of fact or law **common** to all plaintiffs arise in the lawsuit? **No**

Yes

As **another defendant**? *RULE 20(a)(2)*

Would the right to relief be asserted against defendants **jointly**, **severally**, or **alternatively**? **No**

Yes

Would those rights **arise out of** the same transaction or occurrence, or series of transactions or occurrences? **No**

Yes

Would a **question** of fact or law **common** to all defendants arise in the lawsuit? **Yes** / **No**

As a **third-party defendant**? *RULE 13(h) RULE 14(b)*

A defending party may assert a counterclaim back against the original plaintiff (or other claimant). *RULE 13(a)*

Or a third-party added by the defending party may assert a claim against the original plaintiff (or other claimant). *RULE 14(a)(2)(C)-(2)(D)*

If so, the original plaintiff (or other claimant) may add to the lawsuit any new party who "is or may be" liable for "all or part" of that added claim. *RULE 13(h) & 14(b)* **Yes**

Go to Map 3.3

Go to Map 3.2

Go to Map 3.1.1 Map 3.1.2 Map 3.1.3

Is venue proper over the added claim?

Is personal jurisdiction?

Is subject matter jurisdiction?

⚠ **WARNING**

Satisfying RULE 20, 13, or 14 does **not** mean that jurisdiction or venue is automatically proper over the added claim. *RULE 82*

The added party is procedurally proper.

The added party is procedurally improper.

Are the requirements for such a new claim satisfied? *RULE 13(h) RULE 14(b)* **No** / **Yes**

Go To Map 4.2.5

Notes

Claim Joinder By Defenders
Map 4.2.4: *Fed. R. Civ. P. 13*

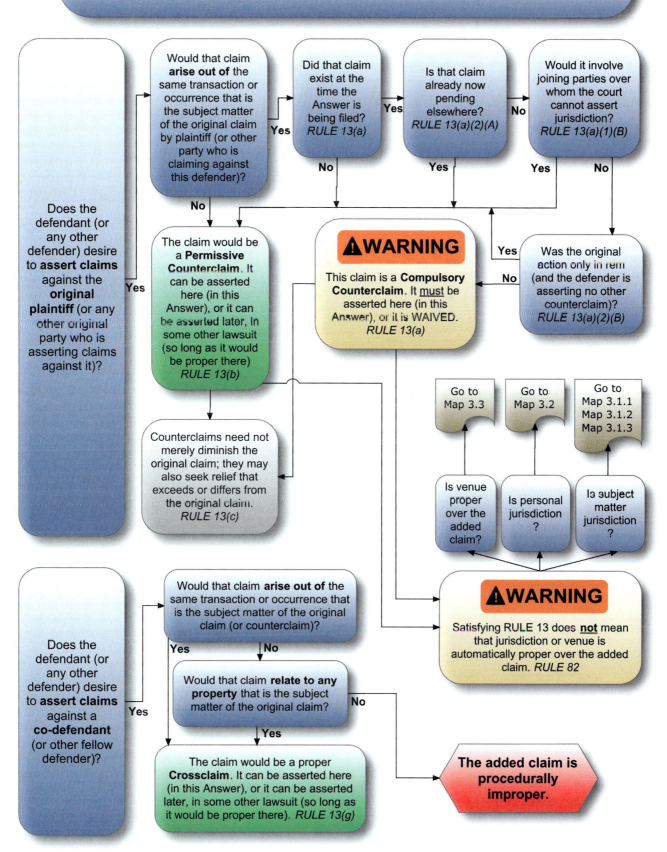

Premise
This Map answers the question asked in Map 4.2: *What CLAIMS Can A Defender Assert In The Lawsuit?*

Does the defendant (or any other defender) desire to **assert claims** against the **original plaintiff** (or any other original party who is asserting claims against it)?

Would that claim **arise out of** the same transaction or occurrence that is the subject matter of the original claim by plaintiff (or other party who is claiming against this defender)?

Did that claim exist at the time the Answer is being filed? *RULE 13(a)*

Is that claim already now pending elsewhere? *RULE 13(a)(2)(A)*

Would it involve joining parties over whom the court cannot assert jurisdiction? *RULE 13(a)(1)(B)*

The claim would be a **Permissive Counterclaim**. It can be asserted here (in this Answer), or it can be asserted later, in some other lawsuit (so long as it would be proper there) *RULE 13(b)*

⚠ **WARNING**
This claim is a **Compulsory Counterclaim**. It <u>must</u> be asserted here (in this Answer), or it is WAIVED. *RULE 13(a)*

Was the original action only in rem (and the defender is asserting no other counterclaim)? *RULE 13(a)(2)(B)*

Counterclaims need not merely diminish the original claim; they may also seek relief that exceeds or differs from the original claim. *RULE 13(c)*

Go to Map 3.3

Go to Map 3.2

Go to Map 3.1.1 Map 3.1.2 Map 3.1.3

Is venue proper over the added claim?

Is personal jurisdiction?

Is subject matter jurisdiction?

Does the defendant (or any other defender) desire to **assert claims** against a **co-defendant** (or other fellow defender)?

Would that claim **arise out of** the same transaction or occurrence that is the subject matter of the original claim (or counterclaim)?

Would that claim **relate to any property** that is the subject matter of the original claim?

The claim would be a proper **Crossclaim**. It can be asserted here (in this Answer), or it can be asserted later, in some other lawsuit (so long as it would be proper there). *RULE 13(g)*

⚠ **WARNING**
Satisfying RULE 13 does **not** mean that jurisdiction or venue is automatically proper over the added claim. *RULE 82*

The added claim is procedurally improper.

93

Notes

Party Joinder By Defenders
Map 4.2.5: *Fed. R. Civ. P. 14 & 19*

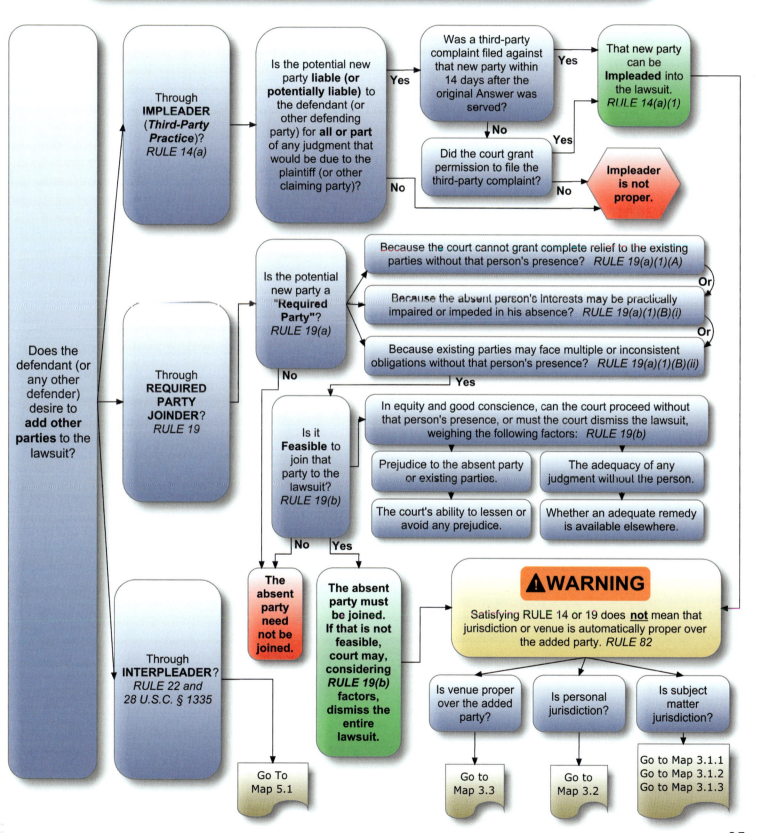

Premise

This Map continues to answer the question asked in Map 4.2: *What PARTIES Can The Defendant (Or Other Defender) Add Into The Lawsuit?*

Does the defendant (or any other defender) desire to **add other parties** to the lawsuit?

Through **IMPLEADER** (*Third-Party Practice*)? *RULE 14(a)*

Is the potential new party **liable (or potentially liable)** to the defendant (or other defending party) for **all or part** of any judgment that would be due to the plaintiff (or other claiming party)?

Yes → Was a third-party complaint filed against that new party within 14 days after the original Answer was served?

Yes → That new party can be **Impleaded** into the lawsuit. *RULE 14(a)(1)*

No → Did the court grant permission to file the third-party complaint?

Yes → (That new party can be Impleaded)

No → **Impleader is not proper.**

No → **Impleader is not proper.**

Through **REQUIRED PARTY JOINDER**? *RULE 19*

Is the potential new party a **"Required Party"**? *RULE 19(a)*

- Because the court cannot grant complete relief to the existing parties without that person's presence? *RULE 19(a)(1)(A)* — Or
- Because the absent person's interests may be practically impaired or impeded in his absence? *RULE 19(a)(1)(B)(i)* — Or
- Because existing parties may face multiple or inconsistent obligations without that person's presence? *RULE 19(a)(1)(B)(ii)*

Yes → In equity and good conscience, can the court proceed without that person's presence, or must the court dismiss the lawsuit, weighing the following factors: *RULE 19(b)*

- Prejudice to the absent party or existing parties.
- The adequacy of any judgment without the person.
- The court's ability to lessen or avoid any prejudice.
- Whether an adequate remedy is available elsewhere.

No → Is it **Feasible** to join that party to the lawsuit? *RULE 19(b)*

No → **The absent party need not be joined.**

Yes → **The absent party must be joined. If that is not feasible, court may, considering *RULE 19(b)* factors, dismiss the entire lawsuit.**

Through **INTERPLEADER**? *RULE 22 and 28 U.S.C. § 1335*

⚠ **WARNING**

Satisfying RULE 14 or 19 does **not** mean that jurisdiction or venue is automatically proper over the added party. *RULE 82*

- Is venue proper over the added party? → Go to Map 3.3
- Is personal jurisdiction? → Go to Map 3.2
- Is subject matter jurisdiction? → Go to Map 3.1.1 / Go to Map 3.1.2 / Go to Map 3.1.3

Go To Map 5.1

Notes

Party Joinder By Non-Parties
Map 4.2.6: *Fed. R. Civ. P. 13, 14, & 24*

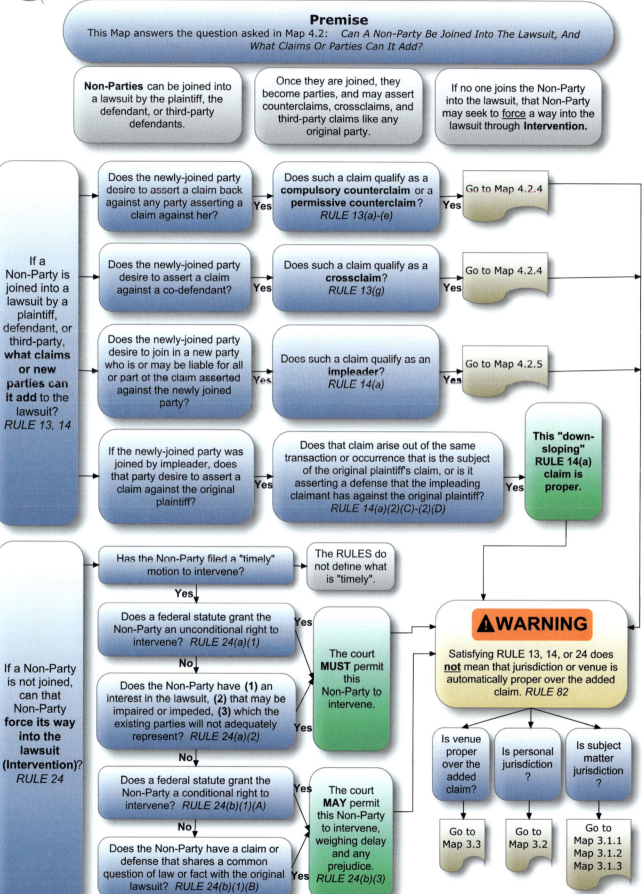

Premise

This Map answers the question asked in Map 4.2: *Can A Non-Party Be Joined Into The Lawsuit, And What Claims Or Parties Can It Add?*

Non-Parties can be joined into a lawsuit by the plaintiff, the defendant, or third-party defendants.

Once they are joined, they become parties, and may assert counterclaims, crossclaims, and third-party claims like any original party.

If no one joins the Non-Party into the lawsuit, that Non-Party may seek to <u>force</u> a way into the lawsuit through **Intervention**.

If a Non-Party is joined into a lawsuit by a plaintiff, defendant, or third-party, **what claims or new parties can it add** to the lawsuit? *RULE 13, 14*

Does the newly-joined party desire to assert a claim back against any party asserting a claim against her? **Yes**

Does such a claim qualify as a **compulsory counterclaim** or a **permissive counterclaim**? *RULE 13(a)-(e)* **Yes**

Go to Map 4.2.4

Does the newly-joined party desire to assert a claim against a co-defendant? **Yes**

Does such a claim qualify as a **crossclaim**? *RULE 13(g)* **Yes**

Go to Map 4.2.4

Does the newly-joined party desire to join in a new party who is or may be liable for all or part of the claim asserted against the newly joined party? **Yes**

Does such a claim qualify as an **impleader**? *RULE 14(a)* **Yes**

Go to Map 4.2.5

If the newly-joined party was joined by impleader, does that party desire to assert a claim against the original plaintiff? **Yes**

Does that claim arise out of the same transaction or occurrence that is the subject of the original plaintiff's claim, or is it asserting a defense that the impleading claimant has against the original plaintiff? *RULE 14(a)(2)(C)-(2)(D)* **Yes**

This "down-sloping" **RULE 14(a)** claim is **proper**.

If a Non-Party is not joined, can that Non-Party **force its way into the lawsuit (Intervention)**? *RULE 24*

Has the Non-Party filed a "timely" motion to intervene?

The RULES do not define what is "timely".

Yes

Does a federal statute grant the Non-Party an unconditional right to intervene? *RULE 24(a)(1)* **Yes**

No

Does the Non-Party have **(1)** an interest in the lawsuit, **(2)** that may be impaired or impeded, **(3)** which the existing parties will not adequately represent? *RULE 24(a)(2)* **Yes**

The court **MUST** permit this Non-Party to intervene.

No

Does a federal statute grant the Non-Party a conditional right to intervene? *RULE 24(b)(1)(A)* **Yes**

No

Does the Non-Party have a claim or defense that shares a common question of law or fact with the original lawsuit? *RULE 24(b)(1)(B)* **Yes**

The court **MAY** permit this Non-Party to intervene, weighing delay and any prejudice. *RULE 24(b)(3)*

⚠**WARNING**

Satisfying RULE 13, 14, or 24 does **not** mean that jurisdiction or venue is automatically proper over the added claim. *RULE 82*

Is venue proper over the added claim?

Is personal jurisdiction?

Is subject matter jurisdiction?

Go to Map 3.3

Go to Map 3.2

Go to Map 3.1.1 Map 3.1.2 Map 3.1.3

Notes

Remedies for Improper / Unfair Joinder
Map 4.2.7: *Fed. R. Civ. P. 21, 25, & 42*

Premise

This Map answers the question from Map 4.0: *What Happens If An Improper Claim Or Improper Party Is Joined Into A Federal Lawsuit, Or The Joinder Is Otherwise Unfair?*

What is the proper remedy for joinder that has occurred, but is **improper** or otherwise **unfair**?

If an **improper claim** is joined?	The entire lawsuit is **not** dismissed. Instead, the improperly joined claimed is severed. *RULE 21*
If an **improper party** is joined or omitted?	The entire lawsuit is **not** dismissed. Instead, the improperly joined party is dropped, or the Improperly omitted party is added. *RULE 21*
If an original party **dies**?	The entire lawsuit is **not** dismissed, *if* the claim survives the death. The decedent's representative may join within 90 days of the date of notice of the death. *RULE 25(a)*
If an original party **becomes incompetent**?	The entire lawsuit is **not** dismissed. The now-incompetent party's representative may, upon motion, continue the litigation. *RULE 25(b)*
If an original party **transfers its interest** in the subject of the lawsuit?	The lawsuit continues with the original party, unless the court orders the successor-in-interest to be substituted into the lawsuit. *RULE 25(c)*
If an original party is **a public officer** who dies or leaves office?	The officer's successor is automatically substituted into the lawsuit. *RULE 25(d)*
If joinder is not improper, but the **effect is unfair**?	The court may order that the various joined claims be tried separately, for convenience, to avoid prejudice, or to expedite and economize. *RULE 42(b)*

Notes

Amending the Pleadings
Map 4.3: *Fed. R. Civ. P. 15*

Premise
This Map answers the question from Map 4.0: *Have all appropriate amendments been made to the pleadings?*

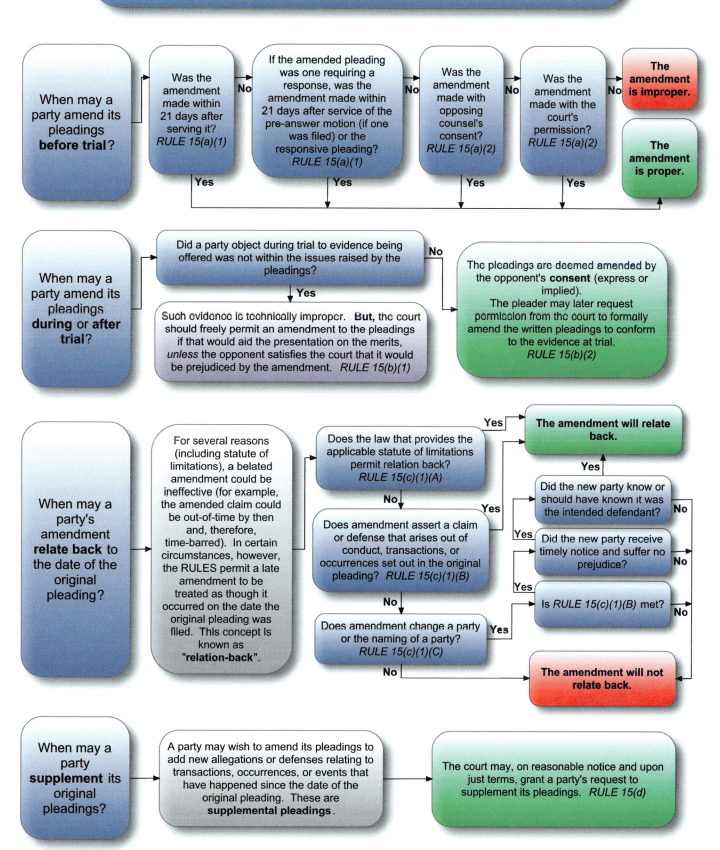

When may a party amend its pleadings before trial?

Was the amendment made within 21 days after serving it? *RULE 15(a)(1)* — **No** →

If the amended pleading was one requiring a response, was the amendment made within 21 days after service of the pre-answer motion (if one was filed) or the responsive pleading? *RULE 15(a)(1)* — **No** →

Was the amendment made with opposing counsel's consent? *RULE 15(a)(2)* — **No** →

Was the amendment made with the court's permission? *RULE 15(a)(2)* — **No** →

The amendment is improper.

The amendment is proper.

(Each "Yes" leads to **The amendment is proper.**)

When may a party amend its pleadings during or after trial?

Did a party object during trial to evidence being offered was not within the issues raised by the pleadings? — **No** →

The pleadings are deemed amended by the opponent's **consent** (express or implied). The pleader may later request permission from the court to formally amend the written pleadings to conform to the evidence at trial. *RULE 15(b)(2)*

Yes ↓

Such evidence is technically improper. **But,** the court should freely permit an amendment to the pleadings if that would aid the presentation on the merits, *unless* the opponent satisfies the court that it would be prejudiced by the amendment. *RULE 15(b)(1)*

When may a party's amendment relate back to the date of the original pleading?

For several reasons (including statute of limitations), a belated amendment could be ineffective (for example, the amended claim could be out-of-time by then and, therefore, time-barred). In certain circumstances, however, the RULES permit a late amendment to be treated as though it occurred on the date the original pleading was filed. This concept is known as **"relation-back"**.

Does the law that provides the applicable statute of limitations permit relation back? *RULE 15(c)(1)(A)* — **Yes** → **The amendment will relate back.**

No ↓

Does amendment assert a claim or defense that arises out of conduct, transactions, or occurrences set out in the original pleading? *RULE 15(c)(1)(B)* — **Yes** →

No ↓

Does amendment change a party or the naming of a party? *RULE 15(c)(1)(C)* — **Yes** →

No ↓

Did the new party know or should have known it was the intended defendant? — **No** →

Yes ↑ (leads to **The amendment will relate back.**)

Did the new party receive timely notice and suffer no prejudice? — **No** →

Yes ↑

Is *RULE 15(c)(1)(B)* met? — **No** →

Yes ↑

The amendment will not relate back.

When may a party supplement its original pleadings?

A party may wish to amend its pleadings to add new allegations or defenses relating to transactions, occurrences, or events that have happened since the date of the original pleading. These are **supplemental pleadings**.

The court may, on reasonable notice and upon just terms, grant a party's request to supplement its pleadings. *RULE 15(d)*

Notes

Post-Pleading Motions

Map 4.4: *Fed. R. Civ. P. 7 & 12*

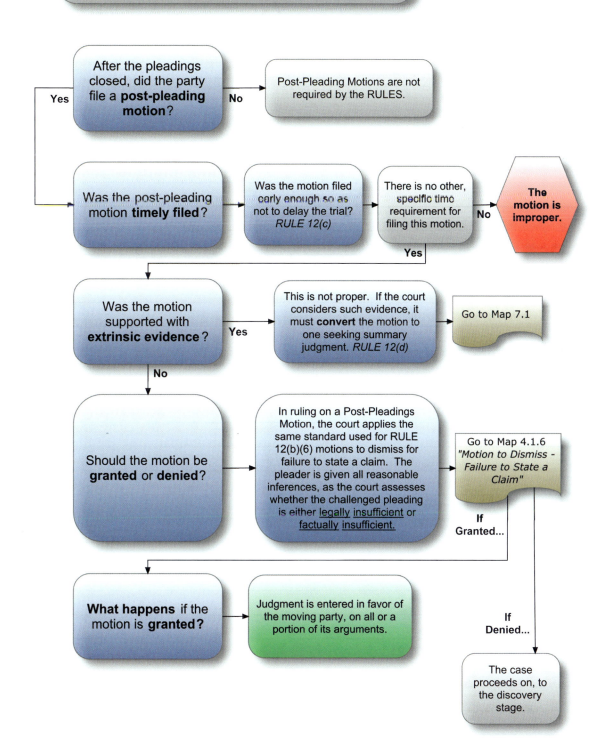

Premise

This Map answers upon the question from Map 4.0:   *Did the lawsuit survive Post-Pleading Motions?*

As the term denotes, **Post-Pleading Motions** (Motions for Judgment on the Pleadings) are motions filed after the pleadings are "closed". Their typical purpose is to seek a dismissal (or other culling) of the pleading to which they are directed, and to do so before the discovery stage begins. This type of motion is infrequently filed, in preference to the timing advantages of a Pre-Answer Motion, and the factually-searching nature of a Summary Judgment Motion.

A "**Motion**" is a request to the court seeking a ruling. *RULE 7(b)(1)*

After the pleadings closed, did the party file a **post-pleading motion**?

No → Post-Pleading Motions are not required by the RULES.

Yes

Was the post-pleading motion **timely filed**?

→ Was the motion filed early enough so as not to delay the trial? *RULE 12(c)*

→ There is no other, specific time requirement for filing this motion.

No → **The motion is improper.**

Yes

Was the motion supported with **extrinsic evidence**?

Yes → This is not proper. If the court considers such evidence, it must **convert** the motion to one seeking summary judgment. *RULE 12(d)*

→ Go to Map 7.1

No

Should the motion be **granted** or **denied**?

→ In ruling on a Post-Pleadings Motion, the court applies the same standard used for RULE 12(b)(6) motions to dismiss for failure to state a claim. The pleader is given all reasonable inferences, as the court assesses whether the challenged pleading is either <u>legally insufficient</u> or <u>factually insufficient.</u>

→ Go to Map 4.1.6 *"Motion to Dismiss - Failure to State a Claim"*

If Granted...

What happens if the motion is **granted**?

→ Judgment is entered in favor of the moving party, on all or a portion of its arguments.

If Denied... → The case proceeds on, to the discovery stage.

Notes

Expeditious Litigation, Generally
Map 4.5: *Fed. R. Civ. P. 1, 16, 26, 37, 41, & 55*

Premise

This Map answers upon the question from Map 4.0: *Is The Lawsuit Proceeding Expeditiously?*

Why is an expeditious federal litigation **necessary**?

→ The "touchstones" of the Federal Rules of Civil Procedure command that the RULES should be administered to achieve the **just, speedy,** and **inexpensive** determination of every federal lawsuit.
RULE 1

How does the court **manage the progress** of federal litigation?

→ The RULES impose a duty on counsel to meet early on in the litigation, and the judge may meet regularly with the litigants to identify problems, provide resolutions, and keep the litigation on pace.
RULE 16 & 26

→ Go to Map 4.5.1

What happens if the **plaintiff** doesn't (or can't) move the **litigation forward**?

→ The plaintiff may voluntarily dismiss the lawsuit. Alternatively, the court may order the lawsuit dismissed in an appropriate case.
RULE 41

→ Go to Map 4.5.2

What happens if the **defendant** (or any defending party) **fails to defend** the lawsuit?

→ The defendant (or other defending party) may be defaulted, and in an appropriate case final judgment may be entered against them.
RULE 55

→ Go to Map 4.5.3

Notes

Litigation Conferences
Map 4.5.1: *Fed. R. Civ. P. 16 & 26*

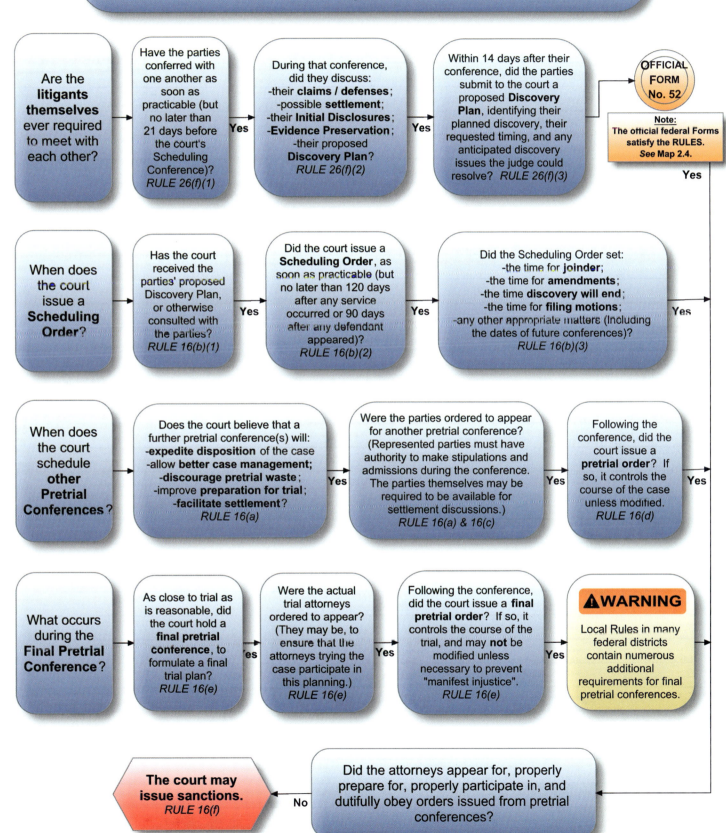

Premise

This Map answers the question posed in Map 4.5: *How Does The Court Manage The Progress Of Federal Litigation?*

Are the **litigants themselves** ever required to meet with each other?

→ **Yes** → Have the parties conferred with one another as soon as practicable (but no later than 21 days before the court's Scheduling Conference)? *RULE 26(f)(1)*

→ **Yes** → During that conference, did they discuss:
- their **claims / defenses**;
- possible **settlement**;
- their **Initial Disclosures**;
- **Evidence Preservation**;
- their proposed **Discovery Plan**? *RULE 26(f)(2)*

→ **Yes** → Within 14 days after their conference, did the parties submit to the court a proposed **Discovery Plan**, identifying their planned discovery, their requested timing, and any anticipated discovery issues the judge could resolve? *RULE 26(f)(3)*

→ **OFFICIAL FORM No. 52**

Note: The official federal Forms satisfy the RULES. *See Map 2.4.*

→ **Yes** ↓

When does the court issue a **Scheduling Order**?

→ **Yes** → Has the court received the parties' proposed Discovery Plan, or otherwise consulted with the parties? *RULE 16(b)(1)*

→ **Yes** → Did the court issue a **Scheduling Order**, as soon as practicable (but no later than 120 days after any service occurred or 90 days after any defendant appeared)? *RULE 16(b)(2)*

→ **Yes** → Did the Scheduling Order set:
- the time for **joinder**;
- the time for **amendments**;
- the time **discovery will end**;
- the time for **filing motions**;
- any other appropriate matters (including the dates of future conferences)? *RULE 16(b)(3)*

→ **Yes** ↓

When does the court schedule **other Pretrial Conferences**?

→ **Yes** → Does the court believe that a further pretrial conference(s) will:
- **expedite disposition** of the case
- allow **better case management;**
- **discourage pretrial waste**;
- improve **preparation for trial**;
- **facilitate settlement**? *RULE 16(a)*

→ **Yes** → Were the parties ordered to appear for another pretrial conference? (Represented parties must have authority to make stipulations and admissions during the conference. The parties themselves may be required to be available for settlement discussions.) *RULE 16(a) & 16(c)*

→ **Yes** → Following the conference, did the court issue a **pretrial order**? If so, it controls the course of the case unless modified. *RULE 16(d)*

→ **Yes** ↓

What occurs during the **Final Pretrial Conference**?

→ **Yes** → As close to trial as is reasonable, did the court hold a **final pretrial conference**, to formulate a final trial plan? *RULE 16(e)*

→ **Yes** → Were the actual trial attorneys ordered to appear? (They may be, to ensure that the attorneys trying the case participate in this planning.) *RULE 16(e)*

→ **Yes** → Following the conference, did the court issue a **final pretrial order**? If so, it controls the course of the trial, and may **not** be modified unless necessary to prevent "manifest injustice". *RULE 16(e)*

→ **Yes** → ⚠ **WARNING** Local Rules in many federal districts contain numerous additional requirements for final pretrial conferences.

→ ↓

Did the attorneys appear for, properly prepare for, properly participate in, and dutifully obey orders issued from pretrial conferences?

→ **No** → **The court may issue sanctions.** *RULE 16(f)*

Notes

Dismissals
Map 4.5.2: *Fed. R. Civ. P. 41*

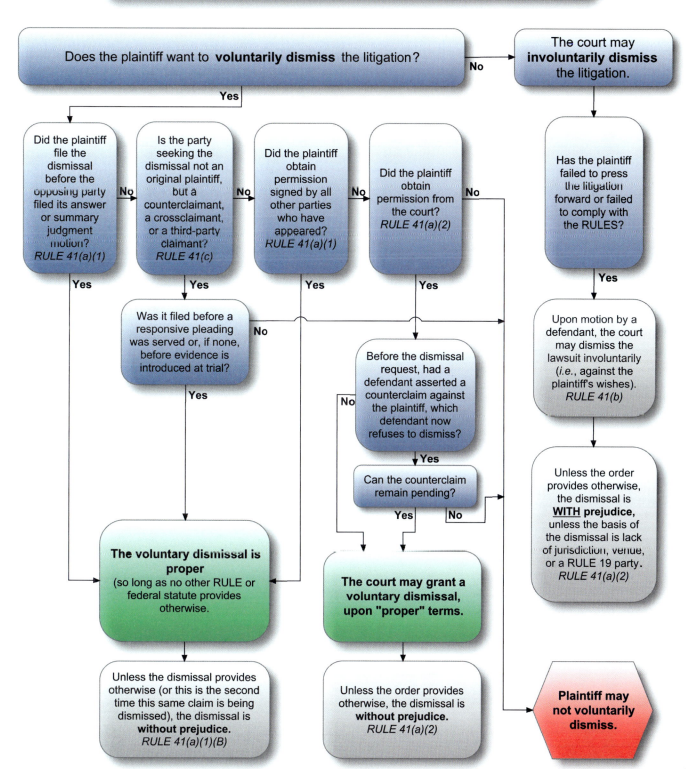

Premise

This Map answers the question posed in Map 4.5: *What Happens If The Plaintiff Doesn't (Or Can't) Move The Litigation Forward?*

A plaintiff may no longer wish to, fail to, or be unable to continue a litigation for many reasons -- for example, the reason for the litigation may have dissipated, the plaintiff's focus may have otherwise moved on, the plaintiff's ability to litigate may have ceased, the litigation facts may have evolved in an unhelpful way, or the defense arguments may now persuade the plaintiff.

Does the plaintiff want to **voluntarily dismiss** the litigation? → No → The court may **involuntarily dismiss** the litigation.

Yes

Did the plaintiff file the dismissal before the opposing party filed its answer or summary judgment motion? *RULE 41(a)(1)* — No → Is the party seeking the dismissal not an original plaintiff, but a counterclaimant, a crossclaimant, or a third-party claimant? *RULE 41(c)* — No → Did the plaintiff obtain permission signed by all other parties who have appeared? *RULE 41(a)(1)* — No → Did the plaintiff obtain permission from the court? *RULE 41(a)(2)* — No →

Yes (below first box) → **The voluntary dismissal is proper** (so long as no other RULE or federal statute provides otherwise.)

Yes (second box) → Was it filed before a responsive pleading was served or, if none, before evidence is introduced at trial? → Yes → **The voluntary dismissal is proper** / No →

Yes (third box) → **The voluntary dismissal is proper**

Yes (fourth box) → Before the dismissal request, had a defendant asserted a counterclaim against the plaintiff, which defendant now refuses to dismiss? — No → **The court may grant a voluntary dismissal, upon "proper" terms.** / Yes → Can the counterclaim remain pending? — Yes → **The court may grant a voluntary dismissal, upon "proper" terms.** / No →

The voluntary dismissal is proper → Unless the dismissal provides otherwise (or this is the second time this same claim is being dismissed), the dismissal is **without prejudice**. *RULE 41(a)(1)(B)*

The court may grant a voluntary dismissal, upon "proper" terms. → Unless the order provides otherwise, the dismissal is **without prejudice**. *RULE 41(a)(2)*

Has the plaintiff failed to press the litigation forward or failed to comply with the RULES? → Yes → Upon motion by a defendant, the court may dismiss the lawsuit involuntarily (*i.e.*, against the plaintiff's wishes). *RULE 41(b)* → Unless the order provides otherwise, the dismissal is **WITH** prejudice, unless the basis of the dismissal is lack of jurisdiction, venue, or a RULE 19 party. *RULE 41(a)(2)*

Plaintiff may not voluntarily dismiss.

Notes

Defaults
Map 4.5.3: *Fed. R. Civ. P. 55*

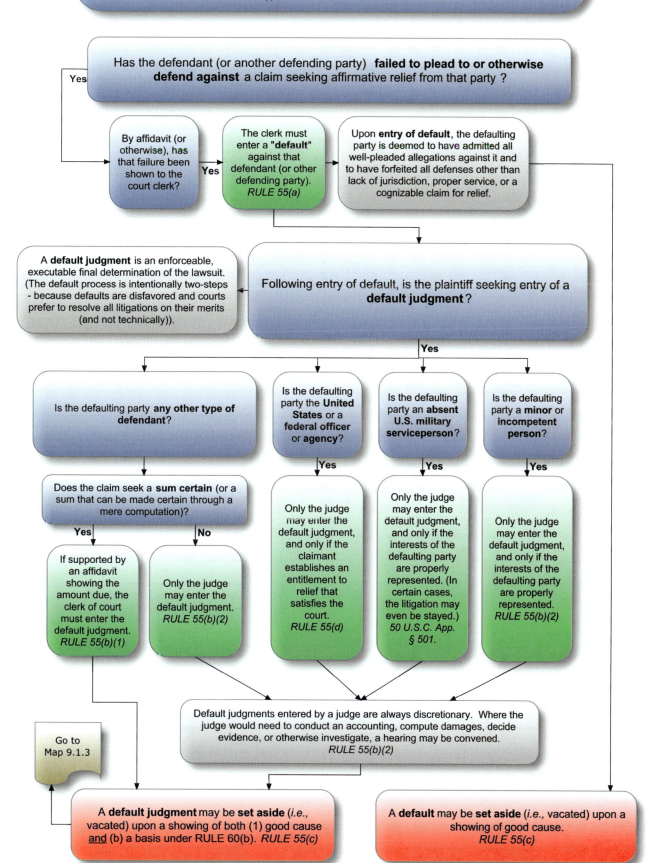

Premise
This Map answers the question posed in Map 4.5: *What Happens If The Defendant (Or Any Defending Party) Fails To Defend The Lawsuit?*

Has the defendant (or another defending party) **failed to plead to or otherwise defend against** a claim seeking affirmative relief from that party?

Yes

By affidavit (or otherwise), has that failure been shown to the court clerk?

Yes

The clerk must enter a **"default"** against that defendant (or other defending party). *RULE 55(a)*

Upon **entry of default**, the defaulting party is deemed to have admitted all well-pleaded allegations against it and to have forfeited all defenses other than lack of jurisdiction, proper service, or a cognizable claim for relief.

A **default judgment** is an enforceable, executable final determination of the lawsuit. (The default process is intentionally two-steps - because defaults are disfavored and courts prefer to resolve all litigations on their merits (and not technically)).

Following entry of default, is the plaintiff seeking entry of a **default judgment**?

Yes

Is the defaulting party **any other type of defendant**?

Is the defaulting party the **United States** or a **federal officer** or **agency**?

Is the defaulting party an **absent U.S. military serviceperson**?

Is the defaulting party a **minor** or **incompetent person**?

Does the claim seek a **sum certain** (or a sum that can be made certain through a mere computation)?

Yes

No

Yes

Yes

Yes

If supported by an affidavit showing the amount due, the clerk of court must enter the default judgment. *RULE 55(b)(1)*

Only the judge may enter the default judgment. *RULE 55(b)(2)*

Only the judge may enter the default judgment, and only if the claimant establishes an entitlement to relief that satisfies the court. *RULE 55(d)*

Only the judge may enter the default judgment, and only if the interests of the defaulting party are properly represented. (In certain cases, the litigation may even be stayed.) *50 U.S.C. App. § 501.*

Only the judge may enter the default judgment, and only if the interests of the defaulting party are properly represented. *RULE 55(b)(2)*

Default judgments entered by a judge are always discretionary. Where the judge would need to conduct an accounting, compute damages, decide evidence, or otherwise investigate, a hearing may be convened. *RULE 55(b)(2)*

Go to Map 9.1.3

A **default judgment** may be **set aside** (*i.e.,* vacated) upon a showing of both (1) good cause <u>and</u> (b) a basis under RULE 60(b). *RULE 55(c)*

A **default** may be **set aside** (*i.e.,* vacated) upon a showing of good cause. *RULE 55(c)*

Notes

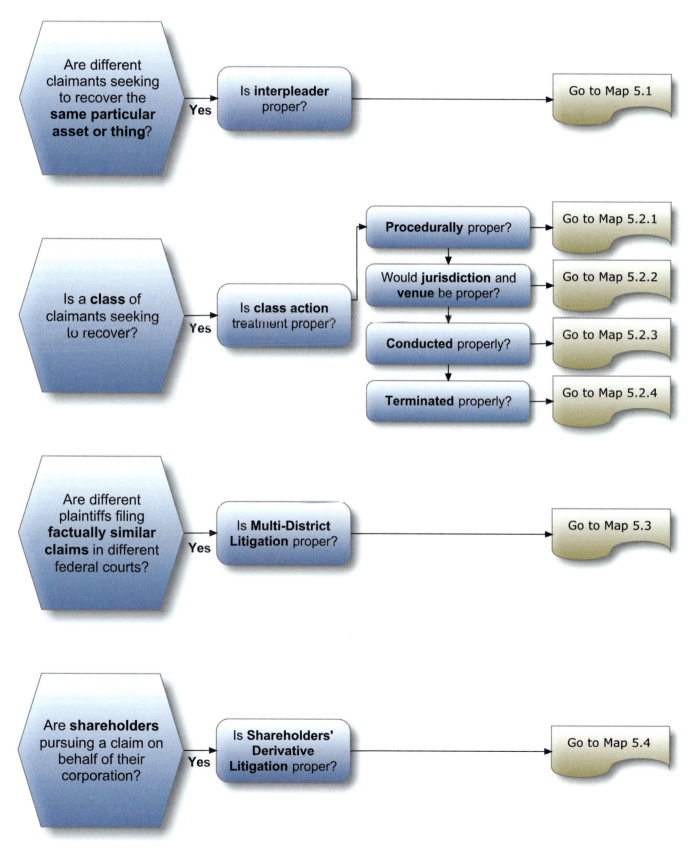

Are different claimants seeking to recover the **same particular asset or thing**?

Yes → Is **interpleader** proper? → Go to Map 5.1

Is a **class** of claimants seeking to recover?

Yes → Is **class action** treatment proper?

- **Procedurally** proper? → Go to Map 5.2.1
- Would **jurisdiction** and **venue** be proper? → Go to Map 5.2.2
- **Conducted** properly? → Go to Map 5.2.3
- **Terminated** properly? → Go to Map 5.2.4

Are different plaintiffs filing **factually similar claims** in different federal courts?

Yes → Is **Multi-District Litigation** proper? → Go to Map 5.3

Are **shareholders** pursuing a claim on behalf of their corporation?

Yes → Is **Shareholders' Derivative Litigation** proper? → Go to Map 5.4

Notes

Interpleader

Map 5.1: *Fed. R. Civ. P. 22 & 28 U.S.C. §§ 1335, 1397, & 2361*

Premise
This Map answers the question asked in Map 5.0: *Is Interpleader Proper?*

Interpleader allows a party who is holding a "stake" that is sought by various different claimants to join those competing claimants into a single litigation, where all their respective claims to the stake can be heard and decided in the same case. Interpleader thus avoids the costs of multiple litigation about a single stake, and the risk of inconsistent rulings.

There are two vehicles for interpleader, "**Rule Interpleader**" (under RULE 22) and "**Statutory Interpleader**" (under 28 U.S.C. § 1335). Each has benefits and weaknesses.

There are two interpleader types:

True Interpleader: where the stake holder asserts no claim to the stake.

In the Nature of Interpleader: where the stake holder does assert a claim to the stake.

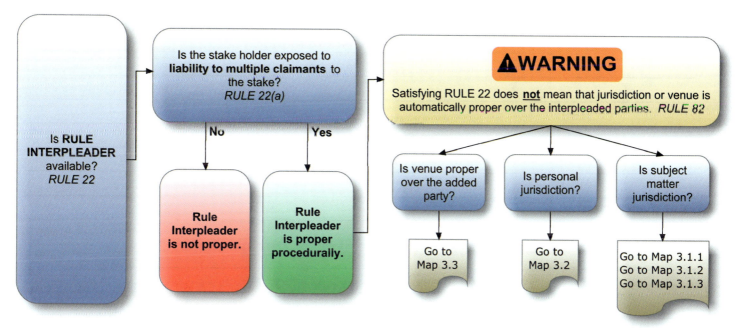

Is **RULE INTERPLEADER** available? *RULE 22*

Is the stake holder exposed to **liability to multiple claimants** to the stake? *RULE 22(a)*

- **No** → **Rule Interpleader is not proper.**
- **Yes** → **Rule Interpleader is proper procedurally.**

⚠️**WARNING**
Satisfying RULE 22 does **not** mean that jurisdiction or venue is automatically proper over the interpleaded parties. *RULE 82*

- Is venue proper over the added party? → Go to Map 3.3
- Is personal jurisdiction? → Go to Map 3.2
- Is subject matter jurisdiction? → Go to Map 3.1.1 / Go to Map 3.1.2 / Go to Map 3.1.3

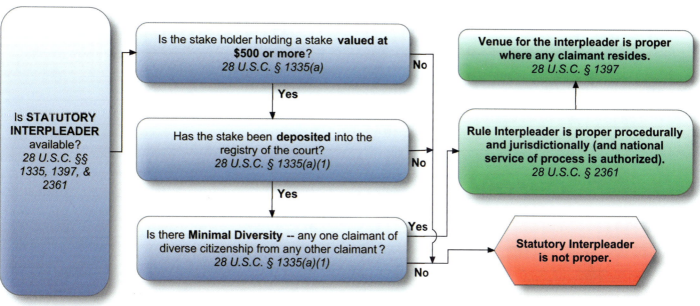

Is **STATUTORY INTERPLEADER** available? *28 U.S.C. §§ 1335, 1397, & 2361*

Is the stake holder holding a stake **valued at $500 or more**? *28 U.S.C. § 1335(a)*
- **No** →
- **Yes** ↓

Has the stake been **deposited** into the registry of the court? *28 U.S.C. § 1335(a)(1)*
- **No** →
- **Yes** ↓

Is there **Minimal Diversity** -- any one claimant of diverse citizenship from any other claimant? *28 U.S.C. § 1335(a)(1)*
- **Yes** →
- **No** →

Venue for the interpleader is proper where any claimant resides. *28 U.S.C. § 1397*

Rule Interpleader is proper procedurally and jurisdictionally (and national service of process is authorized). *28 U.S.C. § 2361*

Statutory Interpleader is not proper.

Notes

Class Actions - Procedural Availability
Map 5.2.1: *Fed. R. Civ. P. 23*

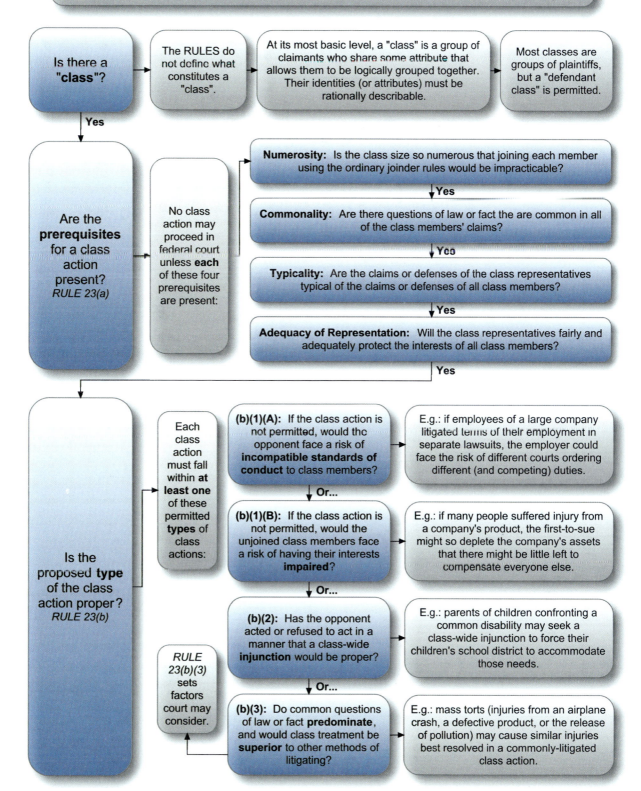

Premise
This Map begins the answer to the question asked in Map 5.0:   *Is Class Action Treatment Proper?*

When the number of parties is so numerous that ordinary joinder procedures are impractical, **class action** may be proper. In a class action, a group of similarly situated claimants (the "class") is represented by one or more lead claimants, who are obliged to litigate the claims for the benefit of the entire class. The result in the lawsuit -- victory or defeat -- binds every class member (except for those who "opt-out" of the class).

Is there a "class"?

The RULES do not define what constitutes a "class".

At its most basic level, a "class" is a group of claimants who share some attribute that allows them to be logically grouped together. Their identities (or attributes) must be rationally describable.

Most classes are groups of plaintiffs, but a "defendant class" is permitted.

Yes

Are the prerequisites for a class action present? *RULE 23(a)*

No class action may proceed in federal court unless **each** of these four prerequisites are present:

Numerosity: Is the class size so numerous that joining each member using the ordinary joinder rules would be impracticable?

↓**Yes**

Commonality: Are there questions of law or fact the are common in all of the class members' claims?

↓**Yes**

Typicality: Are the claims or defenses of the class representatives typical of the claims or defenses of all class members?

↓**Yes**

Adequacy of Representation: Will the class representatives fairly and adequately protect the interests of all class members?

Yes

Is the proposed type of the class action proper? *RULE 23(b)*

Each class action must fall within **at least one** of these permitted **types** of class actions:

RULE 23(b)(3) sets factors court may consider.

(b)(1)(A): If the class action is not permitted, would the opponent face a risk of **incompatible standards of conduct** to class members?

E.g.: if employees of a large company litigated terms of their employment in separate lawsuits, the employer could face the risk of different courts ordering different (and competing) duties.

Or...

(b)(1)(B): If the class action is not permitted, would the unjoined class members face a risk of having their interests **impaired**?

E.g.: if many people suffered injury from a company's product, the first-to-sue might so deplete the company's assets that there might be little left to compensate everyone else.

Or...

(b)(2): Has the opponent acted or refused to act in a manner that a class-wide **injunction** would be proper?

E.g.: parents of children confronting a common disability may seek a class-wide injunction to force their children's school district to accommodate those needs.

Or...

(b)(3): Do common questions of law or fact **predominate**, and would class treatment be **superior** to other methods of litigating?

E.g.: mass torts (injuries from an airplane crash, a defective product, or the release of pollution) may cause similar injuries best resolved in a commonly-litigated class action.

Notes

Class Actions – Proper Jurisdiction & Venue
Map 5.2.2: *28 U.S.C. § 1332(d)*

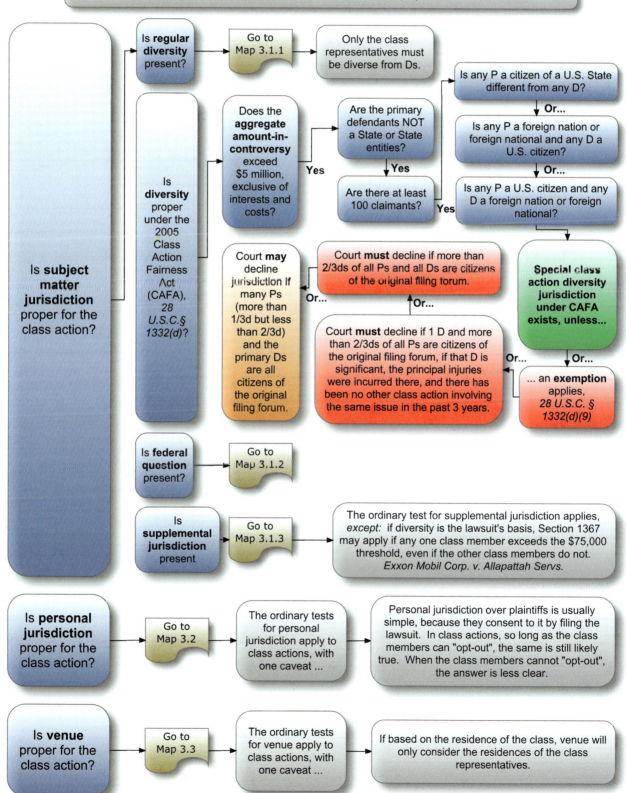

Premise

This Map continues the answer to the question asked in Map 5.0: *Is Class Action Treatment Proper?*

Like any other joinder device, meeting the procedural requirements for class actions does not ensure that subject matter jurisdiction, personal jurisdiction, and venue are proper. Each must be tested.

Is subject matter jurisdiction proper for the class action?

Is **regular diversity** present? → Go to Map 3.1.1 → Only the class representatives must be diverse from Ds.

Is **diversity** proper under the 2005 Class Action Fairness Act (CAFA), *28 U.S.C.§ 1332(d)*?

Does the **aggregate amount-in-controversy** exceed $5 million, exclusive of interests and costs? → **Yes** → Are the primary defendants NOT a State or State entities? → **Yes** → Are there at least 100 claimants? → **Yes** →

Is any P a citizen of a U.S. State different from any D? → **Or...** → Is any P a foreign nation or foreign national and any D a U.S. citizen? → **Or...** → Is any P a U.S. citizen and any D a foreign nation or foreign national?

→ **Special class action diversity jurisdiction under CAFA exists, unless...**

Court **may** decline jurisdiction if many Ps (more than 1/3d but less than 2/3d) and the primary Ds are all citizens of the original filing forum.

Or... Court **must** decline if more than 2/3ds of all Ps and all Ds are citizens of the original filing forum.

Or... Court **must** decline if 1 D and more than 2/3ds of all Ps are citizens of the original filing forum, if that D is significant, the principal injuries were incurred there, and there has been no other class action involving the same issue in the past 3 years. → **Or...**

Or... ... an **exemption** applies, *28 U.S.C. § 1332(d)(9)*

Is **federal question** present? → Go to Map 3.1.2

Is **supplemental jurisdiction** present → Go to Map 3.1.3 → The ordinary test for supplemental jurisdiction applies, *except:* if diversity is the lawsuit's basis, Section 1367 may apply if any one class member exceeds the $75,000 threshold, even if the other class members do not. *Exxon Mobil Corp. v. Allapattah Servs.*

Is personal jurisdiction proper for the class action? → Go to Map 3.2 → The ordinary tests for personal jurisdiction apply to class actions, with one caveat ... → Personal jurisdiction over plaintiffs is usually simple, because they consent to it by filing the lawsuit. In class actions, so long as the class members can "opt-out", the same is still likely true. When the class members cannot "opt-out", the answer is less clear.

Is venue proper for the class action? → Go to Map 3.3 → The ordinary tests for venue apply to class actions, with one caveat ... → If based on the residence of the class, venue will only consider the residences of the class representatives.

119

Notes

Class Actions - Conducting Class Action Lawsuits
Map 5.2.3: *Fed. R. Civ. P. 23*

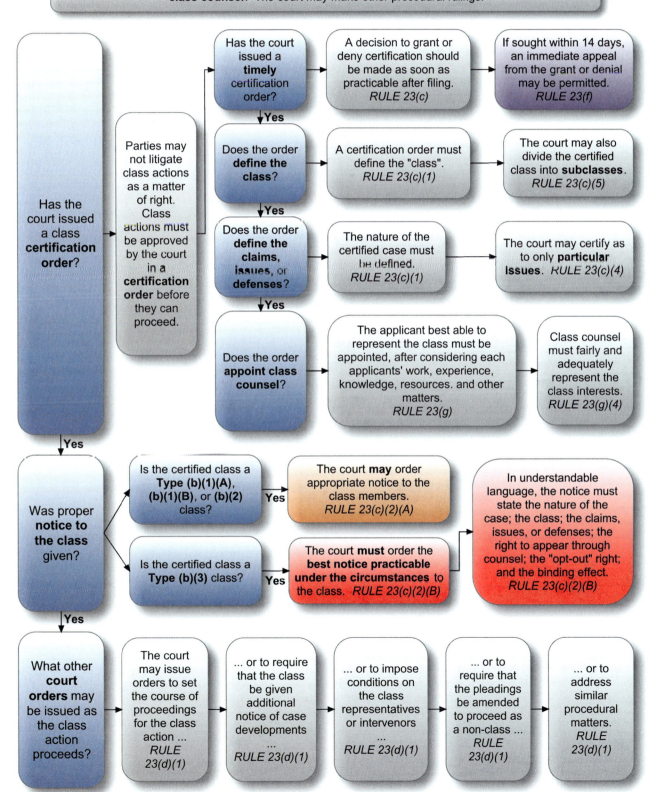

Premise
This Map continues the answer to the question asked in Map 5.0:   *Is Class Action Treatment Proper?*

The court determines that a lawsuit may proceed as a class action by **certifying** the class and **appointing class counsel**. The court may make other procedural rulings.

Has the court issued a class **certification order**?

Parties may not litigate class actions as a matter of right. Class actions must be approved by the court in a **certification order** before they can proceed.

Has the court issued a **timely** certification order?

A decision to grant or deny certification should be made as soon as practicable after filing. *RULE 23(c)*

If sought within 14 days, an immediate appeal from the grant or denial may be permitted. *RULE 23(f)*

Yes

Does the order **define the class**?

A certification order must define the "class". *RULE 23(c)(1)*

The court may also divide the certified class into **subclasses**. *RULE 23(c)(5)*

Yes

Does the order **define the claims, issues, or defenses**?

The nature of the certified case must be defined. *RULE 23(c)(1)*

The court may certify as to only **particular issues**. *RULE 23(c)(4)*

Yes

Does the order **appoint class counsel**?

The applicant best able to represent the class must be appointed, after considering each applicants' work, experience, knowledge, resources. and other matters. *RULE 23(g)*

Class counsel must fairly and adequately represent the class interests. *RULE 23(g)(4)*

Yes

Was proper **notice to the class** given?

Is the certified class a **Type (b)(1)(A), (b)(1)(B), or (b)(2)** class?

Yes The court **may** order appropriate notice to the class members. *RULE 23(c)(2)(A)*

Is the certified class a **Type (b)(3)** class?

Yes The court **must** order the **best notice practicable under the circumstances** to the class. *RULE 23(c)(2)(B)*

In understandable language, the notice must state the nature of the case; the class; the claims, issues, or defenses; the right to appear through counsel; the "opt-out" right; and the binding effect. *RULE 23(c)(2)(B)*

Yes

What other **court orders** may be issued as the class action proceeds?

The court may issue orders to set the course of proceedings for the class action ... *RULE 23(d)(1)*

... or to require that the class be given additional notice of case developments ... *RULE 23(d)(1)*

... or to impose conditions on the class representatives or intervenors ... *RULE 23(d)(1)*

... or to require that the pleadings be amended to proceed as a non-class ... *RULE 23(d)(1)*

... or to address similar procedural matters. *RULE 23(d)(1)*

Notes

Class Actions - Resolving Class Action Lawsuits
Map 5.2.4: *Fed. R. Civ. P. 23*

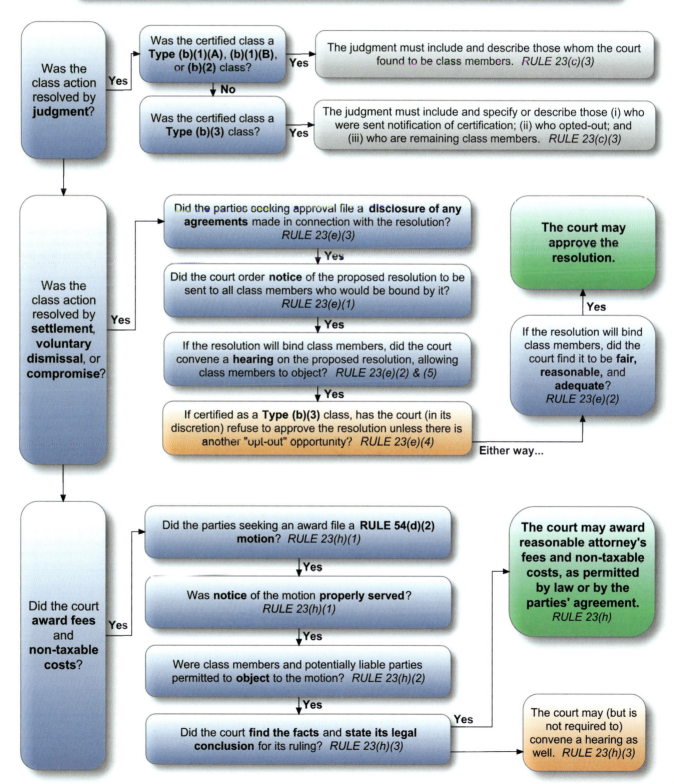

Premise

This Map concludes the answer to the question asked in Map 5.0: *Is Class Action Treatment Proper?*

Although very few of them do, class action lawsuits may end just like any other lawsuit -- with a verdict from a jury or findings and conclusions from a judge. Most class actions, however, are resolved by dismissal or settlement. Because such resolutions can impact the interests of absent parties, court approval is required.

Was the class action resolved by **judgment**?

Yes → Was the certified class a **Type (b)(1)(A), (b)(1)(B), or (b)(2)** class?

Yes → The judgment must include and describe those whom the court found to be class members. *RULE 23(c)(3)*

↓ **No**

Was the certified class a **Type (b)(3)** class?

Yes → The judgment must include and specify or describe those (i) who were sent notification of certification; (ii) who opted-out; and (iii) who are remaining class members. *RULE 23(c)(3)*

Was the class action resolved by **settlement, voluntary dismissal, or compromise**?

Yes → Did the parties seeking approval file a **disclosure of any agreements** made in connection with the resolution? *RULE 23(e)(3)*

↓ **Yes**

Did the court order **notice** of the proposed resolution to be sent to all class members who would be bound by it? *RULE 23(e)(1)*

↓ **Yes**

If the resolution will bind class members, did the court convene a **hearing** on the proposed resolution, allowing class members to object? *RULE 23(e)(2) & (5)*

↓ **Yes**

If certified as a **Type (b)(3)** class, has the court (in its discretion) refuse to approve the resolution unless there is another "opt-out" opportunity? *RULE 23(e)(4)*

Either way... →

If the resolution will bind class members, did the court find it to be **fair, reasonable,** and **adequate**? *RULE 23(e)(2)*

Yes →

The court may approve the resolution.

Did the court **award fees** and **non-taxable costs**?

Yes → Did the parties seeking an award file a **RULE 54(d)(2) motion**? *RULE 23(h)(1)*

↓ **Yes**

Was **notice** of the motion **properly served**? *RULE 23(h)(1)*

↓ **Yes**

Were class members and potentially liable parties permitted to **object** to the motion? *RULE 23(h)(2)*

↓ **Yes**

Did the court **find the facts** and **state its legal conclusion** for its ruling? *RULE 23(h)(3)*

Yes →

The court may award reasonable attorney's fees and non-taxable costs, as permitted by law or by the parties' agreement. *RULE 23(h)*

The court may (but is not required to) convene a hearing as well. *RULE 23(h)(3)*

Notes

Multidistrict Litigation (MDL)
Map 5.3: *28 U.S.C. § 1407*

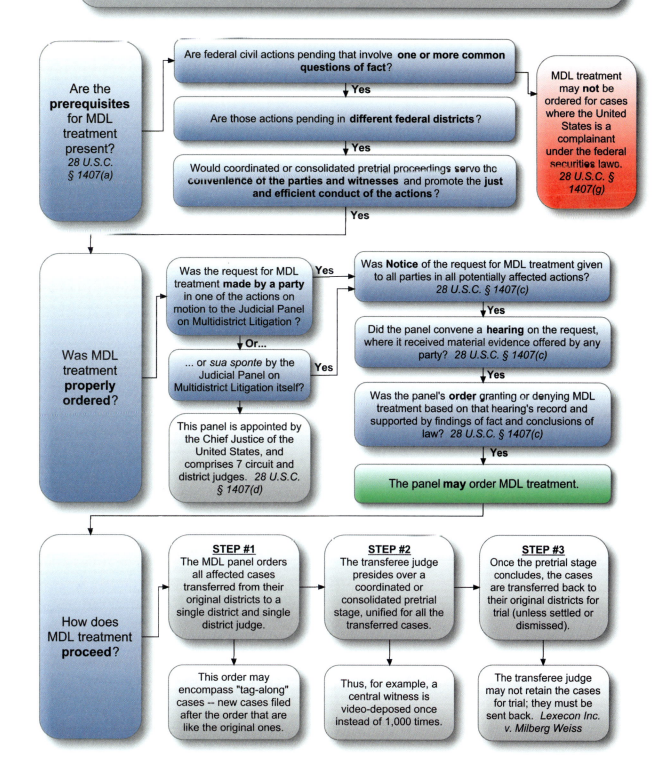

Premise
This Map answers the question asked in Map 5.0: *Is Multidistrict Litigation Proper?*

On occasion, similar lawsuits involving similar types of claims are filed in multiple different federal courts throughout the United States (mass torts, antitrust, and consumer fraud claims are good examples). Class action treatment either is not desired by those litigants or is not proper. But because of the commonality of the claims, and the spectre of duplicative pretrial work (notably, discovery), the **Multidistrict Litigation ("MDL")** statute permits those numerous different cases to all be transferred to a single federal court for a unified pretrial stage of litigation. Once the pretrial work is completed (in a hopefully efficient, coordinated manner) the cases are transferred back to their respective districts for trial.

Are the prerequisites for MDL treatment present? *28 U.S.C. § 1407(a)*

Are federal civil actions pending that involve **one or more common questions of fact**?

↓ **Yes**

Are those actions pending in **different federal districts**?

↓ **Yes**

Would coordinated or consolidated pretrial proceedings serve the **convenience of the parties and witnesses** and promote the **just and efficient conduct of the actions**?

↓ **Yes**

MDL treatment may **not** be ordered for cases where the United States is a complainant under the federal securities laws. *28 U.S.C. § 1407(g)*

Was MDL treatment properly ordered?

Was the request for MDL treatment **made by a party** in one of the actions on motion to the Judicial Panel on Multidistrict Litigation?

↓ **Or...**

... or *sua sponte* by the Judicial Panel on Multidistrict Litigation itself?

↓

This panel is appointed by the Chief Justice of the United States, and comprises 7 circuit and district judges. *28 U.S.C. § 1407(d)*

Yes →

Was **Notice** of the request for MDL treatment given to all parties in all potentially affected actions? *28 U.S.C. § 1407(c)*

↓ **Yes**

Did the panel convene a **hearing** on the request, where it received material evidence offered by any party? *28 U.S.C. § 1407(c)*

↓ **Yes**

Was the panel's **order** granting or denying MDL treatment based on that hearing's record and supported by findings of fact and conclusions of law? *28 U.S.C. § 1407(c)*

↓ **Yes**

The panel **may** order MDL treatment.

How does MDL treatment proceed?

STEP #1
The MDL panel orders all affected cases transferred from their original districts to a single district and single district judge.

This order may encompass "tag-along" cases -- new cases filed after the order that are like the original ones.

STEP #2
The transferee judge presides over a coordinated or consolidated pretrial stage, unified for all the transferred cases.

Thus, for example, a central witness is video-deposed once instead of 1,000 times.

STEP #3
Once the pretrial stage concludes, the cases are transferred back to their original districts for trial (unless settled or dismissed).

The transferee judge may not retain the cases for trial; they must be sent back. *Lexecon Inc. v. Milberg Weiss*

Notes

Shareholders' Derivative Litigation
Map 5.4: *Fed. R. Civ. P. 23.1*

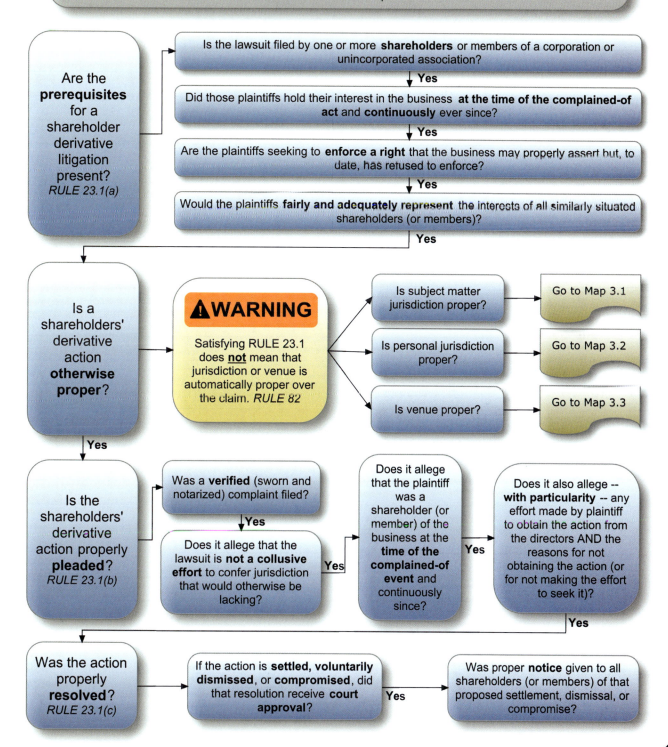

Premise

This Map answers the question asked in Map 5.0: *Is Shareholders' Derivative Litigation Proper?*

Shareholders own corporations (like members own unincorporated associations). When the directors refuse to enforce a right that the business has, the interests of shareholders (or members) may be injured. To remedy that, shareholders (or members) are permitted to bring a lawsuit on behalf of the business -- a **shareholders' derivative action** -- to force the hand of the directors. Because such lawsuits can be expensive, distracting to the business, and filed for improper purposes, special pleading obligations and settlement rules are imposed.

Are the **prerequisites** for a shareholder derivative litigation present? *RULE 23.1(a)*

Is the lawsuit filed by one or more **shareholders** or members of a corporation or unincorporated association?

↓ **Yes**

Did those plaintiffs hold their interest in the business **at the time of the complained-of act** and **continuously** ever since?

↓ **Yes**

Are the plaintiffs seeking to **enforce a right** that the business may properly assert but, to date, has refused to enforce?

↓ **Yes**

Would the plaintiffs **fairly and adequately represent** the interests of all similarly situated shareholders (or members)?

Yes

Is a shareholders' derivative action **otherwise proper**?

⚠ **WARNING**

Satisfying RULE 23.1 does **not** mean that jurisdiction or venue is automatically proper over the claim. *RULE 82*

Is subject matter jurisdiction proper? → Go to Map 3.1

Is personal jurisdiction proper? → Go to Map 3.2

Is venue proper? → Go to Map 3.3

Yes

Is the shareholders' derivative action properly **pleaded**? *RULE 23.1(b)*

Was a **verified** (sworn and notarized) complaint filed?

↓ **Yes**

Does it allege that the lawsuit is **not a collusive effort** to confer jurisdiction that would otherwise be lacking?

Yes →

Does it allege that the plaintiff was a shareholder (or member) of the business at the **time of the complained-of event** and continuously since?

Yes →

Does it also allege -- **with particularity** -- any effort made by plaintiff to obtain the action from the directors AND the reasons for not obtaining the action (or for not making the effort to seek it)?

Yes

Was the action properly **resolved**? *RULE 23.1(c)*

If the action is **settled, voluntarily dismissed**, or **compromised**, did that resolution receive **court approval**?

Yes →

Was proper **notice** given to all shareholders (or members) of that proposed settlement, dismissal, or compromise?

Notes

Federal Civil Litigation Stage 3:
The Discovery Stage - Overview
Map 6.0

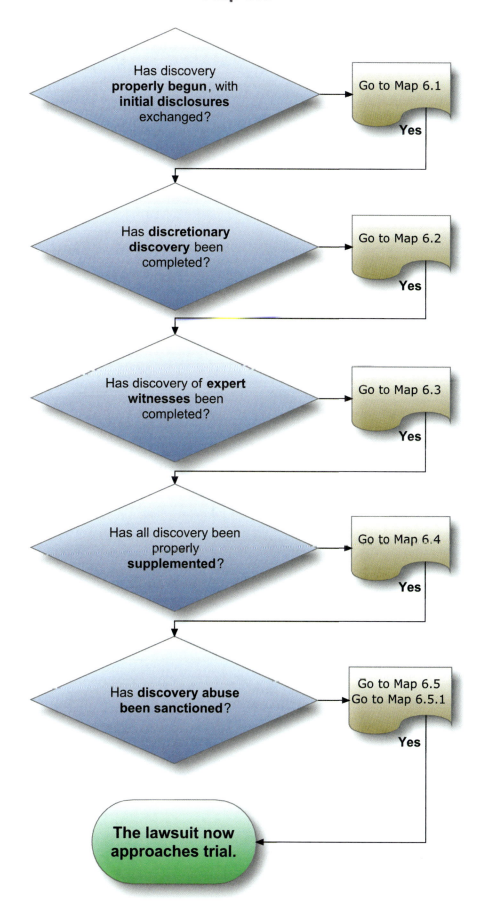

Has discovery **properly begun**, with **initial disclosures** exchanged? — Go to Map 6.1 / **Yes**

Has **discretionary discovery** been completed? — Go to Map 6.2 / **Yes**

Has discovery of **expert witnesses** been completed? — Go to Map 6.3 / **Yes**

Has all discovery been properly **supplemented**? — Go to Map 6.4 / **Yes**

Has **discovery abuse been sanctioned**? — Go to Map 6.5 / Go to Map 6.5.1 / **Yes**

The lawsuit now approaches trial.

Notes

Properly Beginning Discovery
Map 6.1: *Fed. R. Civ. P. 26*

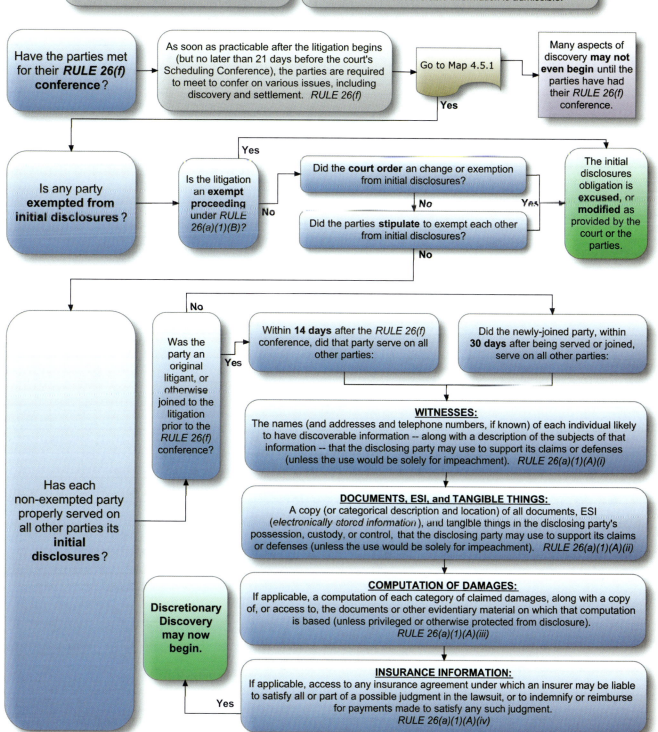

Premise

This Map answers the question from Map 6.0: *Has Discovery Properly Begun, With Initial Disclosures Exchanged?*

Civil Discovery is a litigation stage rarely seen outside the U.S. It authorizes the parties to gather information directly from each other, compels participation by adversaries, and permits information-gathering from non-parties, all of which reduces surprises in litigation and allows all parties to become fully informed of litigation strengths and risks.

The term **informal discovery** is used to refer to information-gathering from cooperative sources, without the use of the formal discovery tools.

Discoverability determines whether information must be exchanged during discovery. **Admissibility** is a far different concept - it determines whether information may be used during trial. Not all discoverable information is admissible.

Have the parties met for their **RULE 26(f) conference**?

As soon as practicable after the litigation begins (but no later than 21 days before the court's Scheduling Conference), the parties are required to meet to confer on various issues, including discovery and settlement. *RULE 26(f)*

Go to Map 4.5.1

Yes

Many aspects of discovery **may not even begin** until the parties have had their *RULE 26(f)* conference.

Is any party **exempted from initial disclosures**?

Is the litigation an **exempt proceeding** under *RULE 26(a)(1)(B)*?

Yes

No

Did the **court order** an change or exemption from initial disclosures?

No

Did the parties **stipulate** to exempt each other from initial disclosures?

Yes

The initial disclosures obligation is **excused**, or **modified** as provided by the court or the parties.

No

No

Has each non-exempted party properly served on all other parties its **initial disclosures**?

Was the party an original litigant, or otherwise joined to the litigation prior to the *RULE 26(f)* conference?

Yes

Within **14 days** after the *RULE 26(f)* conference, did that party serve on all other parties:

Did the newly-joined party, within **30 days** after being served or joined, serve on all other parties:

WITNESSES:
The names (and addresses and telephone numbers, if known) of each individual likely to have discoverable information -- along with a description of the subjects of that information -- that the disclosing party may use to support its claims or defenses (unless the use would be solely for impeachment). *RULE 26(a)(1)(A)(i)*

DOCUMENTS, ESI, and TANGIBLE THINGS:
A copy (or categorical description and location) of all documents, ESI (*electronically stored information*), and tangible things in the disclosing party's possession, custody, or control, that the disclosing party may use to support its claims or defenses (unless the use would be solely for impeachment). *RULE 26(a)(1)(A)(ii)*

Discretionary Discovery may now begin.

COMPUTATION OF DAMAGES:
If applicable, a computation of each category of claimed damages, along with a copy of, or access to, the documents or other evidentiary material on which that computation is based (unless privileged or otherwise protected from disclosure). *RULE 26(a)(1)(A)(iii)*

Yes

INSURANCE INFORMATION:
If applicable, access to any insurance agreement under which an insurer may be liable to satisfy all or part of a possible judgment in the lawsuit, or to indemnify or reimburse for payments made to satisfy any such judgment. *RULE 26(a)(1)(A)(iv)*

Notes

Discretionary Discovery, Generally
Map 6.2: *Fed. R. Civ. P. 26-37 & 45*

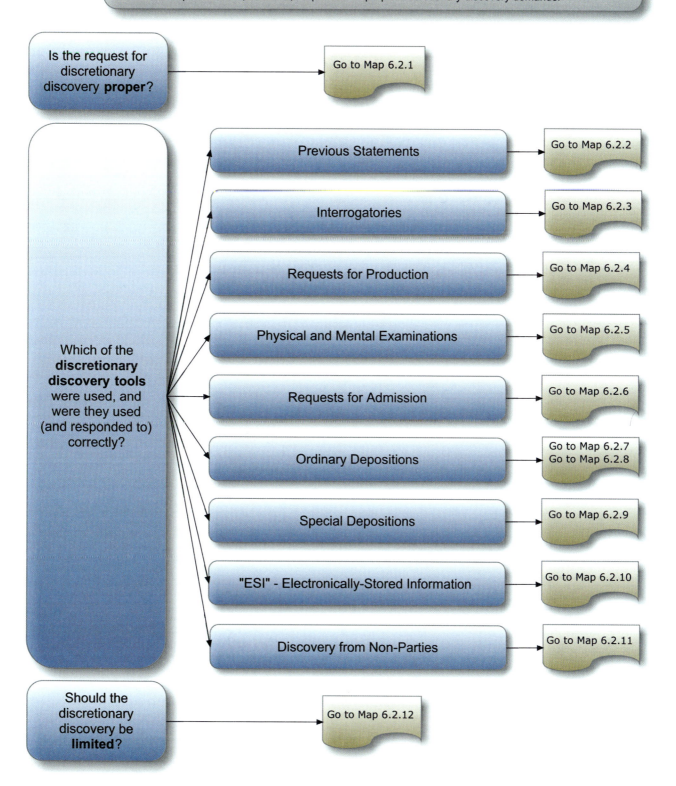

Premise
This Map answers the question from Map 6.0: *Has Discretionary Discovery Been Completed?*

Discretionary Discovery is optional, voluntary discovery. It encompasses a series of information-gathering tools that a party may choose to use to prepare for trial. No party is required to make use of any of these tools, and parties may choose to use some, all, or none as they see fit. But whether they use them or not, parties must, however, respond to all proper discretionary discovery demands.

Is the request for discretionary discovery **proper**? → Go to Map 6.2.1

Which of the **discretionary discovery tools** were used, and were they used (and responded to) correctly?

- Previous Statements → Go to Map 6.2.2
- Interrogatories → Go to Map 6.2.3
- Requests for Production → Go to Map 6.2.4
- Physical and Mental Examinations → Go to Map 6.2.5
- Requests for Admission → Go to Map 6.2.6
- Ordinary Depositions → Go to Map 6.2.7 / Go to Map 6.2.8
- Special Depositions → Go to Map 6.2.9
- "ESI" - Electronically-Stored Information → Go to Map 6.2.10
- Discovery from Non-Parties → Go to Map 6.2.11

Should the discretionary discovery be **limited**? → Go to Map 6.2.12

Notes

Scope of Discretionary Discovery

Map 6.2.1: *Fed. R. Civ. P. 26*

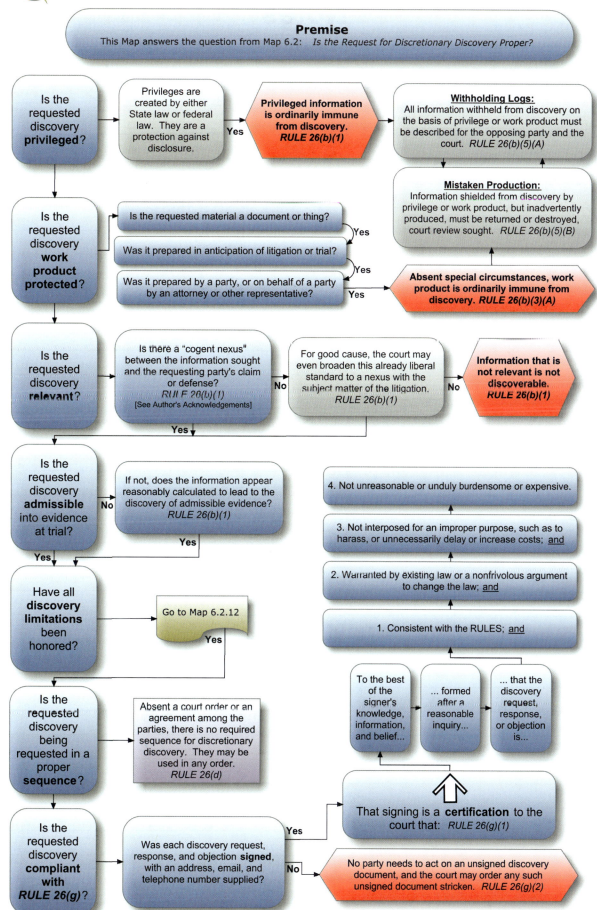

Premise
This Map answers the question from Map 6.2: *Is the Request for Discretionary Discovery Proper?*

Is the requested discovery **privileged**?

Privileges are created by either State law or federal law. They are a protection against disclosure.

Yes → **Privileged information is ordinarily immune from discovery.** *RULE 26(b)(1)*

Withholding Logs: All information withheld from discovery on the basis of privilege or work product must be described for the opposing party and the court. *RULE 26(b)(5)(A)*

Mistaken Production: Information shielded from discovery by privilege or work product, but inadvertently produced, must be returned or destroyed, court review sought. *RULE 26(b)(5)(B)*

Is the requested discovery **work product protected**?

Is the requested material a document or thing?

Was it prepared in anticipation of litigation or trial? **Yes**

Was it prepared by a party, or on behalf of a party by an attorney or other representative? **Yes**

Absent special circumstances, work product is ordinarily immune from discovery. *RULE 26(b)(3)(A)*

Is the requested discovery **relevant**?

Is there a "cogent nexus" between the information sought and the requesting party's claim or defense? *RULE 26(b)(1)* [See Author's Acknowledgements] → **No** → For good cause, the court may even broaden this already liberal standard to a nexus with the subject matter of the litigation. *RULE 26(b)(1)* → **No** → **Information that is not relevant is not discoverable.** *RULE 26(b)(1)*

Yes

Is the requested discovery **admissible** into evidence at trial? → **No** → If not, does the information appear reasonably calculated to lead to the discovery of admissible evidence? *RULE 26(b)(1)* → **Yes**

Yes

4. Not unreasonable or unduly burdensome or expensive.

3. Not interposed for an improper purpose, such as to harass, or unnecessarily delay or increase costs; and

2. Warranted by existing law or a nonfrivolous argument to change the law; and

1. Consistent with the RULES; and

Have all **discovery limitations** been honored? → **Yes** → Go to Map 6.2.12

Is the requested discovery being requested in a proper **sequence**?

Absent a court order or an agreement among the parties, there is no required sequence for discretionary discovery. They may be used in any order. *RULE 26(d)*

To the best of the signer's knowledge, information, and belief... → ... formed after a reasonable inquiry... → ... that the discovery request, response, or objection is...

That signing is a **certification** to the court that: *RULE 26(g)(1)*

Is the requested discovery **compliant with** *RULE 26(g)*? → Was each discovery request, response, and objection **signed**, with an address, email, and telephone number supplied? → **Yes**

→ **No** → No party needs to act on an unsigned discovery document, and the court may order any such unsigned document stricken. *RULE 26(g)(2)*

Notes

Discretionary Discovery - Previous Statements
Map 6.2.2: *Fed. R. Civ. P. 26*

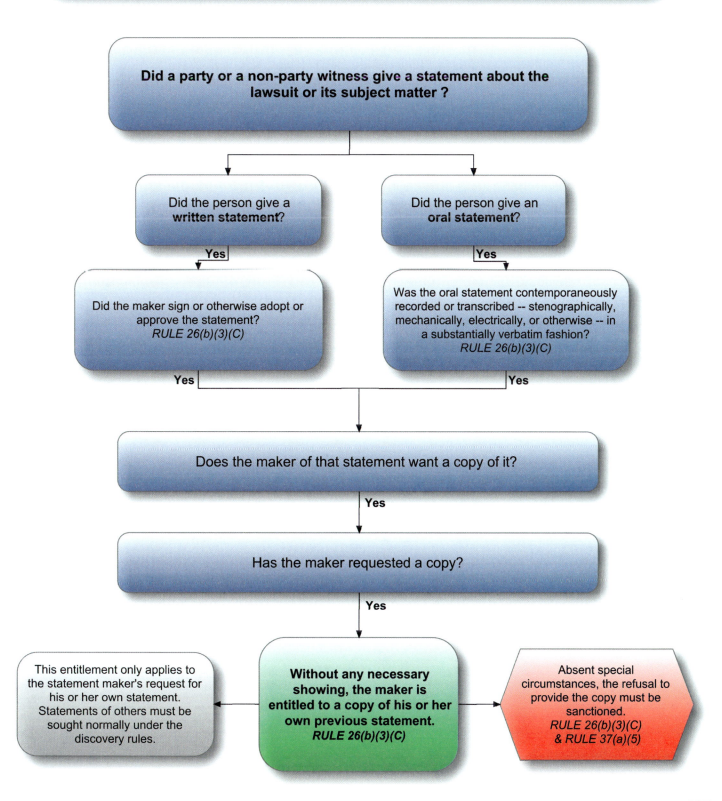

Premise
This Map answers the question from Map 6.2: *Is a Request for Previous Statements Proper?*

Did a party or a non-party witness give a statement about the lawsuit or its subject matter ?

Did the person give a **written statement?**

Did the person give an **oral statement?**

Yes

Yes

Did the maker sign or otherwise adopt or approve the statement?
RULE 26(b)(3)(C)

Was the oral statement contemporaneously recorded or transcribed -- stenographically, mechanically, electrically, or otherwise -- in a substantially verbatim fashion?
RULE 26(b)(3)(C)

Yes

Yes

Does the maker of that statement want a copy of it?

Yes

Has the maker requested a copy?

Yes

This entitlement only applies to the statement maker's request for his or her own statement. Statements of others must be sought normally under the discovery rules.

Without any necessary showing, the maker is entitled to a copy of his or her own previous statement.
RULE 26(b)(3)(C)

Absent special circumstances, the refusal to provide the copy must be sanctioned.
RULE 26(b)(3)(C) & RULE 37(a)(5)

Notes

Discretionary Discovery - Interrogatories
Map 6.2.3: *Fed. R. Civ. P. 33*

Premise
This Map answers the question from Map 6.2: *Are Interrogatories Proper?*

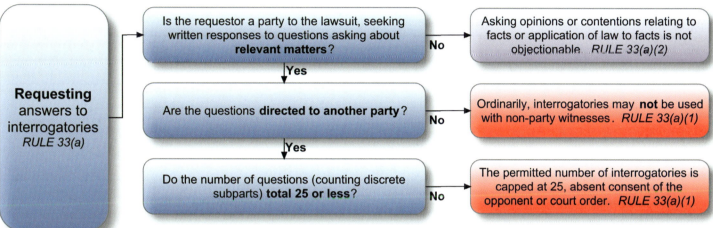

Requesting answers to interrogatories
RULE 33(a)

Is the requestor a party to the lawsuit, seeking written responses to questions asking about **relevant matters**?
— **No** → Asking opinions or contentions relating to facts or application of law to facts is not objectionable. *RULE 33(a)(2)*

↓ **Yes**

Are the questions **directed to another party**?
— **No** → Ordinarily, interrogatories may **not** be used with non-party witnesses. *RULE 33(a)(1)*

↓ **Yes**

Do the number of questions (counting discrete subparts) **total 25 or less**?
— **No** → The permitted number of interrogatories is capped at 25, absent consent of the opponent or court order. *RULE 33(a)(1)*

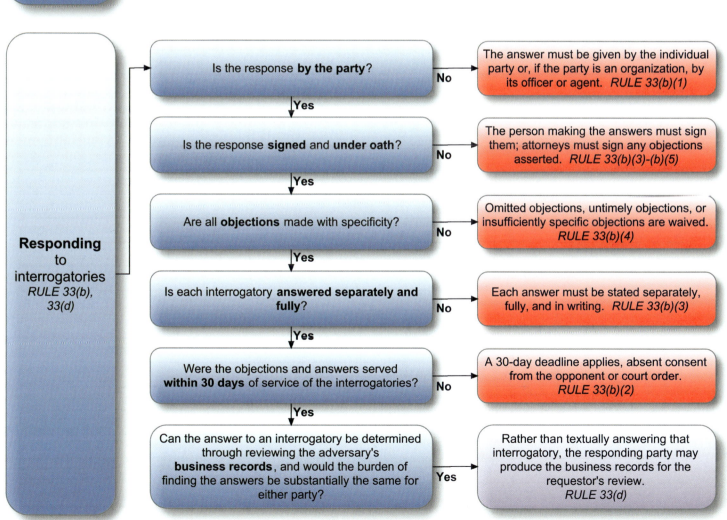

Responding to interrogatories
RULE 33(b), 33(d)

Is the response **by the party**?
— **No** → The answer must be given by the individual party or, if the party is an organization, by its officer or agent. *RULE 33(b)(1)*

↓ **Yes**

Is the response **signed** and **under oath**?
— **No** → The person making the answers must sign them; attorneys must sign any objections asserted. *RULE 33(b)(3)-(b)(5)*

↓ **Yes**

Are all **objections** made with specificity?
— **No** → Omitted objections, untimely objections, or insufficiently specific objections are waived. *RULE 33(b)(4)*

↓ **Yes**

Is each interrogatory **answered separately and fully**?
— **No** → Each answer must be stated separately, fully, and in writing. *RULE 33(b)(3)*

↓ **Yes**

Were the objections and answers served **within 30 days** of service of the interrogatories?
— **No** → A 30-day deadline applies, absent consent from the opponent or court order. *RULE 33(b)(2)*

↓ **Yes**

Can the answer to an interrogatory be determined through reviewing the adversary's **business records**, and would the burden of finding the answers be substantially the same for either party?
— **Yes** → Rather than textually answering that interrogatory, the responding party may produce the business records for the requestor's review. *RULE 33(d)*

Notes

Discretionary Discovery - Requests for Production
Map 6.2.4: *Fed. R. Civ. P. 34*

Premise

This Map answers the question from Map 6.2: *Are Requests for Production Proper?*

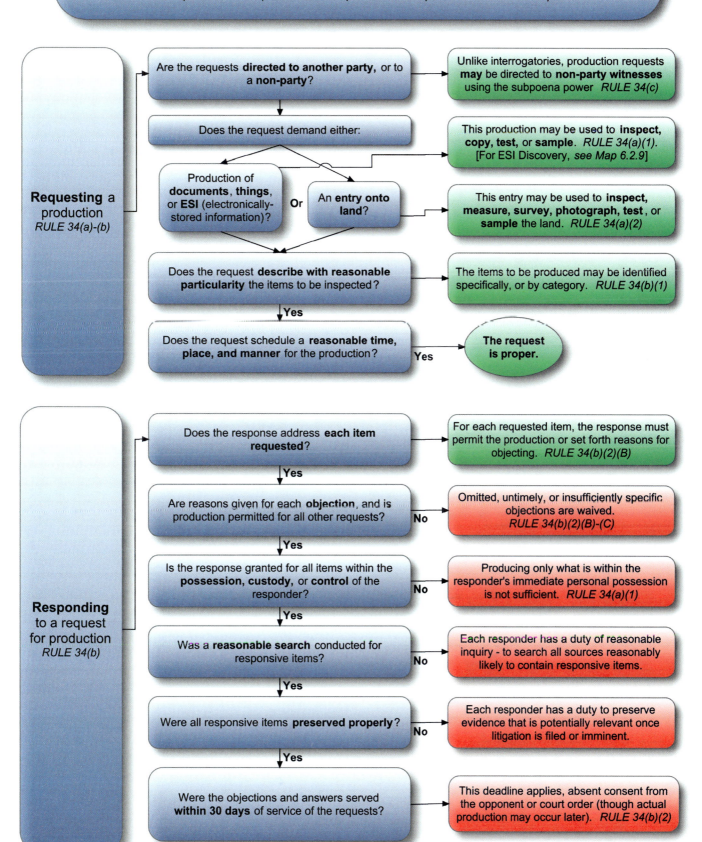

Requesting a production *RULE 34(a)-(b)*

Are the requests **directed to another party**, or to a **non-party**?
→ Unlike interrogatories, production requests **may** be directed to **non-party witnesses** using the subpoena power *RULE 34(c)*

Does the request demand either:
→ This production may be used to **inspect, copy, test,** or **sample**. *RULE 34(a)(1).* [For ESI Discovery, *see Map 6.2.9*]

Production of **documents**, **things**, or **ESI** (electronically-stored information)? **Or** An **entry onto land**?
→ This entry may be used to **inspect, measure, survey, photograph, test,** or **sample** the land. *RULE 34(a)(2)*

Does the request **describe with reasonable particularity** the items to be inspected?
→ The items to be produced may be identified specifically, or by category. *RULE 34(b)(1)*

Yes

Does the request schedule a **reasonable time, place, and manner** for the production? **Yes** →
The request is proper.

Responding to a request for production *RULE 34(b)*

Does the response address **each item requested**?
→ For each requested item, the response must permit the production or set forth reasons for objecting. *RULE 34(b)(2)(B)*

Yes

Are reasons given for each **objection**, and is production permitted for all other requests? **No** →
Omitted, untimely, or insufficiently specific objections are waived. *RULE 34(b)(2)(B)-(C)*

Yes

Is the response granted for all items within the **possession, custody,** or **control** of the responder? **No** →
Producing only what is within the responder's immediate personal possession is not sufficient. *RULE 34(a)(1)*

Yes

Was a **reasonable search** conducted for responsive items? **No** →
Each responder has a duty of reasonable inquiry - to search all sources reasonably likely to contain responsive items.

Yes

Were all responsive items **preserved properly**? **No** →
Each responder has a duty to preserve evidence that is potentially relevant once litigation is filed or imminent.

Yes

Were the objections and answers served **within 30 days** of service of the requests?
→ This deadline applies, absent consent from the opponent or court order (though actual production may occur later). *RULE 34(b)(2)*

Notes

Discretionary Discovery – Physical and Mental Examinations
Map 6.2.5: *Fed. R. Civ. P. 35*

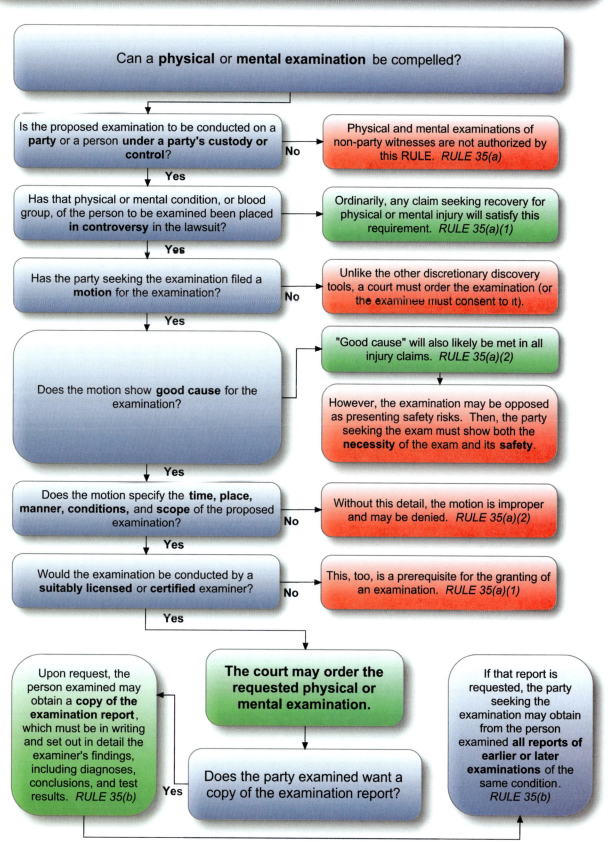

Premise

This Map answers the question from Map 6.2: *Are Requests for Physical or Mental Examinations Proper?*

Can a **physical** or **mental examination** be compelled?

Is the proposed examination to be conducted on a **party** or a person **under a party's custody or control**?

No → Physical and mental examinations of non-party witnesses are not authorized by this RULE. *RULE 35(a)*

Yes ↓

Has that physical or mental condition, or blood group, of the person to be examined been placed **in controversy** in the lawsuit?

→ Ordinarily, any claim seeking recovery for physical or mental injury will satisfy this requirement. *RULE 35(a)(1)*

Yes ↓

Has the party seeking the examination filed a **motion** for the examination?

No → Unlike the other discretionary discovery tools, a court must order the examination (or the examinee must consent to it).

Yes ↓

Does the motion show **good cause** for the examination?

→ "Good cause" will also likely be met in all injury claims. *RULE 35(a)(2)*

→ However, the examination may be opposed as presenting safety risks. Then, the party seeking the exam must show both the **necessity** of the exam and its **safety**.

Yes ↓

Does the motion specify the **time, place, manner, conditions,** and **scope** of the proposed examination?

No → Without this detail, the motion is improper and may be denied. *RULE 35(a)(2)*

Yes ↓

Would the examination be conducted by a **suitably licensed** or **certified** examiner?

No → This, too, is a prerequisite for the granting of an examination. *RULE 35(a)(1)*

Yes ↓

The court may order the requested physical or mental examination.

Does the party examined want a copy of the examination report?

Yes → Upon request, the person examined may obtain a **copy of the examination report**, which must be in writing and set out in detail the examiner's findings, including diagnoses, conclusions, and test results. *RULE 35(b)*

If that report is requested, the party seeking the examination may obtain from the person examined **all reports of earlier or later examinations** of the same condition. *RULE 35(b)*

Notes

Discretionary Discovery - Requests for Admission
Map 6.2.6: *Fed. R. Civ. P. 36*

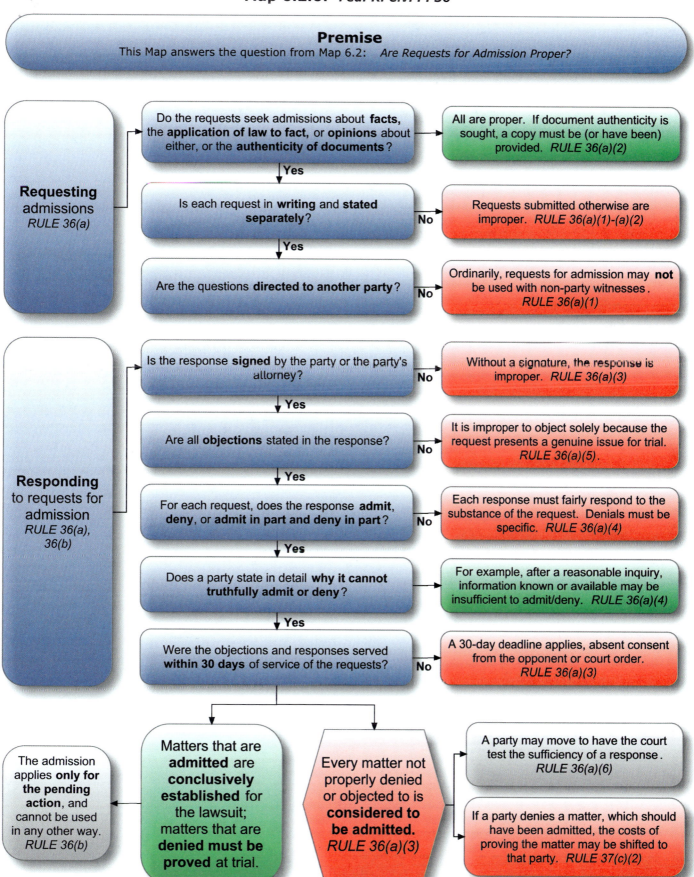

Premise

This Map answers the question from Map 6.2: *Are Requests for Admission Proper?*

Requesting admissions
RULE 36(a)

Do the requests seek admissions about **facts,** the **application of law to fact,** or **opinions** about either, or the **authenticity of documents**?

→ All are proper. If document authenticity is sought, a copy must be (or have been) provided. *RULE 36(a)(2)*

Yes ↓

Is each request in **writing** and **stated separately**?

No → Requests submitted otherwise are improper. *RULE 36(a)(1)-(a)(2)*

Yes ↓

Are the questions **directed to another party**?

No → Ordinarily, requests for admission may **not** be used with non-party witnesses. *RULE 36(a)(1)*

Responding to requests for admission
RULE 36(a), 36(b)

Is the response **signed** by the party or the party's attorney?

No → Without a signature, the response is improper. *RULE 36(a)(3)*

Yes ↓

Are all **objections** stated in the response?

No → It is improper to object solely because the request presents a genuine issue for trial. *RULE 36(a)(5).*

Yes ↓

For each request, does the response **admit, deny,** or **admit in part and deny in part**?

No → Each response must fairly respond to the substance of the request. Denials must be specific. *RULE 36(a)(4)*

Yes ↓

Does a party state in detail **why it cannot truthfully admit or deny**?

→ For example, after a reasonable inquiry, information known or available may be insufficient to admit/deny. *RULE 36(a)(4)*

Yes ↓

Were the objections and responses served **within 30 days** of service of the requests?

No → A 30-day deadline applies, absent consent from the opponent or court order. *RULE 36(a)(3)*

Matters that are **admitted** are **conclusively established** for the lawsuit; matters that are **denied must be proved** at trial.

← The admission applies **only for the pending action**, and cannot be used in any other way. *RULE 36(b)*

Every matter not properly denied or objected to is **considered to be admitted.** *RULE 36(a)(3)*

→ A party may move to have the court test the sufficiency of a response. *RULE 36(a)(6)*

If a party denies a matter, which should have been admitted, the costs of proving the matter may be shifted to that party. *RULE 37(c)(2)*

Notes

Discretionary Discovery - Ordinary Depositions
Map 6.2.7: *Fed. R. Civ. P. 28, 30, & 32*

Premise

This Map answers the question from Map 6.2: *Are Depositions Proper?*

Oral Depositions are among the most frequently used and strategically valuable tools in the discretionary discovery arsenal. They are question-and-answer sessions, between the witness ("deponent") and the deposing attorneys (who can include a party's own attorney). Unlike most written discovery, the answers during a deposition are not drafted artfully by an attorney, but instead are given spontaneously and orally by the witness - under oath. Depositions are also the most agile of all the discovery devices - when a witness answers unclearly or incompletely, or when a witness's answer suggests new questions or lines of questioning, the deposing attorney can react immediately and directly with additional questioning.

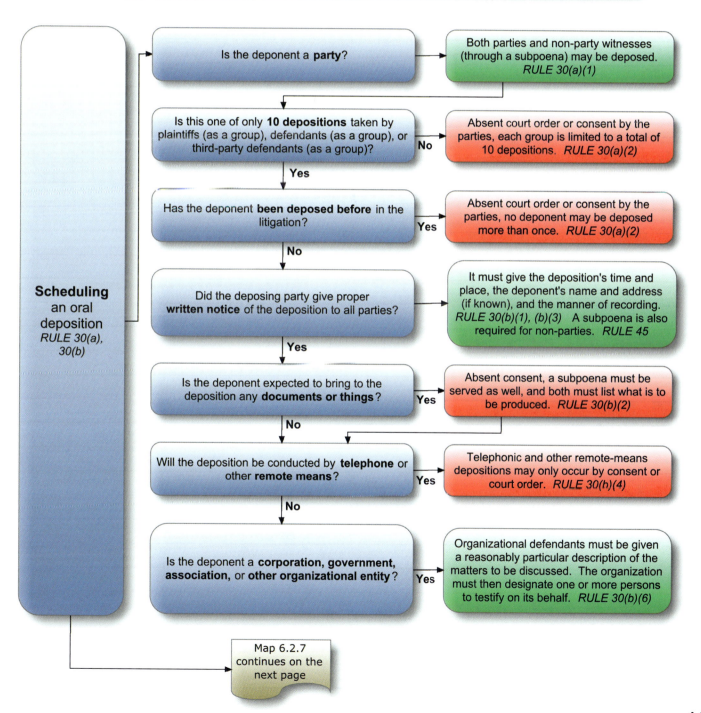

Scheduling an oral deposition *RULE 30(a), 30(b)*

Is the deponent a **party**? → Both parties and non-party witnesses (through a subpoena) may be deposed. *RULE 30(a)(1)*

Is this one of only **10 depositions** taken by plaintiffs (as a group), defendants (as a group), or third-party defendants (as a group)? — **No** → Absent court order or consent by the parties, each group is limited to a total of 10 depositions. *RULE 30(a)(2)*

Yes

Has the deponent **been deposed before** in the litigation? — **Yes** → Absent court order or consent by the parties, no deponent may be deposed more than once. *RULE 30(a)(2)*

No

Did the deposing party give proper **written notice** of the deposition to all parties? → It must give the deposition's time and place, the deponent's name and address (if known), and the manner of recording. *RULE 30(b)(1), (b)(3)* A subpoena is also required for non-parties. *RULE 45*

Yes

Is the deponent expected to bring to the deposition any **documents or things**? — **Yes** → Absent consent, a subpoena must be served as well, and both must list what is to be produced. *RULE 30(b)(2)*

No

Will the deposition be conducted by **telephone** or other **remote means**? — **Yes** → Telephonic and other remote-means depositions may only occur by consent or court order. *RULE 30(b)(4)*

No

Is the deponent a **corporation, government, association**, or **other organizational entity**? — **Yes** → Organizational defendants must be given a reasonably particular description of the matters to be discussed. The organization must then designate one or more persons to testify on its behalf. *RULE 30(b)(6)*

Map 6.2.7 continues on the next page

Notes

Discretionary Discovery - Ordinary Depositions

Map 6.2.7 *continued*: *Fed. R. Civ. P. 28 & 30*

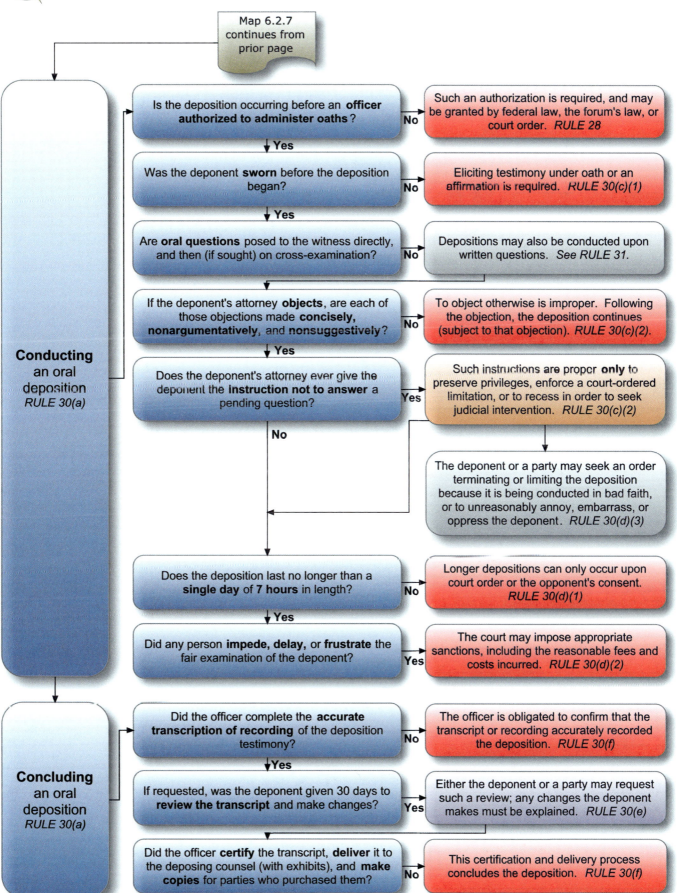

Map 6.2.7 continues from prior page

Conducting an oral deposition *RULE 30(a)*

Is the deposition occurring before an **officer authorized to administer oaths**? — **No** → Such an authorization is required, and may be granted by federal law, the forum's law, or court order. *RULE 28*

↓ **Yes**

Was the deponent **sworn** before the deposition began? — **No** → Eliciting testimony under oath or an affirmation is required. *RULE 30(c)(1)*

↓ **Yes**

Are **oral questions** posed to the witness directly, and then (if sought) on cross-examination? — **No** → Depositions may also be conducted upon written questions. *See RULE 31.*

If the deponent's attorney **objects**, are each of those objections made **concisely, nonargumentatively**, and **nonsuggestively**? — **No** → To object otherwise is improper. Following the objection, the deposition continues (subject to that objection). *RULE 30(c)(2).*

↓ **Yes**

Does the deponent's attorney ever give the deponent the **instruction not to answer** a pending question? — **Yes** → Such instructions are proper **only** to preserve privileges, enforce a court-ordered limitation, or to recess in order to seek judicial intervention. *RULE 30(c)(2)*

↓ **No**

The deponent or a party may seek an order terminating or limiting the deposition because it is being conducted in bad faith, or to unreasonably annoy, embarrass, or oppress the deponent. *RULE 30(d)(3)*

Does the deposition last no longer than a **single day** of **7 hours** in length? — **No** → Longer depositions can only occur upon court order or the opponent's consent. *RULE 30(d)(1)*

↓ **Yes**

Did any person **impede, delay,** or **frustrate** the fair examination of the deponent? — **Yes** → The court may impose appropriate sanctions, including the reasonable fees and costs incurred. *RULE 30(d)(2)*

Concluding an oral deposition *RULE 30(a)*

Did the officer complete the **accurate transcription of recording** of the deposition testimony? — **No** → The officer is obligated to confirm that the transcript or recording accurately recorded the deposition. *RULE 30(f)*

↓ **Yes**

If requested, was the deponent given 30 days to **review the transcript** and make changes? — **Yes** → Either the deponent or a party may request such a review; any changes the deponent makes must be explained. *RULE 30(e)*

Did the officer **certify** the transcript, **deliver** it to the deposing counsel (with exhibits), and **make copies** for parties who purchased them? — **No** → This certification and delivery process concludes the deposition. *RULE 30(f)*

Notes

Discretionary Discovery - Using Depositions at Trial
Map 6.2.8: *Fed. R. Civ. P. 32*

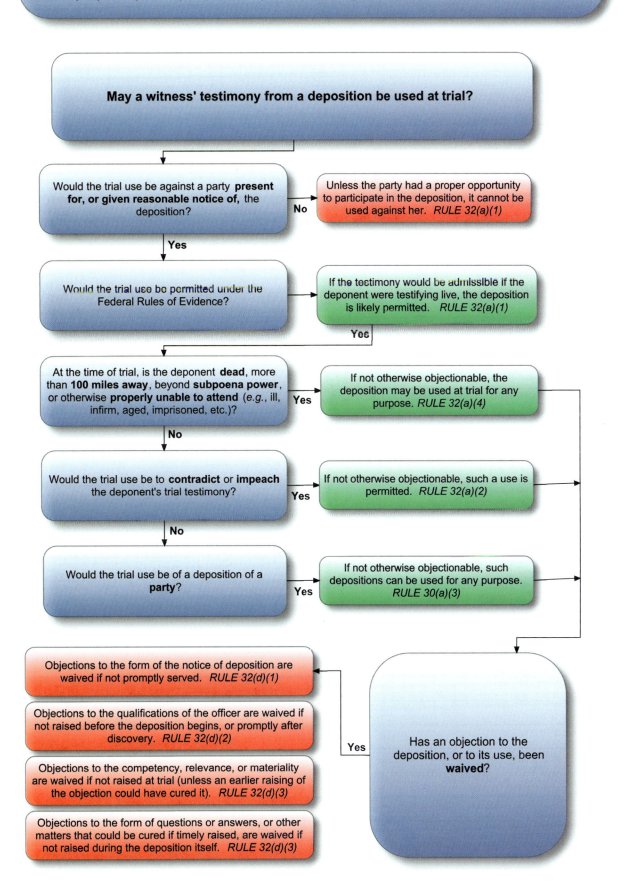

Premise
This Map expands upon the question from Map 6.2, by explaining how depositions are properly used in trials.

May a witness' testimony from a deposition be used at trial?

Would the trial use be against a party **present for, or given reasonable notice of,** the deposition?

No → Unless the party had a proper opportunity to participate in the deposition, it cannot be used against her. *RULE 32(a)(1)*

Yes ↓

Would the trial use be permitted under the Federal Rules of Evidence?

→ If the testimony would be admissible if the deponent were testifying live, the deposition is likely permitted. *RULE 32(a)(1)*

Yes ↓

At the time of trial, is the deponent **dead**, more than **100 miles away**, beyond **subpoena power**, or otherwise **properly unable to attend** (*e.g.*, ill, infirm, aged, imprisoned, etc.)?

Yes → If not otherwise objectionable, the deposition may be used at trial for any purpose. *RULE 32(a)(4)*

No ↓

Would the trial use be to **contradict** or **impeach** the deponent's trial testimony?

Yes → If not otherwise objectionable, such a use is permitted. *RULE 32(a)(2)*

No ↓

Would the trial use be of a deposition of a **party**?

Yes → If not otherwise objectionable, such depositions can be used for any purpose. *RULE 30(a)(3)*

Objections to the form of the notice of deposition are waived if not promptly served. *RULE 32(d)(1)*

Objections to the qualifications of the officer are waived if not raised before the deposition begins, or promptly after discovery. *RULE 32(d)(2)*

Objections to the competency, relevance, or materiality are waived if not raised at trial (unless an earlier raising of the objection could have cured it). *RULE 32(d)(3)*

Objections to the form of questions or answers, or other matters that could be cured if timely raised, are waived if not raised during the deposition itself. *RULE 32(d)(3)*

Yes ← Has an objection to the deposition, or to its use, been **waived**?

Notes

Discretionary Discovery – Special Depositions
Map 6.2.9: *Fed. R. Civ. P. 27, 30, & 31*

Premise

This Map continues to answer the question from Map 6.2:   *Are Special Depositions Proper?*

In appropriate (often atypical) circumstances, special depositions are authorized. Some situations warranting the use of these unusual depositions are described below. Consult the referenced *RULES* themselves for greater explanation of these depositions and the circumstances under which they may be conducted.

Has the deponent been **deposed before**, is the deponent **in prison**, or will the deposition be beyond the **10-deposition limit**?	Is the deponent expected to **leave the U.S.**, and thereafter be unavailable to be deposed?	Do the deposing attorneys wish to interrogate the witness by **written questions** (rather than orally)?	Is the deposition occurring **too early** or **after trial**, but necessary to perpetuate testimony?
Such a deposition can be taken upon court order. Also, other than prisoner-depositions, such a deposition may be taken upon the opponent's consent. *RULE 30(a)(2); RULE 29*	Such a deposition can be taken before the parties' *RULE 26(f)* conference, but only upon a certification of the witness's imminent unavailability. *RULE 30(a)(2)*	Depositions upon written questions may be taken of an individual party or an organizational party, subject to the same limitations as oral depositions. *RULE 31*	Upon a court order, granted to prevent a failure or delay of justice, a party may depose a witness before the lawsuit is filed, or after judgment and before / pending an appeal. *RULE 27*

Organizational parties have the same designation requirement as they do in oral depositions. *RULE 31(a)(4)*

Go to Map 6.2.7

The deposing attorney serves on all other parties: notice of the deposition, the identity of the officer presiding at the deposition, and the deposing attorney's questions. *RULE 31(a)(3)*

Thereafter, cross-examination, re-direct, and re-cross questions must be served. *RULE 31(a)(5)*

All questions are delivered to the officer, who then travels to the witness, reads them to the witness, obtains the witness' sworn testimony, and sends the certified deposition to the deposing attorney. *RULE 31(b)*

Notes

Discretionary Discovery - Electronically-Stored Information ("ESI")

Map 6.2.10: *Fed. R. Civ. P. 26 & 34*

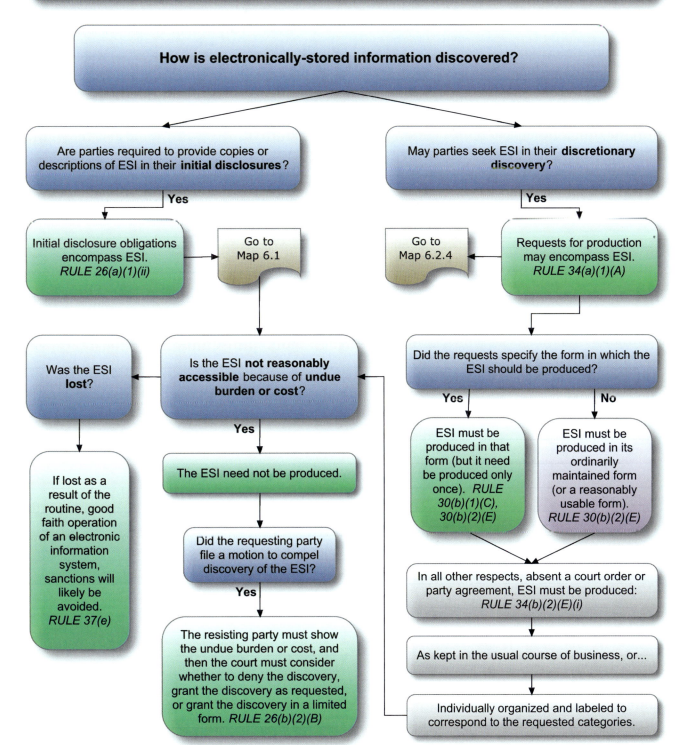

Premise

This Map answers the question from Map 6.2: *Is Seeking Electronically-Stored Information Proper?*

For a time, it was unclear to what extent (if at all) **electronically-stored information** was included within the proper scope of federal civil discovery. That uncertainty is now gone. Like traditional documents and things, electronically-stored information is subject to both disclosure and discretionary discovery in federal civil litigation.

How is electronically-stored information discovered?

Are parties required to provide copies or descriptions of ESI in their **initial disclosures**?

Yes

Initial disclosure obligations encompass ESI. *RULE 26(a)(1)(ii)*

Go to Map 6.1

May parties seek ESI in their **discretionary discovery**?

Yes

Go to Map 6.2.4

Requests for production may encompass ESI. *RULE 34(a)(1)(A)*

Was the ESI **lost**?

Is the ESI **not reasonably accessible** because of **undue burden or cost**?

Yes

The ESI need not be produced.

If lost as a result of the routine, good faith operation of an electronic information system, sanctions will likely be avoided. *RULE 37(e)*

Did the requesting party file a motion to compel discovery of the ESI?

Yes

The resisting party must show the undue burden or cost, and then the court must consider whether to deny the discovery, grant the discovery as requested, or grant the discovery in a limited form. *RULE 26(b)(2)(B)*

Did the requests specify the form in which the ESI should be produced?

Yes

ESI must be produced in that form (but it need be produced only once). *RULE 30(b)(1)(C), 30(b)(2)(E)*

No

ESI must be produced in its ordinarily maintained form (or a reasonably usable form). *RULE 30(b)(2)(E)*

In all other respects, absent a court order or party agreement, ESI must be produced: *RULE 34(b)(2)(E)(i)*

As kept in the usual course of business, or...

Individually organized and labeled to correspond to the requested categories.

Notes

Discretionary Discovery - Discovery From Non-Parties

Map 6.2.11: *Fed. R. Civ. P. 30, 34, & 45*

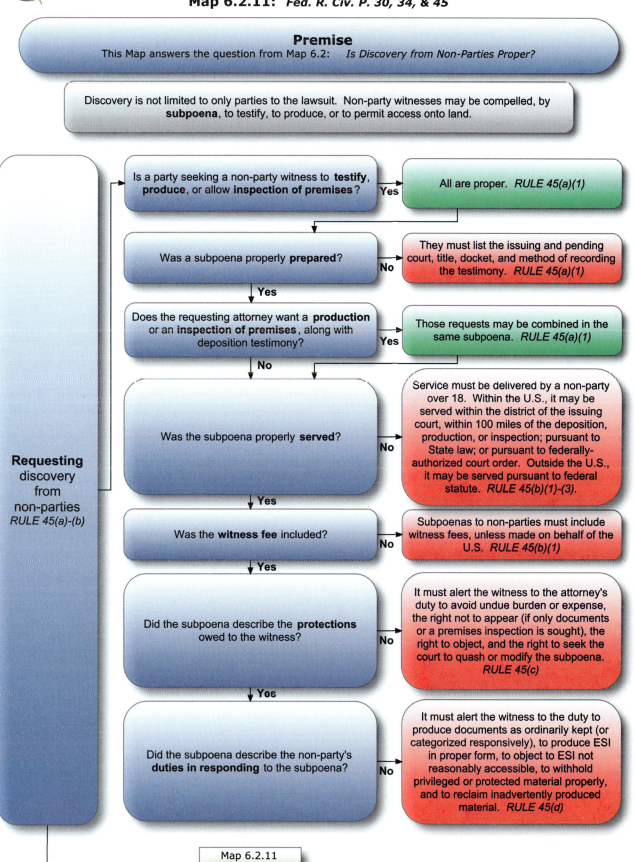

Premise

This Map answers the question from Map 6.2: *Is Discovery from Non-Parties Proper?*

Discovery is not limited to only parties to the lawsuit. Non-party witnesses may be compelled, by **subpoena**, to testify, to produce, or to permit access onto land.

Requesting discovery from non-parties *RULE 45(a)-(b)*

Is a party seeking a non-party witness to **testify**, **produce**, or allow **inspection of premises**? — **Yes** → All are proper. *RULE 45(a)(1)*

Was a subpoena properly **prepared**? — **No** → They must list the issuing and pending court, title, docket, and method of recording the testimony. *RULE 45(a)(1)*

Yes

Does the requesting attorney want a **production** or an **inspection of premises**, along with deposition testimony? — **Yes** → Those requests may be combined in the same subpoena. *RULE 45(a)(1)*

No

Was the subpoena properly **served**? — **No** → Service must be delivered by a non-party over 18. Within the U.S., it may be served within the district of the issuing court, within 100 miles of the deposition, production, or inspection; pursuant to State law; or pursuant to federally-authorized court order. Outside the U.S., it may be served pursuant to federal statute. *RULE 45(b)(1)-(3)*.

Yes

Was the **witness fee** included? — **No** → Subpoenas to non-parties must include witness fees, unless made on behalf of the U.S. *RULE 45(b)(1)*

Yes

Did the subpoena describe the **protections** owed to the witness? — **No** → It must alert the witness to the attorney's duty to avoid undue burden or expense, the right not to appear (if only documents or a premises inspection is sought), the right to object, and the right to seek the court to quash or modify the subpoena. *RULE 45(c)*

Yes

Did the subpoena describe the non-party's **duties in responding** to the subpoena? — **No** → It must alert the witness to the duty to produce documents as ordinarily kept (or categorized responsively), to produce ESI in proper form, to object to ESI not reasonably accessible, to withhold privileged or protected material properly, and to reclaim inadvertently produced material. *RULE 45(d)*

Map 6.2.11 continues on the next page...

Notes

Discretionary Discovery - Discovery From Non-Parties

Map 6.2.11 *continued*: *Fed. R. Civ. P. 30, 34, & 45*

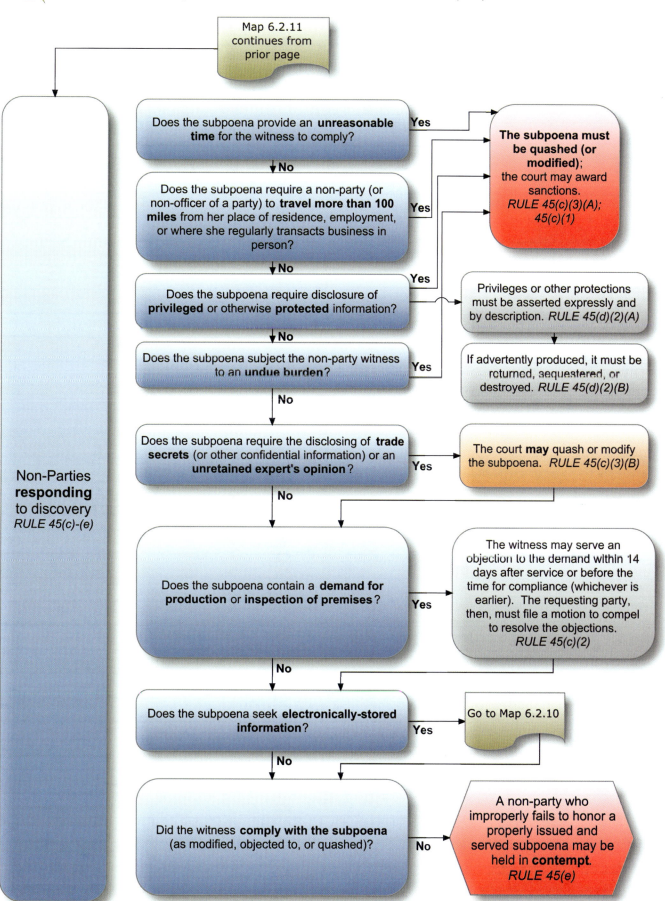

Map 6.2.11 continues from prior page

Non-Parties responding to discovery *RULE 45(c)-(e)*

Does the subpoena provide an **unreasonable time** for the witness to comply? — **Yes** →

 ↓ **No**

Does the subpoena require a non-party (or non-officer of a party) to **travel more than 100 miles** from her place of residence, employment, or where she regularly transacts business in person? — **Yes** →

 ↓ **No**

The subpoena must be quashed (or modified); the court may award sanctions. *RULE 45(c)(3)(A); 45(c)(1)*

Does the subpoena require disclosure of **privileged** or otherwise **protected** information? — **Yes** →

 ↓ **No**

Privileges or other protections must be asserted expressly and by description. *RULE 45(d)(2)(A)*

Does the subpoena subject the non-party witness to an **undue burden**? — **Yes** →

If advertently produced, it must be returned, sequestered, or destroyed. *RULE 45(d)(2)(B)*

 ↓ **No**

Does the subpoena require the disclosing of **trade secrets** (or other confidential information) or an **unretained expert's opinion**? — **Yes** →

The court **may** quash or modify the subpoena. *RULE 45(c)(3)(B)*

 ↓ **No**

Does the subpoena contain a **demand for production** or **inspection of premises**? — **Yes** →

The witness may serve an objection to the demand within 14 days after service or before the time for compliance (whichever is earlier). The requesting party, then, must file a motion to compel to resolve the objections. *RULE 45(c)(2)*

 ↓ **No**

Does the subpoena seek **electronically-stored information**? — **Yes** → Go to Map 6.2.10

 ↓ **No**

Did the witness **comply with the subpoena** (as modified, objected to, or quashed)? — **No** →

A non-party who improperly fails to honor a properly issued and served subpoena may be held in **contempt**. *RULE 45(e)*

159

Notes

Discretionary Discovery - Limiting Discovery
Map 6.2.12: *Fed. R. Civ. P. 26 & 29*

Premise

This Map answers the question from Map 6.2: *Should The Discretionary Discovery Be Limited?*

Although the RULES set parameters and requirements for both discretionary discovery and obligatory disclosures, many of those limitations may be shortened, extended, or otherwise modified by agreement of the parties or court order.

Do the **parties agree** to modify the procedures governing or limiting discovery?

Yes

By written stipulation, the parties can modify the deposition rules or other provisions governing or limiting discovery - provided....

... the agreement will not interfere with the time set by the court for completing discovery, hearing a motion, or the trial date (absent court approval). *RULE 29*

Would the requested discovery:

Be **unreasonably cumulative** or **duplicative**, or...

Be obtained elsewhere **more conveniently**, **less burdensomely**, or **less expensively**, or...

Be sought by a party who has already had **ample opportunity** to obtain the discovery, or...

Be such that the **burden outweighs the likely benefit** of the requested discovery, considering case needs, case value, parties' resources, importance of the issues, and importance of the requested discovery?

Yes

The court may, sua sponte or upon a motion, limit the frequency or extent of discovery that the RULES otherwise permit. *RULE 26(b)(2)(C)*

Would the discovery cause improper **annoyance**, **embarrassment**, **oppression**, or **undue burden or expense**?

Yes

Has the moving party certified that the party has **conferred or attempted to confer** with all other parties, in good faith, to resolve the discovery issue? *RULE 26(c)(1)*

Yes

For good cause, the court may issue a **protective order** to alleviate the objectionable discovery by forbidding it, limiting it, setting terms for it, prescribing different discovery tools, sealing it, or restricting its broader disclosure. *RULE 26(c)(1)*

The court may grant an award of reasonable expenses (including attorney's fees) in favor of the party prevailing on the motion. *RULE 26(c)(3)*

Notes

Discovery of Expert Witnesses

Map 6.3: *Fed. R. Civ. P. 26*

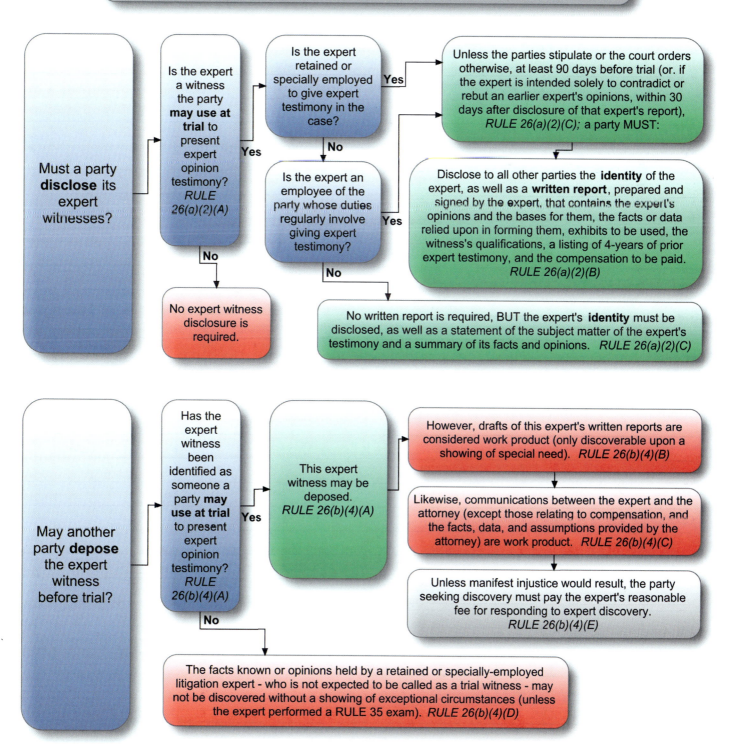

Premise

This Map answers the question from Map 6.0: *Has Discovery of Expert Witnesses Been Completed?*

Ordinarily, opinion testimony can only be offered at trial by percipient witnesses -- those who personally saw, heard, smelled, tasted, or touched the event. An exception, however, is made for **expert witnesses** who, because of their knowledge, skill, experience, training, or education, may offer scientific, technical, or other specialized opinion testimony if it would help the trier of fact.

Must a party disclose its expert witnesses?

→ Is the expert a witness the party **may use at trial** to present expert opinion testimony? *RULE 26(a)(2)(A)*

- **Yes** → Is the expert retained or specially employed to give expert testimony in the case?
  - **Yes** → Unless the parties stipulate or the court orders otherwise, at least 90 days before trial (or, if the expert is intended solely to contradict or rebut an earlier expert's opinions, within 30 days after disclosure of that expert's report), *RULE 26(a)(2)(C)*; a party MUST: → Disclose to all other parties the **identity** of the expert, as well as a **written report**, prepared and signed by the expert, that contains the expert's opinions and the bases for them, the facts or data relied upon in forming them, exhibits to be used, the witness's qualifications, a listing of 4-years of prior expert testimony, and the compensation to be paid. *RULE 26(a)(2)(B)*
  - **No** → Is the expert an employee of the party whose duties regularly involve giving expert testimony?
    - **Yes** → (see above, Disclose to all other parties...)
    - **No** → No written report is required, BUT the expert's **identity** must be disclosed, as well as a statement of the subject matter of the expert's testimony and a summary of its facts and opinions. *RULE 26(a)(2)(C)*
- **No** → No expert witness disclosure is required.

May another party depose the expert witness before trial?

→ Has the expert witness been identified as someone a party **may use at trial** to present expert opinion testimony? *RULE 26(b)(4)(A)*

- **Yes** → This expert witness may be deposed. *RULE 26(b)(4)(A)*
  - → However, drafts of this expert's written reports are considered work product (only discoverable upon a showing of special need). *RULE 26(b)(4)(B)*
  - → Likewise, communications between the expert and the attorney (except those relating to compensation, and the facts, data, and assumptions provided by the attorney) are work product. *RULE 26(b)(4)(C)*
  - → Unless manifest injustice would result, the party seeking discovery must pay the expert's reasonable fee for responding to expert discovery. *RULE 26(b)(4)(E)*
- **No** → The facts known or opinions held by a retained or specially-employed litigation expert - who is not expected to be called as a trial witness - may not be discovered without a showing of exceptional circumstances (unless the expert performed a RULE 35 exam). *RULE 26(b)(4)(D)*

Notes

Duty to Supplement Discovery
Map 6.4: *Fed. R. Civ. P. 26(e)*

Premise

This Map answers the question from Map 6.0: *Has All Discovery Been Properly Supplemented?*

Parties and witnesses are obligated -- on pain of sanctions -- to be accurate and complete in discovery. On occasion, however, new information may arise or inadvertent errors may be uncovered in discovery that has been provided. Parties are under a continuing **duty to supplement** to correct those omissions or errors.

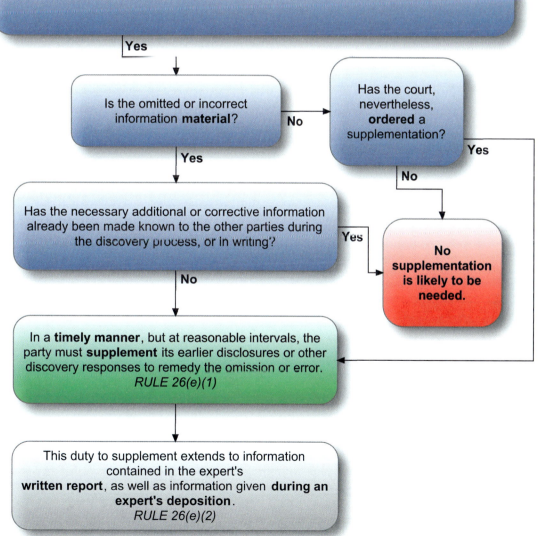

Has the party come to learn that one (or more) of its earlier disclosures or other discovery responses is **incomplete** or **incorrect**?

Yes

Is the omitted or incorrect information **material**?

No

Has the court, nevertheless, **ordered** a supplementation?

Yes

No

Yes

Has the necessary additional or corrective information already been made known to the other parties during the discovery process, or in writing?

Yes

No

No supplementation is likely to be needed.

In a **timely manner**, but at reasonable intervals, the party must **supplement** its earlier disclosures or other discovery responses to remedy the omission or error.
RULE 26(e)(1)

This duty to supplement extends to information contained in the expert's **written report**, as well as information given **during an expert's deposition**.
RULE 26(e)(2)

Notes

Sanctions for Abusive Discovery
Map 6.5: *Fed. R. Civ. P. 37*

Premise

This Map answers the question from Map 6.0: *Has Abusive Discovery Been Sanctioned?*

Did the party fail to participate in **framing the RULE 26(f) discovery plan**?
→ **Yes** → The court may order the party or its attorney to reimburse adversaries for expenses caused by this failure. *RULE 37(f)*

To Learn More About *Motions To Compel*: Go to Map 6.5.1

Did the party fail to make a **RULE 26(a) required disclosure**?
→ **Yes** → Adversaries may file a motion to compel the missing disclosures. *RULE 37(a)(3)* → Also, unless substantially justified or harmless, this failure may cause the court to deny the offending party the use of the information or witness at trial, inform the jury, order a reimbursement of expenses, and impose appropriate sanctions. *RULE 37(c)(1)*

Did the party fail to make a **requested admission**?
→ **Yes** → Unless the request was objectionable, the information sought not substantially important, the refusal had a reasonable basis, or other good reason exists, the failure to admit what later is proven true may cause the court to order a reimbursement of expenses incurred in proving the denied matter. *RULE 37(c)(2)*

Did the party fail to appear for a **deposition**, respond to **interrogatories** or **production requests**?
→ **Yes** → After a good faith conferral with the delinquent party, adversaries may seek sanctions. *RULE 37(d)* → Unless substantially justified (or an award would be unjust), this failure may cause the court to award appropriate sanctions. *RULE 37(d)(3)*

Did the party fail to answer, or evasively answer, **deposition questions, interrogatories**, or **production requests**?
→ **Yes** → Adversaries may file a motion to compel the missing materials and for appropriate sanctions. *RULE 37(a)(3)*

Some Possible Discovery Sanctions:

- matters/facts deemed established;
- prohibiting party to support/oppose;
- striking pleadings;
- staying proceedings until obeyed;
- dismissal or default;
- contempt;
- reimbursement of expenses;

RULE 37(d)(3)

Did the party fail to produce **ESI** that had been **lost**?
→ **Yes** → If lost due to the routine, good faith operation of an electronic information system, this failure will likely not result in sanctions. *RULE 37(e)*

Did the party fail to **appear for a physical / mental examination**?
→ **Yes** → The court may impose appropriate sanctions. *RULE 37(b)(2)(B)*

Did the party fail to make a **RULE 26(e) supplement**?
→ **Yes** → Adversaries may file a motion to compel the missing material. *RULE 37(a)(2)* → Unless substantially justified or harmless, this failure may cause the court to deny the offending party the use of the information or witness at trial, inform the jury, order a reimbursement of expenses, and impose appropriate sanctions. *RULE 37(c)(1)*

Did the party **violate a court's discovery order**?
→ **Yes** → The court may impose appropriate sanctions. *RULE 37(b)(2)(B)*

Notes

Motions to Compel Discovery

Map 6.5.1: *Fed. R. Civ. P. 37*

Premise

This Map completes the answer to question from Map 6.0:   *Has Abusive Discovery Been Sanctioned?*

When confronting an opponent's failure to provide disclosures or discovery (or when the disclosures or discovery that is provided is improper), does the party want the court **to force appropriate discovery** (in addition to the award of sanctions)?

Is there proper cause for filing a motion to compel?

Go to Map 6.5   **No**

Yes

Has the moving party first conferred (or attempted to confer) in a good faith effort to resolve the dispute without court intervention? *RULE 37(a)(1)*   **No**

Yes

Has the moving party served all parties with copies of the motion, and filed the motion with the court (along with a certification of the good faith conferral)? *RULE 37(a)(1)*   **No**

The Motion to Compel is improper.

Yes

If the Requested Discovery is Provided, But Only After the Motion to Compel Is Filed --
the court must order the offending party, attorney, or both to reimburse the moving party for the expenses of making the motion, unless (1) no pre-filing good faith conferral occurred; (2) the offending party's conduct was substantially justified, or (3) an award is otherwise unjust.
RULE 37(a)(5)(A)

If the Motion is Granted --
the court must order the offending party, attorney, or both to reimburse the moving party for the expenses of making the motion, unless (1) no pre-filing good faith conferral occurred; (2) the offending party's conduct was substantially justified, or (3) an award is otherwise unjust.
RULE 37(a)(5)(A)

If the Motion Is Denied --
the court may issue a protective order, and must order the attorney filing the motion, the party, or both to reimburse the opposing party for the expenses of defending the motion, unless (1) the moving party's conduct was substantially justified, or (2) an award is otherwise unjust.
RULE 37(a)(5)(B)

If the Motion Is Granted In Part, and Denied In Part --
the court may issue a protective order, and may order the parties to reimburse one another for their proportionate expenses in litigating the motion.
RULE 37(a)(5)(C)

Notes

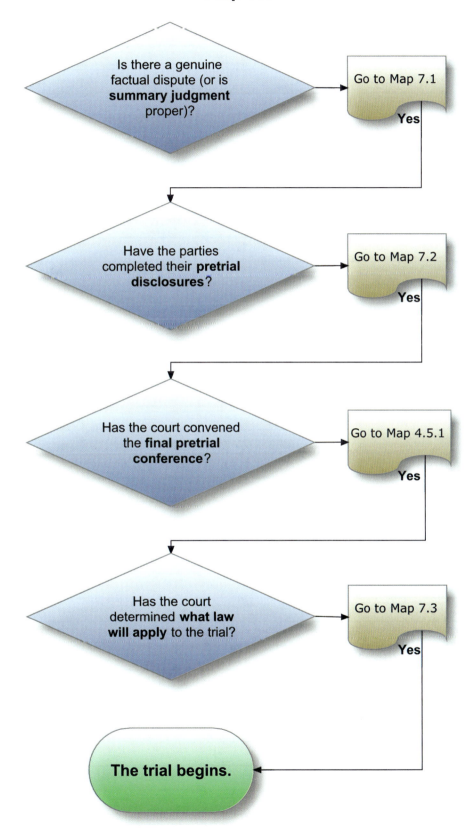

Is there a genuine factual dispute (or is **summary judgment** proper)? → Go to Map 7.1 — **Yes**

Have the parties completed their **pretrial disclosures**? → Go to Map 7.2 — **Yes**

Has the court convened the **final pretrial conference**? → Go to Map 4.5.1 — **Yes**

Has the court determined **what law will apply** to the trial? → Go to Map 7.3 — **Yes**

The trial begins.

Notes

Summary Judgment Motions, Generally

Map 7.1: *Fed. R. Civ. P. 56*

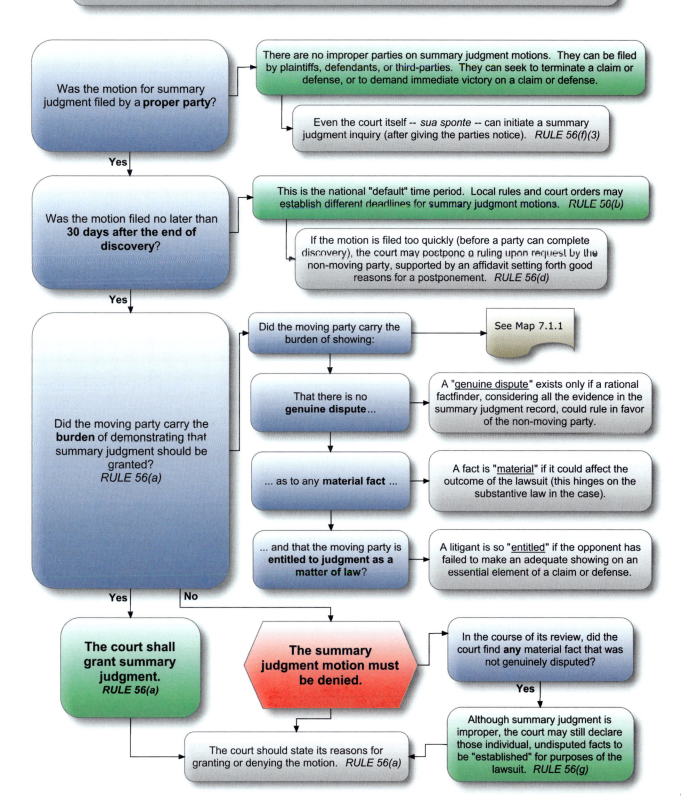

Premise

This Map answers the question from Map 7.0: *Is There A Genuine Factual Dispute (Or Is Summary Judgment Proper)?*

If it becomes clear that a claim or defense has no adequate factual support, there ought to be no need to convene an unnecessary trial to simply announce that result. **Summary judgment** (rather than judgment after trial) is a procedure to identify, and then terminate, factually unsupported claims and defenses.

Was the motion for summary judgment filed by a **proper party**?

There are no improper parties on summary judgment motions. They can be filed by plaintiffs, defendants, or third-parties. They can seek to terminate a claim or defense, or to demand immediate victory on a claim or defense.

Even the court itself -- *sua sponte* -- can initiate a summary judgment inquiry (after giving the parties notice). *RULE 56(f)(3)*

Yes

Was the motion filed no later than **30 days after the end of discovery**?

This is the national "default" time period. Local rules and court orders may establish different deadlines for summary judgment motions. *RULE 56(b)*

If the motion is filed too quickly (before a party can complete discovery), the court may postpone a ruling upon request by the non-moving party, supported by an affidavit setting forth good reasons for a postponement. *RULE 56(d)*

Yes

Did the moving party carry the **burden** of demonstrating that summary judgment should be granted? *RULE 56(a)*

Did the moving party carry the burden of showing:

See Map 7.1.1

That there is no **genuine dispute**...

A "<u>genuine dispute</u>" exists only if a rational factfinder, considering all the evidence in the summary judgment record, could rule in favor of the non-moving party.

... as to any **material fact** ...

A fact is "<u>material</u>" if it could affect the outcome of the lawsuit (this hinges on the substantive law in the case).

... and that the moving party is **entitled to judgment as a matter of law**?

A litigant is so "<u>entitled</u>" if the opponent has failed to make an adequate showing on an essential element of a claim or defense.

Yes   **No**

The court shall grant summary judgment. *RULE 56(a)*

The summary judgment motion must be denied.

In the course of its review, did the court find **any** material fact that was not genuinely disputed?

Yes

Although summary judgment is improper, the court may still declare those individual, undisputed facts to be "established" for purposes of the lawsuit. *RULE 56(g)*

The court should state its reasons for granting or denying the motion. *RULE 56(a)*

Notes

Summary Judgment Motions, Burdens & Procedures

Map 7.1.1: *Fed. R. Civ. P. 56*

Premise

This Map expands on the question from Map 7.0, by explaining the parties' burdens during, and the procedures for, summary judgment motions.

Who has the burden in summary judgment motions?

→ The party moving for summary judgment has the **initial burden** -- of showing that there is no genuine dispute as to any material issue and that he/she is entitled to judgment as a matter of law. *RULE 56(a)*

→ If the moving party makes that showing, the burden then **shifts** to the non-moving party to show that, contrary to the moving party's assertion, there is a genuine dispute as to a material fact which prevents the entry of judgment as a matter of law. *Celotex Corp. v. Catrett*

How are those burdens carried?

→ A party may cite to particular materials submitted to the court in support of (or in opposition to) summary judgment, or... *RULE 56(c)(1)(A)*

→ ... a party may show that none of those submitted materials establish the absence (or presence) of a genuine issue of material fact, or that the opponent cannot produce admissible evidence to support the fact. *RULE 56(c)(1)(B)*

What is used to carry those burdens?

→ Parties may support (or oppose) summary judgment motions with deposition transcripts, documents, ESI, affidavits, declarations, stipulations, admissions, discovery responses, and other materials. *RULE 56(c)(1)(A)*

→ Affidavits and Declarations: must (1) be made upon personal knowledge, (2) set out facts that would be admissible in evidence, and (3) show the author is competent to testify on the matters. *RULE 56(c)(4)*

→ Because affidavits can prove so important in these motions, an affidavit submitted in bad faith may be sanctioned. *RULE 56(h)*

How does the court assess the burdens?

→ The task of the court is a narrow one: Is there an actual, relevant factual disagreement in the lawsuit that requires a trial for resolution?

→ The court does not "weigh" the evidence. Any reasonable doubts or inferences about the evidence, or witness credibility, are resolved in favor of the non-moving party. *Anderson v. Liberty Lobby, Inc.*

→ Such doubts and inferences, however, must be reasonable. If a party's assertion is blatantly contradicted by undisputed evidence, that assertion can be discounted. *Scott v. Harris*

What happens if a party fails to support or address a fact?

→ The court may deem that fact to be undisputed, may grant summary judgment in light of the undisputed fact (if appropriate), may give the delinquent party additional time to respond, or may issue any other appropriate order. *RULE 56(e)*

On summary judgment, how broad are the court's powers?

→ The court may grant summary judgment as the moving party has requested, or may deny it. *RULE 56(a)*

→ The court may enter summary judgment on grounds not raised by any party. *RULE 56(f)(2)*

→ The court may enter summary judgment in favor of the non-moving party. *RULE 56(f)(1)*

→ The court may enter summary judgment *sua sponte* (without a motion), after proper notice to all parties. *RULE 56(f)(3)*

Notes

Pretrial Disclosures
Map 7.2: *Fed. R. Civ. P. 26((a)(3)*

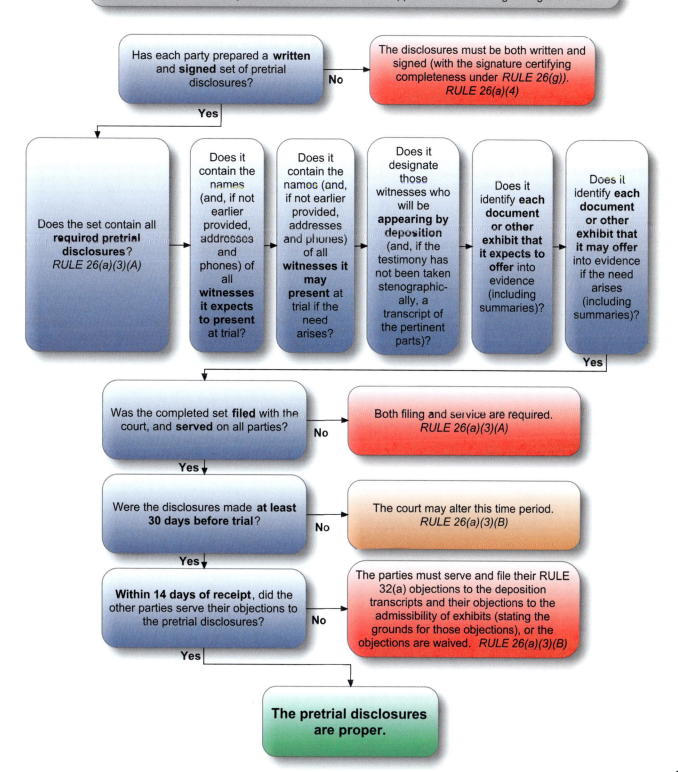

Premise

This Map answers the question from Map 7.0: *Have The Parties Completed Their Pretrial Disclosures?*

One of the guiding principles of the RULES is to avoid inappropriate trial-day surprises. This enables the parties to be better prepared for trial and, it is hoped, more likely to settle their dispute or to assist the factfinder in rendering a just result at trial. **Pretrial Disclosures** ensure that each party -- before trial -- knows the identity of all witnesses and exhibits opponents will be using during the trial.

Has each party prepared a **written** and **signed** set of pretrial disclosures?

No → The disclosures must be both written and signed (with the signature certifying completeness under *RULE 26(g)*). *RULE 26(a)(4)*

Yes

Does the set contain all **required pretrial disclosures**? *RULE 26(a)(3)(A)*

Does it contain the names (and, if not earlier provided, addresses and phones) of all **witnesses it expects to present** at trial?

Does it contain the names (and, if not earlier provided, addresses and phones) of all **witnesses it may present** at trial if the need arises?

Does it designate those witnesses who will be **appearing by deposition** (and, if the testimony has not been taken stenographic-ally, a transcript of the pertinent parts)?

Does it identify **each document or other exhibit that it expects to offer** into evidence (including summaries)?

Does it identify **each document or other exhibit that it may offer** into evidence if the need arises (including summaries)?

Yes

Was the completed set **filed** with the court, and **served** on all parties?

No → Both filing and service are required. *RULE 26(a)(3)(A)*

Yes

Were the disclosures made **at least 30 days before trial**?

No → The court may alter this time period. *RULE 26(a)(3)(B)*

Yes

Within 14 days of receipt, did the other parties serve their objections to the pretrial disclosures?

No → The parties must serve and file their RULE 32(a) objections to the deposition transcripts and their objections to the admissibility of exhibits (stating the grounds for those objections), or the objections are waived. *RULE 26(a)(3)(B)*

Yes

The pretrial disclosures are proper.

Notes

What Law Applies: *Erie*, *Hanna*, and Their Progeny

Map 7.3: *U.S. Constitution; 28 U.S.C. §§ 1652 & 2072*

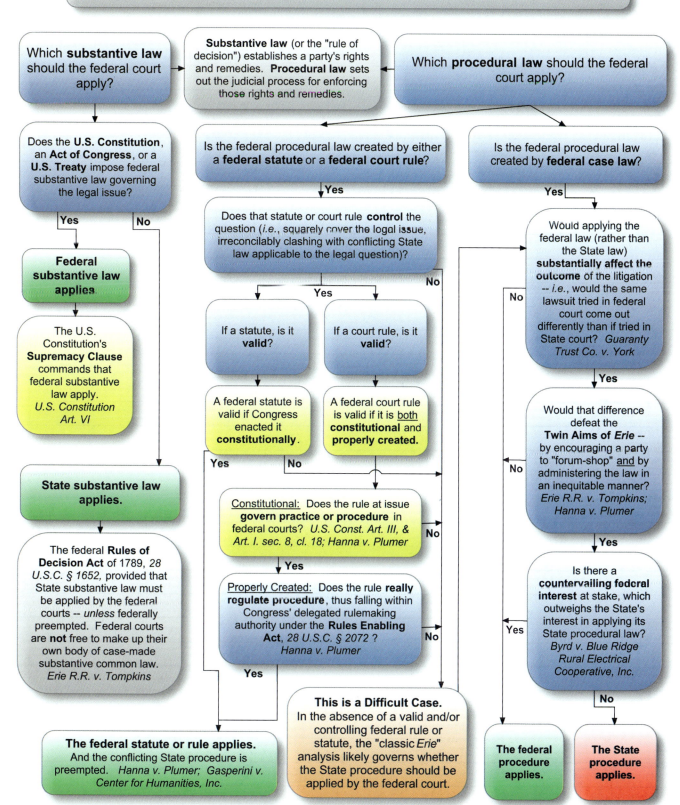

Premise

This Map answers the question from Map 7.0: *Has The Court Determined What Law Will Apply To The Trial?*

Federal courts do not always apply federal law in deciding cases. Especially in diversity cases and supplemental jurisdiction cases, State laws may be implicated. The question of when a federal court should apply State law was addressed in a series of landmark U.S. Supreme Court cases -- those cases are known as the **Erie Doctrine**.

Which **substantive law** should the federal court apply?

Substantive law (or the "rule of decision") establishes a party's rights and remedies. **Procedural law** sets out the judicial process for enforcing those rights and remedies.

Which **procedural law** should the federal court apply?

Does the **U.S. Constitution**, an **Act of Congress**, or a **U.S. Treaty** impose federal substantive law governing the legal issue?

Is the federal procedural law created by either a **federal statute** or a **federal court rule**?

Is the federal procedural law created by **federal case law**?

Yes | **No**

Federal substantive law applies.

The U.S. Constitution's **Supremacy Clause** commands that federal substantive law apply. *U.S. Constitution Art. VI*

Does that statute or court rule **control** the question (*i.e.*, squarely cover the legal issue, irreconcilably clashing with conflicting State law applicable to the legal question)?

Yes

Yes

Would applying the federal law (rather than the State law) **substantially affect the outcome** of the litigation -- *i.e.*, would the same lawsuit tried in federal court come out differently than if tried in State court? *Guaranty Trust Co. v. York*

No

No

Yes

If a statute, is it **valid**?

If a court rule, is it **valid**?

State substantive law applies.

A federal statute is valid if Congress enacted it **constitutionally**.

A federal court rule is valid if it is both **constitutional** and **properly created.**

Would that difference defeat the **Twin Aims of *Erie*** -- by encouraging a party to "forum-shop" and by administering the law in an inequitable manner? *Erie R.R. v. Tompkins; Hanna v. Plumer*

No

Yes | **No**

The federal **Rules of Decision Act** of 1789, *28 U.S.C. § 1652*, provided that State substantive law must be applied by the federal courts -- *unless* federally preempted. Federal courts are **not** free to make up their own body of case-made substantive common law. *Erie R.R. v. Tompkins*

Constitutional: Does the rule at issue **govern practice or procedure** in federal courts? *U.S. Const. Art. III, & Art. I. sec. 8, cl. 18; Hanna v. Plumer*

No

Yes

Yes

Is there a **countervailing federal interest** at stake, which outweighs the State's interest in applying its State procedural law? *Byrd v. Blue Ridge Rural Electrical Cooperative, Inc.*

Yes

Properly Created: Does the rule **really regulate procedure**, thus falling within Congress' delegated rulemaking authority under the **Rules Enabling Act**, *28 U.S.C. § 2072* ? *Hanna v. Plumer*

No

Yes

No

The federal statute or rule applies.
And the conflicting State procedure is preempted. *Hanna v. Plumer; Gasperini v. Center for Humanities, Inc.*

This is a Difficult Case.
In the absence of a valid and/or controlling federal rule or statute, the "classic *Erie*" analysis likely governs whether the State procedure should be applied by the federal court.

The federal procedure applies.

The State procedure applies.

Notes

Discerning the Content of State or Foreign Law

Map 7.3.1: *Fed. R. Civ. P. 44.1*

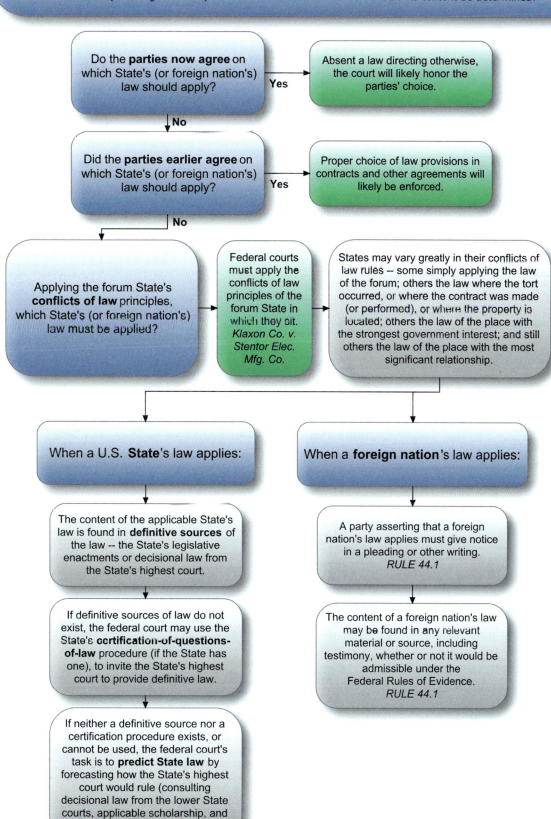

Premise

This Map addresses an issue introduced in Map 7.3 - if non-federal law is to be applied by the federal court, which State's (or foreign nation's) law should be selected and how should its content be determined?

Do the **parties now agree** on which State's (or foreign nation's) law should apply?

Yes → Absent a law directing otherwise, the court will likely honor the parties' choice.

No ↓

Did the **parties earlier agree** on which State's (or foreign nation's) law should apply?

Yes → Proper choice of law provisions in contracts and other agreements will likely be enforced.

No ↓

Applying the forum State's **conflicts of law** principles, which State's (or foreign nation's) law must be applied?

→ Federal courts must apply the conflicts of law principles of the forum State in which they sit. *Klaxon Co. v. Stentor Elec. Mfg. Co.*

→ States may vary greatly in their conflicts of law rules -- some simply applying the law of the forum; others the law where the tort occurred, or where the contract was made (or performed), or where the property is located; others the law of the place with the strongest government interest; and still others the law of the place with the most significant relationship.

When a U.S. State's law applies:

The content of the applicable State's law is found in **definitive sources** of the law -- the State's legislative enactments or decisional law from the State's highest court.

↓

If definitive sources of law do not exist, the federal court may use the State's **certification-of-questions-of-law** procedure (if the State has one), to invite the State's highest court to provide definitive law.

↓

If neither a definitive source nor a certification procedure exists, or cannot be used, the federal court's task is to **predict State law** by forecasting how the State's highest court would rule (consulting decisional law from the lower State courts, applicable scholarship, and other sources).

When a foreign nation's law applies:

A party asserting that a foreign nation's law applies must give notice in a pleading or other writing. *RULE 44.1*

↓

The content of a foreign nation's law may be found in any relevant material or source, including testimony, whether or not it would be admissible under the Federal Rules of Evidence. *RULE 44.1*

Notes

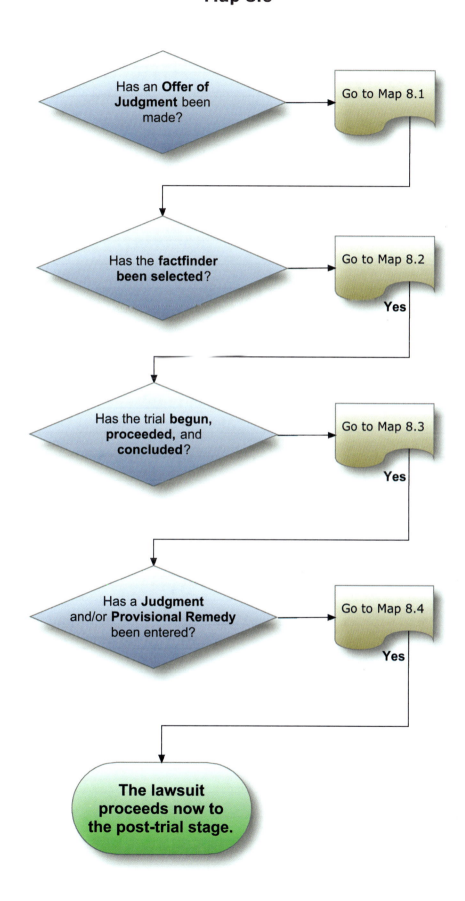

Has an **Offer of Judgment** been made? → Go to Map 8.1

Has the **factfinder been selected**? → Go to Map 8.2 **Yes**

Has the trial **begun, proceeded,** and **concluded**? → Go to Map 8.3 **Yes**

Has a **Judgment** and/or **Provisional Remedy** been entered? → Go to Map 8.4 **Yes**

The lawsuit proceeds now to the post-trial stage.

Notes

Offers of Judgment
Map 8.1: *Fed. R. Civ. P. 68*

Premise
This Map answers the question from Map 8.0: *Has An Offer Of Judgment Been Made?*

At various junctures, the RULES encourage the parties to consider resolving their litigation through a settlement. RULE 26 obligates the parties, at the outset of the litigation, to discuss settlement. RULE 16 permits pretrial conferences with the judge to discuss settlement. **Offers of Judgment** encourage settlement as well, by imposing a penalty on a party's unwise rejection of a settlement offer.

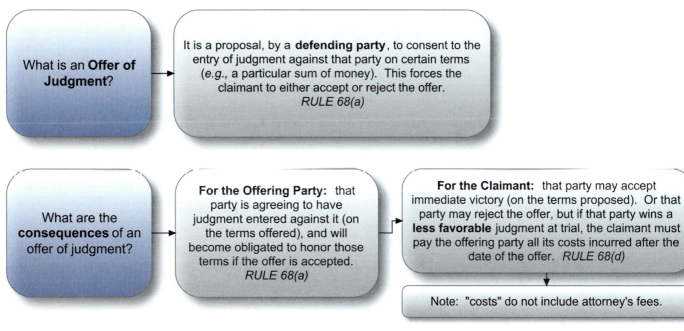

What is an **Offer of Judgment**?

It is a proposal, by a **defending party**, to consent to the entry of judgment against that party on certain terms (*e.g.,* a particular sum of money). This forces the claimant to either accept or reject the offer.
RULE 68(a)

What are the **consequences** of an offer of judgment?

For the Offering Party: that party is agreeing to have judgment entered against it (on the terms offered), and will become obligated to honor those terms if the offer is accepted.
RULE 68(a)

For the Claimant: that party may accept immediate victory (on the terms proposed). Or that party may reject the offer, but if that party wins a **less favorable** judgment at trial, the claimant must pay the offering party all its costs incurred after the date of the offer. *RULE 68(d)*

Note: "costs" do not include attorney's fees.

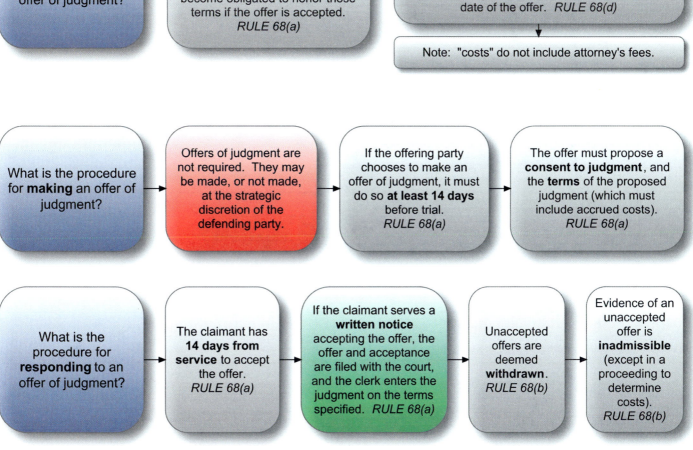

What is the procedure for **making** an offer of judgment?

Offers of judgment are not required. They may be made, or not made, at the strategic discretion of the defending party.

If the offering party chooses to make an offer of judgment, it must do so **at least 14 days** before trial.
RULE 68(a)

The offer must propose a **consent to judgment**, and the **terms** of the proposed judgment (which must include accrued costs).
RULE 68(a)

What is the procedure for **responding** to an offer of judgment?

The claimant has **14 days from service** to accept the offer.
RULE 68(a)

If the claimant serves a **written notice** accepting the offer, the offer and acceptance are filed with the court, and the clerk enters the judgment on the terms specified. *RULE 68(a)*

Unaccepted offers are deemed **withdrawn**.
RULE 68(b)

Evidence of an unaccepted offer is **inadmissible** (except in a proceeding to determine costs).
RULE 68(b)

Notes

Selecting the Factfinder

Map 8.2: *U.S. Constitution; Fed. R. Civ. P. 38, 39, & 73*

Premise
This Map answers the question from Map 8.0: *Has The Factfinder Been Selected?*

Trials occur when there are disputed questions of fact that must be resolved. The decisionmaker who resolves those facts (the "**factfinder**") may be a jury, a judge, or a special panel of lawyers or specialists.

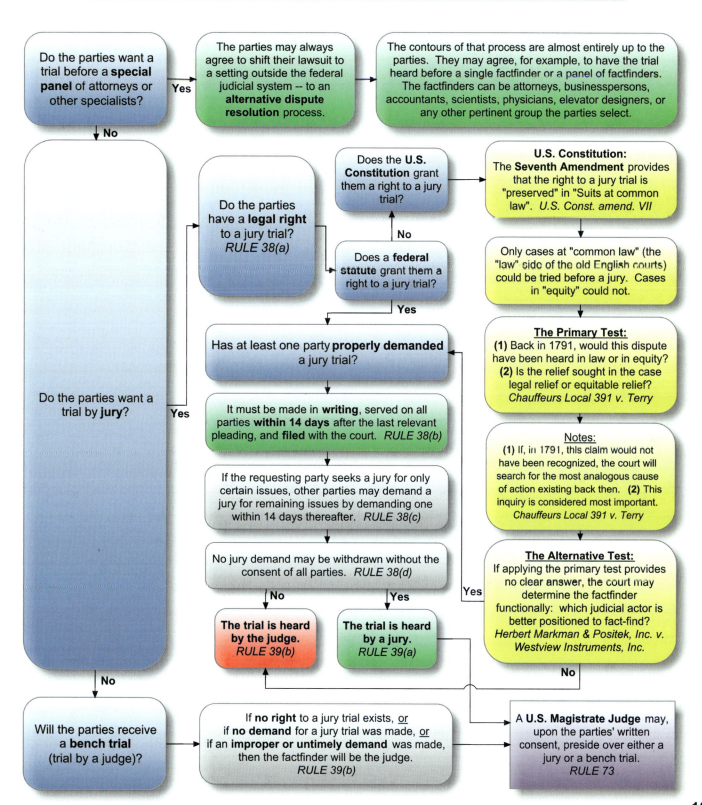

Do the parties want a trial before a **special panel** of attorneys or other specialists?

Yes → The parties may always agree to shift their lawsuit to a setting outside the federal judicial system -- to an **alternative dispute resolution** process.

→ The contours of that process are almost entirely up to the parties. They may agree, for example, to have the trial heard before a single factfinder or a panel of factfinders. The factfinders can be attorneys, businesspersons, accountants, scientists, physicians, elevator designers, or any other pertinent group the parties select.

No

Do the parties want a trial by **jury**?

Yes → Do the parties have a **legal right** to a jury trial? *RULE 38(a)*

Does the **U.S. Constitution** grant them a right to a jury trial?

No → Does a **federal statute** grant them a right to a jury trial? **Yes**

U.S. Constitution:
The **Seventh Amendment** provides that the right to a jury trial is "preserved" in "Suits at common law". *U.S. Const. amend. VII*

Only cases at "common law" (the "law" side of the old English courts) could be tried before a jury. Cases in "equity" could not.

Has at least one party **properly demanded** a jury trial?

It must be made in **writing**, served on all parties **within 14 days** after the last relevant pleading, and **filed** with the court. *RULE 38(b)*

If the requesting party seeks a jury for only certain issues, other parties may demand a jury for remaining issues by demanding one within 14 days thereafter. *RULE 38(c)*

No jury demand may be withdrawn without the consent of all parties. *RULE 38(d)*

The Primary Test:
(1) Back in 1791, would this dispute have been heard in law or in equity? **(2)** Is the relief sought in the case legal relief or equitable relief? *Chauffeurs Local 391 v. Terry*

Notes:
(1) If, in 1791, this claim would not have been recognized, the court will search for the most analogous cause of action existing back then. **(2)** This inquiry is considered most important. *Chauffeurs Local 391 v. Terry*

The Alternative Test:
If applying the primary test provides no clear answer, the court may determine the factfinder functionally: which judicial actor is better positioned to fact-find? *Herbert Markman & Positek, Inc. v. Westview Instruments, Inc.*

No → **The trial is heard by the judge.** *RULE 39(b)*

Yes → **The trial is heard by a jury.** *RULE 39(a)*

Yes

No

Do the parties want a trial by **jury**? **No**

Will the parties receive a **bench trial** (trial by a judge)?

If **no right** to a jury trial exists, <u>or</u> if **no demand** for a jury trial was made, <u>or</u> if an **improper or untimely demand** was made, then the factfinder will be the judge. *RULE 39(b)*

A **U.S. Magistrate Judge** may, upon the parties' written consent, preside over either a jury or a bench trial. *RULE 73*

Notes

Trial Logistics, Generally

Map 8.3: *Fed. R. Civ. P. 42, 43, 45, 46, & 61*

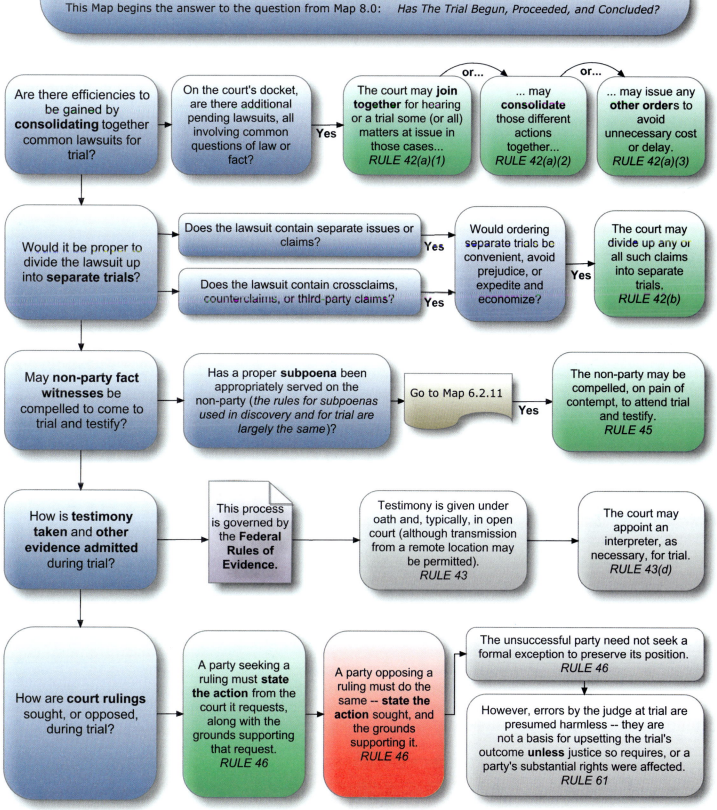

Premise

This Map begins the answer to the question from Map 8.0:   *Has The Trial Begun, Proceeded, and Concluded?*

Are there efficiencies to be gained by **consolidating** together common lawsuits for trial?

On the court's docket, are there additional pending lawsuits, all involving common questions of law or fact?

Yes

or... **or...**

The court may **join together** for hearing or a trial some (or all) matters at issue in those cases...
RULE 42(a)(1)

... may **consolidate** those different actions together...
RULE 42(a)(2)

... may issue any **other order**s to avoid unnecessary cost or delay.
RULE 42(a)(3)

Would it be proper to divide the lawsuit up into **separate trials**?

Does the lawsuit contain separate issues or claims?
Yes

Does the lawsuit contain crossclaims, counterclaims, or third-party claims?
Yes

Would ordering separate trials be convenient, avoid prejudice, or expedite and economize?
Yes

The court may divide up any or all such claims into separate trials.
RULE 42(b)

May **non-party fact witnesses** be compelled to come to trial and testify?

Has a proper **subpoena** been appropriately served on the non-party (*the rules for subpoenas used in discovery and for trial are largely the same*)?

Go to Map 6.2.11

Yes

The non-party may be compelled, on pain of contempt, to attend trial and testify.
RULE 45

How is **testimony taken** and **other evidence admitted** during trial?

This process is governed by the **Federal Rules of Evidence.**

Testimony is given under oath and, typically, in open court (although transmission from a remote location may be permitted).
RULE 43

The court may appoint an interpreter, as necessary, for trial.
RULE 43(d)

How are **court rulings** sought, or opposed, during trial?

A party seeking a ruling must **state the action** from the court it requests, along with the grounds supporting that request.
RULE 46

A party opposing a ruling must do the same -- **state the action** sought, and the grounds supporting it.
RULE 46

The unsuccessful party need not seek a formal exception to preserve its position.
RULE 46

However, errors by the judge at trial are presumed harmless -- they are not a basis for upsetting the trial's outcome **unless** justice so requires, or a party's substantial rights were affected.
RULE 61

Notes

Trial Logistics - Conducting Jury Trials

Map 8.3.1: *28 U.S.C. § 1870; Fed. R. Civ. P. 47, 48, 49, 50, & 51*

Premise
This Map continues to answer the question from Map 8.0 by explaining the logistics of jury trials.

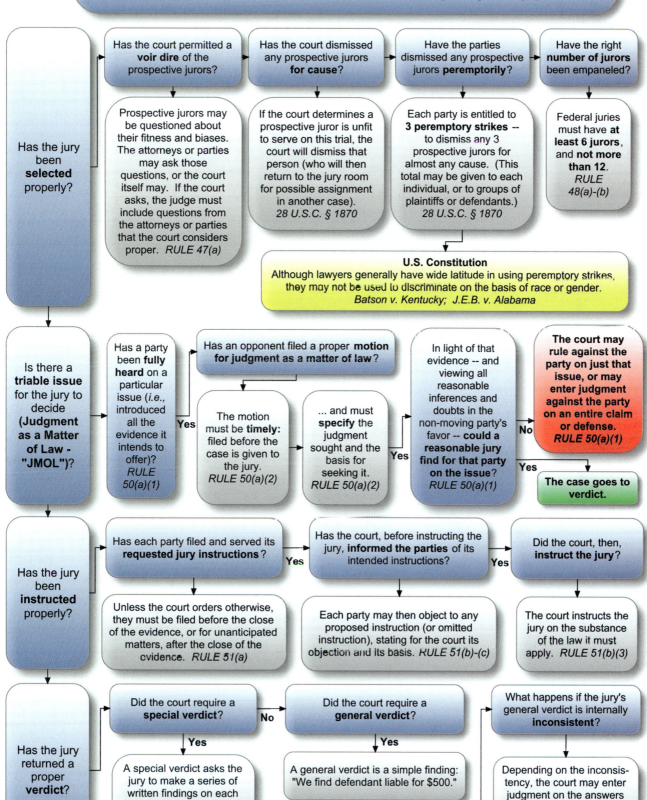

Has the jury been selected properly?

Has the court permitted a **voir dire** of the prospective jurors?

Prospective jurors may be questioned about their fitness and biases. The attorneys or parties may ask those questions, or the court itself may. If the court asks, the judge must include questions from the attorneys or parties that the court considers proper. *RULE 47(a)*

Has the court dismissed any prospective jurors **for cause**?

If the court determines a prospective juror is unfit to serve on this trial, the court will dismiss that person (who will then return to the jury room for possible assignment in another case). *28 U.S.C. § 1870*

Have the parties dismissed any prospective jurors **peremptorily**?

Each party is entitled to **3 peremptory strikes** -- to dismiss any 3 prospective jurors for almost any cause. (This total may be given to each individual, or to groups of plaintiffs or defendants.) *28 U.S.C. § 1870*

Have the right **number of jurors** been empaneled?

Federal juries must have **at least 6 jurors**, and **not more than 12**. *RULE 48(a)-(b)*

U.S. Constitution
Although lawyers generally have wide latitude in using peremptory strikes, they may not be used to discriminate on the basis of race or gender. *Batson v. Kentucky; J.E.B. v. Alabama*

Is there a triable issue for the jury to decide (Judgment as a Matter of Law - "JMOL")?

Has a party been **fully heard** on a particular issue (*i.e.*, introduced all the evidence it intends to offer)? *RULE 50(a)(1)*

Has an opponent filed a proper **motion for judgment as a matter of law**?

The motion must be **timely**: filed before the case is given to the jury. *RULE 50(a)(2)*

... and must **specify** the judgment sought and the basis for seeking it. *RULE 50(a)(2)*

In light of that evidence -- and viewing all reasonable inferences and doubts in the non-moving party's favor -- **could a reasonable jury find for that party on the issue**? *RULE 50(a)(1)*

No → The court may rule against the party on just that issue, or may enter judgment against the party on an entire claim or defense. *RULE 50(a)(1)*

Yes → The case goes to verdict.

Has the jury been instructed properly?

Has each party filed and served its **requested jury instructions**?

Unless the court orders otherwise, they must be filed before the close of the evidence, or for unanticipated matters, after the close of the evidence. *RULE 51(a)*

Yes → Has the court, before instructing the jury, **informed the parties** of its intended instructions?

Each party may then object to any proposed instruction (or omitted instruction), stating for the court its objection and its basis. *RULE 51(b)-(c)*

Yes → Did the court, then, **instruct the jury**?

The court instructs the jury on the substance of the law it must apply. *RULE 51(b)(3)*

Has the jury returned a proper verdict?

Did the court require a **special verdict**?

Yes → A special verdict asks the jury to make a series of written findings on each issue of fact. The court must instruct the jury on how to perform this task. *RULE 49(a)*

No → Did the court require a **general verdict**?

Yes → A general verdict is a simple finding: "We find defendant liable for $500."

This may be combined with a brief series of written questions on one or more issues of fact. *RULE 49(b)*

What happens if the jury's general verdict is internally **inconsistent**?

Depending on the inconsistency, the court may enter judgment on the answers (ignoring the verdict), instruct the jury to review its answers, or order a new trial. *RULE 49(b)*

Notes

Trial Logistics - Conducting Bench Trials
Map 8.3.2: *Fed. R. Civ. P. 52*

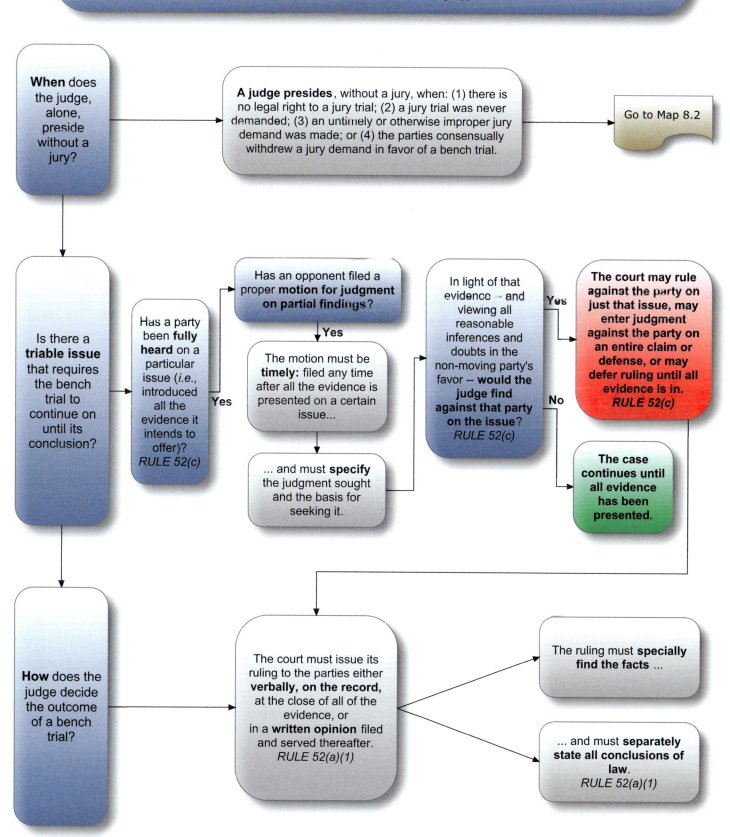

Premise
This Map continues to answer the question from Map 8.0 by explaining the logistics of bench trials (that is, trials before a judge alone, not a jury).

When does the judge, alone, preside without a jury?

A judge presides, without a jury, when: (1) there is no legal right to a jury trial; (2) a jury trial was never demanded; (3) an untimely or otherwise improper jury demand was made; or (4) the parties consensually withdrew a jury demand in favor of a bench trial.

Go to Map 8.2

Is there a **triable issue** that requires the bench trial to continue on until its conclusion?

Has a party been **fully heard** on a particular issue (*i.e.,* introduced all the evidence it intends to offer)? *RULE 52(c)*

Yes

Has an opponent filed a proper **motion for judgment on partial findings**?

Yes

The motion must be **timely**: filed any time after all the evidence is presented on a certain issue...

... and must **specify** the judgment sought and the basis for seeking it.

In light of that evidence -- and viewing all reasonable inferences and doubts in the non-moving party's favor -- **would the judge find against that party on the issue**? *RULE 52(c)*

Yes

No

The court may rule against the party on just that issue, may enter judgment against the party on an entire claim or defense, or may defer ruling until all evidence is in. *RULE 52(c)*

The case continues until all evidence has been presented.

How does the judge decide the outcome of a bench trial?

The court must issue its ruling to the parties either **verbally, on the record,** at the close of all of the evidence, or in a **written opinion** filed and served thereafter. *RULE 52(a)(1)*

The ruling must **specially find the facts** ...

... and must **separately state all conclusions of law**. *RULE 52(a)(1)*

Notes

The Judge's Inability to Proceed
Map 8.3.3: *Fed. R. Civ. P. 63*

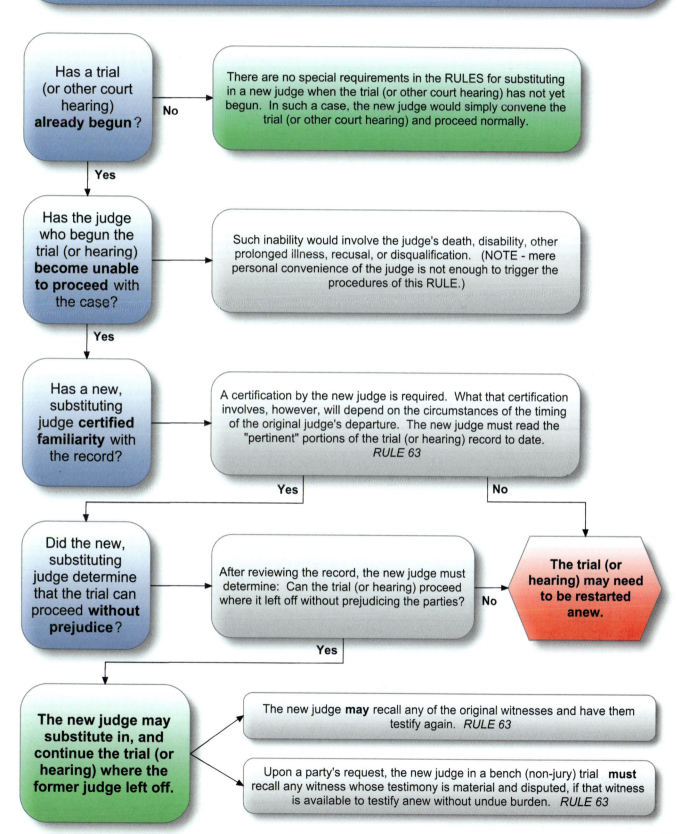

Premise
This Map continues to answer the question from Map 8.0 by explaining the logistics of a trial if the originally presiding judge becomes -- during the course of the trial -- unable to continue.

Has a trial (or other court hearing) **already begun**?

No → There are no special requirements in the RULES for substituting in a new judge when the trial (or other court hearing) has not yet begun. In such a case, the new judge would simply convene the trial (or other court hearing) and proceed normally.

Yes ↓

Has the judge who begun the trial (or hearing) **become unable to proceed** with the case?

Such inability would involve the judge's death, disability, other prolonged illness, recusal, or disqualification. (NOTE - mere personal convenience of the judge is not enough to trigger the procedures of this RULE.)

Yes ↓

Has a new, substituting judge **certified familiarity** with the record?

A certification by the new judge is required. What that certification involves, however, will depend on the circumstances of the timing of the original judge's departure. The new judge must read the "pertinent" portions of the trial (or hearing) record to date. *RULE 63*

Yes ← | **No** →

Did the new, substituting judge determine that the trial can proceed **without prejudice**?

After reviewing the record, the new judge must determine: Can the trial (or hearing) proceed where it left off without prejudicing the parties?

No → **The trial (or hearing) may need to be restarted anew.**

Yes ↓

The new judge may substitute in, and continue the trial (or hearing) where the former judge left off.

→ The new judge **may** recall any of the original witnesses and have them testify again. *RULE 63*

→ Upon a party's request, the new judge in a bench (non-jury) trial **must** recall any witness whose testimony is material and disputed, if that witness is available to testify anew without undue burden. *RULE 63*

Notes

Judgments and Provisional Remedies, Generally

Map 8.4: *U.S. Constitution; Fed. R. Civ. P. 64*

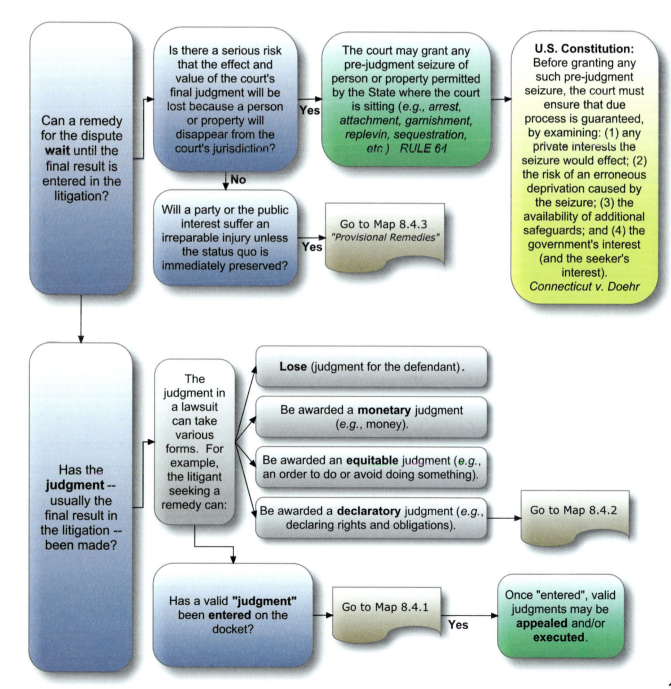

Premise

This Map answers the question from Map 8.0: *Has A Judgment And/Or Provisional Remedy Been Entered?*

A **judgment** is a ruling from the district court from which an appeal may be taken. Although there may be many rulings by the judge in every case (*e.g.*, rulings on motions to dismiss or for summary judgment, rulings on discovery disputes, rulings on joinder motions, rulings on the admissibility of evidence, etc.), there is ordinarily only one "judgment".

A **provisional remedy** is a special order of the court (not granted routinely in every case) that is intended to "freeze" the status quo until the litigation is concluded. These special, interim remedies are usually permitted only when delaying a remedy until the end of the trial would inflict irreparable injury on a party. Provisional remedies last only for a limited time, and ordinarily dissolve when the final judgment is entered.

Can a remedy for the dispute **wait** until the final result is entered in the litigation?

Is there a serious risk that the effect and value of the court's final judgment will be lost because a person or property will disappear from the court's jurisdiction?

Yes → The court may grant any pre-judgment seizure of person or property permitted by the State where the court is sitting (*e.g.*, arrest, attachment, garnishment, replevin, sequestration, etc.) RULE 64

→ **U.S. Constitution:** Before granting any such pre-judgment seizure, the court must ensure that due process is guaranteed, by examining: (1) any private interests the seizure would effect; (2) the risk of an erroneous deprivation caused by the seizure; (3) the availability of additional safeguards; and (4) the government's interest (and the seeker's interest). *Connecticut v. Doehr*

↓**No**

Will a party or the public interest suffer an irreparable injury unless the status quo is immediately preserved?

Yes → Go to Map 8.4.3 *"Provisional Remedies"*

Has the **judgment** -- usually the final result in the litigation -- been made?

The judgment in a lawsuit can take various forms. For example, the litigant seeking a remedy can:

- **Lose** (judgment for the defendant).
- Be awarded a **monetary** judgment (*e.g.*, money).
- Be awarded an **equitable** judgment (*e.g.*, an order to do or avoid doing something).
- Be awarded a **declaratory** judgment (*e.g.*, declaring rights and obligations). → Go to Map 8.4.2

Has a valid **"judgment"** been **entered** on the docket? → Go to Map 8.4.1 **Yes** → Once "entered", valid judgments may be **appealed** and/or **executed**.

Notes

Entry of Judgment

Map 8.4.1: *28 U.S.C. § 1291; Fed. R. Civ. P. 54 & 58*

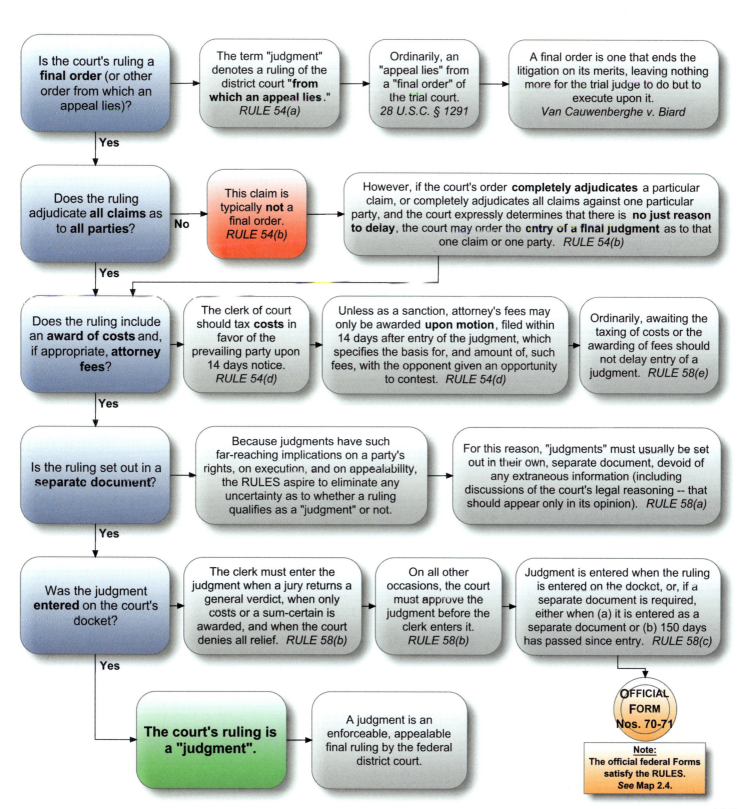

Premise

This Map continues to answer the question from Map 8.0: *Has A Judgment And/Or Provisional Remedy Been Entered?*

Is the court's ruling a **final order** (or other order from which an appeal lies)?

The term "judgment" denotes a ruling of the district court **"from which an appeal lies."** *RULE 54(a)*

Ordinarily, an "appeal lies" from a "final order" of the trial court. *28 U.S.C. § 1291*

A final order is one that ends the litigation on its merits, leaving nothing more for the trial judge to do but to execute upon it. *Van Cauwenberghe v. Biard*

Yes

Does the ruling adjudicate **all claims** as to **all parties**?

No → This claim is typically **not** a final order. *RULE 54(b)*

However, if the court's order **completely adjudicates** a particular claim, or completely adjudicates all claims against one particular party, and the court expressly determines that there is **no just reason to delay**, the court may order the **entry of a final judgment** as to that one claim or one party. *RULE 54(b)*

Yes

Does the ruling include an **award of costs** and, if appropriate, **attorney fees**?

The clerk of court should tax **costs** in favor of the prevailing party upon 14 days notice. *RULE 54(d)*

Unless as a sanction, attorney's fees may only be awarded **upon motion**, filed within 14 days after entry of the judgment, which specifies the basis for, and amount of, such fees, with the opponent given an opportunity to contest. *RULE 54(d)*

Ordinarily, awaiting the taxing of costs or the awarding of fees should not delay entry of a judgment. *RULE 58(e)*

Yes

Is the ruling set out in a **separate document**?

Because judgments have such far-reaching implications on a party's rights, on execution, and on appealability, the RULES aspire to eliminate any uncertainty as to whether a ruling qualifies as a "judgment" or not.

For this reason, "judgments" must usually be set out in their own, separate document, devoid of any extraneous information (including discussions of the court's legal reasoning -- that should appear only in its opinion). *RULE 58(a)*

Yes

Was the judgment **entered** on the court's docket?

The clerk must enter the judgment when a jury returns a general verdict, when only costs or a sum-certain is awarded, and when the court denies all relief. *RULE 58(b)*

On all other occasions, the court must approve the judgment before the clerk enters it. *RULE 58(b)*

Judgment is entered when the ruling is entered on the docket, or, if a separate document is required, either when (a) it is entered as a separate document or (b) 150 days has passed since entry. *RULE 58(c)*

OFFICIAL FORM Nos. 70-71

Note: The official federal Forms satisfy the RULES. *See Map 2.4.*

Yes

The court's ruling is a "judgment".

A judgment is an enforceable, appealable final ruling by the federal district court.

Notes

Declaratory Judgments
Map 8.4.2: *28 U.S.C. §§ 2201-02; Fed. R. Civ. P. 57*

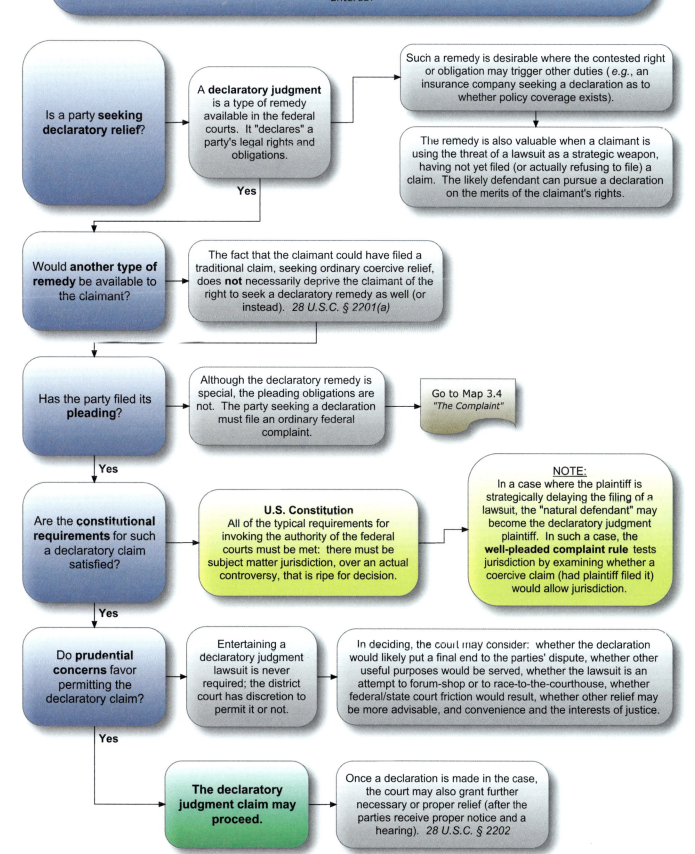

Premise

This Map continues to answer the question from Map 8.0: *Has A Judgment And/Or Provisional Remedy Been Entered?*

Is a party seeking declaratory relief?

A **declaratory judgment** is a type of remedy available in the federal courts. It "declares" a party's legal rights and obligations.

Yes

Such a remedy is desirable where the contested right or obligation may trigger other duties (*e.g.*, an insurance company seeking a declaration as to whether policy coverage exists).

The remedy is also valuable when a claimant is using the threat of a lawsuit as a strategic weapon, having not yet filed (or actually refusing to file) a claim. The likely defendant can pursue a declaration on the merits of the claimant's rights.

Would another type of remedy be available to the claimant?

The fact that the claimant could have filed a traditional claim, seeking ordinary coercive relief, does **not** necessarily deprive the claimant of the right to seek a declaratory remedy as well (or instead). *28 U.S.C. § 2201(a)*

Has the party filed its pleading?

Although the declaratory remedy is special, the pleading obligations are not. The party seeking a declaration must file an ordinary federal complaint.

Go to Map 3.4 *"The Complaint"*

Yes

Are the constitutional requirements for such a declaratory claim satisfied?

U.S. Constitution
All of the typical requirements for invoking the authority of the federal courts must be met: there must be subject matter jurisdiction, over an actual controversy, that is ripe for decision.

NOTE:
In a case where the plaintiff is strategically delaying the filing of a lawsuit, the "natural defendant" may become the declaratory judgment plaintiff. In such a case, the **well-pleaded complaint rule** tests jurisdiction by examining whether a coercive claim (had plaintiff filed it) would allow jurisdiction.

Yes

Do prudential concerns favor permitting the declaratory claim?

Entertaining a declaratory judgment lawsuit is never required; the district court has discretion to permit it or not.

In deciding, the court may consider: whether the declaration would likely put a final end to the parties' dispute, whether other useful purposes would be served, whether the lawsuit is an attempt to forum-shop or to race-to-the-courthouse, whether federal/state court friction would result, whether other relief may be more advisable, and convenience and the interests of justice.

Yes

The declaratory judgment claim may proceed.

Once a declaration is made in the case, the court may also grant further necessary or proper relief (after the parties receive proper notice and a hearing). *28 U.S.C. § 2202*

Notes

Provisional Remedies (TROs and Injunctions)
Map 8.4.3: *Fed. R. Civ. P. 65*

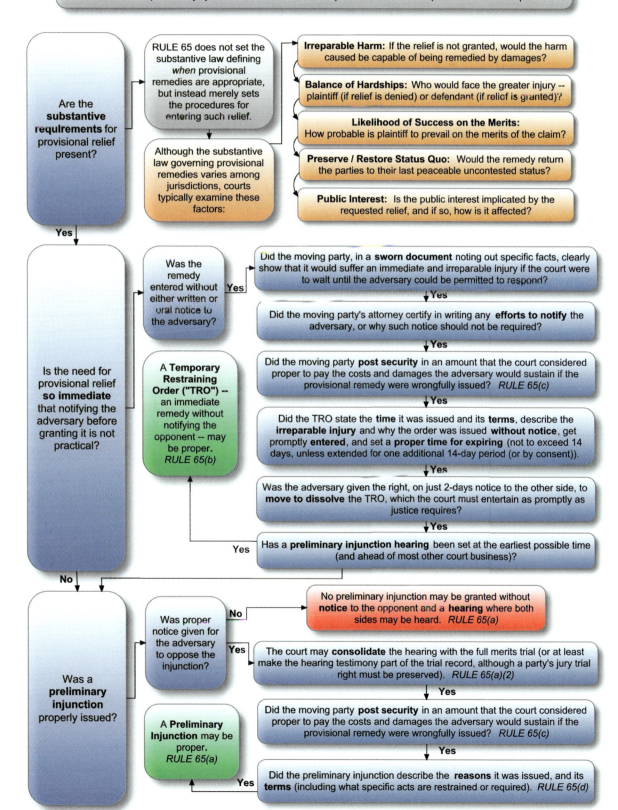

Premise
This Map continues to answer the question from Map 8.0: *Has A Judgment And/Or Provisional Remedy Been Entered?*

Provisional remedies are rulings made by a court before a trial has occurred (and, thus, before the trial judge knows who has won and lost on the merits). Such interim rulings are extraordinary, and granted only where imminent, irreparable injury will occur absent immediate judicial intervention to preserve the status quo.

Are the **substantive requirements** for provisional relief present?

RULE 65 does not set the substantive law defining *when* provisional remedies are appropriate, but instead merely sets the procedures for entering such relief.

Although the substantive law governing provisional remedies varies among jurisdictions, courts typically examine these factors:

Irreparable Harm: If the relief is not granted, would the harm caused be capable of being remedied by damages?

Balance of Hardships: Who would face the greater injury -- plaintiff (if relief is denied) or defendant (if relief is granted)?

Likelihood of Success on the Merits: How probable is plaintiff to prevail on the merits of the claim?

Preserve / Restore Status Quo: Would the remedy return the parties to their last peaceable uncontested status?

Public Interest: Is the public interest implicated by the requested relief, and if so, how is it affected?

Yes

Is the need for provisional relief **so immediate** that notifying the adversary before granting it is not practical?

Was the remedy entered without either written or oral notice to the adversary? **Yes**

Did the moving party, in a **sworn document** noting out specific facts, clearly show that it would suffer an immediate and irreparable injury if the court were to wait until the adversary could be permitted to respond? ↓Yes

Did the moving party's attorney certify in writing any **efforts to notify** the adversary, or why such notice should not be required? ↓Yes

Did the moving party **post security** in an amount that the court considered proper to pay the costs and damages the adversary would sustain if the provisional remedy were wrongfully issued? *RULE 65(c)* ↓Yes

Did the TRO state the **time** it was issued and its **terms**, describe the **irreparable injury** and why the order was issued **without notice**, get promptly **entered**, and set a **proper time for expiring** (not to exceed 14 days, unless extended for one additional 14-day period (or by consent)). ↓Yes

Was the adversary given the right, on just 2-days notice to the other side, to **move to dissolve** the TRO, which the court must entertain as promptly as justice requires? ↓Yes

A **Temporary Restraining Order ("TRO")** -- an immediate remedy without notifying the opponent -- may be proper. *RULE 65(b)*

Yes

Has a **preliminary injunction hearing** been set at the earliest possible time (and ahead of most other court business)?

No

Was a **preliminary injunction** properly issued?

Was proper notice given for the adversary to oppose the injunction? **No**

No preliminary injunction may be granted without **notice** to the opponent and a **hearing** where both sides may be heard. *RULE 65(a)*

Yes

The court may **consolidate** the hearing with the full merits trial (or at least make the hearing testimony part of the trial record, although a party's jury trial right must be preserved). *RULE 65(a)(2)* ↓Yes

Did the moving party **post security** in an amount that the court considered proper to pay the costs and damages the adversary would sustain if the provisional remedy were wrongfully issued? *RULE 65(c)* ↓Yes

A **Preliminary Injunction** may be proper. *RULE 65(a)*

Yes Did the preliminary injunction describe the **reasons** it was issued, and its **terms** (including what specific acts are restrained or required). *RULE 65(d)*

Notes

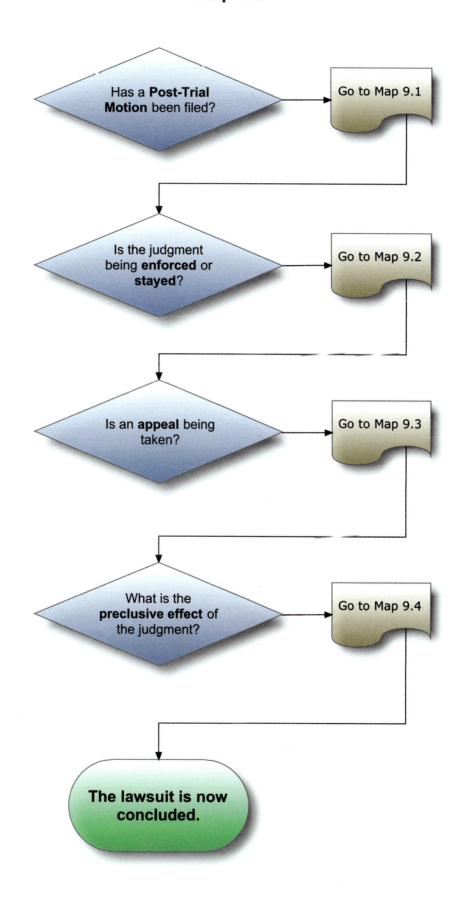

Has a **Post-Trial Motion** been filed? → Go to Map 9.1

Is the judgment being **enforced** or **stayed**? → Go to Map 9.2

Is an **appeal** being taken? → Go to Map 9.3

What is the **preclusive effect** of the judgment? → Go to Map 9.4

The lawsuit is now concluded.

Notes

Post-Trial Motions, Generally
Map 9.1: *Fed. R. Civ. P. 50, 52, 59, & 60*

Premise

This Map answers the question from Map 9.0:   *Has a Post-Trial Motion Been Filed?*

Post-trial motions seek to alter, in some respect, a verdict in a jury trial or the findings of fact and conclusions of law in a bench trial. The moving party either lost the trial (and seeks to win or receive a re-trial) or prevailed but in some unsatisfactory way.

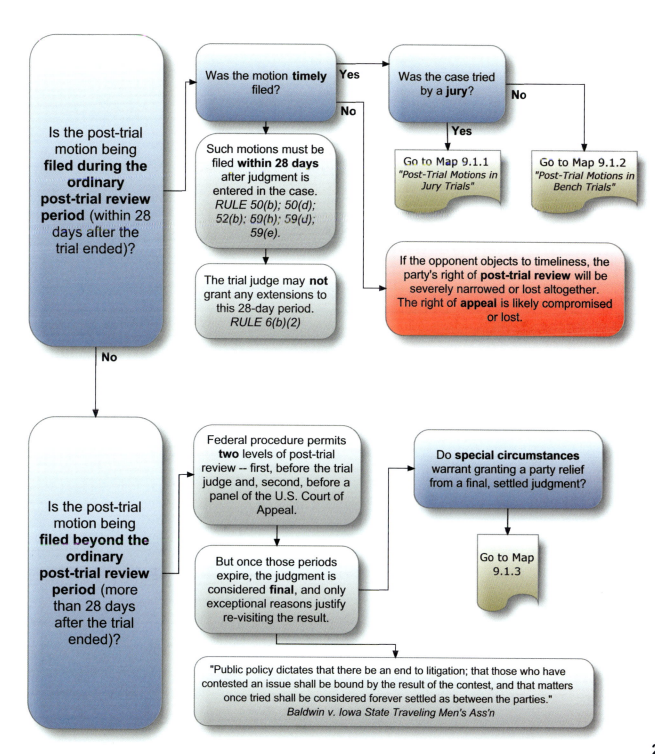

Is the post-trial motion being **filed during the ordinary post-trial review period** (within 28 days after the trial ended)?

Was the motion **timely** filed?

Such motions must be filed **within 28 days** after judgment is entered in the case. *RULE 50(b); 50(d); 52(b); 59(b); 59(d); 59(e).*

The trial judge may **not** grant any extensions to this 28-day period. *RULE 6(b)(2)*

Yes — Was the case tried by a **jury**?

Yes — Go to Map 9.1.1 *"Post-Trial Motions in Jury Trials"*

No — Go to Map 9.1.2 *"Post-Trial Motions in Bench Trials"*

No — If the opponent objects to timeliness, the party's right of **post-trial review** will be severely narrowed or lost altogether. The right of **appeal** is likely compromised or lost.

No

Is the post-trial motion being **filed beyond the ordinary post-trial review period** (more than 28 days after the trial ended)?

Federal procedure permits **two** levels of post-trial review -- first, before the trial judge and, second, before a panel of the U.S. Court of Appeal.

But once those periods expire, the judgment is considered **final**, and only exceptional reasons justify re-visiting the result.

Do **special circumstances** warrant granting a party relief from a final, settled judgment?

Go to Map 9.1.3

"Public policy dictates that there be an end to litigation; that those who have contested an issue shall be bound by the result of the contest, and that matters once tried shall be considered forever settled as between the parties."
Baldwin v. Iowa State Traveling Men's Ass'n

Notes

Post-Trial Motions in Jury Trials

Map 9.1.1: *Fed. R. Civ. P. 50 & 59*

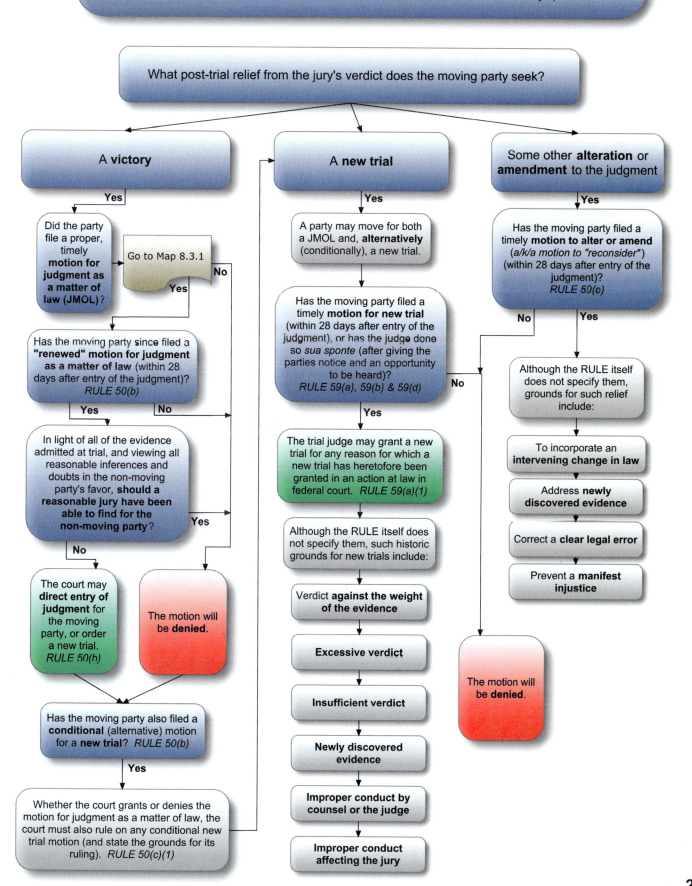

Premise
This Map explains the available post-trial motions that may be filed at the conclusion of jury trials.

What post-trial relief from the jury's verdict does the moving party seek?

A **victory**

Yes

Did the party file a proper, timely **motion for judgment as a matter of law (JMOL)**?

Go to Map 8.3.1

Yes → No

Has the moving party since filed a **"renewed" motion for judgment as a matter of law** (within 28 days after entry of the judgment)? *RULE 50(b)*

Yes — No

In light of all of the evidence admitted at trial, and viewing all reasonable inferences and doubts in the non-moving party's favor, **should a reasonable jury have been able to find for the non-moving party?**

Yes →

No

The court may **direct entry of judgment** for the moving party, or order a new trial. *RULE 50(h)*

The motion will be **denied**.

Has the moving party also filed a **conditional** (alternative) motion for a **new trial**? *RULE 50(b)*

Yes

Whether the court grants or denies the motion for judgment as a matter of law, the court must also rule on any conditional new trial motion (and state the grounds for its ruling). *RULE 50(c)(1)*

A **new trial**

Yes

A party may move for both a JMOL and, **alternatively** (conditionally), a new trial.

Has the moving party filed a timely **motion for new trial** (within 28 days after entry of the judgment), or has the judge done so *sua sponte* (after giving the parties notice and an opportunity to be heard)? *RULE 59(a), 59(b) & 59(d)*

No

Yes

The trial judge may grant a new trial for any reason for which a new trial has heretofore been granted in an action at law in federal court. *RULE 59(a)(1)*

Although the RULE itself does not specify them, such historic grounds for new trials include:

Verdict **against the weight of the evidence**

Excessive verdict

Insufficient verdict

Newly discovered evidence

Improper conduct by counsel or the judge

Improper conduct affecting the jury

Some other **alteration** or **amendment** to the judgment

Yes

Has the moving party filed a timely **motion to alter or amend** (*a/k/a* motion to "reconsider") (within 28 days after entry of the judgment)? *RULE 59(e)*

No — Yes

Although the RULE itself does not specify them, grounds for such relief include:

To incorporate an **intervening change in law**

Address **newly discovered evidence**

Correct a **clear legal error**

Prevent a **manifest injustice**

The motion will be **denied**.

Notes

Post-Trial Motions in Bench Trials
Map 9.1.2: *Fed. R. Civ. P. 52 & 59*

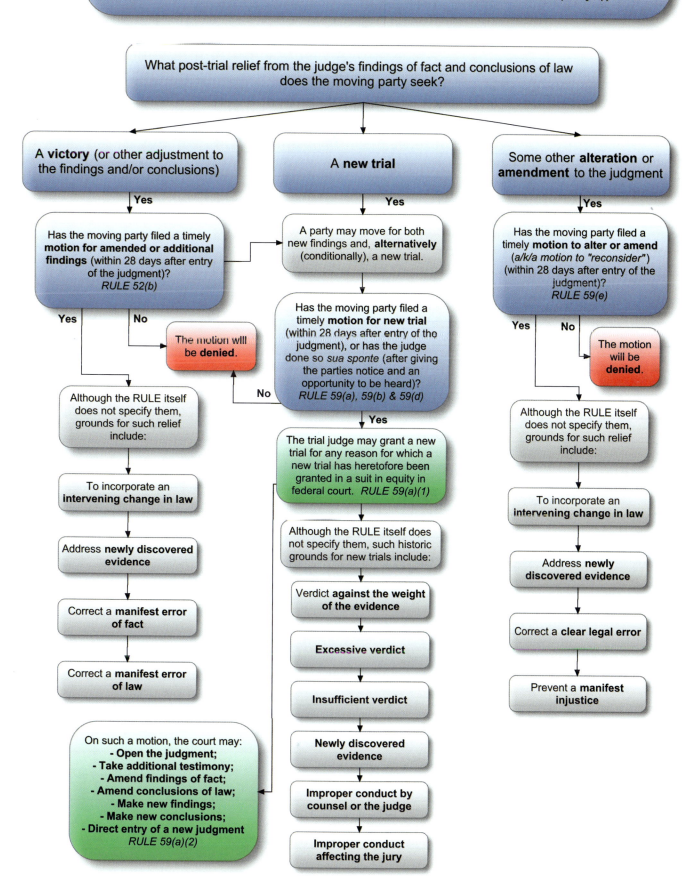

Premise

This Map explains the available post-trial motions that may be filed at the conclusion of bench (non-jury) trials.

What post-trial relief from the judge's findings of fact and conclusions of law does the moving party seek?

A **victory** (or other adjustment to the findings and/or conclusions)

Yes

Has the moving party filed a timely **motion for amended or additional findings** (within 28 days after entry of the judgment)? *RULE 52(b)*

Yes / **No**

The motion will be **denied**.

Although the RULE itself does not specify them, grounds for such relief include:

To incorporate an **intervening change in law**

Address **newly discovered evidence**

Correct a **manifest error of fact**

Correct a **manifest error of law**

On such a motion, the court may:
- Open the judgment;
- Take additional testimony;
- Amend findings of fact;
- Amend conclusions of law;
- Make new findings;
- Make new conclusions;
- Direct entry of a new judgment
RULE 59(a)(2)

A **new trial**

Yes

A party may move for both new findings and, **alternatively** (conditionally), a new trial.

Has the moving party filed a timely **motion for new trial** (within 28 days after entry of the judgment), or has the judge done so *sua sponte* (after giving the parties notice and an opportunity to be heard)? *RULE 59(a), 59(b) & 59(d)*

No / **Yes**

The trial judge may grant a new trial for any reason for which a new trial has heretofore been granted in a suit in equity in federal court. *RULE 59(a)(1)*

Although the RULE itself does not specify them, such historic grounds for new trials include:

Verdict **against the weight of the evidence**

Excessive verdict

Insufficient verdict

Newly discovered evidence

Improper conduct by counsel or the judge

Improper conduct affecting the jury

Some other **alteration** or **amendment** to the judgment

Yes

Has the moving party filed a timely **motion to alter or amend** (a/k/a motion to "reconsider") (within 28 days after entry of the judgment)? *RULE 59(e)*

Yes / **No**

The motion will be **denied**.

Although the RULE itself does not specify them, grounds for such relief include:

To incorporate an **intervening change in law**

Address **newly discovered evidence**

Correct a **clear legal error**

Prevent a **manifest injustice**

Notes

Relief from Settled Judgments

Map 9.1.3: *Fed. R. Civ. P. 60*

Premise

This Map explains the circumstances under which a party may be relieved of a final, settled judgment.

Like all courts, the federal judiciary is mindful of the strong public policy favoring a final end to every civil lawsuit. Once the ordinary avenues for post-trial review by the trial judge and, later, by an appeals court are completed, most cases become permanently final. However, there are rare occasions where special circumstances warrant re-opening a settled judgment to overturn or otherwise adjust it.

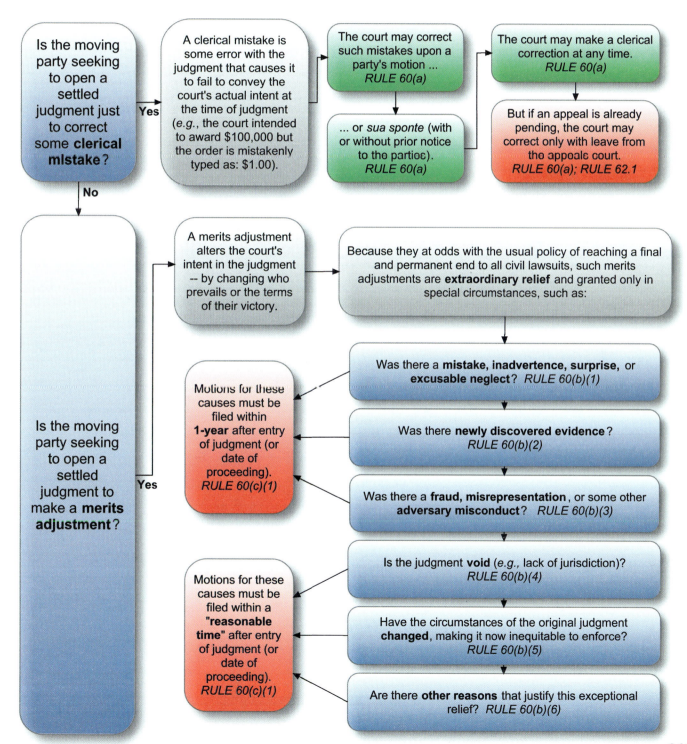

Is the moving party seeking to open a settled judgment just to correct some **clerical mistake**?

Yes → A clerical mistake is some error with the judgment that causes it to fail to convey the court's actual intent at the time of judgment (*e.g.*, the court intended to award $100,000 but the order is mistakenly typed as: $1.00).

The court may correct such mistakes upon a party's motion ... *RULE 60(a)*

... or *sua sponte* (with or without prior notice to the parties). *RULE 60(a)*

The court may make a clerical correction at any time. *RULE 60(a)*

But if an appeal is already pending, the court may correct only with leave from the appeals court. *RULE 60(a); RULE 62.1*

No

Is the moving party seeking to open a settled judgment to make a **merits adjustment**?

Yes → A merits adjustment alters the court's intent in the judgment -- by changing who prevails or the terms of their victory.

Because they at odds with the usual policy of reaching a final and permanent end to all civil lawsuits, such merits adjustments are **extraordinary relief** and granted only in special circumstances, such as:

Was there a **mistake, inadvertence, surprise,** or **excusable neglect**? *RULE 60(b)(1)*

Was there **newly discovered evidence**? *RULE 60(b)(2)*

Was there a **fraud, misrepresentation**, or some other **adversary misconduct**? *RULE 60(b)(3)*

Motions for these causes must be filed within **1-year** after entry of judgment (or date of proceeding). *RULE 60(c)(1)*

Is the judgment **void** (*e.g.*, lack of jurisdiction)? *RULE 60(b)(4)*

Have the circumstances of the original judgment **changed**, making it now inequitable to enforce? *RULE 60(b)(5)*

Are there **other reasons** that justify this exceptional relief? *RULE 60(b)(6)*

Motions for these causes must be filed within a **"reasonable time"** after entry of judgment (or date of proceeding). *RULE 60(c)(1)*

Notes

Enforcement of Judgments
Map 9.2: *Fed. R. Civ. P. 69 & 70*

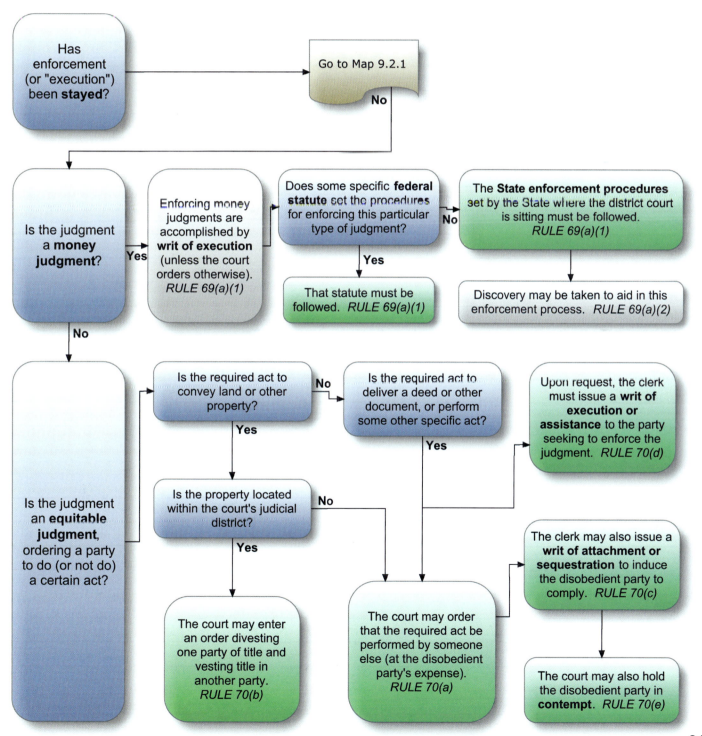

Premise
This Map answers the question from Map 9.0: *Is the Judgment Being Enforced or Stayed?*

Enforcement (or "execution") of a judgment is the process by which a defeated party is compelled to honor a court's judgment, either by paying a monetary judgment or by performing (or refraining to perform) a certain act in an equitable decree.

Has enforcement (or "execution") been **stayed**?

Go to Map 9.2.1

No

Is the judgment a **money judgment**?

Yes

Enforcing money judgments are accomplished by **writ of execution** (unless the court orders otherwise). *RULE 69(a)(1)*

Does some specific **federal statute** set the procedures for enforcing this particular type of judgment?

No

The **State enforcement procedures** set by the State where the district court is sitting must be followed. *RULE 69(a)(1)*

Yes

That statute must be followed. *RULE 69(a)(1)*

Discovery may be taken to aid in this enforcement process. *RULE 69(a)(2)*

No

Is the judgment an **equitable judgment**, ordering a party to do (or not do) a certain act?

Is the required act to convey land or other property?

No

Is the required act to deliver a deed or other document, or perform some other specific act?

Yes

Upon request, the clerk must issue a **writ of execution or assistance** to the party seeking to enforce the judgment. *RULE 70(d)*

Yes

Is the property located within the court's judicial district?

No

Yes

The court may enter an order divesting one party of title and vesting title in another party. *RULE 70(b)*

The court may order that the required act be performed by someone else (at the disobedient party's expense). *RULE 70(a)*

The clerk may also issue a **writ of attachment or sequestration** to induce the disobedient party to comply. *RULE 70(c)*

The court may also hold the disobedient party in **contempt**. *RULE 70(e)*

215

Notes

Staying Enforcement of Judgments
Map 9.2.1: *Fed. R. Civ. P. 62*

Premise

This Map answers the question from Map 9.2: *Has Enforcement Been Stayed?*

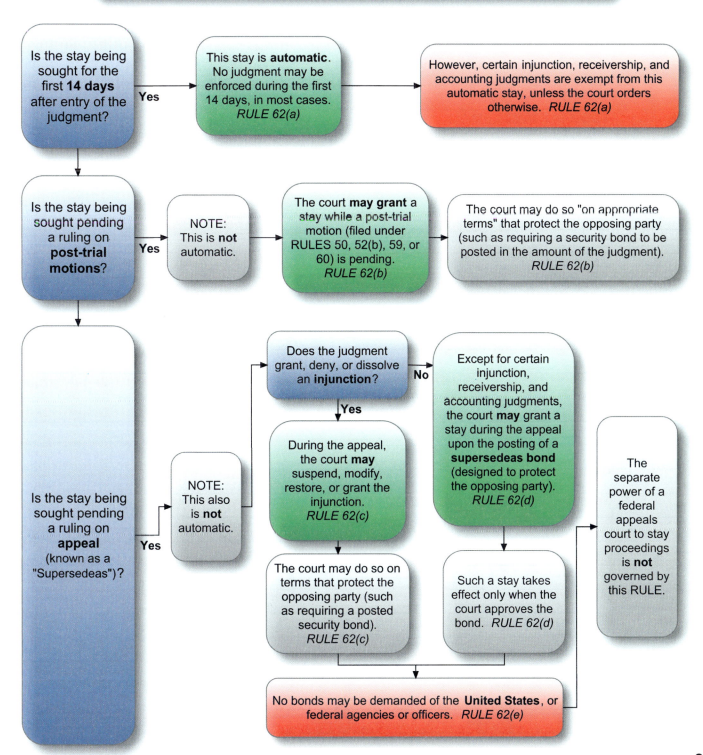

Staying (or "suspending") enforcement procedures postpones the time at which a judgment may be enforced against a defeated party. Stays are usually sought while post-trial motions or appeals are pending, in the hope that the judgment could be reversed or otherwise altered.

Is the stay being sought for the first **14 days** after entry of the judgment?

Yes → This stay is **automatic**. No judgment may be enforced during the first 14 days, in most cases. *RULE 62(a)*

→ However, certain injunction, receivership, and accounting judgments are exempt from this automatic stay, unless the court orders otherwise. *RULE 62(a)*

Is the stay being sought pending a ruling on **post-trial motions**?

Yes → NOTE: This is **not** automatic.

→ The court **may grant** a stay while a post-trial motion (filed under RULES 50, 52(b), 59, or 60) is pending. *RULE 62(b)*

→ The court may do so "on appropriate terms" that protect the opposing party (such as requiring a security bond to be posted in the amount of the judgment). *RULE 62(b)*

Is the stay being sought pending a ruling on **appeal** (known as a "Supersedeas")?

Yes → NOTE: This also is **not** automatic.

Does the judgment grant, deny, or dissolve an **injunction**?

Yes ↓ During the appeal, the court **may** suspend, modify, restore, or grant the injunction. *RULE 62(c)*

→ The court may do so on terms that protect the opposing party (such as requiring a posted security bond). *RULE 62(c)*

No → Except for certain injunction, receivership, and accounting judgments, the court **may** grant a stay during the appeal upon the posting of a **supersedeas bond** (designed to protect the opposing party). *RULE 62(d)*

→ Such a stay takes effect only when the court approves the bond. *RULE 62(d)*

→ The separate power of a federal appeals court to stay proceedings is **not** governed by this RULE.

No bonds may be demanded of the **United States**, or federal agencies or officers. *RULE 62(e)*

Notes

Federal Appeals

Map 9.3: *28 U.S.C. §§ 1291-92; Fed. R. Civ. P. 54 & 62.1; Fed. R. App. P. ("FRAP")*

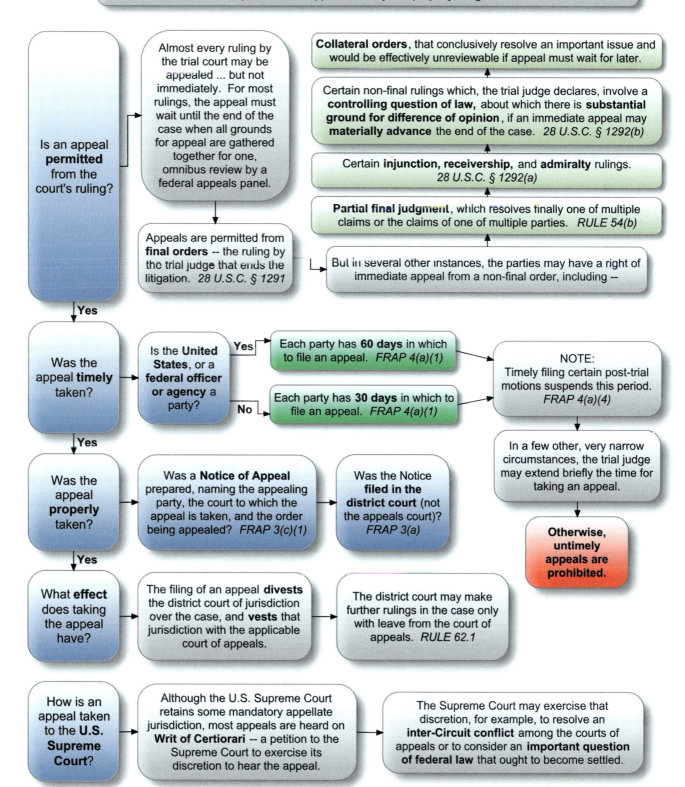

Premise

This Map answers the question from Map 9.0: *Is an Appeal Being Taken?*

The federal courts permit a second-level of post-trial review in civil cases -- by **appeal** to a panel of the local U.S. Court of Appeals. Litigants have a statutory (but not constitutional) right to such an appeal, provided the appeal is timely and properly sought.

Is an appeal permitted from the court's ruling?

Almost every ruling by the trial court may be appealed ... but not immediately. For most rulings, the appeal must wait until the end of the case when all grounds for appeal are gathered together for one, omnibus review by a federal appeals panel.

Appeals are permitted from **final orders** -- the ruling by the trial judge that ends the litigation. *28 U.S.C. § 1291*

But in several other instances, the parties may have a right of immediate appeal from a non-final order, including --

Collateral orders, that conclusively resolve an important issue and would be effectively unreviewable if appeal must wait for later.

Certain non-final rulings which, the trial judge declares, involve a **controlling question of law**, about which there is **substantial ground for difference of opinion**, if an immediate appeal may **materially advance** the end of the case. *28 U.S.C. § 1292(b)*

Certain **injunction, receivership,** and **admiralty** rulings. *28 U.S.C. § 1292(a)*

Partial final judgment, which resolves finally one of multiple claims or the claims of one of multiple parties. *RULE 54(b)*

Yes

Was the appeal timely taken?

Is the **United States**, or a **federal officer or agency** a party?

Yes → Each party has **60 days** in which to file an appeal. *FRAP 4(a)(1)*

No → Each party has **30 days** in which to file an appeal. *FRAP 4(a)(1)*

NOTE: Timely filing certain post-trial motions suspends this period. *FRAP 4(a)(4)*

In a few other, very narrow circumstances, the trial judge may extend briefly the time for taking an appeal.

Yes

Was the appeal properly taken?

Was a **Notice of Appeal** prepared, naming the appealing party, the court to which the appeal is taken, and the order being appealed? *FRAP 3(c)(1)*

Was the Notice **filed in the district court** (not the appeals court)? *FRAP 3(a)*

Otherwise, untimely appeals are prohibited.

Yes

What effect does taking the appeal have?

The filing of an appeal **divests** the district court of jurisdiction over the case, and **vests** that jurisdiction with the applicable court of appeals.

The district court may make further rulings in the case only with leave from the court of appeals. *RULE 62.1*

How is an appeal taken to the U.S. Supreme Court?

Although the U.S. Supreme Court retains some mandatory appellate jurisdiction, most appeals are heard on **Writ of Certiorari** -- a petition to the Supreme Court to exercise its discretion to hear the appeal.

The Supreme Court may exercise that discretion, for example, to resolve an **inter-Circuit conflict** among the courts of appeals or to consider an **important question of federal law** that ought to become settled.

Notes

Claim and Issue Preclusion, Generally
Map 9.4

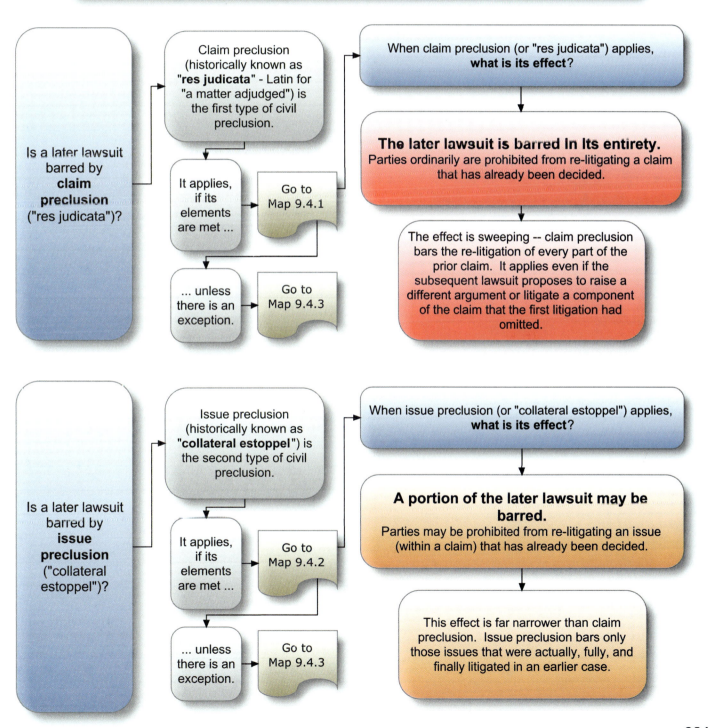

Premise

This Map answers the question from Map 9.0:   *What Is The Preclusive Effect of the Judgment?*

Distilled to its core essence, **preclusion theory** bars a party from re-litigating a matter that it has already litigated earlier to conclusion. It is premised on several policies, including the need to efficiently use judicial resources and the goal that all litigation must come to a final close. Preclusion theory is not grounded in the RULES, but rather has emerged almost entirely through case law.

Is a later lawsuit barred by **claim preclusion** ("res judicata")?

Claim preclusion (historically known as **"res judicata"** - Latin for "a matter adjudged") is the first type of civil preclusion.

It applies, if its elements are met ... → Go to Map 9.4.1

... unless there is an exception. → Go to Map 9.4.3

When claim preclusion (or "res judicata") applies, **what is its effect**?

The later lawsuit is barred in its entirety.
Parties ordinarily are prohibited from re-litigating a claim that has already been decided.

The effect is sweeping -- claim preclusion bars the re-litigation of every part of the prior claim. It applies even if the subsequent lawsuit proposes to raise a different argument or litigate a component of the claim that the first litigation had omitted.

Is a later lawsuit barred by **issue preclusion** ("collateral estoppel")?

Issue preclusion (historically known as **"collateral estoppel"**) is the second type of civil preclusion.

It applies, if its elements are met ... → Go to Map 9.4.2

... unless there is an exception. → Go to Map 9.4.3

When issue preclusion (or "collateral estoppel") applies, **what is its effect**?

A portion of the later lawsuit may be barred.
Parties may be prohibited from re-litigating an issue (within a claim) that has already been decided.

This effect is far narrower than claim preclusion. Issue preclusion bars only those issues that were actually, fully, and finally litigated in an earlier case.

Notes

Claim Preclusion
Map 9.4.1

Premise

This Map answers the question from Map 9.4: *Is The Later Lawsuit Barred By Claim Preclusion?*

Claim preclusion bars the re-litigation of a claim that, earlier, had been litigated to conclusion. Parties get one "bite" from the proverbial litigation "apple", and thereafter are usually foreclosed from trying again. Historically, claim preclusion was known as "res judicata" (Latin for "a matter adjudged"), but that terminology became confusing. Courts and commentators often used "res judicata" to refer to all preclusion concepts collectively. Now, "claim preclusion" is a more precise and descriptive term.

Is the claim in the new lawsuit the **same claim** as one litigated earlier?

Courts have used various different tests to determine whether two claims are the same (consult your local law).

Is it a **torts** claim?

Is it a **contracts** claim?

Do both claims rely on the **same legal theory** (*e.g.,* the negligence of a car driver)?

Do both claims arise from a **single wrongful act**?

Do both claims arise from the **same (or different) primary right invasion** (*e.g.,* right to be free of bodily injury, or right to be free of property loss)?

Will litigating both claims involve largely the **same trial evidence**?

Do both claims arise from the **same transactional package** - arising from the same transaction(s); linked in time, space, origin, or motivation; forming a convenient trial unit; grouped in an expected way?

Do both claims arise from the **same contractual instrument**? (If multiple events of claimed loss occur under the same instrument, only those losses accruing as of the time the lawsuit is filed need be included).

Yes

Yes

Is the claim in the new lawsuit being brought by the **same party** who litigated earlier?

Are the parties the **identically same** ones as earlier?

Or

Are the parties in **privity** with the **identically same** ones as earlier (*e.g.,* the earlier litigant was a predecessor to the same property interest, was litigating on behalf of a current party, was controlled by a current party, etc.)?

Yes

Yes

Are the parties **identically configured** as they were earlier (*i.e.,* the same party is plaintiff again, same party is defendant again)?

Yes

Did the first claim end in a **valid, final** judgment **on the merits**?

VALID: Did the deciding court in the first lawsuit have the legal authority to enter judgment (*e.g.,* jurisdiction)?

FINAL: Was the first ruling a final one (*i.e.,* the trial judge considers the case closed and resolved)?

ON THE MERITS: Was the first ruling a decision on the merits (*e.g.,* not a dismissal for lack of jurisdiction or improper service)?

Yes

The second claim is precluded.

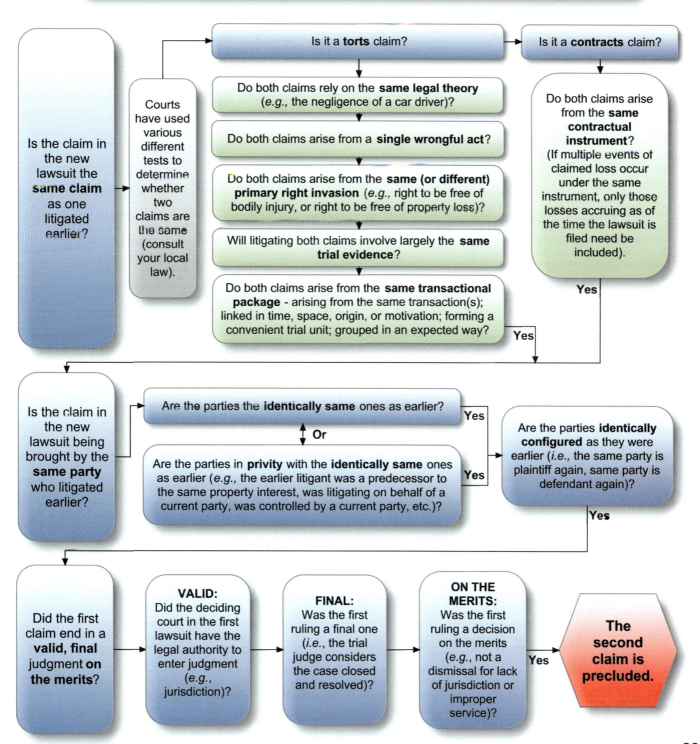

Notes

Issue Preclusion
Map 9.4.2

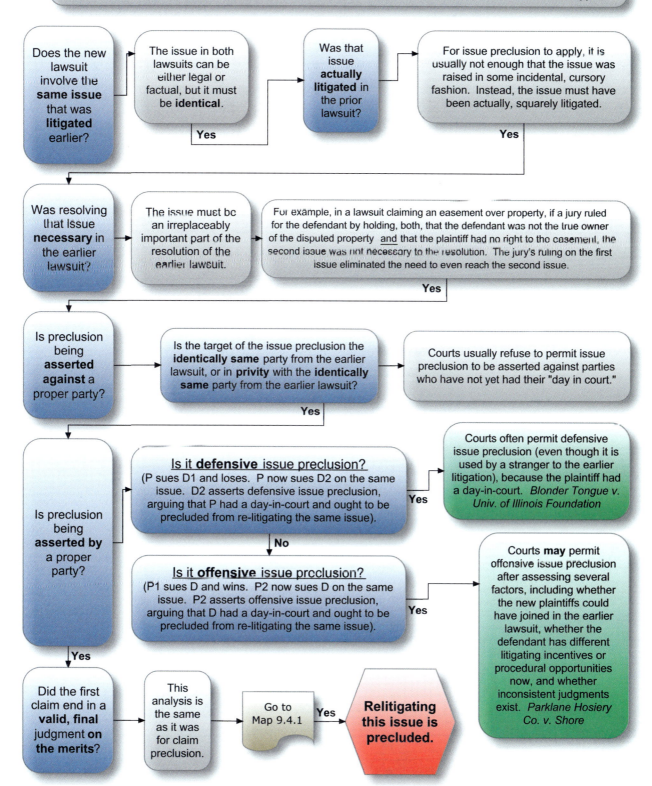

Premise

This Map continues to answer the question from Map 9.4: *Is The Later Lawsuit Barred By Issue Preclusion?*

Issue preclusion bars the re-litigation of an issue that, earlier, had been litigated to conclusion. It differs from claim preclusion because it bars only a portion of a later claim, not the entire claim. Issue preclusion pursues the same broad policy goal as claim preclusion -- to give parties only one bite from the proverbial litigation apple, and thereafter to foreclose them from trying again. Historically, issue preclusion was known as "collateral estoppel".

Does the new lawsuit involve the **same issue** that was **litigated** earlier?

The issue in both lawsuits can be either legal or factual, but it must be **identical**.

Yes

Was that issue **actually litigated** in the prior lawsuit?

For issue preclusion to apply, it is usually not enough that the issue was raised in some incidental, cursory fashion. Instead, the issue must have been actually, squarely litigated.

Yes

Was resolving that issue **necessary** in the earlier lawsuit?

The issue must be an irreplaceably important part of the resolution of the earlier lawsuit.

For example, in a lawsuit claiming an easement over property, if a jury ruled for the defendant by holding, both, that the defendant was not the true owner of the disputed property <u>and</u> that the plaintiff had no right to the easement, the second issue was not necessary to the resolution. The jury's ruling on the first issue eliminated the need to even reach the second issue.

Yes

Is preclusion being **asserted against** a proper party?

Is the target of the issue preclusion the **identically same** party from the earlier lawsuit, or in **privity** with the **identically same** party from the earlier lawsuit?

Courts usually refuse to permit issue preclusion to be asserted against parties who have not yet had their "day in court."

Yes

Is preclusion being **asserted by** a proper party?

Is it **defensive** issue preclusion?
(P sues D1 and loses. P now sues D2 on the same issue. D2 asserts defensive issue preclusion, arguing that P had a day-in-court and ought to be precluded from re-litigating the same issue).

Yes → Courts often permit defensive issue preclusion (even though it is used by a stranger to the earlier litigation), because the plaintiff had a day-in-court. *Blonder Tongue v. Univ. of Illinois Foundation*

No

Is it **offensive** issue preclusion?
(P1 sues D and wins. P2 now sues D on the same issue. P2 asserts offensive issue preclusion, arguing that D had a day-in-court and ought to be precluded from re-litigating the same issue).

Yes → Courts **may** permit offensive issue preclusion after assessing several factors, including whether the new plaintiffs could have joined in the earlier lawsuit, whether the defendant has different litigating incentives or procedural opportunities now, and whether inconsistent judgments exist. *Parklane Hosiery Co. v. Shore*

Yes

Did the first claim end in a **valid, final** judgment **on the merits**?

This analysis is the same as it was for claim preclusion.

Go to Map 9.4.1 **Yes** → **Relitigating this issue is precluded.**

Notes

Exceptions to Claim and Issue Preclusion
Map 9.4.3

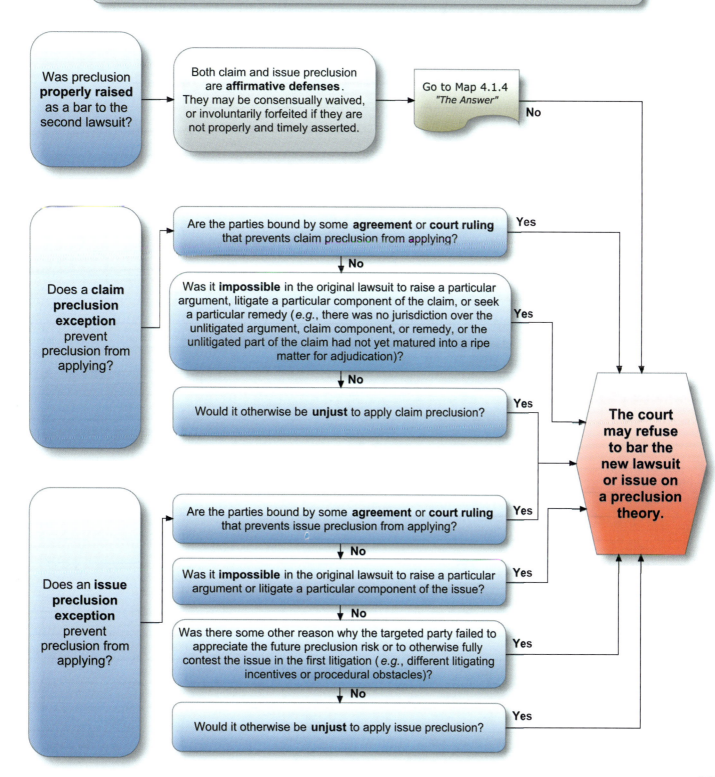

Premise

This Map concludes the answer to the question from Map 9.0: *What Is The Preclusive Effect of the Judgment?*

The bar of preclusion does not always apply, even if its elements are satisfied. It is a waivable defense that may be lost if not asserted, or the court may conclude that applying it would be unjust.

Was preclusion **properly raised** as a bar to the second lawsuit?

Both claim and issue preclusion are **affirmative defenses**. They may be consensually waived, or involuntarily forfeited if they are not properly and timely asserted.

Go to Map 4.1.4 *"The Answer"* — **No**

Does a **claim preclusion exception** prevent preclusion from applying?

Are the parties bound by some **agreement** or **court ruling** that prevents claim preclusion from applying? — **Yes**

No

Was it **impossible** in the original lawsuit to raise a particular argument, litigate a particular component of the claim, or seek a particular remedy (*e.g.*, there was no jurisdiction over the unlitigated argument, claim component, or remedy, or the unlitigated part of the claim had not yet matured into a ripe matter for adjudication)? — **Yes**

No

Would it otherwise be **unjust** to apply claim preclusion? — **Yes**

Does an **issue preclusion exception** prevent preclusion from applying?

Are the parties bound by some **agreement** or **court ruling** that prevents issue preclusion from applying? — **Yes**

No

Was it **impossible** in the original lawsuit to raise a particular argument or litigate a particular component of the issue? — **Yes**

No

Was there some other reason why the targeted party failed to appreciate the future preclusion risk or to otherwise fully contest the issue in the first litigation (*e.g.*, different litigating incentives or procedural obstacles)? — **Yes**

No

Would it otherwise be **unjust** to apply issue preclusion? — **Yes**

The court may refuse to bar the new lawsuit or issue on a preclusion theory.

Notes

X. United States Code
[Selected Sections]
Current with amendments through May 2012

§ 1291. Final decisions of district courts

The courts of appeals (other than the United States Court of Appeals for the Federal Circuit) shall have jurisdiction of appeals from all final decisions of the district courts of the United States, the United States District Court for the District of the Canal Zone, the District Court of Guam, and the District Court of the Virgin Islands, except where a direct review may be had in the Supreme Court. The jurisdiction of the United States Court of Appeals for the Federal Circuit shall be limited to the jurisdiction described in sections 1292 (c) and (d) and 1295 of this title.

§ 1292. Interlocutory decisions

(a) Except as provided in subsections (c) and (d) of this section, the courts of appeals shall have jurisdiction of appeals from:

(1) Interlocutory orders of the district courts of the United States, the United States District Court for the District of the Canal Zone, the District Court of Guam, and the District Court of the Virgin Islands, or of the judges thereof, granting, continuing, modifying, refusing or dissolving injunctions, or refusing to dissolve or modify injunctions, except where a direct review may be had in the Supreme Court;

(2) Interlocutory orders appointing receivers, or refusing orders to wind up receiverships or to take steps to accomplish the purposes thereof, such as directing sales or other disposals of property;

(3) Interlocutory decrees of such district courts or the judges thereof determining the rights and liabilities of the parties to admiralty cases in which appeals from final decrees are allowed.

(b) When a district judge, in making in a civil action an order not otherwise appealable under this section, shall be of the opinion that such order involves a controlling question of law as to which there is substantial ground for difference of opinion and that an immediate appeal from the order may materially advance the ultimate termination of the litigation, he shall so state in writing in such order. The Court of Appeals which would have jurisdiction of an appeal of such action may thereupon, in its discretion, permit an appeal to be taken from such order, if application is made to it within ten days after the entry of the order: Provided, however, That application for an appeal hereunder shall not stay proceedings in the district court unless the district judge or the Court of Appeals or a judge thereof shall so order.

(c) The United States Court of Appeals for the Federal Circuit shall have exclusive jurisdiction—

(1) of an appeal from an interlocutory order or decree described in subsection (a) or (b) of this section in any case over which the court would have jurisdiction of an appeal under section 1295 of this title; and

(2) of an appeal from a judgment in a civil action for patent infringement which would otherwise be appealable to the United States Court of Appeals for the Federal Circuit and is final except for an accounting.

(d)

(1) When the chief judge of the Court of International Trade issues an order under the provisions of section 256 (b) of this title, or when any judge of the Court of International Trade, in issuing any other interlocutory order, includes in the order a statement that a controlling question of law is involved with respect to which there is a substantial ground for difference of opinion and that an immediate appeal from that order may materially advance the ultimate termination of the litigation, the United States Court of Appeals for the Federal Circuit may, in its discretion, permit an appeal to be taken from such order, if application is made to that Court within ten days after the entry of such order.

(2) When the chief judge of the United States Court of Federal Claims issues an order under section 798 (b) of this title, or when any judge of the United States Court of Federal Claims, in issuing an interlocutory order, includes in the order a statement that a controlling question of law is involved with respect to which there is a substantial ground for difference of opinion and that an immediate appeal from that order may materially advance the ultimate termination of the litigation, the United States Court of Appeals for the Federal Circuit may, in its discretion, permit an appeal to be taken from such order, if application is made to that Court within ten days after the entry of such order.

(3) Neither the application for nor the granting of an appeal under this subsection shall stay proceedings in the Court of International Trade or in the Court of Federal Claims, as the case may be, unless a stay is ordered by a judge of the Court of International Trade or of the Court of Federal Claims or by the United States Court of Appeals for the Federal Circuit or a judge of that court.

(4) (A) The United States Court of Appeals for the Federal Circuit shall have exclusive jurisdiction of an appeal from an interlocutory order of a district court of the United States, the District Court of Guam, the District Court of the Virgin Islands, or the District Court for the Northern Mariana Islands, granting or denying, in whole or in part, a motion to transfer an action to the United States Court of Federal Claims under section 1631 of this title. **(B)** When a motion to transfer an action to the Court of Federal Claims is filed in a district court, no further proceedings shall be taken in the district court until 60 days after the court has ruled upon the motion. If an appeal is taken from the district court's grant or denial of the motion, proceedings shall be further stayed until the appeal has been decided by the Court of Appeals for the Federal Circuit. The stay of proceedings in the district court shall not bar the granting of preliminary or injunctive relief, where appropriate and where expedition is reasonably necessary. However, during the period in which proceedings are stayed as provided in this subparagraph, no transfer to the Court of Federal Claims pursuant to the motion shall be carried out.

(e) The Supreme Court may prescribe rules, in accordance with section 2072 of this title, to provide for an appeal of an interlocutory decision to the courts of appeals that is not otherwise provided for under subsection (a), (b), (c), or (d).

§ 1331. Federal question

The district courts shall have original jurisdiction of all civil actions arising under the Constitution, laws, or treaties of the United States.

§ 1332. Diversity of citizenship; amount in controversy; costs

(a) The district courts shall have original jurisdiction of all civil actions where the matter in controversy exceeds the sum or value of $75,000, exclusive of interest and costs, and is between—

(1) citizens of different States;

(2) citizens of a State and citizens or subjects of a foreign state, except that the district courts shall not have original jurisdiction under this subsection of an action between citizens of a State and citizens or subjects of a foreign state who are lawfully admitted for permanent residence in the United States and are domiciled in the same State;

(3) citizens of different States and in which citizens or subjects of a foreign state are additional parties; and

(4) a foreign state, defined in section 1603(a) of this title, as plaintiff and citizens of a State or of different States.

(b) Except when express provision therefor is otherwise made in a statute of the United States, where the plaintiff who files the case originally in the Federal courts is finally adjudged to be entitled to recover less than the sum or value of $75,000, computed without regard to any setoff or counterclaim to which the defendant may be adjudged to be entitled, and exclusive of interest and costs, the district court may deny costs to the plaintiff and, in addition, may impose costs on the plaintiff.

(c) For the purposes of this section and section 1441 of this title—

(1) a corporation shall be deemed to be a citizen of every State and foreign state by which it has been incorporated and of the State or foreign state where it has its principal place of business, except that in any direct action against the insurer of a policy or contract of liability insurance, whether incorporated or unincorporated, to which action the insured is not joined as a party-defendant, such insurer shall be deemed a citizen of—

    (A) every State and foreign state of which the insured is a citizen;

    (B) every State and foreign state by which the insurer has been incorporated; and

    (C) the State or foreign state where the insurer has its principal place of business; and

(2) the legal representative of the estate of a decedent shall be deemed to be a citizen only of the same State as the decedent, and the legal representative of an infant or incompetent shall be deemed to be a citizen only of the same State as the infant or incompetent.

(d)

(1) In this subsection—

    (A) the term "class" means all of the class members in a class action;

    (B) the term "class action" means any civil action filed under rule 23 of the Federal Rules of Civil Procedure or similar State statute or rule of judicial procedure authorizing an action to be brought by 1 or more representative persons as a class action;

    (C) the term "class certification order" means an order issued by a court approving the treatment of some or all aspects of a civil action as a class action; and

    (D) the term "class members" means the persons (named or unnamed) who fall within the definition of the proposed or certified class in a class action

(2) The district courts shall have original jurisdiction of any civil action in which the matter in controversy exceeds the sum or value of $5,000,000, exclusive of interest and costs, and is a class action in which—

    (A) any member of a class of plaintiffs is a citizen of a State different from any defendant;

    (B) any member of a class of plaintiffs is a foreign state or a citizen or subject of a foreign state and any defendant is a citizen of a State; or

    (C) any member of a class of plaintiffs is a citizen of a State and any defendant is a foreign state or a citizen or subject of a foreign state.

(3) A district court may, in the interests of justice and looking at the totality of the circumstances, decline to exercise jurisdiction under paragraph (2) over a class action in which greater than one-third but less than two-thirds of the members of all proposed plaintiff classes in the aggregate and the primary defendants are citizens of the State in which the action was originally filed based on consideration of—

> **(A)** whether the claims asserted involve matters of national or interstate interest;
>
> **(B)** whether the claims asserted will be governed by laws of the State in which the action was originally filed or by the laws of other States;
>
> **(C)** whether the class action has been pleaded in a manner that seeks to avoid Federal jurisdiction;
>
> **(D)** whether the action was brought in a forum with a distinct nexus with the class members, the alleged harm, or the defendants;
>
> **(E)** whether the number of citizens of the State in which the action was originally filed in all proposed plaintiff classes in the aggregate is substantially larger than the number of citizens from any other State, and the citizenship of the other members of the proposed class is dispersed among a substantial number of States; and
>
> **(F)** whether, during the 3-year period preceding the filing of that class action, 1 or more other class actions asserting the same or similar claims on behalf of the same or other persons have been filed.

(4) A district court shall decline to exercise jurisdiction under paragraph (2)—

> **(A)**
>
> > **(i)** over a class action in which—
> >
> > > **(I)** greater than two-thirds of the members of all proposed plaintiff classes in the aggregate are citizens of the State in which the action was originally filed;
> > >
> > > **(II)** at least 1 defendant is a defendant—**(aa)** from whom significant relief is sought by members of the plaintiff class; **(bb)** whose alleged conduct forms a significant basis for the claims asserted by the proposed plaintiff class; and **(cc)** who is a citizen of the State in which the action was originally filed; and
> > >
> > > **(III)** principal injuries resulting from the alleged conduct or any related conduct of each defendant were incurred in the State in which the action was originally filed; and
> >
> > **(ii)** during the 3-year period preceding the filing of that class action, no other class action has been filed asserting the same or similar factual allegations against any of the defendants on behalf of the same or other persons; or
>
> **(B)** two-thirds or more of the members of all proposed plaintiff classes in the aggregate, and the primary defendants, are citizens of the State in which the action was originally filed.

(5) Paragraphs (2) through (4) shall not apply to any class action in which—

> **(A)** the primary defendants are States, State officials, or other governmental entities against whom the district court may be foreclosed from ordering relief; or
>
> **(B)** the number of members of all proposed plaintiff classes in the aggregate is less than 100.

(6) In any class action, the claims of the individual class members shall be aggregated to determine whether the matter in controversy exceeds the sum or value of $5,000,000, exclusive of interest and costs.

(7) Citizenship of the members of the proposed plaintiff classes shall be determined for purposes of paragraphs (2) through (6) as of the date of filing of the complaint or amended complaint, or, if the case stated by the initial pleading is not subject to Federal jurisdiction, as of the date of service by plaintiffs of an amended pleading, motion, or other paper, indicating the existence of Federal jurisdiction.

(8) This subsection shall apply to any class action before or after the entry of a class certification order by the court with respect to that action.

(9) Paragraph (2) shall not apply to any class action that solely involves a claim—

> **(A)** concerning a covered security as defined under 16(f)(3) [1] of the Securities Act of 1933 (15 U.S.C. 78p (f)(3) [2]) and section 28(f)(5)(E) of the Securities Exchange Act of 1934 (15 U.S.C. 78bb (f)(5)(E));
>
> **(B)** that relates to the internal affairs or governance of a corporation or other form of business enterprise and that arises under or by virtue of the laws of the State in which such corporation or business enterprise is incorporated or organized; or
>
> **(C)** that relates to the rights, duties (including fiduciary duties), and obligations relating to or created by or pursuant to any security (as defined under section 2(a)(1) of the Securities Act of 1933 (15 U.S.C. 77b (a)(1)) and the regulations issued thereunder).

(10) For purposes of this subsection and section 1453, an unincorporated association shall be deemed to be a citizen of the State where it has its principal place of business and the State under whose laws it is organized.

(11)

> **(A)** For purposes of this subsection and section 1453, a mass action shall be deemed to be a class action removable under paragraphs (2) through (10) if it otherwise meets the provisions of those paragraphs.
>
> **(B)**
>
> > **(i)** As used in subparagraph (A), the term "mass action" means any civil action (except a civil action within the scope of section 1711 (2)) in which monetary relief claims of 100 or more persons are proposed to be tried jointly on the ground that the plaintiffs' claims involve common questions of law or fact, except that jurisdiction shall exist only over those plaintiffs whose claims in a mass action satisfy the jurisdictional amount requirements under subsection (a).
> >
> > **(ii)** As used in subparagraph (A), the term "mass action" shall not include any civil action in which—
> >
> > > **(I)** all of the claims in the action arise from an event or occurrence in the State in which the action was filed, and that allegedly resulted in injuries in that State or in States contiguous to that State;
> > >
> > > **(II)** the claims are joined upon motion of a defendant;
> > >
> > > **(III)** all of the claims in the action are asserted on behalf of the general public (and not on behalf of individual claimants or members of a purported class) pursuant to a State statute specifically authorizing such action; or
> > >
> > > **(IV)** the claims have been consolidated or coordinated solely for pretrial proceedings.
>
> **(C)**
>
> > **(i)** Any action(s) removed to Federal court pursuant to this subsection shall not thereafter be transferred to any other court pursuant to section 1407, or the rules promulgated thereunder, unless a majority of the plaintiffs in the action request transfer pursuant to section 1407.
> >
> > **(ii)** This subparagraph will not apply—
> >
> > > **(I)** to cases certified pursuant to rule 23 of the Federal Rules of Civil Procedure; or
> > >
> > > **(II)** if plaintiffs propose that the action proceed as a class action pursuant to rule 23 of the Federal Rules of Civil Procedure.

(D) The limitations periods on any claims asserted in a mass action that is removed to Federal court pursuant to this subsection shall be deemed tolled during the period that the action is pending in Federal court.

(e) The word "States", as used in this section, includes the Territories, the District of Columbia, and the Commonwealth of Puerto Rico.

§ 1335. Interpleader

(a) The district courts shall have original jurisdiction of any civil action of interpleader or in the nature of interpleader filed by any person, firm, or corporation, association, or society having in his or its custody or possession money or property of the value of $500 or more, or having issued a note, bond, certificate, policy of insurance, or other instrument of value or amount of $500 or more, or providing for the delivery or payment or the loan of money or property of such amount or value, or being under any obligation written or unwritten to the amount of $500 or more, if

> **(1)** Two or more adverse claimants, of diverse citizenship as defined in subsection (a) or (d) of section 1332 of this title, are claiming or may claim to be entitled to such money or property, or to any one or more of the benefits arising by virtue of any note, bond, certificate, policy or other instrument, or arising by virtue of any such obligation; and if
>
> **(2)** the plaintiff has deposited such money or property or has paid the amount of or the loan or other value of such instrument or the amount due under such obligation into the registry of the court, there to abide the judgment of the court, or has given bond payable to the clerk of the court in such amount and with such surety as the court or judge may deem proper, conditioned upon the compliance by the plaintiff with the future order or judgment of the court with respect to the subject matter of the controversy.

(b) Such an action may be entertained although the titles or claims of the conflicting claimants do not have a common origin, or are not identical, but are adverse to and independent of one another.

§ 1367. Supplemental jurisdiction

(a) Except as provided in subsections (b) and (c) or as expressly provided otherwise by Federal statute, in any civil action of which the district courts have original jurisdiction, the district courts shall have supplemental jurisdiction over all other claims that are so related to claims in the action within such original jurisdiction that they form part of the same case or controversy under Article III of the United States Constitution. Such supplemental jurisdiction shall include claims that involve the joinder or intervention of additional parties.

(b) In any civil action of which the district courts have original jurisdiction founded solely on section 1332 of this title, the district courts shall not have supplemental jurisdiction under subsection (a) over claims by plaintiffs against persons made parties under Rule 14, 19, 20, or 24 of the Federal Rules of Civil Procedure, or over claims by persons proposed to be joined as plaintiffs under Rule 19 of such rules, or seeking to intervene as plaintiffs under Rule 24 of such rules, when exercising supplemental jurisdiction over such claims would be inconsistent with the jurisdictional requirements of section 1332.

(c) The district courts may decline to exercise supplemental jurisdiction over a claim under subsection (a) if—

> **(1)** the claim raises a novel or complex issue of State law,

(2) the claim substantially predominates over the claim or claims over which the district court has original jurisdiction,

(3) the district court has dismissed all claims over which it has original jurisdiction, or

(4) in exceptional circumstances, there are other compelling reasons for declining jurisdiction.

(d) The period of limitations for any claim asserted under subsection (a), and for any other claim in the same action that is voluntarily dismissed at the same time as or after the dismissal of the claim under subsection (a), shall be tolled while the claim is pending and for a period of 30 days after it is dismissed unless State law provides for a longer tolling period.

(e) As used in this section, the term "State" includes the District of Columbia, the Commonwealth of Puerto Rico, and any territory or possession of the United States.

§ 1390. Venue - Scope

(a) Venue Defined.— As used in this chapter, the term "venue" refers to the geographic specification of the proper court or courts for the litigation of a civil action that is within the subject-matter jurisdiction of the district courts in general, and does not refer to any grant or restriction of subject-matter jurisdiction providing for a civil action to be adjudicated only by the district court for a particular district or districts.

(b) Exclusion of Certain Cases.— Except as otherwise provided by law, this chapter shall not govern the venue of a civil action in which the district court exercises the jurisdiction conferred by section 1333, except that such civil actions may be transferred between district courts as provided in this chapter.

(c) Clarification Regarding Cases Removed From State Courts.— This chapter shall not determine the district court to which a civil action pending in a State court may be removed, but shall govern the transfer of an action so removed as between districts and divisions of the United States district courts.

§ 1391. Venue generally

(a) Applicability of Section.— Except as otherwise provided by law—

> **(1)** this section shall govern the venue of all civil actions brought in district courts of the United States; and
> **(2)** the proper venue for a civil action shall be determined without regard to whether the action is local or transitory in nature.

(b) Venue in General.— A civil action may be brought in—

> **(1)** a judicial district in which any defendant resides, if all defendants are residents of the State in which the district is located;
> **(2)** a judicial district in which a substantial part of the events or omissions giving rise to the claim occurred, or a substantial part of property that is the subject of the action is situated; or
> **(3)** if there is no district in which an action may otherwise be brought as provided in this section, any judicial district in which any defendant is subject to the court's personal jurisdiction with respect to such action.

(c) Residency.— For all venue purposes—

> **(1)** a natural person, including an alien lawfully admitted for permanent residence in the United States, shall be deemed to reside in the judicial district in which that person is domiciled;

(2) an entity with the capacity to sue and be sued in its common name under applicable law, whether or not incorporated, shall be deemed to reside, if a defendant, in any judicial district in which such defendant is subject to the court's personal jurisdiction with respect to the civil action in question and, if a plaintiff, only in the judicial district in which it maintains its principal place of business; and

(3) a defendant not resident in the United States may be sued in any judicial district, and the joinder of such a defendant shall be disregarded in determining where the action may be brought with respect to other defendants.

(d) Residency of Corporations in States With Multiple Districts.— For purposes of venue under this chapter, in a State which has more than one judicial district and in which a defendant that is a corporation is subject to personal jurisdiction at the time an action is commenced, such corporation shall be deemed to reside in any district in that State within which its contacts would be sufficient to subject it to personal jurisdiction if that district were a separate State, and, if there is no such district, the corporation shall be deemed to reside in the district within which it has the most significant contacts.

(e) Actions Where Defendant Is Officer or Employee of the United States.—

(1) In general.— A civil action in which a defendant is an officer or employee of the United States or any agency thereof acting in his official capacity or under color of legal authority, or an agency of the United States, or the United States, may, except as otherwise provided by law, be brought in any judicial district in which

(A) a defendant in the action resides,

(B) a substantial part of the events or omissions giving rise to the claim occurred, or a substantial part of property that is the subject of the action is situated, or

(C) the plaintiff resides if no real property is involved in the action. Additional persons may be joined as parties to any such action in accordance with the Federal Rules of Civil Procedure and with such other venue requirements as would be applicable if the United States or one of its officers, employees, or agencies were not a party.

(2) Service.— The summons and complaint in such an action shall be served as provided by the Federal Rules of Civil Procedure except that the delivery of the summons and complaint to the officer or agency as required by the rules may be made by certified mail beyond the territorial limits of the district in which the action is brought.

(f) Civil Actions Against a Foreign State.— A civil action against a foreign state as defined in section 1603(a) of this title may be brought—

(1) in any judicial district in which a substantial part of the events or omissions giving rise to the claim occurred, or a substantial part of property that is the subject of the action is situated;

(2) in any judicial district in which the vessel or cargo of a foreign state is situated, if the claim is asserted under section 1605(b) of this title;

(3) in any judicial district in which the agency or instrumentality is licensed to do business or is doing business, if the action is brought against an agency or instrumentality of a foreign state as defined in section 1603(b) of this title; or

(4) in the United States District Court for the District of Columbia if the action is brought against a foreign state or political subdivision thereof.

(g) Multiparty, Multiforum Litigation.— A civil action in which jurisdiction of the district court is based upon section 1369 of this title may be brought in any district in which any defendant resides or in which a substantial part of the accident giving rise to the action took place.

§ 1397. Interpleader

Any civil action of interpleader or in the nature of interpleader under section 1335 of this title may be brought in the judicial district in which one or more of the claimants reside.

§ 1404. Change of venue

(a) For the convenience of parties and witnesses, in the interest of justice, a district court may transfer any civil action to any other district or division where it might have been brought or to any district or division to which all parties have consented.

(b) Upon motion, consent or stipulation of all parties, any action, suit or proceeding of a civil nature or any motion or hearing thereof, may be transferred, in the discretion of the court, from the division in which pending to any other division in the same district. Transfer of proceedings in rem brought by or on behalf of the United States may be transferred under this section without the consent of the United States where all other parties request transfer.

(c) A district court may order any civil action to be tried at any place within the division in which it is pending.

(d) Transfers from a district court of the United States to the District Court of Guam, the District Court for the Northern Mariana Islands, or the District Court of the Virgin Islands shall not be permitted under this section. As otherwise used in this section, the term "district court" includes the District Court of Guam, the District Court for the Northern Mariana Islands, and the District Court of the Virgin Islands, and the term "district" includes the territorial jurisdiction of each such court.

§ 1406. Cure or waiver of defects

(a) The district court of a district in which is filed a case laying venue in the wrong division or district shall dismiss, or if it be in the interest of justice, transfer such case to any district or division in which it could have been brought.

(b) Nothing in this chapter shall impair the jurisdiction of a district court of any matter involving a party who does not interpose timely and sufficient objection to the venue.

(c) As used in this section, the term "district court" includes the District Court of Guam, the District Court for the Northern Mariana Islands, and the District Court of the Virgin Islands, and the term "district" includes the territorial jurisdiction of each such court.

§ 1407. Multidistrict litigation

(a) When civil actions involving one or more common questions of fact are pending in different districts, such actions may be transferred to any district for coordinated or consolidated pretrial proceedings. Such transfers shall be made by the judicial panel on multidistrict litigation authorized by this section upon its determination that transfers for such proceedings will be for the convenience of parties and witnesses and will promote the just and efficient conduct of such actions. Each action so transferred shall be remanded by the panel at or before the conclusion of such pretrial proceedings to the district from which it was transferred unless it shall have been previously terminated: Provided, however, That the panel may separate any claim, cross-claim, counter-claim, or third-party claim and remand any of such claims before the remainder of the action is remanded.

(b) Such coordinated or consolidated pretrial proceedings shall be conducted by a judge or judges to whom such actions are assigned by the judicial panel on multidistrict litigation. For this purpose, upon request of the panel, a circuit judge or a district judge may be designated and assigned temporarily for service in the transferee district by the Chief Justice of the United States or the chief judge of the circuit, as may be required, in accordance with the provisions of chapter 13 of this title. With the consent of the transferee district court, such actions may be assigned by the panel to a judge or judges of such district. The judge or judges to whom such actions are assigned, the members of the judicial panel on multidistrict litigation, and other circuit and district judges designated when needed by the panel may exercise the powers of a district judge in any district for the purpose of conducting pretrial depositions in such coordinated or consolidated pretrial proceedings.

(c) Proceedings for the transfer of an action under this section may be initiated by—
    (i) the judicial panel on multidistrict litigation upon its own initiative, or
    (ii) motion filed with the panel by a party in any action in which transfer for coordinated or consolidated pretrial proceedings under this section may be appropriate. A copy of such motion shall be filed in the district court in which the moving party's action is pending.
The panel shall give notice to the parties in all actions in which transfers for coordinated or consolidated pretrial proceedings are contemplated, and such notice shall specify the time and place of any hearing to determine whether such transfer shall be made. Orders of the panel to set a hearing and other orders of the panel issued prior to the order either directing or denying transfer shall be filed in the office of the clerk of the district court in which a transfer hearing is to be or has been held. The panel's order of transfer shall be based upon a record of such hearing at which material evidence may be offered by any party to an action pending in any district that would be affected by the proceedings under this section, and shall be supported by findings of fact and conclusions of law based upon such record. Orders of transfer and such other orders as the panel may make thereafter shall be filed in the office of the clerk of the district court of the transferee district and shall be effective when thus filed. The clerk of the transferee district court shall forthwith transmit a certified copy of the panel's order to transfer to the clerk of the district court from which the action is being transferred. An order denying transfer shall be filed in each district wherein there is a case pending in which the motion for transfer has been made.

(d) The judicial panel on multidistrict litigation shall consist of seven circuit and district judges designated from time to time by the Chief Justice of the United States, no two of whom shall be from the same circuit. The concurrence of four members shall be necessary to any action by the panel.

(e) No proceedings for review of any order of the panel may be permitted except by extraordinary writ pursuant to the provisions of title 28, section 1651, United States Code. Petitions for an extraordinary writ to review an order of the panel to set a transfer hearing and other orders of the panel issued prior to the order either directing or denying transfer shall be filed only in the court of appeals having jurisdiction over the district in which a hearing is to be or has been held. Petitions for an extraordinary writ to review an order to transfer or orders subsequent to transfer shall be filed only in the court of appeals having jurisdiction over the transferee district. There shall be no appeal or review of an order of the panel denying a motion to transfer for consolidated or coordinated proceedings.

(f) The panel may prescribe rules for the conduct of its business not inconsistent with Acts of Congress and the Federal Rules of Civil Procedure.

(g) Nothing in this section shall apply to any action in which the United States is a complainant arising under the antitrust laws. "Antitrust laws" as used herein include those acts referred to in the Act of

October 15, 1914, as amended (38 Stat. 730; 15 U.S.C. 12), and also include the Act of June 19, 1936 (49 Stat. 1526; 15 U.S.C. 13, 13a, and 13b) and the Act of September 26, 1914, as added March 21, 1938 (52 Stat. 116, 117; 15 U.S.C. 56); but shall not include section 4A of the Act of October 15, 1914, as added July 7, 1955 (69 Stat. 282; 15 U.S.C. 15a).

(h) Notwithstanding the provisions of section 1404 or subsection (f) of this section, the judicial panel on multidistrict litigation may consolidate and transfer with or without the consent of the parties, for both pretrial purposes and for trial, any action brought under section 4C of the Clayton Act.

§ 1441. Actions removable generally

(a) Generally.— Except as otherwise expressly provided by Act of Congress, any civil action brought in a State court of which the district courts of the United States have original jurisdiction, may be removed by the defendant or the defendants, to the district court of the United States for the district and division embracing the place where such action is pending.

(b) Removal Based on Diversity of Citizenship.—

> **(1)** In determining whether a civil action is removable on the basis of the jurisdiction under section 1332(a) of this title, the citizenship of defendants sued under fictitious names shall be disregarded.
> **(2)** A civil action otherwise removable solely on the basis of the jurisdiction under section 1332(a) of this title may not be removed if any of the parties in interest properly joined and served as defendants is a citizen of the State in which such action is brought.

(c) Joinder of Federal Law Claims and State Law Claims.—

> **(1)** If a civil action includes—
>> **(A)** a claim arising under the Constitution, laws, or treaties of the United States (within the meaning of section 1331 of this title), and
>> **(B)** a claim not within the original or supplemental jurisdiction of the district court or a claim that has been made nonremovable by statute,
> the entire action may be removed if the action would be removable without the inclusion of the claim described in subparagraph (B).

(2) Upon removal of an action described in paragraph (1), the district court shall sever from the action all claims described in paragraph (1)(B) and shall remand the severed claims to the State court from which the action was removed. Only defendants against whom a claim described in paragraph (1)(A) has been asserted are required to join in or consent to the removal under paragraph (1).

(d) Actions Against Foreign States.— Any civil action brought in a State court against a foreign state as defined in section 1603(a) of this title may be removed by the foreign state to the district court of the United States for the district and division embracing the place where such action is pending. Upon removal the action shall be tried by the court without jury. Where removal is based upon this subsection, the time limitations of section 1446(b) of this chapter may be enlarged at any time for cause shown.

(e) Multiparty, Multiforum Jurisdiction.—

> **(1)** Notwithstanding the provisions of subsection (b) of this section, a defendant in a civil action in a State court may remove the action to the district court of the United States for the district and division embracing the place where the action is pending if—

(A) the action could have been brought in a United States district court under section 1369 of this title; or

(B) the defendant is a party to an action which is or could have been brought, in whole or in part, under section 1369 in a United States district court and arises from the same accident as the action in State court, even if the action to be removed could not have been brought in a district court as an original matter.

The removal of an action under this subsection shall be made in accordance with section 1446 of this title, except that a notice of removal may also be filed before trial of the action in State court within 30 days after the date on which the defendant first becomes a party to an action under section 1369 in a United States district court that arises from the same accident as the action in State court, or at a later time with leave of the district court.

(2) Whenever an action is removed under this subsection and the district court to which it is removed or transferred under section 1407(j) has made a liability determination requiring further proceedings as to damages, the district court shall remand the action to the State court from which it had been removed for the determination of damages, unless the court finds that, for the convenience of parties and witnesses and in the interest of justice, the action should be retained for the determination of damages.

(3) Any remand under paragraph (2) shall not be effective until 60 days after the district court has issued an order determining liability and has certified its intention to remand the removed action for the determination of damages. An appeal with respect to the liability determination of the district court may be taken during that 60-day period to the court of appeals with appellate jurisdiction over the district court. In the event a party files such an appeal, the remand shall not be effective until the appeal has been finally disposed of. Once the remand has become effective, the liability determination shall not be subject to further review by appeal or otherwise.

(4) Any decision under this subsection concerning remand for the determination of damages shall not be reviewable by appeal or otherwise.

(5) An action removed under this subsection shall be deemed to be an action under section 1369 and an action in which jurisdiction is based on section 1369 of this title for purposes of this section and sections 1407, 1697, and 1785 of this title.

(6) Nothing in this subsection shall restrict the authority of the district court to transfer or dismiss an action on the ground of inconvenient forum.

(f) Derivative Removal Jurisdiction.— The court to which a civil action is removed under this section is not precluded from hearing and determining any claim in such civil action because the State court from which such civil action is removed did not have jurisdiction over that claim.

§ 1446. Procedure for removal

(a) Generally.— A defendant or defendants desiring to remove any civil action from a State court shall file in the district court of the United States for the district and division within which such action is pending a notice of removal signed pursuant to Rule 11 of the Federal Rules of Civil Procedure and containing a short and plain statement of the grounds for removal, together with a copy of all process, pleadings, and orders served upon such defendant or defendants in such action.

(b) Requirements; Generally.—

(1) The notice of removal of a civil action or proceeding shall be filed within 30 days after the receipt by the defendant, through service or otherwise, of a copy of the initial pleading setting forth the claim for relief upon which such action or proceeding is based, or within 30 days after the service of summons upon the defendant if such initial pleading has then been filed in court and is not required to be served on the defendant, whichever period is shorter.

(2)

    (A) When a civil action is removed solely under section 1441(a), all defendants who have been properly joined and served must join in or consent to the removal of the action.
    (B) Each defendant shall have 30 days after receipt by or service on that defendant of the initial pleading or summons described in paragraph (1) to file the notice of removal.
    (C) If defendants are served at different times, and a later-served defendant files a notice of removal, any earlier-served defendant may consent to the removal even though that earlier-served defendant did not previously initiate or consent to removal.

(3) Except as provided in subsection (c), if the case stated by the initial pleading is not removable, a notice of removal may be filed within thirty days after receipt by the defendant, through service or otherwise, of a copy of an amended pleading, motion, order or other paper from which it may first be ascertained that the case is one which is or has become removable.

(c) Requirements; Removal Based on Diversity of Citizenship.—

(1) A case may not be removed under subsection (b)(3) on the basis of jurisdiction conferred by section 1332 more than 1 year after commencement of the action, unless the district court finds that the plaintiff has acted in bad faith in order to prevent a defendant from removing the action.

(2) If removal of a civil action is sought on the basis of the jurisdiction conferred by section 1332(a), the sum demanded in good faith in the initial pleading shall be deemed to be the amount in controversy, except that—
    (A) the notice of removal may assert the amount in controversy if the initial pleading seeks—
        (i) nonmonetary relief; or
        (ii) a money judgment, but the State practice either does not permit demand for a specific sum or permits recovery of damages in excess of the amount demanded; and
    (B) removal of the action is proper on the basis of an amount in controversy asserted under subparagraph (A) if the district court finds, by the preponderance of the evidence, that the amount in controversy exceeds the amount specified in section 1332(a).

(3)

    (A) If the case stated by the initial pleading is not removable solely because the amount in controversy does not exceed the amount specified in section 1332(a), information relating to the amount in controversy in the record of the State proceeding, or in responses to discovery, shall be treated as an "other paper" under subsection (b)(3).
    (B) If the notice of removal is filed more than 1 year after commencement of the action and the district court finds that the plaintiff deliberately failed to disclose the actual amount in controversy to prevent removal, that finding shall be deemed bad faith under paragraph (1).

(d) Notice to Adverse Parties and State Court.— Promptly after the filing of such notice of removal of a civil action the defendant or defendants shall give written notice thereof to all adverse parties and shall file a copy of the notice with the clerk of such State court, which shall effect the removal and the State court shall proceed no further unless and until the case is remanded.

(e) Counterclaim in 337 Proceeding.— With respect to any counterclaim removed to a district court pursuant to section 337(c) of the Tariff Act of 1930, the district court shall resolve such counterclaim in the same manner as an original complaint under the Federal Rules of Civil Procedure, except that the payment of a filing fee shall not be required in such cases and the counterclaim shall relate back to the date of the original complaint in the proceeding before the International Trade Commission under section 337 of that Act.

(f) [Omitted]

(g) Where the civil action or criminal prosecution that is removable under section 1442(a) is a proceeding in which a judicial order for testimony or documents is sought or issued or sought to be enforced, the 30-day requirement of subsection (b) of this section and paragraph (1) of section 1455(b) is satisfied if the person or entity desiring to remove the proceeding files the notice of removal not later than 30 days after receiving, through service, notice of any such proceeding.

§ 1447. Procedure after removal generally

(a) In any case removed from a State court, the district court may issue all necessary orders and process to bring before it all proper parties whether served by process issued by the State court or otherwise.

(b) It may require the removing party to file with its clerk copies of all records and proceedings in such State court or may cause the same to be brought before it by writ of certiorari issued to such State court.

(c) A motion to remand the case on the basis of any defect other than lack of subject matter jurisdiction must be made within 30 days after the filing of the notice of removal under section 1446 (a). If at any time before final judgment it appears that the district court lacks subject matter jurisdiction, the case shall be remanded. An order remanding the case may require payment of just costs and any actual expenses, including attorney fees, incurred as a result of the removal. A certified copy of the order of remand shall be mailed by the clerk to the clerk of the State court. The State court may thereupon proceed with such case.

(d) An order remanding a case to the State court from which it was removed is not reviewable on appeal or otherwise, except that an order remanding a case to the State court from which it was removed pursuant to section 1443 of this title shall be reviewable by appeal or otherwise.

(e) If after removal the plaintiff seeks to join additional defendants whose joinder would destroy subject matter jurisdiction, the court may deny joinder, or permit joinder and remand the action to the State court.

§ 1927. Counsel's liability for excessive costs

Any attorney or other person admitted to conduct cases in any court of the United States or any Territory thereof who so multiplies the proceedings in any case unreasonably and vexatiously may be required by the court to satisfy personally the excess costs, expenses, and attorneys' fees reasonably incurred because of such conduct.

§ 1652. State laws as rules of decision

The laws of the several states, except where the Constitution or treaties of the United States or Acts of Congress otherwise require or provide, shall be regarded as rules of decision in civil actions in the courts of the United States, in cases where they apply.

§ 2072. Rules of procedure and evidence; power to prescribe

(a) The Supreme Court shall have the power to prescribe general rules of practice and procedure and rules of evidence for cases in the United States district courts (including proceedings before magistrate judges thereof) and courts of appeals.

(b) Such rules shall not abridge, enlarge or modify any substantive right. All laws in conflict with such rules shall be of no further force or effect after such rules have taken effect.

(c) Such rules may define when a ruling of a district court is final for the purposes of appeal under section 1291 of this title.

§ 2361. Process and procedure

In any civil action of interpleader or in the nature of interpleader under section 1335 of this title, a district court may issue its process for all claimants and enter its order restraining them from instituting or prosecuting any proceeding in any State or United States court affecting the property, instrument or obligation involved in the interpleader action until further order of the court. Such process and order shall be returnable at such time as the court or judge thereof directs, and shall be addressed to and served by the United States marshals for the respective districts where the claimants reside or may be found.

Such district court shall hear and determine the case, and may discharge the plaintiff from further liability, make the injunction permanent, and make all appropriate orders to enforce its judgment.

XI. *Federal Rules of Civil Procedure*

Originally effective September 16, 1938;
Current with amendments through December 1, 2010

Title I. Scope of the Rules; Form of Action

Rule 1. Scope and Purpose

These rules govern the procedure in all civil actions and proceedings in the United States district courts, except as stated in Rule 81. They should be construed and administered to secure the just, speedy, and inexpensive determination of every action and proceeding.

Rule 2. One Form of Action

There is one form of action—the civil action.

Title II. Commencing an Action; Service of Process, Pleadings, Motions, and Orders

Rule 3. Commencing an Action

A civil action is commenced by filing a complaint with the court.

Rule 4. Summons

(a) CONTENTS; AMENDMENTS.

  (1) *Contents.* A summons must:
    (A) name the court and the parties;
    (B) be directed to the defendant;
    (C) state the name and address of the plaintiff's attorney or—if unrepresented—of the plaintiff;
    (D) state the time within which the defendant must appear and defend;
    (E) notify the defendant that a failure to appear and defend will result in a default judgment against the defendant for the relief demanded in the complaint;
    (F) be signed by the clerk; and
    (G) bear the court's seal.
  (2) *Amendments.* The court may permit a summons to be amended.

(b) ISSUANCE. On or after filing the complaint, the plaintiff may present a summons to the clerk for signature and seal. If the summons is properly completed, the clerk must sign, seal, and issue it to the plaintiff for service on the defendant. A summons—or a copy of a summons that is addressed to multiple defendants—must be issued for each defendant to be served.

(c) SERVICE.

(1) *In General.* A summons must be served with a copy of the complaint. The plaintiff is responsible for having the summons and complaint served within the time allowed by Rule 4(m) and must furnish the necessary copies to the person who makes service.

(2) *By Whom.* Any person who is at least 18 years old and not a party may serve a summons and complaint.

(3) *By a Marshal or Someone Specially Appointed.* At the plaintiff's request, the court may order that service be made by a United States marshal or deputy marshal or by a person specially appointed by the court. The court must so order if the plaintiff is authorized to proceed in forma pauperis under 28 U.S.C. § 1915 or as a seaman under 28 U.S.C. § 1916.

(d) WAIVING SERVICE.

(1) *Requesting a Waiver.* An individual, corporation, or association that is subject to service under Rule 4(e), (f), or (h) has a duty to avoid unnecessary expenses of serving the summons. The plaintiff may notify such a defendant that an action has been commenced and request that the defendant waive service of a summons. The notice and request must:

    (A) be in writing and be addressed: (i) to the individual defendant; or (ii) for a defendant subject to service under Rule 4(h), to an officer, a managing or general agent, or any other agent authorized by appointment or by law to receive service of process;

    (B) name the court where the complaint was filed;

    (C) be accompanied by a copy of the complaint, 2 copies of a waiver form, and a prepaid means for returning the form;

    (D) inform the defendant, using text prescribed in Form 5, of the consequences of waiving and not waiving service;

    (E) state the date when the request is sent;

    (F) give the defendant a reasonable time of at least 30 days after the request was sent—or at least 60 days if sent to the defendant outside any judicial district of the United States—to return the waiver; and

    (G) be sent by first-class mail or other reliable means.

(2) *Failure to Waive.* If a defendant located within the United States fails, without good cause, to sign and return a waiver requested by a plaintiff located within the United States, the court must impose on the defendant:

    (A) the expenses later incurred in making service; and

    (B) the reasonable expenses, including attorney's fees, of any motion required to collect those service expenses.

(3) *Time to Answer After a Waiver.* A defendant who, before being served with process, timely returns a waiver need not serve an answer to the complaint until 60 days after the request was sent—or until 90 days after it was sent to the defendant outside any judicial district of the United States.

(4) *Results of Filing a Waiver.* When the plaintiff files a waiver, proof of service is not required and these rules apply as if a summons and complaint had been served at the time of filing the waiver.

(5) *Jurisdiction and Venue Not Waived.* Waiving service of a summons does not waive any objection to personal jurisdiction or to venue.

(e) SERVING AN INDIVIDUAL WITHIN A JUDICIAL DISTRICT OF THE UNITED STATES. Unless federal law provides otherwise, an individual—other than a minor, an incompetent person, or a person whose waiver has been filed—may be served in a judicial district of the United States by:

(1) following state law for serving a summons in an action brought in courts of general jurisdiction in the state where the district court is located or where service is made; or
(2) doing any of the following:
(A) delivering a copy of the summons and of the complaint to the individual personally;
(B) leaving a copy of each at the individual's dwelling or usual place of abode with someone of suitable age and discretion who resides there; or
(C) delivering a copy of each to an agent authorized by appointment or by law to receive service of process.

(f) SERVING AN INDIVIDUAL IN A FOREIGN COUNTRY. Unless federal law provides otherwise, an individual—other than a minor, an incompetent person, or a person whose waiver has been filed—may be served at a place not within any judicial district of the United States:

(1) by any internationally agreed means of service that is reasonably calculated to give notice, such as those authorized by the Hague Convention on the Service Abroad of Judicial and Extrajudicial Documents;
(2) if there is no internationally agreed means, or if an international agreement allows but does not specify other means, by a method that is reasonably calculated to give notice:
(A) as prescribed by the foreign country's law for service in that country in an action in its courts of general jurisdiction;
(B) as the foreign authority directs in response to a letter rogatory or letter of request; or
(C) unless prohibited by the foreign country's law, by: (i) delivering a copy of the summons and of the complaint to the individual personally; or (ii) using any form of mail that the clerk addresses and sends to the individual and that requires a signed receipt; or
(3) by other means not prohibited by international agreement, as the court orders.

(g) SERVING A MINOR OR AN INCOMPETENT PERSON. A minor or an incompetent person in a judicial district of the United States must be served by following state law for serving a summons or like process on such a defendant in an action brought in the courts of general jurisdiction of the state where service is made. A minor or an incompetent person who is not within any judicial district of the United States must be served in the manner prescribed by Rule 4(f)(2)(A), (f)(2)(B), or (f)(3).

(h) SERVING A CORPORATION, PARTNERSHIP, OR ASSOCIATION. Unless federal law provides otherwise or the defendant's waiver has been filed, a domestic or foreign corporation, or a partnership or other unincorporated association that is subject to suit under a common name, must be served:

(1) in a judicial district of the United States:
(A) in the manner prescribed by Rule 4(e)(1) for serving an individual; or
(B) by delivering a copy of the summons and of the complaint to an officer, a managing or general agent, or any other agent authorized by appointment or by law to receive service of process and—if the agent is one authorized by statute and the statute so requires—by also mailing a copy of each to the defendant; or
(2) at a place not within any judicial district of the United States, in any manner prescribed by Rule 4(f) for serving an individual, except personal delivery under (f)(2)(C)(i).

(i) SERVING THE UNITED STATES AND ITS AGENCIES, CORPORATIONS, OFFICERS, OR EMPLOYEES.

(1) *United States.* To serve the United States, a party must:

(A)(i) deliver a copy of the summons and of the complaint to the United States attorney for the district where the action is brought—or to an assistant United States attorney or clerical employee whom the United States attorney designates in a writing filed with the court clerk—or (ii) send a copy of each by registered or certified mail to the civil-process clerk at the United States attorney's office;

(B) send a copy of each by registered or certified mail to the Attorney General of the United States at Washington, D.C.; and

(C) if the action challenges an order of a nonparty agency or officer of the United States, send a copy of each by registered or certified mail to the agency or officer.

(2) *Agency; Corporation; Officer or Employee Sued in an Official Capacity.* To serve a United States agency or corporation, or a United States officer or employee sued only in an official capacity, a party must serve the United States and also send a copy of the summons and of the complaint by registered or certified mail to the agency, corporation, officer, or employee.

(3) *Officer or Employee Sued Individually.* To serve a United States officer or employee sued in an individual capacity for an act or omission occurring in connection with duties performed on the United States' behalf (whether or not the officer or employee is also sued in an official capacity), a party must serve the United States and also serve the officer or employee under Rule 4(e), (f), or (g).

(4) *Extending Time.* The court must allow a party a reasonable time to cure its failure to:

(A) serve a person required to be served under Rule 4(i)(2), if the party has served either the United States attorney or the Attorney General of the United States; or

(B) serve the United States under Rule 4(i)(3), if the party has served the United States officer or employee.

(j) SERVING A FOREIGN, STATE, OR LOCAL GOVERNMENT.

(1) *Foreign State.* A foreign state or its political subdivision, agency, or instrumentality must be served in accordance with 28 U.S.C. § 1608.

(2) *State or Local Government.* A state, a municipal corporation, or any other state-created governmental organization that is subject to suit must be served by:

(A) delivering a copy of the summons and of the complaint to its chief executive officer; or

(B) serving a copy of each in the manner prescribed by that state's law for serving a summons or like process on such a defendant.

(k) TERRITORIAL LIMITS OF EFFECTIVE SERVICE.

(1) *In General.* Serving a summons or filing a waiver of service establishes personal jurisdiction over a defendant:

(A) who is subject to the jurisdiction of a court of general jurisdiction in the state where the district court is located;

(B) who is a party joined under Rule 14 or 19 and is served within a judicial district of the United States and not more than 100 miles from where the summons was issued; or

(C) when authorized by a federal statute.

(2) *Federal Claim Outside State-Court Jurisdiction.* For a claim that arises under federal law, serving a summons or filing a waiver of service establishes personal jurisdiction over a defendant if:

(A) the defendant is not subject to jurisdiction in any state's courts of general jurisdiction; and

(B) exercising jurisdiction is consistent with the United States Constitution and laws.

(*l*) PROVING SERVICE.

(1) *Affidavit Required.* Unless service is waived, proof of service must be made to the court. Except for service by a United States marshal or deputy marshal, proof must be by the server's affidavit.

(2) *Service Outside the United States.* Service not within any judicial district of the United States must be proved as follows:

(A) if made under Rule 4(f)(1), as provided in the applicable treaty or convention; or

(B) if made under Rule 4(f)(2) or (f)(3), by a receipt signed by the addressee, or by other evidence satisfying the court that the summons and complaint were delivered to the addressee.

(3) *Validity of Service; Amending Proof.* Failure to prove service does not affect the validity of service. The court may permit proof of service to be amended.

(m) TIME LIMIT FOR SERVICE. If a defendant is not served within 120 days after the complaint is filed, the court—on motion or on its own after notice to the plaintiff—must dismiss the action without prejudice against that defendant or order that service be made within a specified time. But if the plaintiff shows good cause for the failure, the court must extend the time for service for an appropriate period. This subdivision (m) does not apply to service in a foreign country under Rule 4(f) or 4(j)(1).

(n) ASSERTING JURISDICTION OVER PROPERTY OR ASSETS.

(1) *Federal Law.* The court may assert jurisdiction over property if authorized by a federal statute. Notice to claimants of the property must be given as provided in the statute or by serving a summons under this rule.

(2) *State Law.* On a showing that personal jurisdiction over a defendant cannot be obtained in the district where the action is brought by reasonable efforts to serve a summons under this rule, the court may assert jurisdiction over the defendant's assets found in the district. Jurisdiction is acquired by seizing the assets under the circumstances and in the manner provided by state law in that district.

Rule 4.1. Serving Other Process

(a) IN GENERAL. Process—other than a summons under Rule 4 or a subpoena under Rule 45—must be served by a United States marshal or deputy marshal or by a person specially appointed for that purpose. It may be served anywhere within the territorial limits of the state where the district court is located and, if authorized by a federal statute, beyond those limits. Proof of service must be made under Rule 4(*l*).

(b) ENFORCING ORDERS: COMMITTING FOR CIVIL CONTEMPT. An order committing a person for civil contempt of a decree or injunction issued to enforce federal law may be served and enforced in any district. Any other order in a civil-contempt proceeding may be served only in the state where the issuing court is located or elsewhere in the United States within 100 miles from where the order was issued.

Rule 5. Serving and Filing Pleadings and Other Papers

(a) SERVICE: WHEN REQUIRED.

(1) *In General.* Unless these rules provide otherwise, each of the following papers must be served on every party:
    (A) an order stating that service is required;
    (B) a pleading filed after the original complaint, unless the court orders otherwise under Rule 5(c) because there are numerous defendants;
    (C) a discovery paper required to be served on a party, unless the court orders otherwise;
    (D) a written motion, except one that may be heard ex parte; and
    (E) a written notice, appearance, demand, or offer of judgment, or any similar paper.

(2) *If a Party Fails to Appear.* No service is required on a party who is in default for failing to appear. But a pleading that asserts a new claim for relief against such a party must be served on that party under Rule 4.

(3) *Seizing Property.* If an action is begun by seizing property and no person is or need be named as a defendant, any service required before the filing of an appearance, answer, or claim must be made on the person who had custody or possession of the property when it was seized.

(b) SERVICE: HOW MADE.

(1) *Serving an Attorney.* If a party is represented by an attorney, service under this rule must be made on the attorney unless the court orders service on the party.

(2) *Service in General.* A paper is served under this rule by:
    (A) handing it to the person;
    (B) leaving it: (i) at the person's office with a clerk or other person in charge or, if no one is in charge, in a conspicuous place in the office; or (ii) if the person has no office or the office is closed, at the person's dwelling or usual place of abode with someone of suitable age and discretion who resides there;
    (C) mailing it to the person's last known address—in which event service is complete upon mailing;
    (D) leaving it with the court clerk if the person has no known address;
    (E) sending it by electronic means if the person consented in writing—in which event service is complete upon transmission, but is not effective if the serving party learns that it did not reach the person to be served; or
    (F) delivering it by any other means that the person consented to in writing—in which event service is complete when the person making service delivers it to the agency designated to make delivery.

(3) *Using Court Facilities.* If a local rule so authorizes, a party may use the court's transmission facilities to make service under Rule 5(b)(2)(E).

(c) SERVING NUMEROUS DEFENDANTS.

(1) *In General.* If an action involves an unusually large number of defendants, the court may, on motion or on its own, order that:
    (A) defendants' pleadings and replies to them need not be served on other defendants;
    (B) any crossclaim, counterclaim, avoidance, or affirmative defense in those pleadings and replies to them will be treated as denied or avoided by all other parties; and
    (C) filing any such pleading and serving it on the plaintiff constitutes notice of the pleading to all parties.

(2) *Notifying Parties.* A copy of every such order must be served on the parties as the court directs.

(d) FILING.

(1) *Required Filings; Certificate of Service.* Any paper after the complaint that is required to be served—together with a certificate of service—must be filed within a reasonable time after service. But disclosures under Rule 26(a)(1) or (2) and the following discovery requests and responses must not be filed until they are used in the proceeding or the court orders filing: depositions, interrogatories, requests for documents or tangible things or to permit entry onto land, and requests for admission.

(2) *How Filing Is Made—In General.* A paper is filed by delivering it:
    (A) to the clerk; or
    (B) to a judge who agrees to accept it for filing, and who must then note the filing date on the paper and promptly send it to the clerk.

(3) *Electronic Filing, Signing, or Verification.* A court may, by local rule, allow papers to be filed, signed, or verified by electronic means that are consistent with any technical standards established by the Judicial Conference of the United States. A local rule may require electronic filing only if reasonable exceptions are allowed. A paper filed electronically in compliance with a local rule is a written paper for purposes of these rules.

(4) *Acceptance by the Clerk.* The clerk must not refuse to file a paper solely because it is not in the form prescribed by these rules or by a local rule or practice.

Rule 5.1. Constitutional Challenge to a Statute—Notice, Certification, and Intervention

(a) NOTICE BY A PARTY. A party that files a pleading, written motion, or other paper drawing into question the constitutionality of a federal or state statute must promptly:

(1) file a notice of constitutional question stating the question and identifying the paper that raises it, if:
    (A) a federal statute is questioned and the parties do not include the United States, one of its agencies, or one of its officers or employees in an official capacity; or
    (B) a state statute is questioned and the parties do not include the state, one of its agencies, or one of its officers or employees in an official capacity; and
(2) serve the notice and paper on the Attorney General of the United States if a federal statute is questioned—or on the state attorney general if a state statute is questioned—either by certified or registered mail or by sending it to an electronic address designated by the attorney general for this purpose.

(b) CERTIFICATION BY THE COURT. The court must, under 28 U.S.C. § 2403, certify to the appropriate attorney general that a statute has been questioned.

(c) INTERVENTION; FINAL DECISION ON THE MERITS. Unless the court sets a later time, the attorney general may intervene within 60 days after the notice is filed or after the court certifies the challenge, whichever is earlier. Before the time to intervene expires, the court may reject the constitutional challenge, but may not enter a final judgment holding the statute unconstitutional.

(d) NO FORFEITURE. A party's failure to file and serve the notice, or the court's failure to certify, does not forfeit a constitutional claim or defense that is otherwise timely asserted.

Rule 5.2. Privacy Protection For Filings Made with the Court

(a) REDACTED FILINGS. Unless the court orders otherwise, in an electronic or paper filing with the court that contains an individual's social-security number, taxpayer-identification number, or birth date, the name of an individual known to be a minor, or a financial-account number, a party or nonparty making the filing may include only:

> (1) the last four digits of the social-security number and taxpayer-identification number; (2) the year of the individual's birth;
> (3) the minor's initials; and
> (4) the last four digits of the financial-account number.

(b) EXEMPTIONS FROM THE REDACTION REQUIREMENT. The redaction requirement does not apply to the following:

> (1) a financial-account number that identifies the property allegedly subject to forfeiture in a forfeiture proceeding;
> (2) the record of an administrative or agency proceeding;
> (3) the official record of a state-court proceeding;
> (4) the record of a court or tribunal, if that record was not subject to the redaction requirement when originally filed;
> (5) a filing covered by Rule 5.2(c) or (d); and
> (6) a pro se filing in an action brought under 28 U.S.C. §§ 2241, 2254, or 2255.

(c) LIMITATIONS ON REMOTE ACCESS TO ELECTRONIC FILES; SOCIALSECURITY APPEALS AND IMMIGRATION CASES. Unless the court orders otherwise, in an action for benefits under the Social Security Act, and in an action or proceeding relating to an order of removal, to relief from removal, or to immigration benefits or detention, access to an electronic file is authorized as follows:

> (1) the parties and their attorneys may have remote electronic access to any part of the case file, including the administrative record;
> (2) any other person may have electronic access to the full record at the courthouse, but may have remote electronic access only to:
>> (A) the docket maintained by the court; and
>> (B) an opinion, order, judgment, or other disposition of the court, but not any other part of the case file or the administrative record.

(d) FILINGS MADE UNDER SEAL. The court may order that a filing be made under seal without redaction. The court may later unseal the filing or order the person who made the filing to file a redacted version for the public record.

(e) PROTECTIVE ORDERS. For good cause, the court may by order in a case:

> (1) require redaction of additional information; or
> (2) limit or prohibit a nonparty's remote electronic access to a document filed with the court.

(f) OPTION FOR ADDITIONAL UNREDACTED FILING UNDER SEAL. A person making a redacted filing may also file an unredacted copy under seal. The court must retain the unredacted copy as part of the record.

(g) OPTION FOR FILING A REFERENCE LIST. A filing that contains redacted information may be filed together with a reference list that identifies each item of redacted information and specifies an appropriate identifier that uniquely corresponds to each item listed. The list must be filed under seal and may be amended as of right. Any reference in the case to a listed identifier will be construed to refer to the corresponding item of information.

(h) WAIVER OF PROTECTION OF IDENTIFIERS. A person waives the protection of Rule 5.2(a) as to the person's own information by filing it without redaction and not under seal.

Rule 6. Computing and Extending Time; Time for Motion Papers

(a) COMPUTING TIME. The following rules apply in computing any time period specified in these rules, in any local rule or court order, or in any statute that does not specify a method of computing time.

(1) *Period Stated in Days or a Longer Unit.* When the period is stated in days or a longer unit of time:
    (A) exclude the day of the event that triggers the period;
    (B) count every day, including intermediate Saturdays, Sundays, and legal holidays; and
    (C) include the last day of the period, but if the last day is a Saturday, Sunday, or legal holiday, the period continues to run until the end of the next day that is not a Saturday, Sunday, or legal holiday.
(2) *Period Stated in Hours.* When the period is stated in hours:
    (A) begin counting immediately on the occurrence of the event that triggers the period;
    (B) count every hour, including hours during intermediate Saturdays, Sundays, and legal holidays; and
    (C) if the period would end on a Saturday, Sunday, or legal holiday, the period continues to run until the same time on the next day that is not a Saturday, Sunday, or legal holiday.
(3) *Inaccessibility of the Clerk's Office.* Unless the court orders otherwise, if the clerk's office is inaccessible:
    (A) on the last day for filing under Rule 6(a)(1), then the time for filing is extended to the first accessible day that is not a Saturday, Sunday, or legal holiday; or
    (B) during the last hour for filing under Rule 6(a)(2), then the time for filing is extended to the same time on the first accessible day that is not a Saturday, Sunday, or legal holiday.
(4) *"Last Day" Defined.* Unless a different time is set by a statute, local rule, or court order, the last day ends:
    (A) for electronic filing, at midnight in the court's time zone; and
    (B) for filing by other means, when the clerk's office is scheduled to close.
(5) *"Next Day" Defined.* The "next day" is determined by continuing to count forward when the period is measured after an event and backward when measured before an event.
(6) *"Legal Holiday" Defined.* "Legal holiday" means:
    (A) the day set aside by statute for observing New Year's Day, Martin Luther King Jr.'s Birthday, Washington's Birthday, Memorial Day, Independence Day, Labor Day, Columbus Day, Veterans' Day, Thanksgiving Day, or Christmas Day; (B) any day declared a holiday by the President or Congress; and
    (C) for periods that are measured after an event, any other day declared a holiday by the state where the district court is located.

(b) EXTENDING TIME.

(1) *In General.* When an act may or must be done within a specified time, the court may, for good cause, extend the time:
> (A) with or without motion or notice if the court acts, or if a request is made, before the original time or its extension expires; or
> (B) on motion made after the time has expired if the party failed to act because of excusable neglect.

(2) *Exceptions.* A court must not extend the time to act under Rules 50(b) and (d), 52(b), 59(b), (d), and (e), and 60(b).

(c) MOTIONS, NOTICES OF HEARING, AND AFFIDAVITS.

(1) *In General.* A written motion and notice of the hearing must be served at least 14 days before the time specified for the hearing, with the following exceptions:
> (A) when the motion may be heard ex parte;
> (B) when these rules set a different time; or
> (C) when a court order—which a party may, for good cause, apply for ex parte—sets a different time.

(2) *Supporting Affidavit.* Any affidavit supporting a motion must be served with the motion. Except as Rule 59(c) provides otherwise, any opposing affidavit must be served at least 7 days before the hearing, unless the court permits service at another time.

(d) ADDITIONAL TIME AFTER CERTAIN KINDS OF SERVICE. When a party may or must act within a specified time after service and service is made under Rule 5(b)(2)(C), (D), (E), or (F), 3 days are added after the period would otherwise expire under Rule 6(a).

Title III. Pleadings and Motions

Rule 7. Pleadings Allowed; Form of Motions and Other Papers

(a) PLEADINGS. Only these pleadings are allowed:

(1) a complaint;
(2) an answer to a complaint;
(3) an answer to a counterclaim designated as a counterclaim;
(4) an answer to a crossclaim;
(5) a third-party complaint;
(6) an answer to a third-party complaint; and
(7) if the court orders one, a reply to an answer.

(b) MOTIONS AND OTHER PAPERS.

(1) *In General.* A request for a court order must be made by motion. The motion must:
> (A) be in writing unless made during a hearing or trial;
> (B) state with particularity the grounds for seeking the order; and
> (C) state the relief sought.

(2) *Form.* The rules governing captions and other matters of form in pleadings apply to motions and other papers.

Rule 7.1. Disclosure Statement

(a) WHO MUST FILE; CONTENTS. A nongovernmental corporate party must file 2 copies of a disclosure statement that:

>(1) identifies any parent corporation and any publicly held corporation owning 10% or more of its stock; or
>(2) states that there is no such corporation.

(b) TIME TO FILE; SUPPLEMENTAL FILING. A party must:

>(1) file the disclosure statement with its first appearance, pleading, petition, motion, response, or other request addressed to the court; and
>(2) promptly file a supplemental statement if any required information changes.

Rule 8. General Rules of Pleading

(a) CLAIM FOR RELIEF. A pleading that states a claim for relief must contain:

>(1) a short and plain statement of the grounds for the court's jurisdiction, unless the court already has jurisdiction and the claim needs no new jurisdictional support;
>(2) a short and plain statement of the claim showing that the pleader is entitled to relief; and
>(3) a demand for the relief sought, which may include relief in the alternative or different types of relief.

(b) DEFENSES; ADMISSIONS AND DENIALS.

>(1) *In General.* In responding to a pleading, a party must:
>>(A) state in short and plain terms its defenses to each claim asserted against it; and
>>(B) admit or deny the allegations asserted against it by an opposing party.
>
>(2) *Denials—Responding to the Substance.* A denial must fairly respond to the substance of the allegation.
>(3) *General and Specific Denials.* A party that intends in good faith to deny all the allegations of a pleading—including the jurisdictional grounds—may do so by a general denial. A party that does not intend to deny all the allegations must either specifically deny designated allegations or generally deny all except those specifically admitted.
>(4) *Denying Part of an Allegation.* A party that intends in good faith to deny only part of an allegation must admit the part that is true and deny the rest.
>(5) *Lacking Knowledge or Information.* A party that lacks knowledge or information sufficient to form a belief about the truth of an allegation must so state, and the statement has the effect of a denial.
>(6) *Effect of Failing to Deny.* An allegation—other than one relating to the amount of damages— is admitted if a responsive pleading is required and the allegation is not denied. If a responsive pleading is not required, an allegation is considered denied or avoided.

(c) AFFIRMATIVE DEFENSES.

>(1) *In General.* In responding to a pleading, a party must affirmatively state any avoidance or affirmative defense, including:

- accord and satisfaction;
- arbitration and award;
- assumption of risk;
- contributory negligence;
- duress;
- estoppel;
- failure of consideration;
- fraud;
- illegality;
- injury by fellow servant;
- laches;
- license;
- payment;
- release;
- res judicata;
- statute of frauds;
- statute of limitations; and
- waiver.

(2) *Mistaken Designation.* If a party mistakenly designates a defense as a counterclaim, or a counterclaim as a defense, the court must, if justice requires, treat the pleading as though it were correctly designated, and may impose terms for doing so.

(d) PLEADING TO BE CONCISE AND DIRECT; ALTERNATIVE STATEMENTS; INCONSISTENCY.

(1) *In General.* Each allegation must be simple, concise, and direct. No technical form is required.
(2) *Alternative Statements of a Claim or Defense.* A party may set out 2 or more statements of a claim or defense alternatively or hypothetically, either in a single count or defense or in separate ones. If a party makes alternative statements, the pleading is sufficient if any one of them is sufficient.
(3) *Inconsistent Claims or Defenses.* A party may state as many separate claims or defenses as it has, regardless of consistency.

(e) CONSTRUING PLEADINGS. Pleadings must be construed so as to do justice.

Rule 9. Pleading Special Matters

(a) CAPACITY OR AUTHORITY TO SUE; LEGAL EXISTENCE.

(1) *In General.* Except when required to show that the court has jurisdiction, a pleading need not allege:
    (A) a party's capacity to sue or be sued;
    (B) a party's authority to sue or be sued in a representative capacity; or
    (C) the legal existence of an organized association of persons that is made a party.
(2) *Raising Those Issues.* To raise any of those issues, a party must do so by a specific denial, which must state any supporting facts that are peculiarly within the party's knowledge.

(b) FRAUD OR MISTAKE; CONDITIONS OF MIND. In alleging fraud or mistake, a party must state with particularity the circumstances constituting fraud or mistake. Malice, intent, knowledge, and other conditions of a person's mind may be alleged generally.

(c) CONDITIONS PRECEDENT. In pleading conditions precedent, it suffices to allege generally that all conditions precedent have occurred or been performed. But when denying that a condition precedent has occurred or been performed, a party must do so with particularity.

(d) OFFICIAL DOCUMENT OR ACT. In pleading an official document or official act, it suffices to allege that the document was legally issued or the act legally done.

(e) JUDGMENT. In pleading a judgment or decision of a domestic or foreign court, a judicial or quasi-judicial tribunal, or a board or officer, it suffices to plead the judgment or decision without showing jurisdiction to render it.

(f) TIME AND PLACE. An allegation of time or place is material when testing the sufficiency of a pleading.

(g) SPECIAL DAMAGES. If an item of special damage is claimed, it must be specifically stated.

(h) ADMIRALTY OR MARITIME CLAIM.

> (1) *How Designated.* If a claim for relief is within the admiralty or maritime jurisdiction and also within the court's subject-matter jurisdiction on some other ground, the pleading may designate the claim as an admiralty or maritime claim for purposes of Rules 14(c), 38(e), and 82 and the Supplemental Rules for Admiralty or Maritime Claims and Asset Forfeiture Actions. A claim cognizable only in the admiralty or maritime jurisdiction is an admiralty or maritime claim for those purposes, whether or not so designated.
>
> (2) *Designation for Appeal.* A case that includes an admiralty or maritime claim within this subdivision (h) is an admiralty case within 28 U.S.C. § 1292(a)(3).

Rule 10. Form of Pleadings

(a) CAPTION; NAMES OF PARTIES. Every pleading must have a caption with the court's name, a title, a file number, and a Rule 7(a) designation. The title of the complaint must name all the parties; the title of other pleadings, after naming the first party on each side, may refer generally to other parties.

(b) PARAGRAPHS; SEPARATE STATEMENTS. A party must state its claims or defenses in numbered paragraphs, each limited as far as practicable to a single set of circumstances. A later pleading may refer by number to a paragraph in an earlier pleading. If doing so would promote clarity, each claim founded on a separate transaction or occurrence—and each defense other than a denial—must be stated in a separate count or defense.

(c) ADOPTION BY REFERENCE; EXHIBITS. A statement in a pleading may be adopted by reference elsewhere in the same pleading or in any other pleading or motion. A copy of a written instrument that is an exhibit to a pleading is a part of the pleading for all purposes.

Rule 11. Signing Pleadings, Motions, and Other Papers; Representations to the Court; Sanctions

(a) SIGNATURE. Every pleading, written motion, and other paper must be signed by at least one attorney of record in the attorney's name—or by a party personally if the party is unrepresented. The paper must state the signer's address, e-mail address, and telephone number. Unless a rule or statute specifically states otherwise, a pleading need not be verified or accompanied by an affidavit. The court must strike an unsigned paper unless the omission is promptly corrected after being called to the attorney's or party's attention.

(b) REPRESENTATIONS TO THE COURT. By presenting to the court a pleading, written motion, or other paper—whether by signing, filing, submitting, or later advocating it—an attorney or unrepresented party certifies that to the best of the person's knowledge, information, and belief, formed after an inquiry reasonable under the circumstances:

> (1) it is not being presented for any improper purpose, such as to harass, cause unnecessary delay, or needlessly increase the cost of litigation;
> (2) the claims, defenses, and other legal contentions are warranted by existing law or by a nonfrivolous argument for extending, modifying, or reversing existing law or for establishing new law;
> (3) the factual contentions have evidentiary support or, if specifically so identified, will likely have evidentiary support after a reasonable opportunity for further investigation or discovery; and
> (4) the denials of factual contentions are warranted on the evidence or, if specifically so identified, are reasonably based on belief or a lack of information.

(c) SANCTIONS.

> (1) *In General.* If, after notice and a reasonable opportunity to respond, the court determines that Rule 11(b) has been violated, the court may impose an appropriate sanction on any attorney, law firm, or party that violated the rule or is responsible for the violation. Absent exceptional circumstances, a law firm must be held jointly responsible for a violation committed by its partner, associate, or employee.
> (2) *Motion for Sanctions.* A motion for sanctions must be made separately from any other motion and must describe the specific conduct that allegedly violates Rule 11(b). The motion must be served under Rule 5, but it must not be filed or be presented to the court if the challenged paper, claim, defense, contention, or denial is withdrawn or appropriately corrected within 21 days after service or within another time the court sets. If warranted, the court may award to the prevailing party the reasonable expenses, including attorney's fees, incurred for the motion.
> (3) *On the Court's Initiative.* On its own, the court may order an attorney, law firm, or party to show cause why conduct specifically described in the order has not violated Rule 11(b).
> (4) *Nature of a Sanction.* A sanction imposed under this rule must be limited to what suffices to deter repetition of the conduct or comparable conduct by others similarly situated. The sanction may include nonmonetary directives; an order to pay a penalty into court; or, if imposed on motion and warranted for effective deterrence, an order directing payment to the movant of part or all of the reasonable attorney's fees and other expenses directly resulting from the violation.
> (5) *Limitations on Monetary Sanctions.* The court must not impose a monetary sanction:
>> (A) against a represented party for violating Rule 11(b)(2); or
>> (B) on its own, unless it issued the show-cause order under Rule 11(c)(3) before voluntary dismissal or settlement of the claims made by or against the party that is, or whose attorneys are, to be sanctioned.
> (6) *Requirements for an Order.* An order imposing a sanction must describe the sanctioned conduct and explain the basis for the sanction.

(d) INAPPLICABILITY TO DISCOVERY. This rule does not apply to disclosures and discovery requests, responses, objections, and motions under Rules 26 through 37.

Rule 12. Defenses and Objections: When and How Presented; Motion for Judgment on the Pleadings; Consolidating Motions; Waiving Defenses; Pretrial Hearing

(a) TIME TO SERVE A RESPONSIVE PLEADING.

(1) *In General.* Unless another time is specified by this rule or a federal statute, the time for serving a responsive pleading is as follows:

(A) A defendant must serve an answer: (i) within 21 days after being served with the summons and complaint; or (ii) if it has timely waived service under Rule 4(d), within 60 days after the request for a waiver was sent, or within 90 days after it was sent to the defendant outside any judicial district of the United States. (B) A party must serve an answer to a counterclaim or crossclaim within 21 days after being served with the pleading that states the counterclaim or crossclaim.

(C) A party must serve a reply to an answer within 21 days after being served with an order to reply, unless the order specifies a different time.

(2) *United States and Its Agencies, Officers, or Employees Sued in an Official Capacity.* The United States, a United States agency, or a United States officer or employee sued only in an official capacity must serve an answer to a complaint, counterclaim, or crossclaim within 60 days after service on the United States attorney.

(3) *United States Officers or Employees Sued in an Individual Capacity.* A United States officer or employee sued in an individual capacity for an act or omission occurring in connection with duties performed on the United States' behalf must serve an answer to a complaint, counterclaim, or crossclaim within 60 days after service on the officer or employee or service on the United States attorney, whichever is later.

(4) *Effect of a Motion.* Unless the court sets a different time, serving a motion under this rule alters these periods as follows:

(A) if the court denies the motion or postpones its disposition until trial, the responsive pleading must be served within 14 days after notice of the court's action; or

(B) if the court grants a motion for a more definite statement, the responsive pleading must be served within 14 days after the more definite statement is served.

(b) HOW TO PRESENT DEFENSES. Every defense to a claim for relief in any pleading must be asserted in the responsive pleading if one is required. But a party may assert the following defenses by motion:

(1) lack of subject-matter jurisdiction;
(2) lack of personal jurisdiction;
(3) improper venue;
(4) insufficient process;
(5) insufficient service of process;
(6) failure to state a claim upon which relief can be granted; and
(7) failure to join a party under Rule 19.

A motion asserting any of these defenses must be made before pleading if a responsive pleading is allowed. If a pleading sets out a claim for relief that does not require a responsive pleading, an opposing party may assert at trial any defense to that claim. No defense or objection is waived by joining it with one or more other defenses or objections in a responsive pleading or in a motion.

(c) MOTION FOR JUDGMENT ON THE PLEADINGS. After the pleadings are closed—but early enough not to delay trial—a party may move for judgment on the pleadings.

(d) RESULT OF PRESENTING MATTERS OUTSIDE THE PLEADINGS. If, on a motion under Rule 12(b)(6) or 12(c), matters outside the pleadings are presented to and not excluded by the court, the motion must be treated as one for summary judgment under Rule 56. All parties must be given a reasonable opportunity to present all the material that is pertinent to the motion.

(e) MOTION FOR A MORE DEFINITE STATEMENT. A party may move for a more definite statement of a pleading to which a responsive pleading is allowed but which is so vague or ambiguous that the party cannot reasonably prepare a response. The motion must be made before filing a responsive pleading and must point out the defects complained of and the details desired. If the court orders a more definite statement and the order is not obeyed within 14 days after notice of the order or within the time the court sets, the court may strike the pleading or issue any other appropriate order.

(f) MOTION TO STRIKE. The court may strike from a pleading an insufficient defense or any redundant, immaterial, impertinent, or scandalous matter. The court may act:

>   (1) on its own; or
>   (2) on motion made by a party either before responding to the pleading or, if a response is not allowed, within 21 days after being served with the pleading.

(g) JOINING MOTIONS.

>   (1) *Right to Join.* A motion under this rule may be joined with any other motion allowed by this rule.
>   (2) *Limitation on Further Motions.* Except as provided in Rule 12(h)(2) or (3), a party that makes a motion under this rule must not make another motion under this rule raising a defense or objection that was available to the party but omitted from its earlier motion.

(h) WAIVING AND PRESERVING CERTAIN DEFENSES.

>   (1) *When Some Are Waived.* A party waives any defense listed in Rule 12(b)(2)–(5) by:
>   (A) omitting it from a motion in the circumstances described in Rule 12(g)(2); or
>   (B) failing to either: (i) make it by motion under this rule; or (ii) include it in a responsive pleading or in an amendment allowed by Rule 15(a)(1) as a matter of course.
>   (2) *When to Raise Others.* Failure to state a claim upon which relief can be granted, to join a person required by Rule 19(b), or to state a legal defense to a claim may be raised:
>   (A) in any pleading allowed or ordered under Rule 7(a);
>   (B) by a motion under Rule 12(c); or
>   (C) at trial.
>   (3) *Lack of Subject-Matter Jurisdiction.* If the court determines at any time that it lacks subject-matter jurisdiction, the court must dismiss the action.

(i) HEARING BEFORE TRIAL. If a party so moves, any defense listed in Rule 12(b)(1)–(7)—whether made in a pleading or by motion—and a motion under Rule 12(c) must be heard and decided before trial unless the court orders a deferral until trial.

Rule 13. Counterclaim and Crossclaim

(a) COMPULSORY COUNTERCLAIM.

(1) *In General.* A pleading must state as a counterclaim any claim that—at the time of its service—the pleader has against an opposing party if the claim:

(A) arises out of the transaction or occurrence that is the subject matter of the opposing party's claim; and

(B) does not require adding another party over whom the court cannot acquire jurisdiction.

(2) *Exceptions.* The pleader need not state the claim if:

(A) when the action was commenced, the claim was the subject of another pending action; or

(B) the opposing party sued on its claim by attachment or other process that did not establish personal jurisdiction over the pleader on that claim, and the pleader does not assert any counterclaim under this rule.

(b) PERMISSIVE COUNTERCLAIM. A pleading may state as a counterclaim against an opposing party any claim that is not compulsory.

(c) RELIEF SOUGHT IN A COUNTERCLAIM. A counterclaim need not diminish or defeat the recovery sought by the opposing party. It may request relief that exceeds in amount or differs in kind from the relief sought by the opposing party.

(d) COUNTERCLAIM AGAINST THE UNITED STATES. These rules do not expand the right to assert a counterclaim—or to claim a credit—against the United States or a United States officer or agency.

(e) COUNTERCLAIM MATURING OR ACQUIRED AFTER PLEADING. The court may permit a party to file a supplemental pleading asserting a counterclaim that matured or was acquired by the party after serving an earlier pleading.

(f) [ABROGATED.]

(g) CROSSCLAIM AGAINST A COPARTY. A pleading may state as a crossclaim any claim by one party against a coparty if the claim arises out of the transaction or occurrence that is the subject matter of the original action or of a counterclaim, or if the claim relates to any property that is the subject matter of the original action. The crossclaim may include a claim that the coparty is or may be liable to the crossclaimant for all or part of a claim asserted in the action against the crossclaimant.

(h) JOINING ADDITIONAL PARTIES. Rules 19 and 20 govern the addition of a person as a party to a counterclaim or crossclaim.

(i) SEPARATE TRIALS; SEPARATE JUDGMENTS. If the court orders separate trials under Rule 42(b), it may enter judgment on a counterclaim or crossclaim under Rule 54(b) when it has jurisdiction to do so, even if the opposing party's claims have been dismissed or otherwise resolved.

Rule 14. Third-Party Practice

(a) WHEN A DEFENDING PARTY MAY BRING IN A THIRD PARTY.

(1) *Timing of the Summons and Complaint.* A defending party may, as third-party plaintiff, serve a summons and complaint on a nonparty who is or may be liable to it for all or part of the claim against it. But the third-party plaintiff must, by motion, obtain the court's leave if it files the third-party complaint more than 14 days after serving its original answer.

(2) *Third-Party Defendant's Claims and Defenses.* The person served with the summons and third-party complaint—the "third-party defendant":

    (A) must assert any defense against the third-party plaintiff's claim under Rule 12;

    (B) must assert any counterclaim against the third-party plaintiff under Rule 13(a), and may assert any counterclaim against the third-party plaintiff under Rule 13(b) or any crossclaim against another third-party defendant under Rule 13(g);

    (C) may assert against the plaintiff any defense that the third-party plaintiff has to the plaintiff's claim; and

    (D) may also assert against the plaintiff any claim arising out of the transaction or occurrence that is the subject matter of the plaintiff's claim against the third-party plaintiff.

(3) *Plaintiff's Claims Against a Third-Party Defendant.* The plaintiff may assert against the third-party defendant any claim arising out of the transaction or occurrence that is the subject matter of the plaintiff's claim against the third-party plaintiff. The third-party defendant must then assert any defense under Rule 12 and any counterclaim under Rule 13(a), and may assert any counterclaim under Rule 13(b) or any crossclaim under Rule 13(g).

(4) *Motion to Strike, Sever, or Try Separately.* Any party may move to strike the third-party claim, to sever it, or to try it separately.

(5) *Third-Party Defendant's Claim Against a Nonparty.* A third-party defendant may proceed under this rule against a nonparty who is or may be liable to the third-party defendant for all or part of any claim against it.

(6) *Third-Party Complaint In Rem.* If it is within the admiralty or maritime jurisdiction, a third-party complaint may be in rem. In that event, a reference in this rule to the "summons" includes the warrant of arrest, and a reference to the defendant or third-party plaintiff includes, when appropriate, a person who asserts a right under Supplemental Rule C(6)(a)(i) in the property arrested.

(b) WHEN A PLAINTIFF MAY BRING IN A THIRD PARTY. When a claim is asserted against a plaintiff, the plaintiff may bring in a third party if this rule would allow a defendant to do so.

(c) ADMIRALTY OR MARITIME CLAIM.

(1) *Scope of Impleader.* If a plaintiff asserts an admiralty or maritime claim under Rule 9(h), the defendant or a person who asserts a right under Supplemental Rule C(6)(a)(i) may, as a third-party plaintiff, bring in a third-party defendant who may be wholly or partly liable—either to the plaintiff or to the third-party plaintiff—for remedy over, contribution, or otherwise on account of the same transaction, occurrence, or series of transactions or occurrences.

(2) *Defending Against a Demand for Judgment for the Plaintiff.* The third-party plaintiff may demand judgment in the plaintiff's favor against the third-party defendant. In that event, the third-party defendant must defend under Rule 12 against the plaintiff's claim as well as the third-party plaintiff's claim; and the action proceeds as if the plaintiff had sued both the third-party defendant and the third-party plaintiff.

Rule 15. Amended and Supplemental Pleadings

(a) AMENDMENTS BEFORE TRIAL.

(1) *Amending as a Matter of Course.* A party may amend its pleading once as a matter of course within:
>
> (A) 21 days after serving it, or
>
> (B) if the pleading is one to which a responsive pleading is required, 21 days after service of a responsive pleading or 21 days after service of a motion under Rule 12(b), (e), or (f), whichever is earlier.

(2) *Other Amendments.* In all other cases, a party may amend its pleading only with the opposing party's written consent or the court's leave. The court should freely give leave when justice so requires.

(3) *Time to Respond.* Unless the court orders otherwise, any required response to an amended pleading must be made within the time remaining to respond to the original pleading or within 14 days after service of the amended pleading, whichever is later.

(b) AMENDMENTS DURING AND AFTER TRIAL.

(1) *Based on an Objection at Trial.* If, at trial, a party objects that evidence is not within the issues raised in the pleadings, the court may permit the pleadings to be amended. The court should freely permit an amendment when doing so will aid in presenting the merits and the objecting party fails to satisfy the court that the evidence would prejudice that party's action or defense on the merits. The court may grant a continuance to enable the objecting party to meet the evidence.

(2) *For Issues Tried by Consent.* When an issue not raised by the pleadings is tried by the parties' express or implied consent, it must be treated in all respects as if raised in the pleadings. A party may move—at any time, even after judgment—to amend the pleadings to conform them to the evidence and to raise an unpleaded issue. But failure to amend does not affect the result of the trial of that issue.

(c) RELATION BACK OF AMENDMENTS.

(1) *When an Amendment Relates Back.* An amendment to a pleading relates back to the date of the original pleading when:
>
> (A) the law that provides the applicable statute of limitations allows relation back; (B) the amendment asserts a claim or defense that arose out of the conduct, transaction, or occurrence set out—or attempted to be set out—in the original pleading; or
>
> (C) the amendment changes the party or the naming of the party against whom a claim is asserted, if Rule 15(c)(1)(B) is satisfied and if, within the period provided by Rule 4(m) for serving the summons and complaint, the party to be brought in by amendment: (i) received such notice of the action that it will not be prejudiced in defending on the merits; and (ii) knew or should have known that the action would have been brought against it, but for a mistake concerning the proper party's identity.

(2) *Notice to the United States.* When the United States or a United States officer or agency is added as a defendant by amendment, the notice requirements of Rule 15(c)(1)(C)(i) and (ii) are satisfied if, during the stated period, process was delivered or mailed to the United States attorney or the United States attorney's designee, to the Attorney General of the United States, or to the officer or agency.

(d) SUPPLEMENTAL PLEADINGS. On motion and reasonable notice, the court may, on just terms, permit a party to serve a supplemental pleading setting out any transaction, occurrence, or event that happened after the date of the pleading to be supplemented. The court may permit supplementation even though the original pleading is defective in stating a claim or defense. The court may order that the opposing party plead to the supplemental pleading within a specified time.

Rule 16. Pretrial Conferences; Scheduling; Management

(a) PURPOSES OF A PRETRIAL CONFERENCE. In any action, the court may order the attorneys and any unrepresented parties to appear for one or more pretrial conferences for such purposes as:

(1) expediting disposition of the action;
(2) establishing early and continuing control so that the case will not be protracted because of lack of management;
(3) discouraging wasteful pretrial activities;
(4) improving the quality of the trial through more thorough preparation; and
(5) facilitating settlement.

(b) SCHEDULING.

(1) *Scheduling Order.* Except in categories of actions exempted by local rule, the district judge— or a magistrate judge when authorized by local rule—must issue a scheduling order:
   (A) after receiving the parties' report under Rule 26(f); or
   (B) after consulting with the parties' attorneys and any unrepresented parties at a scheduling conference or by telephone, mail, or other means.
(2) *Time to Issue.* The judge must issue the scheduling order as soon as practicable, but in any event within the earlier of 120 days after any defendant has been served with the complaint or 90 days after any defendant has appeared.
(3) *Contents of the Order.*
   (A) *Required Contents.* The scheduling order must limit the time to join other parties, amend the pleadings, complete discovery, and file motions.
   (B) *Permitted Contents.* The scheduling order may: (i) modify the timing of disclosures under Rules 26(a) and 26(e)(1); (ii) modify the extent of discovery; (iii) provide for disclosure or discovery of electronically stored information; (iv) include any agreements the parties reach for asserting claims of privilege or of protection as trial preparation material after information is produced; (v) set dates for pretrial conferences and for trial; and (vi) include other appropriate matters.
(4) *Modifying a Schedule.* A schedule may be modified only for good cause and with the judge's consent.

(c) ATTENDANCE AND MATTERS FOR CONSIDERATION AT A PRETRIAL CONFERENCE.

(1) *Attendance.* A represented party must authorize at least one of its attorneys to make stipulations and admissions about all matters that can reasonably be anticipated for discussion at a pretrial conference. If appropriate, the court may require that a party or its representative be present or reasonably available by other means to consider possible settlement.
(2) *Matters for Consideration.* At any pretrial conference, the court may consider and take appropriate action on the following matters:

(A) formulating and simplifying the issues, and eliminating frivolous claims or defenses;

(B) amending the pleadings if necessary or desirable;

(C) obtaining admissions and stipulations about facts and documents to avoid unnecessary proof, and ruling in advance on the admissibility of evidence;

(D) avoiding unnecessary proof and cumulative evidence, and limiting the use of testimony under Federal Rule of Evidence 702;

(E) determining the appropriateness and timing of summary adjudication under Rule 56;

(F) controlling and scheduling discovery, including orders affecting disclosures and discovery under Rule 26 and Rules 29 through 37;

(G) identifying witnesses and documents, scheduling the filing and exchange of any pretrial briefs, and setting dates for further conferences and for trial;

(H) referring matters to a magistrate judge or a master;

(I) settling the case and using special procedures to assist in resolving the dispute when authorized by statute or local rule;

(J) determining the form and content of the pretrial order;

(K) disposing of pending motions;

(L) adopting special procedures for managing potentially difficult or protracted actions that may involve complex issues, multiple parties, difficult legal questions, or unusual proof problems;

(M) ordering a separate trial under Rule 42(b) of a claim, counterclaim, crossclaim, third-party claim, or particular issue;

(N) ordering the presentation of evidence early in the trial on a manageable issue that might, on the evidence, be the basis for a judgment as a matter of law under Rule 50(a) or a judgment on partial findings under Rule 52(c);

(O) establishing a reasonable limit on the time allowed to present evidence; and

(P) facilitating in other ways the just, speedy, and inexpensive disposition of the action.

(d) PRETRIAL ORDERS. After any conference under this rule, the court should issue an order reciting the action taken. This order controls the course of the action unless the court modifies it.

(e) FINAL PRETRIAL CONFERENCE AND ORDERS. The court may hold a final pretrial conference to formulate a trial plan, including a plan to facilitate the admission of evidence. The conference must be held as close to the start of trial as is reasonable, and must be attended by at least one attorney who will conduct the trial for each party and by any unrepresented party. The court may modify the order issued after a final pretrial conference only to prevent manifest injustice.

(f) SANCTIONS.

(1) *In General.* On motion or on its own, the court may issue any just orders, including those authorized by Rule 37(b)(2)(A)(ii)–(vii), if a party or its attorney:

(A) fails to appear at a scheduling or other pretrial conference;

(B) is substantially unprepared to participate—or does not participate in good faith—in the conference; or

(C) fails to obey a scheduling or other pretrial order.

(2) *Imposing Fees and Costs.* Instead of or in addition to any other sanction, the court must order the party, its attorney, or both to pay the reasonable expenses—including attorney's fees—incurred because of any noncompliance with this rule, unless the noncompliance was substantially justified or other circumstances make an award of expenses unjust.

Title IV. Parties

Rule 17. Plaintiff and Defendant; Capacity; Public Officers

(a) REAL PARTY IN INTEREST.

(1) *Designation in General.* An action must be prosecuted in the name of the real party in interest. The following may sue in their own names without joining the person for whose benefit the action is brought:
> (A) an executor;
> (B) an administrator;
> (C) a guardian;
> (D) a bailee;
> (E) a trustee of an express trust;
> (F) a party with whom or in whose name a contract has been made for another's benefit; and
> (G) a party authorized by statute.

(2) *Action in the Name of the United States for Another's Use or Benefit.* When a federal statute so provides, an action for another's use or benefit must be brought in the name of the United States.

(3) *Joinder of the Real Party in Interest.* The court may not dismiss an action for failure to prosecute in the name of the real party in interest until, after an objection, a reasonable time has been allowed for the real party in interest to ratify, join, or be substituted into the action. After ratification, joinder, or substitution, the action proceeds as if it had been originally commenced by the real party in interest.

(b) CAPACITY TO SUE OR BE SUED. Capacity to sue or be sued is determined as follows:

(1) for an individual who is not acting in a representative capacity, by the law of the individual's domicile;

(2) for a corporation, by the law under which it was organized; and

(3) for all other parties, by the law of the state where the court is located, except that:
> (A) a partnership or other unincorporated association with no such capacity under that state's law may sue or be sued in its common name to enforce a substantive right existing under the United States Constitution or laws; and
> (B) 28 U.S.C. §§ 754 and 959(a) govern the capacity of a receiver appointed by a United States court to sue or be sued in a United States court.

(c) MINOR OR INCOMPETENT PERSON.

(1) *With a Representative.* The following representatives may sue or defend on behalf of a minor or an incompetent person:
> (A) a general guardian;
> (B) a committee;
> (C) a conservator; or
> (D) a like fiduciary.

(2) *Without a Representative.* A minor or an incompetent person who does not have a duly appointed representative may sue by a next friend or by a guardian ad litem. The court must appoint a guardian ad litem—or issue another appropriate order—to protect a minor or incompetent person who is unrepresented in an action.

(d) PUBLIC OFFICER'S TITLE AND NAME. A public officer who sues or is sued in an official capacity may be designated by official title rather than by name, but the court may order that the officer's name be added.

Rule 18. Joinder of Claims

(a) IN GENERAL. A party asserting a claim, counterclaim, crossclaim, or third-party claim may join, as independent or alternative claims, as many claims as it has against an opposing party.

(b) JOINDER OF CONTINGENT CLAIMS. A party may join two claims even though one of them is contingent on the disposition of the other; but the court may grant relief only in accordance with the parties' relative substantive rights. In particular, a plaintiff may state a claim for money and a claim to set aside a conveyance that is fraudulent as to that plaintiff, without first obtaining a judgment for the money.

Rule 19. Required Joinder of Parties

(a) PERSONS REQUIRED TO BE JOINED IF FEASIBLE.

(1) *Required Party.* A person who is subject to service of process and whose joinder will not deprive the court of subject matter jurisdiction must be joined as a party if:
    (A) in that person's absence, the court cannot accord complete relief among existing parties; or
    (B) that person claims an interest relating to the subject of the action and is so situated that disposing of the action in the person's absence may: (i) as a practical matter impair or impede the person's ability to protect the interest; or (ii) leave an existing party subject to a substantial risk of incurring double, multiple, or otherwise inconsistent obligations because of the interest.
(2) *Joinder by Court Order.* If a person has not been joined as required, the court must order that the person be made a party. A person who refuses to join as a plaintiff may be made either a defendant or, in a proper case, an involuntary plaintiff.
(3) *Venue.* If a joined party objects to venue and the joinder would make venue improper, the court must dismiss that party.

(b) WHEN JOINDER IS NOT FEASIBLE. If a person who is required to be joined if feasible cannot be joined, the court must determine whether, in equity and good conscience, the action should proceed among the existing parties or should be dismissed. The factors for the court to consider include:

(1) the extent to which a judgment rendered in the person's absence might prejudice that person or the existing parties;
(2) the extent to which any prejudice could be lessened or avoided by:
    (A) protective provisions in the judgment;
    (B) shaping the relief; or
    (C) other measures;
(3) whether a judgment rendered in the person's absence would be adequate; and
(4) whether the plaintiff would have an adequate remedy if the action were dismissed for nonjoinder.

(c) PLEADING THE REASONS FOR NONJOINDER. When asserting a claim for relief, a party must state:

> (1) the name, if known, of any person who is required to be joined if feasible but is not joined; and
>
> (2) the reasons for not joining that person.

(d) EXCEPTION FOR CLASS ACTIONS. This rule is subject to Rule 23.

Rule 20. Permissive Joinder of Parties

(a) PERSONS WHO MAY JOIN OR BE JOINED.

> (1) *Plaintiffs.* Persons may join in one action as plaintiffs if:
>> (A) they assert any right to relief jointly, severally, or in the alternative with respect to or arising out of the same transaction, occurrence, or series of transactions or occurrences; and
>>
>> (B) any question of law or fact common to all plaintiffs will arise in the action.
>
> (2) *Defendants.* Persons—as well as a vessel, cargo, or other property subject to admiralty process in rem—may be joined in one action as defendants if:
>> (A) any right to relief is asserted against them jointly, severally, or in the alternative with respect to or arising out of the same transaction, occurrence, or series of transactions or occurrences; and
>>
>> (B) any question of law or fact common to all defendants will arise in the action.
>
> (3) *Extent of Relief.* Neither a plaintiff nor a defendant need be interested in obtaining or defending against all the relief demanded. The court may grant judgment to one or more plaintiffs according to their rights, and against one or more defendants according to their liabilities.

(b) PROTECTIVE MEASURES. The court may issue orders—including an order for separate trials—to protect a party against embarrassment, delay, expense, or other prejudice that arises from including a person against whom the party asserts no claim and who asserts no claim against the party.

Rule 21. Misjoinder and Nonjoinder of Parties

Misjoinder of parties is not a ground for dismissing an action. On motion or on its own, the court may at any time, on just terms, add or drop a party. The court may also sever any claim against a party.

Rule 22. Interpleader

(a) GROUNDS.

> (1) *By a Plaintiff.* Persons with claims that may expose a plaintiff to double or multiple liability may be joined as defendants and required to interplead. Joinder for interpleader is proper even though:
>> (A) the claims of the several claimants, or the titles on which their claims depend, lack a common origin or are adverse and independent rather than identical; or
>>
>> (B) the plaintiff denies liability in whole or in part to any or all of the claimants.
>
> (2) *By a Defendant.* A defendant exposed to similar liability may seek interpleader through a crossclaim or counterclaim.

(b) RELATION TO OTHER RULES AND STATUTES. This rule supplements—and does not limit—the joinder of parties allowed by Rule 20. The remedy this rule provides is in addition to—and does not supersede or limit—the remedy provided by 28 U.S.C. §§ 1335, 1397, and 2361. An action under those statutes must be conducted under these rules.

Rule 23. Class Actions

(a) PREREQUISITES. One or more members of a class may sue or be sued as representative parties on behalf of all members only if:

> (1) the class is so numerous that joinder of all members is impracticable;
> (2) there are questions of law or fact common to the class;
> (3) the claims or defenses of the representative parties are typical of the claims or defenses of the class; and
> (4) the representative parties will fairly and adequately protect the interests of the class.

(b) TYPES OF CLASS ACTIONS. A class action may be maintained if Rule 23(a) is satisfied and if:

> (1) prosecuting separate actions by or against individual class members would create a risk of:
>> (A) inconsistent or varying adjudications with respect to individual class members that would establish incompatible standards of conduct for the party opposing the class; or
>> (B) adjudications with respect to individual class members that, as a practical matter, would be dispositive of the interests of the other members not parties to the individual adjudications or would substantially impair or impede their ability to protect their interests;
> (2) the party opposing the class has acted or refused to act on grounds that apply generally to the class, so that final injunctive relief or corresponding declaratory relief is appropriate respecting the class as a whole; or
> (3) the court finds that the questions of law or fact common to class members predominate over any questions affecting only individual members, and that a class action is superior to other available methods for fairly and efficiently adjudicating the controversy. The matters pertinent to these findings include:
>> (A) the class members' interests in individually controlling the prosecution or defense of separate actions;
>> (B) the extent and nature of any litigation concerning the controversy already begun by or against class members;
>> (C) the desirability or undesirability of concentrating the litigation of the claims in the particular forum; and
>> (D) the likely difficulties in managing a class action.

(c) CERTIFICATION ORDER; NOTICE TO CLASS MEMBERS; JUDGMENT; ISSUES CLASSES; SUBCLASSES.

> (1) *Certification Order.*
>> (A) *Time to Issue.* At an early practicable time after a person sues or is sued as a class representative, the court must determine by order whether to certify the action as a class action.

(B) *Defining the Class; Appointing Class Counsel.* An order that certifies a class action must define the class and the class claims, issues, or defenses, and must appoint class counsel under Rule 23(g).

(C) *Altering or Amending the Order.* An order that grants or denies class certification may be altered or amended before final judgment.

(2) *Notice.*

(A) *For (b)(1) or (b)(2) Classes.* For any class certified under Rule 23(b)(1) or (b)(2), the court may direct appropriate notice to the class.

(B) *For (b)(3) Classes.* For any class certified under Rule 23(b)(3), the court must direct to class members the best notice that is practicable under the circumstances, including individual notice to all members who can be identified through reasonable effort. The notice must clearly and concisely state in plain, easily understood language: (i) the nature of the action; (ii) the definition of the class certified; (iii) the class claims, issues, or defenses; (iv) that a class member may enter an appearance through an attorney if the member so desires; (v) that the court will exclude from the class any member who requests exclusion; (vi) the time and manner for requesting exclusion; and (vii) the binding effect of a class judgment on members under Rule 23(c)(3).

(3) *Judgment.* Whether or not favorable to the class, the judgment in a class action must:

(A) for any class certified under Rule 23(b)(1) or (b)(2), include and describe those whom the court finds to be class members; and

(B) for any class certified under Rule 23(b)(3), include and specify or describe those to whom the Rule 23(c)(2) notice was directed, who have not requested exclusion, and whom the court finds to be class members.

(4) *Particular Issues.* When appropriate, an action may be brought or maintained as a class action with respect to particular issues.

(5) *Subclasses.* When appropriate, a class may be divided into subclasses that are each treated as a class under this rule.

(d) CONDUCTING THE ACTION.

(1) *In General.* In conducting an action under this rule, the court may issue orders that:

(A) determine the course of proceedings or prescribe measures to prevent undue repetition or complication in presenting evidence or argument;

(B) require—to protect class members and fairly conduct the action—giving appropriate notice to some or all class members of: (i) any step in the action; (ii) the proposed extent of the judgment; or (iii) the members' opportunity to signify whether they consider the representation fair and adequate, to intervene and present claims or defenses, or to otherwise come into the action;

(C) impose conditions on the representative parties or on intervenors;

(D) require that the pleadings be amended to eliminate allegations about representation of absent persons and that the action proceed accordingly; or

(E) deal with similar procedural matters.

(2) *Combining and Amending Orders.* An order under Rule 23(d)(1) may be altered or amended from time to time and may be combined with an order under Rule 16.

(e) SETTLEMENT, VOLUNTARY DISMISSAL, OR COMPROMISE. The claims, issues, or defenses of a certified class may be settled, voluntarily dismissed, or compromised only with the court's approval. The following procedures apply to a proposed settlement, voluntary dismissal, or compromise:

(1) The court must direct notice in a reasonable manner to all class members who would be bound by the proposal.

(2) If the proposal would bind class members, the court may approve it only after a hearing and on finding that it is fair, reasonable, and adequate.

(3) The parties seeking approval must file a statement identifying any agreement made in connection with the proposal.

(4) If the class action was previously certified under Rule 23(b)(3), the court may refuse to approve a settlement unless it affords a new opportunity to request exclusion to individual class members who had an earlier opportunity to request exclusion but did not do so.

(5) Any class member may object to the proposal if it requires court approval under this subdivision (e); the objection may be withdrawn only with the court's approval.

(f) APPEALS. A court of appeals may permit an appeal from an order granting or denying class-action certification under this rule if a petition for permission to appeal is filed with the circuit clerk within 14 days after the order is entered. An appeal does not stay proceedings in the district court unless the district judge or the court of appeals so orders.

(g) CLASS COUNSEL.

(1) *Appointing Class Counsel.* Unless a statute provides otherwise, a court that certifies a class must appoint class counsel. In appointing class counsel, the court:

(A) must consider: (i) the work counsel has done in identifying or investigating potential claims in the action; (ii) counsel's experience in handling class actions, other complex litigation, and the types of claims asserted in the action; (iii) counsel's knowledge of the applicable law; and (iv) the resources that counsel will commit to representing the class;

(B) may consider any other matter pertinent to counsel's ability to fairly and adequately represent the interests of the class;

(C) may order potential class counsel to provide information on any subject pertinent to the appointment and to propose terms for attorney's fees and nontaxable costs;

(D) may include in the appointing order provisions about the award of attorney's fees or nontaxable costs under Rule 23(h); and

(E) may make further orders in connection with the appointment.

(2) *Standard for Appointing Class Counsel.* When one applicant seeks appointment as class counsel, the court may appoint that applicant only if the applicant is adequate under Rule 23(g)(1) and (4). If more than one adequate applicant seeks appointment, the court must appoint the applicant best able to represent the interests of the class.

(3) *Interim Counsel.* The court may designate interim counsel to act on behalf of a putative class before determining whether to certify the action as a class action.

(4) *Duty of Class Counsel.* Class counsel must fairly and adequately represent the interests of the class.

(h) ATTORNEY'S FEES AND NONTAXABLE COSTS. In a certified class action, the court may award reasonable attorney's fees and nontaxable costs that are authorized by law or by the parties' agreement. The following procedures apply:

(1) A claim for an award must be made by motion under Rule 54(d)(2), subject to the provisions of this subdivision (h), at a time the court sets. Notice of the motion must be served on all parties and, for motions by class counsel, directed to class members in a reasonable manner.

(2) A class member, or a party from whom payment is sought, may object to the motion.

(3) The court may hold a hearing and must find the facts and state its legal conclusions under Rule 52(a).

(4) The court may refer issues related to the amount of the award to a special master or a magistrate judge, as provided in Rule 54(d)(2)(D).

Rule 23.1. Derivative Actions

(a) PREREQUISITES. This rule applies when one or more shareholders or members of a corporation or an unincorporated association bring a derivative action to enforce a right that the corporation or association may properly assert but has failed to enforce. The derivative action may not be maintained if it appears that the plaintiff does not fairly and adequately represent the interests of shareholders or members who are similarly situated in enforcing the right of the corporation or association.

(b) PLEADING REQUIREMENTS. The complaint must be verified and must:

> (1) allege that the plaintiff was a shareholder or member at the time of the transaction complained of, or that the plaintiff's share or membership later devolved on it by operation of law;
> (2) allege that the action is not a collusive one to confer jurisdiction that the court would otherwise lack; and
> (3) state with particularity:
>> (A) any effort by the plaintiff to obtain the desired action from the directors or comparable authority and, if necessary, from the shareholders or members; and
>> (B) the reasons for not obtaining the action or not making the effort.

(c) SETTLEMENT, DISMISSAL, AND COMPROMISE. A derivative action may be settled, voluntarily dismissed, or compromised only with the court's approval. Notice of a proposed settlement, voluntary dismissal, or compromise must be given to shareholders or members in the manner that the court orders.

Rule 23.2. Actions Relating to Unincorporated Associations

This rule applies to an action brought by or against the members of an unincorporated association as a class by naming certain members as representative parties. The action may be maintained only if it appears that those parties will fairly and adequately protect the interests of the association and its members. In conducting the action, the court may issue any appropriate orders corresponding with those in Rule 23(d), and the procedure for settlement, voluntary dismissal, or compromise must correspond with the procedure in Rule 23(e).

Rule 24. Intervention

(a) INTERVENTION OF RIGHT. On timely motion, the court must permit anyone to intervene who:

> (1) is given an unconditional right to intervene by a federal statute; or
> (2) claims an interest relating to the property or transaction that is the subject of the action, and is so situated that disposing of the action may as a practical matter impair or impede the movant's ability to protect its interest, unless existing parties adequately represent that interest.

(b) PERMISSIVE INTERVENTION.

> (1) *In General.* On timely motion, the court may permit anyone to intervene who:
>> (A) is given a conditional right to intervene by a federal statute; or
>> (B) has a claim or defense that shares with the main action a common question of law or fact.

(2) *By a Government Officer or Agency.* On timely motion, the court may permit a federal or state governmental officer or agency to intervene if a party's claim or defense is based on:

(A) a statute or executive order administered by the officer or agency; or

(B) any regulation, order, requirement, or agreement issued or made under the statute or executive order.

(3) *Delay or Prejudice.* In exercising its discretion, the court must consider whether the intervention will unduly delay or prejudice the adjudication of the original parties' rights.

(c) NOTICE AND PLEADING REQUIRED. A motion to intervene must be served on the parties as provided in Rule 5. The motion must state the grounds for intervention and be accompanied by a pleading that sets out the claim or defense for which intervention is sought.

Rule 25. Substitution of Parties

(a) DEATH.

(1) *Substitution if the Claim Is Not Extinguished.* If a party dies and the claim is not extinguished, the court may order substitution of the proper party. A motion for substitution may be made by any party or by the decedent's successor or representative. If the motion is not made within 90 days after service of a statement noting the death, the action by or against the decedent must be dismissed.

(2) *Continuation Among the Remaining Parties.* After a party's death, if the right sought to be enforced survives only to or against the remaining parties, the action does not abate, but proceeds in favor of or against the remaining parties. The death should be noted on the record.

(3) *Service.* A motion to substitute, together with a notice of hearing, must be served on the parties as provided in Rule 5 and on nonparties as provided in Rule 4. A statement noting death must be served in the same manner. Service may be made in any judicial district.

(b) INCOMPETENCY. If a party becomes incompetent, the court may, on motion, permit the action to be continued by or against the party's representative. The motion must be served as provided in Rule 25(a)(3).

(c) TRANSFER OF INTEREST. If an interest is transferred, the action may be continued by or against the original party unless the court, on motion, orders the transferee to be substituted in the action or joined with the original party. The motion must be served as provided in Rule 25(a)(3).

(d) PUBLIC OFFICERS; DEATH OR SEPARATION FROM OFFICE. An action does not abate when a public officer who is a party in an official capacity dies, resigns, or otherwise ceases to hold office while the action is pending. The officer's successor is automatically substituted as a party. Later proceedings should be in the substituted party's name, but any misnomer not affecting the parties' substantial rights must be disregarded. The court may order substitution at any time, but the absence of such an order does not affect the substitution.

Title V. Disclosures and Discovery

Rule 26. Duty to Disclose; General Provisions Governing Discovery

(a) REQUIRED DISCLOSURES.

(1) *Initial Disclosure.*

(A) *In General.* Except as exempted by Rule 26(a)(1)(B) or as otherwise stipulated or ordered by the court, a party must, without awaiting a discovery request, provide to the other parties:

(i) the name and, if known, the address and telephone number of each individual likely to have discoverable information—along with the subjects of that information—that the disclosing party may use to support its claims or defenses, unless the use would be solely for impeachment;

(ii) a copy—or a description by category and location—of all documents, electronically stored information, and tangible things that the disclosing party has in its possession, custody, or control and may use to support its claims or defenses, unless the use would be solely for impeachment;

(iii) a computation of each category of damages claimed by the disclosing party—who must also make available for inspection and copying as under Rule 34 the documents or other evidentiary material, unless privileged or protected from disclosure, on which each computation is based, including materials bearing on the nature and extent of injuries suffered; and

(iv) for inspection and copying as under Rule 34, any insurance agreement under which an insurance business may be liable to satisfy all or part of a possible judgment in the action or to indemnify or reimburse for payments made to satisfy the judgment.

(B) *Proceedings Exempt from Initial Disclosure.* The following proceedings are exempt from initial disclosure:

(i) an action for review on an administrative record;

(ii) a forfeiture action in rem arising from a federal statute;

(iii) a petition for habeas corpus or any other proceeding to challenge a criminal conviction or sentence;

(iv) an action brought without an attorney by a person in the custody of the United States, a state, or a state subdivision;

(v) an action to enforce or quash an administrative summons or subpoena;

(vi) an action by the United States to recover benefit payments;

(vii) an action by the United States to collect on a student loan guaranteed by the United States;

(viii) a proceeding ancillary to a proceeding in another court; and

(ix) an action to enforce an arbitration award

(C) *Time for Initial Disclosures—In General.* A party must make the initial disclosures at or within 14 days after the parties' Rule 26(f) conference unless a different time is set by stipulation or court order, or unless a party objects during the conference that initial disclosures are not appropriate in this action and states the objection in the proposed discovery plan. In ruling on the objection, the court must determine what disclosures, if any, are to be made and must set the time for disclosure.

(D) *Time for Initial Disclosures—For Parties Served or Joined Later.* A party that is first served or otherwise joined after the Rule 26(f) conference must make the initial disclosures within 30 days after being served or joined, unless a different time is set by stipulation or court order.

(E) *Basis for Initial Disclosure; Unacceptable Excuses.* A party must make its initial disclosures based on the information then reasonably available to it. A party is not excused from making its disclosures because it has not fully investigated the case or because it challenges the sufficiency of another party's disclosures or because another party has not made its disclosures.

(2) *Disclosure of Expert Testimony.*

(A) *In General.* In addition to the disclosures required by Rule 26(a)(1), a party must disclose to the other parties the identity of any witness it may use at trial to present evidence under Federal Rule of Evidence 702, 703, or 705.

(B) *Witnesses Who Must Provide a Written Report.* Unless otherwise stipulated or ordered by the court, this disclosure must be accompanied by a written report—prepared and signed by the witness—if the witness is one retained or specially employed to provide expert testimony in the case or one whose duties as the party's employee regularly involve giving expert testimony. The report must contain:

(i) a complete statement of all opinions the witness will express and the basis and reasons for them;

(ii) the facts or data considered by the witness in forming them;

(iii) any exhibits that will be used to summarize or support them;

(iv) the witness's qualifications, including a list of all publications authored in the previous 10 years;

(v) a list of all other cases in which, during the previous 4 years, the witness testified as an expert at trial or by deposition; and

(vi) a statement of the compensation to be paid for the study and testimony in the case.

(C) *Witnesses Who Do Not Provide a Written Report.* Unless otherwise stipulated or ordered by the court, if the witness is not required to provide a written report, this disclosure must state:

(i) the subject matter on which the witness is expected to present evidence under Federal Rule of Evidence 702, 703, or 705; and

(ii) a summary of the facts and opinions to which the witness is expected to testify.

(D) *Time to Disclose Expert Testimony.* A party must make these disclosures at the times and in the sequence that the court orders. Absent a stipulation or a court order, the disclosures must be made:

(i) at least 90 days before the date set for trial or for the case to be ready for trial; or

(ii) if the evidence is intended solely to contradict or rebut evidence on the same subject matter identified by another party under Rule 26(a)(2)(B) or (C), within 30 days after the other party's disclosure.

(E) *Supplementing the Disclosure.* The parties must supplement these disclosures when required under Rule 26(e).

(3) *Pretrial Disclosures.*

(A) *In General.* In addition to the disclosures required by Rule 26(a)(1) and (2), a party must provide to the other parties and promptly file the following information about the evidence that it may present at trial other than solely for impeachment:

(i) the name and, if not previously provided, the address and telephone number of each witness—separately identifying those the party expects to present and those it may call if the need arises;

(ii) the designation of those witnesses whose testimony the party expects to present by deposition and, if not taken stenographically, a transcript of the pertinent parts of the deposition; and

(iii) an identification of each document or other exhibit, including summaries of other evidence—separately identifying those items the party expects to offer and those it may offer if the need arises.

(B) *Time for Pretrial Disclosures; Objections.* Unless the court orders otherwise, these disclosures must be made at least 30 days before trial. Within 14 days after they are made, unless the court sets a different time, a party may serve and promptly file a list of the following objections: any objections to the use under Rule 32(a) of a deposition designated by another party under Rule 26(a)(3)(A)(ii); and any objection, together with the grounds for it, that may be made to the admissibility of materials identified under Rule 26(a)(3)(A)(iii). An objection not so made—except for one under Federal Rule of Evidence 402 or 403—is waived unless excused by the court for good cause.

(4) *Form of Disclosures.* Unless the court orders otherwise, all disclosures under Rule 26(a) must be in writing, signed, and served.

(b) DISCOVERY SCOPE AND LIMITS.

(1) *Scope in General.* Unless otherwise limited by court order, the scope of discovery is as follows: Parties may obtain discovery regarding any nonprivileged matter that is relevant to any party's claim or defense—including the existence, description, nature, custody, condition, and location of any documents or other tangible things and the identity and location of persons who know of any discoverable matter. For good cause, the court may order discovery of any matter relevant to the subject matter involved in the action. Relevant information need not be admissible at the trial if the discovery appears reasonably calculated to lead to the discovery of admissible evidence. All discovery is subject to the limitations imposed by Rule 26(b)(2)(C).

(2) *Limitations on Frequency and Extent.*

(A) *When Permitted.* By order, the court may alter the limits in these rules on the number of depositions and interrogatories or on the length of depositions under Rule 30. By order or local rule, the court may also limit the number of requests under Rule 36.

(B) *Specific Limitations on Electronically Stored Information.* A party need not provide discovery of electronically stored information from sources that the party identifies as not reasonably accessible because of undue burden or cost. On motion to compel discovery or for a protective order, the party from whom discovery is sought must show that the information is not reasonably accessible because of undue burden or cost. If that showing is made, the court may nonetheless order discovery from such sources if the requesting party shows good cause, considering the limitations of Rule 26(b)(2)(C). The court may specify conditions for the discovery.

(C) *When Required.* On motion or on its own, the court must limit the frequency or extent of discovery otherwise allowed by these rules or by local rule if it determines that:

(i) the discovery sought is unreasonably cumulative or duplicative, or can be obtained from some other source that is more convenient, less burdensome, or less expensive;

(ii) the party seeking discovery has had ample opportunity to obtain the information by discovery in the action; or

(iii) the burden or expense of the proposed discovery outweighs its likely benefit, considering the needs of the case, the amount in controversy, the parties' resources, the importance of the issues at stake in the action, and the importance of the discovery in resolving the issues.

(3) *Trial Preparation: Materials.*

(A) *Documents and Tangible Things.* Ordinarily, a party may not discover documents and tangible things that are prepared in anticipation of litigation or for trial by or for another party or its representative (including the other party's attorney, consultant, surety, indemnitor, insurer, or agent). But, subject to Rule 26(b)(4), those materials may be discovered if: (i) they are otherwise discoverable under Rule 26(b)(1); and (ii) the party shows that it has substantial need for the materials to prepare its case and cannot, without undue hardship, obtain their substantial equivalent by other means.

(B) *Protection Against Disclosure.* If the court orders discovery of those materials, it must protect against disclosure of the mental impressions, conclusions, opinions, or legal theories of a party's attorney or other representative concerning the litigation.

(C) *Previous Statement.* Any party or other person may, on request and without the required showing, obtain the person's own previous statement about the action or its subject matter. If the request is refused, the person may move for a court order, and Rule 37(a)(5) applies to the award of expenses. A previous statement is either: (i) a written statement that the person has signed or otherwise adopted or approved; or (ii) a contemporaneous stenographic, mechanical, electrical, or other recording—or a transcription of it—that recites substantially verbatim the person's oral statement.

(4) *Trial Preparation: Experts.*

(A) *Deposition of an Expert Who May Testify.* A party may depose any person who has been identified as an expert whose opinions may be presented at trial. If Rule 26(a)(2)(B) requires a report from the expert, the deposition may be conducted only after the report is provided.

(B) *Trial-Preparation Protection for Draft Reports or Disclosures.* Rules 26(b)(3)(A) and (B) protect drafts of any report or disclosure required under Rule 26(a)(2), regardless of the form in which the draft is recorded.

(C) *Trial-Preparation Protection for Communications Between a Party's Attorney and Expert Witnesses.* Rules 26(b)(3)(A) and (B) protect communications between the party's attorney and any witness required to provide a report under Rule 26(a)(2)(B), regardless of the form of the communications, except to the extent that the communications: (i) relate to compensation for the expert's study or testimony; (ii) identify facts or data that the party's attorney provided and that the expert considered in forming the opinions to be expressed; or (iii) identify assumptions that the party's attorney provided and that the expert relied on in forming the opinions to be expressed.

(D) *Expert Employed Only for Trial Preparation.* Ordinarily, a party may not, by interrogatories or deposition, discover facts known or opinions held by an expert who has been retained or specially employed by another party in anticipation of litigation or to prepare for trial and who is not expected to be called as a witness at trial. But a party may do so only: (i) as provided in Rule 35(b); or (ii) on showing exceptional circumstances under which it is impracticable for the party to obtain facts or opinions on the same subject by other means.

(E) *Payment.* Unless manifest injustice would result, the court must require that the party seeking discovery: (i) pay the expert a reasonable fee for time spent in responding to discovery under Rule 26(b)(4)(A) or (D); and (ii) for discovery under (D), also pay the other party a fair portion of the fees and expenses it reasonably incurred in obtaining the expert's facts and opinions.

(5) *Claiming Privilege or Protecting Trial-Preparation Materials.*

(A) *Information Withheld.* When a party withholds information otherwise discoverable by claiming that the information is privileged or subject to protection as trial-preparation material, the party must: (i) expressly make the claim; and (ii) describe the nature of the documents, communications, or tangible things not produced or disclosed—and do so in a manner that, without revealing information itself privileged or protected, will enable other parties to assess the claim.

(B) *Information Produced.* If information produced in discovery is subject to a claim of privilege or of protection as trial-preparation material, the party making the claim may notify any party that received the information of the claim and the basis for it. After being notified, a party must promptly return, sequester, or destroy the specified information and any copies it has; must not use or disclose the information until the claim is resolved; must take reasonable steps to retrieve the information if the party disclosed it before being notified; and may promptly present the information to the court under seal for a determination of the claim. The producing party must preserve the information until the claim is resolved.

(c) PROTECTIVE ORDERS.

(1) *In General.* A party or any person from whom discovery is sought may move for a protective order in the court where the action is pending—or as an alternative on matters relating to a deposition, in the court for the district where the deposition will be taken. The motion must include a certification that the movant has in good faith conferred or attempted to confer with other affected parties in an effort to resolve the dispute without court action. The court may, for good cause, issue an order to protect a party or person from annoyance, embarrassment, oppression, or undue burden or expense, including one or more of the following:

(A) forbidding the disclosure or discovery;

(B) specifying terms, including time and place, for the disclosure or discovery;

(C) prescribing a discovery method other than the one selected by the party seeking discovery;

(D) forbidding inquiry into certain matters, or limiting the scope of disclosure or discovery to certain matters;

(E) designating the persons who may be present while the discovery is conducted;

(F) requiring that a deposition be sealed and opened only on court order;

(G) requiring that a trade secret or other confidential research, development, or commercial information not be revealed or be revealed only in a specified way; and

(H) requiring that the parties simultaneously file specified documents or information in sealed envelopes, to be opened as the court directs.

(2) *Ordering Discovery.* If a motion for a protective order is wholly or partly denied, the court may, on just terms, order that any party or person provide or permit discovery.

(3) *Awarding Expenses.* Rule 37(a)(5) applies to the award of expenses.

(d) TIMING AND SEQUENCE OF DISCOVERY.

(1) *Timing.* A party may not seek discovery from any source before the parties have conferred as required by Rule 26(f), except in a proceeding exempted from initial disclosure under Rule 26(a)(1)(B), or when authorized by these rules, by stipulation, or by court order.

(2) *Sequence.* Unless, on motion, the court orders otherwise for the parties' and witnesses' convenience and in the interests of justice:

(A) methods of discovery may be used in any sequence; and

(B) discovery by one party does not require any other party to delay its discovery.

(e) SUPPLEMENTING DISCLOSURES AND RESPONSES.

    (1) *In General.* A party who has made a disclosure under Rule 26(a)—or who has responded to an interrogatory, request for production, or request for admission—must supplement or correct its disclosure or response:

        (A) in a timely manner if the party learns that in some material respect the disclosure or response is incomplete or incorrect, and if the additional or corrective information has not otherwise been made known to the other parties during the discovery process or in writing; or

        (B) as ordered by the court.

    (2) *Expert Witness.* For an expert whose report must be disclosed under Rule 26(a)(2)(B), the party's duty to supplement extends both to information included in the report and to information given during the expert's deposition. Any additions or changes to this information must be disclosed by the time the party's pretrial disclosures under Rule 26(a)(3) are due.

(f) CONFERENCE OF THE PARTIES; PLANNING FOR DISCOVERY.

    (1) *Conference Timing.* Except in a proceeding exempted from initial disclosure under Rule 26(a)(1)(B) or when the court orders otherwise, the parties must confer as soon as practicable—and in any event at least 21 days before a scheduling conference is to be held or a scheduling order is due under Rule 16(b).

    (2) *Conference Content; Parties' Responsibilities.* In conferring, the parties must consider the nature and basis of their claims and defenses and the possibilities for promptly settling or resolving the case; make or arrange for the disclosures required by Rule 26(a)(1); discuss any issues about preserving discoverable information; and develop a proposed discovery plan. The attorneys of record and all unrepresented parties that have appeared in the case are jointly responsible for arranging the conference, for attempting in good faith to agree on the proposed discovery plan, and for submitting to the court within 14 days after the conference a written report outlining the plan. The court may order the parties or attorneys to attend the conference in person.

    (3) *Discovery Plan.* A discovery plan must state the parties' views and proposals on:

        (A) what changes should be made in the timing, form, or requirement for disclosures under Rule 26(a), including a statement of when initial disclosures were made or will be made;

        (B) the subjects on which discovery may be needed, when discovery should be completed, and whether discovery should be conducted in phases or be limited to or focused on particular issues;

        (C) any issues about disclosure or discovery of electronically stored information, including the form or forms in which it should be produced;

        (D) any issues about claims of privilege or of protection as trial-preparation materials, including—if the parties agree on a procedure to assert these claims after production—whether to ask the court to include their agreement in an order;

        (E) what changes should be made in the limitations on discovery imposed under these rules or by local rule, and what other limitations should be imposed; and

        (F) any other orders that the court should issue under Rule 26(c) or under Rule 16(b) and (c).

    (4) *Expedited Schedule.* If necessary to comply with its expedited schedule for Rule 16(b) conferences, a court may by local rule:

        (A) require the parties' conference to occur less than 21 days before the scheduling conference is held or a scheduling order is due under Rule 16(b); and

(B) require the written report outlining the discovery plan to be filed less than 14 days after the parties' conference, or excuse the parties from submitting a written report and permit them to report orally on their discovery plan at the Rule 16(b) conference.

(g) SIGNING DISCLOSURES AND DISCOVERY REQUESTS, RESPONSES, AND OBJECTIONS.

(1) *Signature Required; Effect of Signature.* Every disclosure under Rule 26(a)(1) or (a)(3) and every discovery request, response, or objection must be signed by at least one attorney of record in the attorney's own name—or by the party personally, if unrepresented—and must state the signer's address, email address, and telephone number. By signing, an attorney or party certifies that to the best of the person's knowledge, information, and belief formed after a reasonable inquiry:
> (A) with respect to a disclosure, it is complete and correct as of the time it is made; and
> (B) with respect to a discovery request, response, or objection, it is:
>> (i) consistent with these rules and warranted by existing law or by a nonfrivolous argument for extending, modifying, or reversing existing law, or for establishing new law;
>> (ii) not interposed for any improper purpose, such as to harass, cause unnecessary delay, or needlessly increase the cost of litigation; and
>> (iii) neither unreasonable nor unduly burdensome or expensive, considering the needs of the case, prior discovery in the case, the amount in controversy, and the importance of the issues at stake in the action.

(2) *Failure to Sign.* Other parties have no duty to act on an unsigned disclosure, request, response, or objection until it is signed, and the court must strike it unless a signature is promptly supplied after the omission is called to the attorney's or party's attention.

(3) *Sanction for Improper Certification.* If a certification violates this rule without substantial justification, the court, on motion or on its own, must impose an appropriate sanction on the signer, the party on whose behalf the signer was acting, or both. The sanction may include an order to pay the reasonable expenses, including attorney's fees, caused by the violation.

Rule 27. Depositions to Perpetuate Testimony

(a) BEFORE AN ACTION IS FILED.

(1) *Petition.* A person who wants to perpetuate testimony about any matter cognizable in a United States court may file a verified petition in the district court for the district where any expected adverse party resides. The petition must ask for an order authorizing the petitioner to depose the named persons in order to perpetuate their testimony. The petition must be titled in the petitioner's name and must show:
> (A) that the petitioner expects to be a party to an action cognizable in a United States court but cannot presently bring it or cause it to be brought;
> (B) the subject matter of the expected action and the petitioner's interest;
> (C) the facts that the petitioner wants to establish by the proposed testimony and the reasons to perpetuate it;
> (D) the names or a description of the persons whom the petitioner expects to be adverse parties and their addresses, so far as known; and
> (E) the name, address, and expected substance of the testimony of each deponent.

(2) *Notice and Service.* At least 21 days before the hearing date, the petitioner must serve each expected adverse party with a copy of the petition and a notice stating the time and place of the hearing. The notice may be served either inside or outside the district or state in the manner

provided in Rule 4. If that service cannot be made with reasonable diligence on an expected adverse party, the court may order service by publication or otherwise. The court must appoint an attorney to represent persons not served in the manner provided in Rule 4 and to cross-examine the deponent if an unserved person is not otherwise represented. If any expected adverse party is a minor or is incompetent, Rule 17(c) applies.

(3) *Order and Examination.* If satisfied that perpetuating the testimony may prevent a failure or delay of justice, the court must issue an order that designates or describes the persons whose depositions may be taken, specifies the subject matter of the examinations, and states whether the depositions will be taken orally or by written interrogatories. The depositions may then be taken under these rules, and the court may issue orders like those authorized by Rules 34 and 35. A reference in these rules to the court where an action is pending means, for purposes of this rule, the court where the petition for the deposition was filed.

(4) *Using the Deposition.* A deposition to perpetuate testimony may be used under Rule 32(a) in any later-filed district court action involving the same subject matter if the deposition either was taken under these rules or, although not so taken, would be admissible in evidence in the courts of the state where it was taken.

(b) PENDING APPEAL.

(1) *In General.* The court where a judgment has been rendered may, if an appeal has been taken or may still be taken, permit a party to depose witnesses to perpetuate their testimony for use in the event of further proceedings in that court.

(2) *Motion.* The party who wants to perpetuate testimony may move for leave to take the depositions, on the same notice and service as if the action were pending in the district court. The motion must show:

> (A) the name, address, and expected substance of the testimony of each deponent; and
> (B) the reasons for perpetuating the testimony.

(3) *Court Order.* If the court finds that perpetuating the testimony may prevent a failure or delay of justice, the court may permit the depositions to be taken and may issue orders like those authorized by Rules 34 and 35. The depositions may be taken and used as any other deposition taken in a pending district court action.

(c) PERPETUATION BY AN ACTION. This rule does not limit a court's power to entertain an action to perpetuate testimony.

Rule 28. Persons Before Whom Depositions May Be Taken

(a) WITHIN THE UNITED STATES.

(1) *In General.* Within the United States or a territory or insular possession subject to United States jurisdiction, a deposition must be taken before:

> (A) an officer authorized to administer oaths either by federal law or by the law in the place of examination; or
> (B) a person appointed by the court where the action is pending to administer oaths and take testimony.

(2) *Definition of "Officer."* The term "officer" in Rules 30, 31, and 32 includes a person appointed by the court under this rule or designated by the parties under Rule 29(a).

(b) IN A FOREIGN COUNTRY.

(1) *In General.* A deposition may be taken in a foreign country:

(A) under an applicable treaty or convention;

(B) under a letter of request, whether or not captioned a ''letter rogatory'';

(C) on notice, before a person authorized to administer oaths either by federal law or by the law in the place of examination; or

(D) before a person commissioned by the court to administer any necessary oath and take testimony.

(2) *Issuing a Letter of Request or a Commission.* A letter of request, a commission, or both may be issued:

(A) on appropriate terms after an application and notice of it; and

(B) without a showing that taking the deposition in another manner is impracticable or inconvenient.

(3) *Form of a Request, Notice, or Commission.* When a letter of request or any other device is used according to a treaty or convention, it must be captioned in the form prescribed by that treaty or convention. A letter of request may be addressed ''To the Appropriate Authority in [name of country].'' A deposition notice or a commission must designate by name or descriptive title the person before whom the deposition is to be taken.

(4) *Letter of Request—Admitting Evidence.* Evidence obtained in response to a letter of request need not be excluded merely because it is not a verbatim transcript, because the testimony was not taken under oath, or because of any similar departure from the requirements for depositions taken within the United States.

(c) DISQUALIFICATION. A deposition must not be taken before a person who is any party's relative, employee, or attorney; who is related to or employed by any party's attorney; or who is financially interested in the action.

Rule 29. Stipulations About Discovery Procedure

Unless the court orders otherwise, the parties may stipulate that:

(a) a deposition may be taken before any person, at any time or place, on any notice, and in the manner specified—in which event it may be used in the same way as any other deposition; and

(b) other procedures governing or limiting discovery be modified—but a stipulation extending the time for any form of discovery must have court approval if it would interfere with the time set for completing discovery, for hearing a motion, or for trial.

Rule 30. Depositions by Oral Examination

(a) WHEN A DEPOSITION MAY BE TAKEN.

(1) *Without Leave.* A party may, by oral questions, depose any person, including a party, without leave of court except as provided in Rule 30(a)(2). The deponent's attendance may be compelled by subpoena under Rule 45.

(2) *With Leave.* A party must obtain leave of court, and the court must grant leave to the extent consistent with Rule 26(b)(2):

(A) if the parties have not stipulated to the deposition and:

    (i) the deposition would result in more than 10 depositions being taken under this rule or Rule 31 by the plaintiffs, or by the defendants, or by the third-party defendants;

    (ii) the deponent has already been deposed in the case; or

    (iii) the party seeks to take the deposition before the time specified in Rule 26(d), unless the party certifies in the notice, with supporting facts, that the deponent is expected to leave the United States and be unavailable for examination in this country after that time; or

(B) if the deponent is confined in prison.

(b) NOTICE OF THE DEPOSITION; OTHER FORMAL REQUIREMENTS.

(1) *Notice in General.* A party who wants to depose a person by oral questions must give reasonable written notice to every other party. The notice must state the time and place of the deposition and, if known, the deponent's name and address. If the name is unknown, the notice must provide a general description sufficient to identify the person or the particular class or group to which the person belongs.

(2) *Producing Documents.* If a subpoena duces tecum is to be served on the deponent, the materials designated for production, as set out in the subpoena, must be listed in the notice or in an attachment. The notice to a party deponent may be accompanied by a request under Rule 34 to produce documents and tangible things at the deposition.

(3) *Method of Recording.*

    (A) *Method Stated in the Notice.* The party who notices the deposition must state in the notice the method for recording the testimony. Unless the court orders otherwise, testimony may be recorded by audio, audiovisual, or stenographic means. The noticing party bears the recording costs. Any party may arrange to transcribe a deposition.

    (B) *Additional Method.* With prior notice to the deponent and other parties, any party may designate another method for recording the testimony in addition to that specified in the original notice. That party bears the expense of the additional record or transcript unless the court orders otherwise.

(4) *By Remote Means.* The parties may stipulate—or the court may on motion order—that a deposition be taken by telephone or other remote means. For the purpose of this rule and Rules 28(a), 37(a)(2), and 37(b)(1), the deposition takes place where the deponent answers the questions.

(5) *Officer's Duties.*

    (A) *Before the Deposition.* Unless the parties stipulate otherwise, a deposition must be conducted before an officer appointed or designated under Rule 28. The officer must begin the deposition with an on-the-record statement that includes:

        (i) the officer's name and business address;

        (ii) the date, time, and place of the deposition;

        (iii) the deponent's name;

        (iv) the officer's administration of the oath or affirmation to the deponent; and

        (v) the identity of all persons present.

    (B) *Conducting the Deposition; Avoiding Distortion.* If the deposition is recorded nonstenographically, the officer must repeat the items in Rule 30(b)(5)(A)(i)–(iii) at the beginning of each unit of the recording medium. The deponent's and attorneys' appearance or demeanor must not be distorted through recording techniques.

    (C) *After the Deposition.* At the end of a deposition, the officer must state on the record that the deposition is complete and must set out any stipulations made by the attorneys about custody of the transcript or recording and of the exhibits, or about any other pertinent matters.

(6) *Notice or Subpoena Directed to an Organization.* In its notice or subpoena, a party may name as the deponent a public or private corporation, a partnership, an association, a governmental agency, or other entity and must describe with reasonable particularity the matters for examination. The named organization must then designate one or more officers, directors, or managing agents, or designate other persons who consent to testify on its behalf; and it may set out the matters on which each person designated will testify. A subpoena must advise a nonparty organization of its duty to make this designation. The persons designated must testify about information known or reasonably available to the organization. This paragraph (6) does not preclude a deposition by any other procedure allowed by these rules.

(c) EXAMINATION AND CROSS-EXAMINATION; RECORD OF THE EXAMINATION; OBJECTIONS; WRITTEN QUESTIONS.

(1) *Examination and Cross-Examination.* The examination and cross-examination of a deponent proceed as they would at trial under the Federal Rules of Evidence, except Rules 103 and 615. After putting the deponent under oath or affirmation, the officer must record the testimony by the method designated under Rule 30(b)(3)(A). The testimony must be recorded by the officer personally or by a person acting in the presence and under the direction of the officer.

(2) *Objections.* An objection at the time of the examination—whether to evidence, to a party's conduct, to the officer's qualifications, to the manner of taking the deposition, or to any other aspect of the deposition—must be noted on the record, but the examination still proceeds; the testimony is taken subject to any objection. An objection must be stated concisely in a nonargumentative and nonsuggestive manner. A person may instruct a deponent not to answer only when necessary to preserve a privilege, to enforce a limitation ordered by the court, or to present a motion under Rule 30(d)(3).

(3) *Participating Through Written Questions.* Instead of participating in the oral examination, a party may serve written questions in a sealed envelope on the party noticing the deposition, who must deliver them to the officer. The officer must ask the deponent those questions and record the answers verbatim.

(d) DURATION; SANCTION; MOTION TO TERMINATE OR LIMIT.

(1) *Duration.* Unless otherwise stipulated or ordered by the court, a deposition is limited to 1 day of 7 hours. The court must allow additional time consistent with Rule 26(b)(2) if needed to fairly examine the deponent or if the deponent, another person, or any other circumstance impedes or delays the examination.

(2) *Sanction.* The court may impose an appropriate sanction—including the reasonable expenses and attorney's fees incurred by any party—on a person who impedes, delays, or frustrates the fair examination of the deponent.

(3) *Motion to Terminate or Limit.*

(A) *Grounds.* At any time during a deposition, the deponent or a party may move to terminate or limit it on the ground that it is being conducted in bad faith or in a manner that unreasonably annoys, embarrasses, or oppresses the deponent or party. The motion may be filed in the court where the action is pending or the deposition is being taken. If the objecting deponent or party so demands, the deposition must be suspended for the time necessary to obtain an order.

(B) *Order.* The court may order that the deposition be terminated or may limit its scope and manner as provided in Rule 26(c). If terminated, the deposition may be resumed only by order of the court where the action is pending.

(C) *Award of Expenses.* Rule 37(a)(5) applies to the award of expenses.

(e) REVIEW BY THE WITNESS; CHANGES.

(1) *Review; Statement of Changes.* On request by the deponent or a party before the deposition is completed, the deponent must be allowed 30 days after being notified by the officer that the transcript or recording is available in which:
(A) to review the transcript or recording; and
(B) if there are changes in form or substance, to sign a statement listing the changes and the reasons for making them.
(2) *Changes Indicated in the Officer's Certificate.* The officer must note in the certificate prescribed by Rule 30(f)(1) whether a review was requested and, if so, must attach any changes the deponent makes during the 30-day period.

(f) CERTIFICATION AND DELIVERY; EXHIBITS; COPIES OF THE TRANSCRIPT OR RECORDING; FILING.

(1) *Certification and Delivery.* The officer must certify in writing that the witness was duly sworn and that the deposition accurately records the witness's testimony. The certificate must accompany the record of the deposition. Unless the court orders otherwise, the officer must seal the deposition in an envelope or package bearing the title of the action and marked "Deposition of [witness's name]" and must promptly send it to the attorney who arranged for the transcript or recording. The attorney must store it under conditions that will protect it against loss, destruction, tampering, or deterioration.
(2) *Documents and Tangible Things.*
(A) *Originals and Copies.* Documents and tangible things produced for inspection during a deposition must, on a party's request, be marked for identification and attached to the deposition. Any party may inspect and copy them. But if the person who produced them wants to keep the originals, the person may:
(i) offer copies to be marked, attached to the deposition, and then used as originals—after giving all parties a fair opportunity to verify the copies by comparing them with the originals; or
(ii) give all parties a fair opportunity to inspect and copy the originals after they are marked—in which event the originals may be used as if attached to the deposition.
(B) *Order Regarding the Originals.* Any party may move for an order that the originals be attached to the deposition pending final disposition of the case.
(3) *Copies of the Transcript or Recording.* Unless otherwise stipulated or ordered by the court, the officer must retain the stenographic notes of a deposition taken stenographically or a copy of the recording of a deposition taken by another method. When paid reasonable charges, the officer must furnish a copy of the transcript or recording to any party or the deponent.
(4) *Notice of Filing.* A party who files the deposition must promptly notify all other parties of the filing.

(g) FAILURE TO ATTEND A DEPOSITION OR SERVE A SUBPOENA; EXPENSES.

A party who, expecting a deposition to be taken, attends in person or by an attorney may recover reasonable expenses for attending, including attorney's fees, if the noticing party failed to:

(1) attend and proceed with the deposition; or
(2) serve a subpoena on a nonparty deponent, who consequently did not attend.

Rule 31. Depositions by Written Questions

(a) WHEN A DEPOSITION MAY BE TAKEN.

(1) *Without Leave.* A party may, by written questions, depose any person, including a party, without leave of court except as provided in Rule 31(a)(2). The deponent's attendance may be compelled by subpoena under Rule 45.

(2) *With Leave.* A party must obtain leave of court, and the court must grant leave to the extent consistent with Rule 26(b)(2):

(A) if the parties have not stipulated to the deposition and:

(i) the deposition would result in more than 10 depositions being taken under this rule or Rule 30 by the plaintiffs, or by the defendants, or by the third-party defendants;

(ii) the deponent has already been deposed in the case; or

(iii) the party seeks to take a deposition before the time specified in Rule 26(d); or

(B) if the deponent is confined in prison.

(3) *Service; Required Notice.* A party who wants to depose a person by written questions must serve them on every other party, with a notice stating, if known, the deponent's name and address. If the name is unknown, the notice must provide a general description sufficient to identify the person or the particular class or group to which the person belongs. The notice must also state the name or descriptive title and the address of the officer before whom the deposition will be taken.

(4) *Questions Directed to an Organization.* A public or private corporation, a partnership, an association, or a governmental agency may be deposed by written questions in accordance with Rule 30(b)(6).

(5) *Questions from Other Parties.* Any questions to the deponent from other parties must be served on all parties as follows: cross-questions, within 14 days after being served with the notice and direct questions; redirect questions, within 7 days after being served with cross-questions; and recross-questions, within 7 days after being served with redirect questions. The court may, for good cause, extend or shorten these times.

(b) DELIVERY TO THE OFFICER; OFFICER'S DUTIES. The party who noticed the deposition must deliver to the officer a copy of all the questions served and of the notice. The officer must promptly proceed in the manner provided in Rule 30(c), (e), and (f) to:

(1) take the deponent's testimony in response to the questions;

(2) prepare and certify the deposition; and

(3) send it to the party, attaching a copy of the questions and of the notice.

(c) NOTICE OF COMPLETION OR FILING.

(1) *Completion.* The party who noticed the deposition must notify all other parties when it is completed.

(2) *Filing.* A party who files the deposition must promptly notify all other parties of the filing.

Rule 32. Using Depositions in Court Proceedings

(a) USING DEPOSITIONS.

(1) *In General.* At a hearing or trial, all or part of a deposition may be used against a party on these conditions:
> (A) the party was present or represented at the taking of the deposition or had reasonable notice of it;
> (B) it is used to the extent it would be admissible under the Federal Rules of Evidence if the deponent were present and testifying; and
> (C) the use is allowed by Rule 32(a)(2) through (8).

(2) *Impeachment and Other Uses.* Any party may use a deposition to contradict or impeach the testimony given by the deponent as a witness, or for any other purpose allowed by the Federal Rules of Evidence.

(3) *Deposition of Party, Agent, or Designee.* An adverse party may use for any purpose the deposition of a party or anyone who, when deposed, was the party's officer, director, managing agent, or designee under Rule 30(b)(6) or 31(a)(4).

(4) *Unavailable Witness.* A party may use for any purpose the deposition of a witness, whether or not a party, if the court finds:
> (A) that the witness is dead;
> (B) that the witness is more than 100 miles from the place of hearing or trial or is outside the United States, unless it appears that the witness's absence was procured by the party offering the deposition;
> (C) that the witness cannot attend or testify because of age, illness, infirmity, or imprisonment;
> (D) that the party offering the deposition could not procure the witness's attendance by subpoena; or
> (E) on motion and notice, that exceptional circumstances make it desirable—in the interest of justice and with due regard to the importance of live testimony in open court—to permit the deposition to be used.

(5) *Limitations on Use.*
> (A) *Deposition Taken on Short Notice.* A deposition must not be used against a party who, having received less than 14 days' notice of the deposition, promptly moved for a protective order under Rule 26(c)(1)(B) requesting that it not be taken or be taken at a different time or place—and this motion was still pending when the deposition was taken.
> (B) *Unavailable Deponent; Party Could Not Obtain an Attorney.* A deposition taken without leave of court under the unavailability provision of Rule 30(a)(2)(A)(iii) must not be used against a party who shows that, when served with the notice, it could not, despite diligent efforts, obtain an attorney to represent it at the deposition.

(6) *Using Part of a Deposition.* If a party offers in evidence only part of a deposition, an adverse party may require the offeror to introduce other parts that in fairness should be considered with the part introduced, and any party may itself introduce any other parts.

(7) *Substituting a Party.* Substituting a party under Rule 25 does not affect the right to use a deposition previously taken.

(8) *Deposition Taken in an Earlier Action.* A deposition lawfully taken and, if required, filed in any federal- or state-court action may be used in a later action involving the same subject matter between the same parties, or their representatives or successors in interest, to the same extent as if taken in the later action. A deposition previously taken may also be used as allowed by the Federal Rules of Evidence.

(b) OBJECTIONS TO ADMISSIBILITY. Subject to Rules 28(b) and 32(d)(3), an objection may be made at a hearing or trial to the admission of any deposition testimony that would be inadmissible if the witness were present and testifying.

(c) FORM OF PRESENTATION. Unless the court orders otherwise, a party must provide a transcript of any deposition testimony the party offers, but may provide the court with the testimony in nontranscript form as well. On any party's request, deposition testimony offered in a jury trial for any purpose other than impeachment must be presented in nontranscript form, if available, unless the court for good cause orders otherwise.

(d) WAIVER OF OBJECTIONS.

(1) *To the Notice.* An objection to an error or irregularity in a deposition notice is waived unless promptly served in writing on the party giving the notice.

(2) *To the Officer's Qualification.* An objection based on disqualification of the officer before whom a deposition is to be taken is waived if not made:
   (A) before the deposition begins; or
   (B) promptly after the basis for disqualification becomes known or, with reasonable diligence, could have been known.

(3) *To the Taking of the Deposition.*
   (A) *Objection to Competence, Relevance, or Materiality.* An objection to a deponent's competence—or to the competence, relevance, or materiality of testimony—is not waived by a failure to make the objection before or during the deposition, unless the ground for it might have been corrected at that time.
   (B) *Objection to an Error or Irregularity.* An objection to an error or irregularity at an oral examination is waived if:
      (i) it relates to the manner of taking the deposition, the form of a question or answer, the oath or affirmation, a party's conduct, or other matters that might have been corrected at that time; and
      (ii) it is not timely made during the deposition.
   (C) *Objection to a Written Question.* An objection to the form of a written question under Rule 31 is waived if not served in writing on the party submitting the question within the time for serving responsive questions or, if the question is a recross-question, within 7 days after being served with it.

(4) *To Completing and Returning the Deposition.* An objection to how the officer transcribed the testimony—or prepared, signed, certified, sealed, endorsed, sent, or otherwise dealt with the deposition—is waived unless a motion to suppress is made promptly after the error or irregularity becomes known or, with reasonable diligence, could have been known.

Rule 33. Interrogatories to Parties

(a) IN GENERAL.

(1) *Number.* Unless otherwise stipulated or ordered by the court, a party may serve on any other party no more than 25 written interrogatories, including all discrete subparts. Leave to serve additional interrogatories may be granted to the extent consistent with Rule 26(b)(2).

(2) *Scope.* An interrogatory may relate to any matter that may be inquired into under Rule 26(b). An interrogatory is not objectionable merely because it asks for an opinion or contention that relates to fact or the application of law to fact, but the court may order that the interrogatory need

not be answered until designated discovery is complete, or until a pretrial conference or some other time.

(b) ANSWERS AND OBJECTIONS.

(1) *Responding Party.* The interrogatories must be answered:
(A) by the party to whom they are directed; or
(B) if that party is a public or private corporation, a partnership, an association, or a governmental agency, by any officer or agent, who must furnish the information available to the party.

(2) *Time to Respond.* The responding party must serve its answers and any objections within 30 days after being served with the interrogatories. A shorter or longer time may be stipulated to under Rule 29 or be ordered by the court.

(3) *Answering Each Interrogatory.* Each interrogatory must, to the extent it is not objected to, be answered separately and fully in writing under oath.

(4) *Objections.* The grounds for objecting to an interrogatory must be stated with specificity. Any ground not stated in a timely objection is waived unless the court, for good cause, excuses the failure.

(5) *Signature.* The person who makes the answers must sign them, and the attorney who objects must sign any objections.

(c) USE. An answer to an interrogatory may be used to the extent allowed by the Federal Rules of Evidence.

(d) OPTION TO PRODUCE BUSINESS RECORDS. If the answer to an interrogatory may be determined by examining, auditing, compiling, abstracting, or summarizing a party's business records (including electronically stored information), and if the burden of deriving or ascertaining the answer will be substantially the same for either party, the responding party may answer by:

(1) specifying the records that must be reviewed, in sufficient detail to enable the interrogating party to locate and identify them as readily as the responding party could; and
(2) giving the interrogating party a reasonable opportunity to examine and audit the records and to make copies, compilations, abstracts, or summaries.

Rule 34. Producing Documents, Electronically Stored Information, and Tangible Things, or Entering onto Land, for Inspection and Other Purposes

(a) IN GENERAL. A party may serve on any other party a request within the scope of Rule 26(b):

(1) to produce and permit the requesting party or its representative to inspect, copy, test, or sample the following items in the responding party's possession, custody, or control:
(A) any designated documents or electronically stored information—including writings, drawings, graphs, charts, photographs, sound recordings, images, and other data or data compilations—stored in any medium from which information can be obtained either directly or, if necessary, after translation by the responding party into a reasonably usable form; or
(B) any designated tangible things; or
(2) to permit entry onto designated land or other property possessed or controlled by the responding party, so that the requesting party may inspect, measure, survey, photograph, test, or sample the property or any designated object or operation on it.

(b) PROCEDURE.

(1) *Contents of the Request.* The request:
    (A) must describe with reasonable particularity each item or category of items to be inspected;
    (B) must specify a reasonable time, place, and manner for the inspection and for performing the related acts; and
    (C) may specify the form or forms in which electronically stored information is to be produced.

(2) *Responses and Objections.*
    (A) *Time to Respond.* The party to whom the request is directed must respond in writing within 30 days after being served. A shorter or longer time may be stipulated to under Rule 29 or be ordered by the court.
    (B) *Responding to Each Item.* For each item or category, the response must either state that inspection and related activities will be permitted as requested or state an objection to the request, including the reasons.
    (C) *Objections.* An objection to part of a request must specify the part and permit inspection of the rest.
    (D) *Responding to a Request for Production of Electronically Stored Information.* The response may state an objection to a requested form for producing electronically stored information. If the responding party objects to a requested form— or if no form was specified in the request—the party must state the form or forms it intends to use.
    (E) *Producing the Documents or Electronically Stored Information.* Unless otherwise stipulated or ordered by the court, these procedures apply to producing documents or electronically stored information:
        (i) A party must produce documents as they are kept in the usual course of business or must organize and label them to correspond to the categories in the request;
        (ii) If a request does not specify a form for producing electronically stored information, a party must produce it in a form or forms in which it is ordinarily maintained or in a reasonably usable form or forms; and
        (iii) A party need not produce the same electronically stored information in more than one form.

(c) NONPARTIES. As provided in Rule 45, a nonparty may be compelled to produce documents and tangible things or to permit an inspection.

Rule 35. Physical and Mental Examinations

(a) ORDER FOR AN EXAMINATION.

(1) *In General.* The court where the action is pending may order a party whose mental or physical condition—including blood group—is in controversy to submit to a physical or mental examination by a suitably licensed or certified examiner. The court has the same authority to order a party to produce for examination a person who is in its custody or under its legal control.

(2) *Motion and Notice; Contents of the Order.* The order:
    (A) may be made only on motion for good cause and on notice to all parties and the person to be examined; and

(B) must specify the time, place, manner, conditions, and scope of the examination, as well as the person or persons who will perform it.

(b) EXAMINER'S REPORT.

(1) *Request by the Party or Person Examined.* The party who moved for the examination must, on request, deliver to the requester a copy of the examiner's report, together with like reports of all earlier examinations of the same condition. The request may be made by the party against whom the examination order was issued or by the person examined.

(2) *Contents.* The examiner's report must be in writing and must set out in detail the examiner's findings, including diagnoses, conclusions, and the results of any tests.

(3) *Request by the Moving Party.* After delivering the reports, the party who moved for the examination may request—and is entitled to receive—from the party against whom the examination order was issued like reports of all earlier or later examinations of the same condition. But those reports need not be delivered by the party with custody or control of the person examined if the party shows that it could not obtain them.

(4) *Waiver of Privilege.* By requesting and obtaining the examiner's report, or by deposing the examiner, the party examined waives any privilege it may have—in that action or any other action involving the same controversy—concerning testimony about all examinations of the same condition.

(5) *Failure to Deliver a Report.* The court on motion may order—on just terms—that a party deliver the report of an examination. If the report is not provided, the court may exclude the examiner's testimony at trial.

(6) *Scope.* This subdivision (b) applies also to an examination made by the parties' agreement, unless the agreement states otherwise. This subdivision does not preclude obtaining an examiner's report or deposing an examiner under other rules.

Rule 36. Requests for Admission

(a) SCOPE AND PROCEDURE.

(1) *Scope.* A party may serve on any other party a written request to admit, for purposes of the pending action only, the truth of any matters within the scope of Rule 26(b)(1) relating to:
    (A) facts, the application of law to fact, or opinions about either; and
    (B) the genuineness of any described documents.

(2) *Form; Copy of a Document.* Each matter must be separately stated. A request to admit the genuineness of a document must be accompanied by a copy of the document unless it is, or has been, otherwise furnished or made available for inspection and copying.

(3) *Time to Respond; Effect of Not Responding.* A matter is admitted unless, within 30 days after being served, the party to whom the request is directed serves on the requesting party a written answer or objection addressed to the matter and signed by the party or its attorney. A shorter or longer time for responding may be stipulated to under Rule 29 or be ordered by the court.

(4) *Answer.* If a matter is not admitted, the answer must specifically deny it or state in detail why the answering party cannot truthfully admit or deny it. A denial must fairly respond to the substance of the matter; and when good faith requires that a party qualify an answer or deny only a part of a matter, the answer must specify the part admitted and qualify or deny the rest. The answering party may assert lack of knowledge or information as a reason for failing to admit or deny only if the party states that it has made reasonable inquiry and that the information it knows or can readily obtain is insufficient to enable it to admit or deny.

(5) *Objections.* The grounds for objecting to a request must be stated. A party must not object solely on the ground that the request presents a genuine issue for trial.

(6) *Motion Regarding the Sufficiency of an Answer or Objection.* The requesting party may move to determine the sufficiency of an answer or objection. Unless the court finds an objection justified, it must order that an answer be served. On finding that an answer does not comply with this rule, the court may order either that the matter is admitted or that an amended answer be served. The court may defer its final decision until a pretrial conference or a specified time before trial. Rule 37(a)(5) applies to an award of expenses.

(b) EFFECT OF AN ADMISSION; WITHDRAWING OR AMENDING IT. A matter admitted under this rule is conclusively established unless the court, on motion, permits the admission to be withdrawn or amended. Subject to Rule 16(e), the court may permit withdrawal or amendment if it would promote the presentation of the merits of the action and if the court is not persuaded that it would prejudice the requesting party in maintaining or defending the action on the merits. An admission under this rule is not an admission for any other purpose and cannot be used against the party in any other proceeding.

Rule 37. Failure to Make Disclosures or to Cooperate in Discovery; Sanctions

(a) MOTION FOR AN ORDER COMPELLING DISCLOSURE OR DISCOVERY.

(1) *In General.* On notice to other parties and all affected persons, a party may move for an order compelling disclosure or discovery. The motion must include a certification that the movant has in good faith conferred or attempted to confer with the person or party failing to make disclosure or discovery in an effort to obtain it without court action.

(2) *Appropriate Court.* A motion for an order to a party must be made in the court where the action is pending. A motion for an order to a nonparty must be made in the court where the discovery is or will be taken.

(3) *Specific Motions.*

(A) *To Compel Disclosure.* If a party fails to make a disclosure required by Rule 26(a), any other party may move to compel disclosure and for appropriate sanctions.

(B) *To Compel a Discovery Response.* A party seeking discovery may move for an order compelling an answer, designation, production, or inspection. This motion may be made if:

(i) a deponent fails to answer a question asked under Rule 30 or 31;

(ii) a corporation or other entity fails to make a designation under Rule 30(b)(6) or 31(a)(4);

(iii) a party fails to answer an interrogatory submitted under Rule 33; or

(iv) a party fails to respond that inspection will be permitted—or fails to permit inspection—as requested under Rule 34.

(C) *Related to a Deposition.* When taking an oral deposition, the party asking a question may complete or adjourn the examination before moving for an order.

(4) *Evasive or Incomplete Disclosure, Answer, or Response.* For purposes of this subdivision (a), an evasive or incomplete disclosure, answer, or response must be treated as a failure to disclose, answer, or respond.

(5) *Payment of Expenses; Protective Orders.*

(A) *If the Motion Is Granted (or Disclosure or Discovery Is Provided After Filing).* If the motion is granted—or if the disclosure or requested discovery is provided after the motion was filed—the court must, after giving an opportunity to be heard, require the party or deponent whose conduct necessitated the motion, the party or attorney advising that conduct, or both to pay the movant's reasonable expenses incurred in making the motion, including attorney's fees. But the court must not order this payment if:

> (i) the movant filed the motion before attempting in good faith to obtain the disclosure or discovery without court action;
>
> (ii) the opposing party's nondisclosure, response, or objection was substantially justified; or
>
> (iii) other circumstances make an award of expenses unjust.

(B) *If the Motion Is Denied.* If the motion is denied, the court may issue any protective order authorized under Rule 26(c) and must, after giving an opportunity to be heard, require the movant, the attorney filing the motion, or both to pay the party or deponent who opposed the motion its reasonable expenses incurred in opposing the motion, including attorney's fees. But the court must not order this payment if the motion was substantially justified or other circumstances make an award of expenses unjust.

(C) *If the Motion Is Granted in Part and Denied in Part.* If the motion is granted in part and denied in part, the court may issue any protective order authorized under Rule 26(c) and may, after giving an opportunity to be heard, apportion the reasonable expenses for the motion.

(b) FAILURE TO COMPLY WITH A COURT ORDER.

(1) *Sanctions in the District Where the Deposition Is Taken.* If the court where the discovery is taken orders a deponent to be sworn or to answer a question and the deponent fails to obey, the failure may be treated as contempt of court.

(2) *Sanctions in the District Where the Action Is Pending.*

> (A) *For Not Obeying a Discovery Order.* If a party or a party's officer, director, or managing agent—or a witness designated under Rule 30(b)(6) or 31(a)(4)—fails to obey an order to provide or permit discovery, including an order under Rule 26(f), 35, or 37(a), the court where the action is pending may issue further just orders. They may include the following:
>
>> (i) directing that the matters embraced in the order or other designated facts be taken as established for purposes of the action, as the prevailing party claims;
>>
>> (ii) prohibiting the disobedient party from supporting or opposing designated claims or defenses, or from introducing designated matters in evidence;
>>
>> (iii) striking pleadings in whole or in part;
>>
>> (iv) staying further proceedings until the order is obeyed;
>>
>> (v) dismissing the action or proceeding in whole or in part;
>>
>> (vi) rendering a default judgment against the disobedient party; or
>>
>> (vii) treating as contempt of court the failure to obey any order except an order to submit to a physical or mental examination.
>
> (B) *For Not Producing a Person for Examination.* If a party fails to comply with an order under Rule 35(a) requiring it to produce another person for examination, the court may issue any of the orders listed in Rule 37(b)(2)(A)(i)–(vi), unless the disobedient party shows that it cannot produce the other person.
>
> (C) *Payment of Expenses.* Instead of or in addition to the orders above, the court must order the disobedient party, the attorney advising that party, or both to pay the reasonable expenses, including attorney's fees, caused by the failure, unless the failure was substantially justified or other circumstances make an award of expenses unjust.

(c) FAILURE TO DISCLOSE, TO SUPPLEMENT AN EARLIER RESPONSE, OR TO ADMIT.

(1) *Failure to Disclose or Supplement.* If a party fails to provide information or identify a witness as required by Rule 26(a) or (e), the party is not allowed to use that information or witness to supply evidence on a motion, at a hearing, or at a trial, unless the failure was substantially justified or is harmless. In addition to or instead of this sanction, the court, on motion and after giving an opportunity to be heard:

(A) may order payment of the reasonable expenses, including attorney's fees, caused by the failure;

(B) may inform the jury of the party's failure; and

(C) may impose other appropriate sanctions, including any of the orders listed in Rule 37(b)(2)(A)(i)–(vi).

(2) *Failure to Admit.* If a party fails to admit what is requested under Rule 36 and if the requesting party later proves a document to be genuine or the matter true, the requesting party may move that the party who failed to admit pay the reasonable expenses, including attorney's fees, incurred in making that proof. The court must so order unless:

(A) the request was held objectionable under Rule 36(a);

(B) the admission sought was of no substantial importance;

(C) the party failing to admit had a reasonable ground to believe that it might prevail on the matter; or

(D) there was other good reason for the failure to admit.

(d) PARTY'S FAILURE TO ATTEND ITS OWN DEPOSITION, SERVE ANSWERS TO INTERROGATORIES, OR RESPOND TO A REQUEST FOR INSPECTION.

(1) *In General.*

(A) *Motion; Grounds for Sanctions.* The court where the action is pending may, on motion, order sanctions if:

(i) a party or a party's officer, director, or managing agent—or a person designated under Rule 30(b)(6) or 31(a)(4)—fails, after being served with proper notice, to appear for that person's deposition; or

(ii) a party, after being properly served with interrogatories under Rule 33 or a request for inspection under Rule 34, fails to serve its answers, objections, or written response.

(B) *Certification.* A motion for sanctions for failing to answer or respond must include a certification that the movant has in good faith conferred or attempted to confer with the party failing to act in an effort to obtain the answer or response without court action.

(2) *Unacceptable Excuse for Failing to Act.* A failure described in Rule 37(d)(1)(A) is not excused on the ground that the discovery sought was objectionable, unless the party failing to act has a pending motion for a protective order under Rule 26(c).

(3) *Types of Sanctions.* Sanctions may include any of the orders listed in Rule 37(b)(2)(A)(i)–(vi). Instead of or in addition to these sanctions, the court must require the party failing to act, the attorney advising that party, or both to pay the reasonable expenses, including attorney's fees, caused by the failure, unless the failure was substantially justified or other circumstances make an award of expenses unjust.

(e) FAILURE TO PROVIDE ELECTRONICALLY STORED INFORMATION. Absent exceptional circumstances, a court may not impose sanctions under these rules on a party for failing to provide electronically stored information lost as a result of the routine, good-faith operation of an electronic information system.

(f) FAILURE TO PARTICIPATE IN FRAMING A DISCOVERY PLAN. If a party or its attorney fails to participate in good faith in developing and submitting a proposed discovery plan as required by Rule 26(f), the court may, after giving an opportunity to be heard, require that party or attorney to pay to any other party the reasonable expenses, including attorney's fees, caused by the failure.

Title VI. Trials

Rule 38. Right to a Jury Trial; Demand

(a) RIGHT PRESERVED. The right of trial by jury as declared by the Seventh Amendment to the Constitution—or as provided by a federal statute—is preserved to the parties inviolate.

(b) DEMAND. On any issue triable of right by a jury, a party may demand a jury trial by:

> (1) serving the other parties with a written demand—which may be included in a pleading—no later than 14 days after the last pleading directed to the issue is served; and
> (2) filing the demand in accordance with Rule 5(d).

(c) SPECIFYING ISSUES. In its demand, a party may specify the issues that it wishes to have tried by a jury; otherwise, it is considered to have demanded a jury trial on all the issues so triable. If the party has demanded a jury trial on only some issues, any other party may—within 14 days after being served with the demand or within a shorter time ordered by the court—serve a demand for a jury trial on any other or all factual issues triable by jury.

(d) WAIVER; WITHDRAWAL. A party waives a jury trial unless its demand is properly served and filed. A proper demand may be withdrawn only if the parties consent.

(e) ADMIRALTY AND MARITIME CLAIMS. These rules do not create a right to a jury trial on issues in a claim that is an admiralty or maritime claim under Rule 9(h).

Rule 39. Trial by Jury or by the Court

(a) WHEN A DEMAND IS MADE. When a jury trial has been demanded under Rule 38, the action must be designated on the docket as a jury action. The trial on all issues so demanded must be by jury unless:

> (1) the parties or their attorneys file a stipulation to a nonjury trial or so stipulate on the record; or
> (2) the court, on motion or on its own, finds that on some or all of those issues there is no federal right to a jury trial.

(b) WHEN NO DEMAND IS MADE. Issues on which a jury trial is not properly demanded are to be tried by the court. But the court may, on motion, order a jury trial on any issue for which a jury might have been demanded.

(c) ADVISORY JURY; JURY TRIAL BY CONSENT. In an action not triable of right by a jury, the court, on motion or on its own:
> (1) may try any issue with an advisory jury; or
> (2) may, with the parties' consent, try any issue by a jury whose verdict has the same effect as if a jury trial had been a matter of right, unless the action is against the United States and a federal statute provides for a nonjury trial.

Rule 40. Scheduling Cases for Trial

Each court must provide by rule for scheduling trials. The court must give priority to actions entitled to priority by a federal statute.

Rule 41. Dismissal of Actions

(a) VOLUNTARY DISMISSAL.

> (1) *By the Plaintiff.*
>> (A) *Without a Court Order.* Subject to Rules 23(e), 23.1(c), 23.2, and 66 and any applicable federal statute, the plaintiff may dismiss an action without a court order by filing:
>>> (i) a notice of dismissal before the opposing party serves either an answer or a motion for summary judgment; or
>>> (ii) a stipulation of dismissal signed by all parties who have appeared.
>> (B) *Effect.* Unless the notice or stipulation states otherwise, the dismissal is without prejudice. But if the plaintiff previously dismissed any federal- or state-court action based on or including the same claim, a notice of dismissal operates as an adjudication on the merits.
> (2) *By Court Order; Effect.* Except as provided in Rule 41(a)(1), an action may be dismissed at the plaintiff's request only by court order, on terms that the court considers proper. If a defendant has pleaded a counterclaim before being served with the plaintiff's motion to dismiss, the action may be dismissed over the defendant's objection only if the counterclaim can remain pending for independent adjudication. Unless the order states otherwise, a dismissal under this paragraph (2) is without prejudice.

(b) INVOLUNTARY DISMISSAL; EFFECT. If the plaintiff fails to prosecute or to comply with these rules or a court order, a defendant may move to dismiss the action or any claim against it. Unless the dismissal order states otherwise, a dismissal under this subdivision (b) and any dismissal not under this rule—except one for lack of jurisdiction, improper venue, or failure to join a party under Rule 19—operates as an adjudication on the merits.

(c) DISMISSING A COUNTERCLAIM, CROSSCLAIM, OR THIRD-PARTY CLAIM. This rule applies to a dismissal of any counterclaim, crossclaim, or third-party claim. A claimant's voluntary dismissal under Rule 41(a)(1)(A)(i) must be made:

> (1) before a responsive pleading is served; or
> (2) if there is no responsive pleading, before evidence is introduced at a hearing or trial.

(d) COSTS OF A PREVIOUSLY DISMISSED ACTION. If a plaintiff who previously dismissed an action in any court files an action based on or including the same claim against the same defendant, the court:
> (1) may order the plaintiff to pay all or part of the costs of that previous action; and
> (2) may stay the proceedings until the plaintiff has complied.

Rule 42. Consolidation; Separate Trials

(a) CONSOLIDATION. If actions before the court involve a common question of law or fact, the court may:

>> (1) join for hearing or trial any or all matters at issue in the actions;
>> (2) consolidate the actions; or
>> (3) issue any other orders to avoid unnecessary cost or delay.

(b) SEPARATE TRIALS. For convenience, to avoid prejudice, or to expedite and economize, the court may order a separate trial of one or more separate issues, claims, crossclaims, counterclaims, or third-party claims. When ordering a separate trial, the court must preserve any federal right to a jury trial.

Rule 43. Taking Testimony

(a) IN OPEN COURT. At trial, the witnesses' testimony must be taken in open court unless a federal statute, the Federal Rules of Evidence, these rules, or other rules adopted by the Supreme Court provide otherwise. For good cause in compelling circumstances and with appropriate safeguards, the court may permit testimony in open court by contemporaneous transmission from a different location.

(b) AFFIRMATION INSTEAD OF AN OATH. When these rules require an oath, a solemn affirmation suffices.

(c) EVIDENCE ON A MOTION. When a motion relies on facts outside the record, the court may hear the matter on affidavits or may hear it wholly or partly on oral testimony or on depositions.

(d) INTERPRETER. The court may appoint an interpreter of its choosing; fix reasonable compensation to be paid from funds provided by law or by one or more parties; and tax the compensation as costs.

Rule 44. Proving an Official Record

(a) MEANS OF PROVING.

>> (1) *Domestic Record.* Each of the following evidences an official record—or an entry in it—that is otherwise admissible and is kept within the United States, any state, district, or commonwealth, or any territory subject to the administrative or judicial jurisdiction of the United States:
>>> (A) an official publication of the record; or
>>> (B) a copy attested by the officer with legal custody of the record—or by the officer's deputy—and accompanied by a certificate that the officer has custody. The certificate must be made under seal:
>>>> (i) by a judge of a court of record in the district or political subdivision where the record is kept; or
>>>> (ii) by any public officer with a seal of office and with official duties in the district or political subdivision where the record is kept.
>> (2) *Foreign Record.*
>>> (A) *In General.* Each of the following evidences a foreign official record—or an entry in it—that is otherwise admissible:
>>>> (i) an official publication of the record; or
>>>> (ii) the record—or a copy—that is attested by an authorized person and is accompanied either by a final certification of genuineness or by a certification

under a treaty or convention to which the United States and the country where the record is located are parties.

(B) *Final Certification of Genuineness.* A final certification must certify the genuineness of the signature and official position of the attester or of any foreign official whose certificate of genuineness relates to the attestation or is in a chain of certificates of genuineness relating to the attestation. A final certification may be made by a secretary of a United States embassy or legation; by a consul general, vice consul, or consular agent of the United States; or by a diplomatic or consular official of the foreign country assigned or accredited to the United States.

(C) *Other Means of Proof.* If all parties have had a reasonable opportunity to investigate a foreign record's authenticity and accuracy, the court may, for good cause, either:

(i) admit an attested copy without final certification; or

(ii) permit the record to be evidenced by an attested summary with or without a final certification.

(b) LACK OF A RECORD. A written statement that a diligent search of designated records revealed no record or entry of a specified tenor is admissible as evidence that the records contain no such record or entry. For domestic records, the statement must be authenticated under Rule 44(a)(1). For foreign records, the statement must comply with (a)(2)(C)(ii).

(c) OTHER PROOF. A party may prove an official record—or an entry or lack of an entry in it—by any other method authorized by law.

Rule 44.1. Determining Foreign Law

A party who intends to raise an issue about a foreign country's law must give notice by a pleading or other writing. In determining foreign law, the court may consider any relevant material or source, including testimony, whether or not submitted by a party or admissible under the Federal Rules of Evidence. The court's determination must be treated as a ruling on a question of law.

Rule 45. Subpoena

(a) IN GENERAL.

(1) *Form and Contents.*

(A) *Requirements—In General.* Every subpoena must:

(i) state the court from which it issued;

(ii) state the title of the action, the court in which it is pending, and its civil-action number;

(iii) command each person to whom it is directed to do the following at a specified time and place: attend and testify; produce designated documents, electronically stored information, or tangible things in that person's possession, custody, or control; or permit the inspection of premises; and

(iv) set out the text of Rule 45(c) and (d).

(B) *Command to Attend a Deposition—Notice of the Recording Method.* A subpoena commanding attendance at a deposition must state the method for recording the testimony.

(C) *Combining or Separating a Command to Produce or to Permit Inspection; Specifying the Form for Electronically Stored Information.* A command to produce documents, electronically stored information, or tangible things or to permit the inspection of premises may be included in a subpoena commanding attendance at a deposition, hearing, or trial, or may be set out in a separate subpoena. A subpoena may specify the form or forms in which electronically stored information is to be produced.

(D) *Command to Produce; Included Obligations.* A command in a subpoena to produce documents, electronically stored information, or tangible things requires the responding party to permit inspection, copying, testing, or sampling of the materials.

(2) *Issued from Which Court.* A subpoena must issue as follows:

(A) for attendance at a hearing or trial, from the court for the district where the hearing or trial is to be held;

(B) for attendance at a deposition, from the court for the district where the deposition is to be taken; and

(C) for production or inspection, if separate from a subpoena commanding a person's attendance, from the court for the district where the production or inspection is to be made.

(3) *Issued by Whom.* The clerk must issue a subpoena, signed but otherwise in blank, to a party who requests it. That party must complete it before service. An attorney also may issue and sign a subpoena as an officer of:

(A) a court in which the attorney is authorized to practice; or

(B) a court for a district where a deposition is to be taken or production is to be made, if the attorney is authorized to practice in the court where the action is pending.

(b) SERVICE.

(1) *By Whom; Tendering Fees; Serving a Copy of Certain Subpoenas.* Any person who is at least 18 years old and not a party may serve a subpoena. Serving a subpoena requires delivering a copy to the named person and, if the subpoena requires that person's attendance, tendering the fees for 1 day's attendance and the mileage allowed by law. Fees and mileage need not be tendered when the subpoena issues on behalf of the United States or any of its officers or agencies. If the subpoena commands the production of documents, electronically stored information, or tangible things or the inspection of premises before trial, then before it is served, a notice must be served on each party.

(2) *Service in the United States.* Subject to Rule 45(c)(3)(A)(ii), a subpoena may be served at any place:

(A) within the district of the issuing court;

(B) outside that district but within 100 miles of the place specified for the deposition, hearing, trial, production, or inspection;

(C) within the state of the issuing court if a state statute or court rule allows service at that place of a subpoena issued by a state court of general jurisdiction sitting in the place specified for the deposition, hearing, trial, production, or inspection; or

(D) that the court authorizes on motion and for good cause, if a federal statute so provides.

(3) *Service in a Foreign Country.* 28 U.S.C. § 1783 governs issuing and serving a subpoena directed to a United States national or resident who is in a foreign country.

(4) *Proof of Service.* Proving service, when necessary, requires filing with the issuing court a statement showing the date and manner of service and the names of the persons served. The statement must be certified by the server.

(c) PROTECTING A PERSON SUBJECT TO A SUBPOENA.

(1) *Avoiding Undue Burden or Expense; Sanctions.* A party or attorney responsible for issuing and serving a subpoena must take reasonable steps to avoid imposing undue burden or expense on

a person subject to the subpoena. The issuing court must enforce this duty and impose an appropriate sanction—which may include lost earnings and reasonable attorney's fees—on a party or attorney who fails to comply.

(2) *Command to Produce Materials or Permit Inspection.*

    (A) *Appearance Not Required.* A person commanded to produce documents, electronically stored information, or tangible things, or to permit the inspection of premises, need not appear in person at the place of production or inspection unless also commanded to appear for a deposition, hearing, or trial.

    (B) *Objections.* A person commanded to produce documents or tangible things or to permit inspection may serve on the party or attorney designated in the subpoena a written objection to inspecting, copying, testing or sampling any or all of the materials or to inspecting the premises—or to producing electronically stored information in the form or forms requested. The objection must be served before the earlier of the time specified for compliance or 14 days after the subpoena is served. If an objection is made, the following rules apply:

        (i) At any time, on notice to the commanded person, the serving party may move the issuing court for an order compelling production or inspection.

        (ii) These acts may be required only as directed in the order, and the order must protect a person who is neither a party nor a party's officer from significant expense resulting from compliance.

(3) *Quashing or Modifying a Subpoena.*

    (A) *When Required.* On timely motion, the issuing court must quash or modify a subpoena that:

        (i) fails to allow a reasonable time to comply;

        (ii) requires a person who is neither a party nor a party's officer to travel more than 100 miles from where that person resides, is employed, or regularly transacts business in person—except that, subject to Rule 45(c)(3)(B)(iii), the person may be commanded to attend a trial by traveling from any such place within the state where the trial is held;

        (iii) requires disclosure of privileged or other protected matter, if no exception or waiver applies; or

        (iv) subjects a person to undue burden.

    (B) *When Permitted.* To protect a person subject to or affected by a subpoena, the issuing court may, on motion, quash or modify the subpoena if it requires:

        (i) disclosing a trade secret or other confidential research, development, or commercial information;

        (ii) disclosing an unretained expert's opinion or information that does not describe specific occurrences in dispute and results from the expert's study that was not requested by a party; or

        (iii) a person who is neither a party nor a party's officer to incur substantial expense to travel more than 100 miles to attend trial.

    (C) *Specifying Conditions as an Alternative.* In the circumstances described in Rule 45(c)(3)(B), the court may, instead of quashing or modifying a subpoena, order appearance or production under specified conditions if the serving party:

        (i) shows a substantial need for the testimony or material that cannot be otherwise met without undue hardship; and

        (ii) ensures that the subpoenaed person will be reasonably compensated.

(d) DUTIES IN RESPONDING TO A SUBPOENA.

(1) *Producing Documents or Electronically Stored Information.* These procedures apply to producing documents or electronically stored information:

(A) *Documents.* A person responding to a subpoena to produce documents must produce them as they are kept in the ordinary course of business or must organize and label them to correspond to the categories in the demand.

(B) *Form for Producing Electronically Stored Information Not Specified.* If a subpoena does not specify a form for producing electronically stored information, the person responding must produce it in a form or forms in which it is ordinarily maintained or in a reasonably usable form or forms.

(C) *Electronically Stored Information Produced in Only One Form.* The person responding need not produce the same electronically stored information in more than one form.

(D) *Inaccessible Electronically Stored Information.* The person responding need not provide discovery of electronically stored information from sources that the person identifies as not reasonably accessible because of undue burden or cost. On motion to compel discovery or for a protective order, the person responding must show that the information is not reasonably accessible because of undue burden or cost. If that showing is made, the court may nonetheless order discovery from such sources if the requesting party shows good cause, considering the limitations of Rule 26(b)(2)(C). The court may specify conditions for the discovery.

(2) *Claiming Privilege or Protection.*

(A) *Information Withheld.* A person withholding subpoenaed information under a claim that it is privileged or subject to protection as trial-preparation material must:

(i) expressly make the claim; and

(ii) describe the nature of the withheld documents, communications, or tangible things in a manner that, without revealing information itself privileged or protected, will enable the parties to assess the claim.

(B) *Information Produced.* If information produced in response to a subpoena is subject to a claim of privilege or of protection as trial-preparation material, the person making the claim may notify any party that received the information of the claim and the basis for it. After being notified, a party must promptly return, sequester, or destroy the specified information and any copies it has; must not use or disclose the information until the claim is resolved; must take reasonable steps to retrieve the information if the party disclosed it before being notified; and may promptly present the information to the court under seal for a determination of the claim. The person who produced the information must preserve the information until the claim is resolved.

(e) CONTEMPT. The issuing court may hold in contempt a person who, having been served, fails without adequate excuse to obey the subpoena. A nonparty's failure to obey must be excused if the subpoena purports to require the nonparty to attend or produce at a place outside the limits of Rule 45(c)(3)(A)(ii).

Rule 46. Objecting to a Ruling or Order

A formal exception to a ruling or order is unnecessary. When the ruling or order is requested or made, a party need only state the action that it wants the court to take or objects to, along with the grounds for the request or objection. Failing to object does not prejudice a party who had no opportunity to do so when the ruling or order was made.

Rule 47. Selecting Jurors

(a) EXAMINING JURORS. The court may permit the parties or their attorneys to examine prospective jurors or may itself do so. If the court examines the jurors, it must permit the parties or their attorneys to make any further inquiry it considers proper, or must itself ask any of their additional questions it considers proper.

(b) PEREMPTORY CHALLENGES. The court must allow the number of peremptory challenges provided by 28 U.S.C. § 1870.

(c) EXCUSING A JUROR. During trial or deliberation, the court may excuse a juror for good cause.

Rule 48. Number of Jurors; Verdict; Polling

(a) NUMBER OF JURORS. A jury must begin with at least 6 and no more than 12 members, and each juror must participate in the verdict unless excused under Rule 47(c).

(b) VERDICT. Unless the parties stipulate otherwise, the verdict must be unanimous and must be returned by a jury of at least 6 members.

(c) POLLING. After a verdict is returned but before the jury is discharged, the court must on a party's request, or may on its own, poll the jurors individually. If the poll reveals a lack of unanimity or lack of assent by the number of jurors that the parties stipulated to, the court may direct the jury to deliberate further or may order a new trial.

Rule 49. Special Verdict; General Verdict and Questions

(a) SPECIAL VERDICT.

(1) *In General.* The court may require a jury to return only a special verdict in the form of a special written finding on each issue of fact. The court may do so by:
(A) submitting written questions susceptible of a categorical or other brief answer;
(B) submitting written forms of the special findings that might properly be made under the pleadings and evidence; or
(C) using any other method that the court considers appropriate.
(2) *Instructions.* The court must give the instructions and explanations necessary to enable the jury to make its findings on each submitted issue.
(3) *Issues Not Submitted.* A party waives the right to a jury trial on any issue of fact raised by the pleadings or evidence but not submitted to the jury unless, before the jury retires, the party demands its submission to the jury. If the party does not demand submission, the court may make a finding on the issue. If the court makes no finding, it is considered to have made a finding consistent with its judgment on the special verdict.

(b) GENERAL VERDICT WITH ANSWERS TO WRITTEN QUESTIONS.

(1) *In General.* The court may submit to the jury forms for a general verdict, together with written questions on one or more issues of fact that the jury must decide. The court must give the instructions and explanations necessary to enable the jury to render a general verdict and answer the questions in writing, and must direct the jury to do both.

(2) *Verdict and Answers Consistent.* When the general verdict and the answers are consistent, the court must approve, for entry under Rule 58, an appropriate judgment on the verdict and answers.

(3) *Answers Inconsistent with the Verdict.* When the answers are consistent with each other but one or more is inconsistent with the general verdict, the court may:

> (A) approve, for entry under Rule 58, an appropriate judgment according to the answers, notwithstanding the general verdict;
> (B) direct the jury to further consider its answers and verdict; or
> (C) order a new trial.

(4) *Answers Inconsistent with Each Other and the Verdict.* When the answers are inconsistent with each other and one or more is also inconsistent with the general verdict, judgment must not be entered; instead, the court must direct the jury to further consider its answers and verdict, or must order a new trial.

Rule 50. Judgment as a Matter of Law in a Jury Trial; Related Motion for a New Trial; Conditional Ruling

(a) JUDGMENT AS A MATTER OF LAW.

(1) *In General.* If a party has been fully heard on an issue during a jury trial and the court finds that a reasonable jury would not have a legally sufficient evidentiary basis to find for the party on that issue, the court may:

> (A) resolve the issue against the party; and
> (B) grant a motion for judgment as a matter of law against the party on a claim or defense that, under the controlling law, can be maintained or defeated only with a favorable finding on that issue.

(2) *Motion.* A motion for judgment as a matter of law may be made at any time before the case is submitted to the jury. The motion must specify the judgment sought and the law and facts that entitle the movant to the judgment.

(b) RENEWING THE MOTION AFTER TRIAL; ALTERNATIVE MOTION FOR A NEW TRIAL. If the court does not grant a motion for judgment as a matter of law made under Rule 50(a), the court is considered to have submitted the action to the jury subject to the court's later deciding the legal questions raised by the motion. No later than 28 days after the entry of judgment—or if the motion addresses a jury issue not decided by a verdict, no later than 28 days after the jury was discharged—the movant may file a renewed motion for judgment as a matter of law and may include an alternative or joint request for a new trial under Rule 59. In ruling on the renewed motion, the court may:

> (1) allow judgment on the verdict, if the jury returned a verdict;
> (2) order a new trial; or
> (3) direct the entry of judgment as a matter of law.

(c) GRANTING THE RENEWED MOTION; CONDITIONAL RULING ON A MOTION FOR A NEW TRIAL.

(1) *In General.* If the court grants a renewed motion for judgment as a matter of law, it must also conditionally rule on any motion for a new trial by determining whether a new trial should be granted if the judgment is later vacated or reversed. The court must state the grounds for conditionally granting or denying the motion for a new trial.

(2) *Effect of a Conditional Ruling.* Conditionally granting the motion for a new trial does not affect the judgment's finality; if the judgment is reversed, the new trial must proceed unless the

appellate court orders otherwise. If the motion for a new trial is conditionally denied, the appellee may assert error in that denial; if the judgment is reversed, the case must proceed as the appellate court orders.

(d) TIME FOR A LOSING PARTY'S NEW-TRIAL MOTION. Any motion for a new trial under Rule 59 by a party against whom judgment as a matter of law is rendered must be filed no later than 28 days after the entry of the judgment.

(e) DENYING THE MOTION FOR JUDGMENT AS A MATTER OF LAW; REVERSAL ON APPEAL. If the court denies the motion for judgment as a matter of law, the prevailing party may, as appellee, assert grounds entitling it to a new trial should the appellate court conclude that the trial court erred in denying the motion. If the appellate court reverses the judgment, it may order a new trial, direct the trial court to determine whether a new trial should be granted, or direct the entry of judgment.

Rule 51. Instructions to the Jury; Objections; Preserving a Claim of Error

(a) REQUESTS.

(1) *Before or at the Close of the Evidence.* At the close of the evidence or at any earlier reasonable time that the court orders, a party may file and furnish to every other party written requests for the jury instructions it wants the court to give.
(2) *After the Close of the Evidence.* After the close of the evidence, a party may:
(A) file requests for instructions on issues that could not reasonably have been anticipated by an earlier time that the court set for requests; and
(B) with the court's permission, file untimely requests for instructions on any issue.

(b) INSTRUCTIONS. The court:

(1) must inform the parties of its proposed instructions and proposed action on the requests before instructing the jury and before final jury arguments;
(2) must give the parties an opportunity to object on the record and out of the jury's hearing before the instructions and arguments are delivered; and
(3) may instruct the jury at any time before the jury is discharged.

(c) OBJECTIONS.

(1) *How to Make.* A party who objects to an instruction or the failure to give an instruction must do so on the record, stating distinctly the matter objected to and the grounds for the objection.
(2) *When to Make.* An objection is timely if:
(A) a party objects at the opportunity provided under Rule 51(b)(2); or
(B) a party was not informed of an instruction or action on a request before that opportunity to object, and the party objects promptly after learning that the instruction or request will be, or has been, given or refused.

(d) ASSIGNING ERROR; PLAIN ERROR.

(1) *Assigning Error.* A party may assign as error:
(A) an error in an instruction actually given, if that party properly objected; or
(B) a failure to give an instruction, if that party properly requested it and—unless the court rejected the request in a definitive ruling on the record—also properly objected.

(2) *Plain Error.* A court may consider a plain error in the instructions that has not been preserved as required by Rule 51(d)(1) if the error affects substantial rights.

Rule 52. Findings and Conclusions by the Court; Judgment on Partial Findings

(a) FINDINGS AND CONCLUSIONS.

(1) *In General.* In an action tried on the facts without a jury or with an advisory jury, the court must find the facts specially and state its conclusions of law separately. The findings and conclusions may be stated on the record after the close of the evidence or may appear in an opinion or a memorandum of decision filed by the court. Judgment must be entered under Rule 58.

(2) *For an Interlocutory Injunction.* In granting or refusing an interlocutory injunction, the court must similarly state the findings and conclusions that support its action.

(3) *For a Motion.* The court is not required to state findings or conclusions when ruling on a motion under Rule 12 or 56 or, unless these rules provide otherwise, on any other motion.

(4) *Effect of a Master's Findings.* A master's findings, to the extent adopted by the court, must be considered the court's findings.

(5) *Questioning the Evidentiary Support.* A party may later question the sufficiency of the evidence supporting the findings, whether or not the party requested findings, objected to them, moved to amend them, or moved for partial findings.

(6) *Setting Aside the Findings.* Findings of fact, whether based on oral or other evidence, must not be set aside unless clearly erroneous, and the reviewing court must give due regard to the trial court's opportunity to judge the witnesses' credibility.

(b) AMENDED OR ADDITIONAL FINDINGS. On a party's motion filed no later than 28 days after the entry of judgment, the court may amend its findings—or make additional findings—and may amend the judgment accordingly. The motion may accompany a motion for a new trial under Rule 59.

(c) JUDGMENT ON PARTIAL FINDINGS. If a party has been fully heard on an issue during a nonjury trial and the court finds against the party on that issue, the court may enter judgment against the party on a claim or defense that, under the controlling law, can be maintained or defeated only with a favorable finding on that issue. The court may, however, decline to render any judgment until the close of the evidence. A judgment on partial findings must be supported by findings of fact and conclusions of law as required by Rule 52(a).

Rule 53. Masters

(a) APPOINTMENT.

(1) *Scope.* Unless a statute provides otherwise, a court may appoint a master only to:
(A) perform duties consented to by the parties;
(B) hold trial proceedings and make or recommend findings of fact on issues to be decided without a jury if appointment is warranted by:
(i) some exceptional condition; or
(ii) the need to perform an accounting or resolve a difficult computation of damages; or
(C) address pretrial and posttrial matters that cannot be effectively and timely addressed by an available district judge or magistrate judge of the district.

(2) *Disqualification.* A master must not have a relationship to the parties, attorneys, action, or court that would require disqualification of a judge under 28 U.S.C. § 455, unless the parties, with the court's approval, consent to the appointment after the master discloses any potential grounds for disqualification.

(3) *Possible Expense or Delay.* In appointing a master, the court must consider the fairness of imposing the likely expenses on the parties and must protect against unreasonable expense or delay.

(b) ORDER APPOINTING A MASTER.

(1) *Notice.* Before appointing a master, the court must give the parties notice and an opportunity to be heard. Any party may suggest candidates for appointment.

(2) *Contents.* The appointing order must direct the master to proceed with all reasonable diligence and must state:

> (A) the master's duties, including any investigation or enforcement duties, and any limits on the master's authority under Rule 53(c);
>
> (B) the circumstances, if any, in which the master may communicate ex parte with the court or a party;
>
> (C) the nature of the materials to be preserved and filed as the record of the master's activities;
>
> (D) the time limits, method of filing the record, other procedures, and standards for reviewing the master's orders, findings, and recommendations; and (E) the basis, terms, and procedure for fixing the master's compensation under Rule 53(g).

(3) *Issuing.* The court may issue the order only after:

> (A) the master files an affidavit disclosing whether there is any ground for disqualification under 28 U.S.C. § 455; and
>
> (B) if a ground is disclosed, the parties, with the court's approval, waive the disqualification.

(4) *Amending.* The order may be amended at any time after notice to the parties and an opportunity to be heard.

(c) MASTER'S AUTHORITY.

(1) *In General.* Unless the appointing order directs otherwise, a master may:

> (A) regulate all proceedings;
>
> (B) take all appropriate measures to perform the assigned duties fairly and efficiently; and
>
> (C) if conducting an evidentiary hearing, exercise the appointing court's power to compel, take, and record evidence.

(2) *Sanctions.* The master may by order impose on a party any noncontempt sanction provided by Rule 37 or 45, and may recommend a contempt sanction against a party and sanctions against a nonparty.

(d) MASTER'S ORDERS. A master who issues an order must file it and promptly serve a copy on each party. The clerk must enter the order on the docket.

(e) MASTER'S REPORTS. A master must report to the court as required by the appointing order. The master must file the report and promptly serve a copy on each party, unless the court orders otherwise.

(f) ACTION ON THE MASTER'S ORDER, REPORT, OR RECOMMENDATIONS.

(1) *Opportunity for a Hearing; Action in General.* In acting on a master's order, report, or recommendations, the court must give the parties notice and an opportunity to be heard; may receive evidence; and may adopt or affirm, modify, wholly or partly reject or reverse, or resubmit to the master with instructions.

(2) *Time to Object or Move to Adopt or Modify.* A party may file objections to—or a motion to adopt or modify—the master's order, report, or recommendations no later than 21 days after a copy is served, unless the court sets a different time.

(3) *Reviewing Factual Findings.* The court must decide de novo all objections to findings of fact made or recommended by a master, unless the parties, with the court's approval, stipulate that:

(A) the findings will be reviewed for clear error; or

(B) the findings of a master appointed under Rule 53(a)(1)(A) or (C) will be final.

(4) *Reviewing Legal Conclusions.* The court must decide de novo all objections to conclusions of law made or recommended by a master.

(5) *Reviewing Procedural Matters.* Unless the appointing order establishes a different standard of review, the court may set aside a master's ruling on a procedural matter only for an abuse of discretion.

(g) COMPENSATION.

(1) *Fixing Compensation.* Before or after judgment, the court must fix the master's compensation on the basis and terms stated in the appointing order, but the court may set a new basis and terms after giving notice and an opportunity to be heard.

(2) *Payment.* The compensation must be paid either:

(A) by a party or parties; or

(B) from a fund or subject matter of the action within the court's control.

(3) *Allocating Payment.* The court must allocate payment among the parties after considering the nature and amount of the controversy, the parties' means, and the extent to which any party is more responsible than other parties for the reference to a master. An interim allocation may be amended to reflect a decision on the merits.

(h) APPOINTING A MAGISTRATE JUDGE. A magistrate judge is subject to this rule only when the order referring a matter to the magistrate judge states that the reference is made under this rule.

Title VII. Judgment

Rule 54. Judgment; Costs

(a) DEFINITION; FORM. "Judgment" as used in these rules includes a decree and any order from which an appeal lies. A judgment should not include recitals of pleadings, a master's report, or a record of prior proceedings.

(b) JUDGMENT ON MULTIPLE CLAIMS OR INVOLVING MULTIPLE PARTIES. When an action presents more than one claim for relief—whether as a claim, counterclaim, crossclaim, or third-party claim—or when multiple parties are involved, the court may direct entry of a final judgment as to one or more, but fewer than all, claims or parties only if the court expressly determines that there is no just reason for delay. Otherwise, any order or other decision, however designated, that adjudicates fewer than all the claims or the rights and liabilities of fewer than all the parties does not end the action as to any of the claims or parties and may be revised at any time before the entry of a judgment adjudicating all the claims and all the parties' rights and liabilities.

(c) DEMAND FOR JUDGMENT; RELIEF TO BE GRANTED. A default judgment must not differ in kind from, or exceed in amount, what is demanded in the pleadings. Every other final judgment should grant the relief to which each party is entitled, even if the party has not demanded that relief in its pleadings.

(d) COSTS; ATTORNEY'S FEES.

(1) *Costs Other Than Attorney's Fees.* Unless a federal statute, these rules, or a court order provides otherwise, costs—other than attorney's fees—should be allowed to the prevailing party. But costs against the United States, its officers, and its agencies may be imposed only to the extent allowed by law. The clerk may tax costs on 14 days' notice. On motion served within the next 7 days, the court may review the clerk's action.

(2) *Attorney's Fees.*

(A) *Claim to Be by Motion.* A claim for attorney's fees and related nontaxable expenses must be made by motion unless the substantive law requires those fees to be proved at trial as an element of damages.

(B) *Timing and Contents of the Motion.* Unless a statute or a court order provides otherwise, the motion must:

(i) be filed no later than 14 days after the entry of judgment;

(ii) specify the judgment and the statute, rule, or other grounds entitling the movant to the award;

(iii) state the amount sought or provide a fair estimate of it; and

(iv) disclose, if the court so orders, the terms of any agreement about fees for the services for which the claim is made.

(C) *Proceedings.* Subject to Rule 23(h), the court must, on a party's request, give an opportunity for adversary submissions on the motion in accordance with Rule 43(c) or 78. The court may decide issues of liability for fees before receiving submissions on the value of services. The court must find the facts and state its conclusions of law as provided in Rule 52(a).

(D) *Special Procedures by Local Rule; Reference to a Master or a Magistrate Judge.* By local rule, the court may establish special procedures to resolve fee-related issues without extensive evidentiary hearings. Also, the court may refer issues concerning the value of services to a special master under Rule 53 without regard to the limitations of Rule 53(a)(1), and may refer a motion for attorney's fees to a magistrate judge under Rule 72(b) as if it were a dispositive pretrial matter.

(E) *Exceptions.* Subparagraphs (A)–(D) do not apply to claims for fees and expenses as sanctions for violating these rules or as sanctions under 28 U.S.C. § 1927.

Rule 55. Default; Default Judgment

(a) ENTERING A DEFAULT. When a party against whom a judgment for affirmative relief is sought has failed to plead or otherwise defend, and that failure is shown by affidavit or otherwise, the clerk must enter the party's default.

(b) ENTERING A DEFAULT JUDGMENT.

(1) *By the Clerk.* If the plaintiff's claim is for a sum certain or a sum that can be made certain by computation, the clerk—on the plaintiff's request, with an affidavit showing the amount due—must enter judgment for that amount and costs against a defendant who has been defaulted for not appearing and who is neither a minor nor an incompetent person.

(2) *By the Court.* In all other cases, the party must apply to the court for a default judgment. A default judgment may be entered against a minor or incompetent person only if represented by a general guardian, conservator, or other like fiduciary who has appeared. If the party against whom a default judgment is sought has appeared personally or by a representative, that party or its representative must be served with written notice of the application at least 7 days before the hearing. The court may conduct hearings or make referrals—preserving any federal statutory right to a jury trial—when, to enter or effectuate judgment, it needs to:

(A) conduct an accounting;

(B) determine the amount of damages;

(C) establish the truth of any allegation by evidence; or

(D) investigate any other matter.

(c) SETTING ASIDE A DEFAULT OR A DEFAULT JUDGMENT. The court may set aside an entry of default for good cause, and it may set aside a default judgment under Rule 60(b).

(d) JUDGMENT AGAINST THE UNITED STATES. A default judgment may be entered against the United States, its officers, or its agencies only if the claimant establishes a claim or right to relief by evidence that satisfies the court.

Rule 56. Summary Judgment

(a) MOTION FOR SUMMARY JUDGMENT OR PARTIAL SUMMARY JUDGMENT. A party may move for summary judgment, identifying each claim or defense—or the part of each claim or defense—on which summary judgment is sought. The court shall grant summary judgment if the movant shows that there is no genuine dispute as to any material fact and the movant is entitled to judgment as a matter of law. The court should state on the record the reasons for granting or denying the motion.

(b) TIME TO FILE A MOTION. Unless a different time is set by local rule or the court orders otherwise, a party may file a motion for summary judgment at any time until 30 days after the close of all discovery.

(c) PROCEDURES.

(1) *Supporting Factual Positions.* A party asserting that a fact cannot be or is genuinely disputed must support the assertion by:

(A) citing to particular parts of materials in the record, including depositions, documents, electronically stored information, affidavits or declarations, stipulations (including those made for purposes of the motion only), admissions, interrogatory answers, or other materials; or

(B) showing that the materials cited do not establish the absence or presence of a genuine dispute, or that an adverse party cannot produce admissible evidence to support the fact.

(2) *Objection That a Fact Is Not Supported by Admissible Evidence.* A party may object that the material cited to support or dispute a fact cannot be presented in a form that would be admissible in evidence.

(3) *Materials Not Cited.* The court need consider only the cited materials, but it may consider other materials in the record.

(4) *Affidavits or Declarations.* An affidavit or declaration used to support or oppose a motion must be made on personal knowledge, set out facts that would be admissible in evidence, and show that the affiant or declarant is competent to testify on the matters stated.

(d) WHEN FACTS ARE UNAVAILABLE TO THE NONMOVANT. If a nonmovant shows by affidavit or declaration that, for specified reasons, it cannot present facts essential to justify its opposition, the court may:

    (1) defer considering the motion or deny it;

    (2) allow time to obtain affidavits or declarations or to take discovery; or

    (3) issue any other appropriate order.

(e) FAILING TO PROPERLY SUPPORT OR ADDRESS A FACT. If a party fails to properly support an assertion of fact or fails to properly address another party's assertion of fact as required by Rule 56(c), the court may:

    (1) give an opportunity to properly support or address the fact;

    (2) consider the fact undisputed for purposes of the motion;

    (3) grant summary judgment if the motion and supporting materials—including the facts considered undisputed—show that the movant is entitled to it; or

    (4) issue any other appropriate order.

(f) JUDGMENT INDEPENDENT OF THE MOTION. After giving notice and a reasonable time to respond, the court may:

    (1) grant summary judgment for a nonmovant;

    (2) grant the motion on grounds not raised by a party; or

    (3) consider summary judgment on its own after identifying for the parties material facts that may not be genuinely in dispute.

(g) FAILING TO GRANT ALL THE REQUESTED RELIEF. If the court does not grant all the relief requested by the motion, it may enter an order stating any material fact—including an item of damages or other relief—that is not genuinely in dispute and treating the fact as established in the case.

(h) AFFIDAVIT OR DECLARATION SUBMITTED IN BAD FAITH. If satisfied that an affidavit or declaration under this rule is submitted in bad faith or solely for delay, the court—after notice and a reasonable time to respond—may order the submitting party to pay the other party the reasonable expenses, including attorney's fees, it incurred as a result. An offending party or attorney may also be held in contempt or subjected to other appropriate sanctions.

Rule 57. Declaratory Judgment

These rules govern the procedure for obtaining a declaratory judgment under 28 U.S.C. § 2201. Rules 38 and 39 govern a demand for a jury trial. The existence of another adequate remedy does not preclude a declaratory judgment that is otherwise appropriate. The court may order a speedy hearing of a declaratory judgment action.

Rule 58. Entering Judgment

(a) SEPARATE DOCUMENT. Every judgment and amended judgment must be set out in a separate document, but a separate document is not required for an order disposing of a motion:

> (1) for judgment under Rule 50(b);
> (2) to amend or make additional findings under Rule 52(b);
> (3) for attorney's fees under Rule 54;
> (4) for a new trial, or to alter or amend the judgment, under Rule 59; or
> (5) for relief under Rule 60.

(b) ENTERING JUDGMENT.

> (1) *Without the Court's Direction.* Subject to Rule 54(b) and unless the court orders otherwise, the clerk must, without awaiting the court's direction, promptly prepare, sign, and enter the judgment when:
>> (A) the jury returns a general verdict;
>> (B) the court awards only costs or a sum certain; or
>> (C) the court denies all relief.
> (2) *Court's Approval Required.* Subject to Rule 54(b), the court must promptly approve the form of the judgment, which the clerk must promptly enter, when:
>> (A) the jury returns a special verdict or a general verdict with answers to written questions; or
>> (B) the court grants other relief not described in this subdivision (b).

(c) TIME OF ENTRY. For purposes of these rules, judgment is entered at the following times:

> (1) if a separate document is not required, when the judgment is entered in the civil docket under Rule 79(a); or
> (2) if a separate document is required, when the judgment is entered in the civil docket under Rule 79(a) and the earlier of these events occurs:
>> (A) it is set out in a separate document; or
>> (B) 150 days have run from the entry in the civil docket.

(d) REQUEST FOR ENTRY. A party may request that judgment be set out in a separate document as required by Rule 58(a).

(e) COST OR FEE AWARDS. Ordinarily, the entry of judgment may not be delayed, nor the time for appeal extended, in order to tax costs or award fees. But if a timely motion for attorney's fees is made under Rule 54(d)(2), the court may act before a notice of appeal has been filed and become effective to order that the motion have the same effect under Federal Rule of Appellate Procedure 4(a)(4) as a timely motion under Rule 59.

Rule 59. New Trial; Altering or Amending a Judgment

(a) IN GENERAL.

> (1) *Grounds for New Trial.* The court may, on motion, grant a new trial on all or some of the issues—and to any party—as follows:

(A) after a jury trial, for any reason for which a new trial has heretofore been granted in an action at law in federal court; or

(B) after a nonjury trial, for any reason for which a rehearing has heretofore been granted in a suit in equity in federal court.

(2) *Further Action After a Nonjury Trial.* After a nonjury trial, the court may, on motion for a new trial, open the judgment if one has been entered, take additional testimony, amend findings of fact and conclusions of law or make new ones, and direct the entry of a new judgment.

(b) TIME TO FILE A MOTION FOR A NEW TRIAL. A motion for a new trial must be filed no later than 28 days after the entry of judgment.

(c) TIME TO SERVE AFFIDAVITS. When a motion for a new trial is based on affidavits, they must be filed with the motion. The opposing party has 14 days after being served to file opposing affidavits. The court may permit reply affidavits.

(d) NEW TRIAL ON THE COURT'S INITIATIVE OR FOR REASONS NOT IN THE MOTION. No later than 28 days after the entry of judgment, the court, on its own, may order a new trial for any reason that would justify granting one on a party's motion. After giving the parties notice and an opportunity to be heard, the court may grant a timely motion for a new trial for a reason not stated in the motion. In either event, the court must specify the reasons in its order.

(e) MOTION TO ALTER OR AMEND A JUDGMENT. A motion to alter or amend a judgment must be filed no later than 28 days after the entry of the judgment.

Rule 60. Relief from a Judgment or Order

(a) CORRECTIONS BASED ON CLERICAL MISTAKES; OVERSIGHTS AND OMISSIONS. The court may correct a clerical mistake or a mistake arising from oversight or omission whenever one is found in a judgment, order, or other part of the record. The court may do so on motion or on its own, with or without notice. But after an appeal has been docketed in the appellate court and while it is pending, such a mistake may be corrected only with the appellate
court's leave.

(b) GROUNDS FOR RELIEF FROM A FINAL JUDGMENT, ORDER, OR PROCEEDING. On motion and just terms, the court may relieve a party or its legal representative from a final judgment, order, or proceeding for the following reasons:

(1) mistake, inadvertence, surprise, or excusable neglect;
(2) newly discovered evidence that, with reasonable diligence, could not have been discovered in time to move for a new trial under Rule 59(b);
(3) fraud (whether previously called intrinsic or extrinsic), misrepresentation, or misconduct by an opposing party;
(4) the judgment is void;
(5) the judgment has been satisfied, released, or discharged; it is based on an earlier judgment that has been reversed or vacated; or applying it prospectively is no longer equitable; or
(6) any other reason that justifies relief.

(c) TIMING AND EFFECT OF THE MOTION.

(1) *Timing.* A motion under Rule 60(b) must be made within a reasonable time—and for reasons (1), (2), and (3) no more than a year after the entry of the judgment or order or the date of the proceeding.

(2) *Effect on Finality.* The motion does not affect the judgment's finality or suspend its operation.

(d) OTHER POWERS TO GRANT RELIEF. This rule does not limit a court's power to:

(1) entertain an independent action to relieve a party from a judgment, order, or proceeding;

(2) grant relief under 28 U.S.C. § 1655 to a defendant who was not personally notified of the action; or

(3) set aside a judgment for fraud on the court.

(e) BILLS AND WRITS ABOLISHED. The following are abolished: bills of review, bills in the nature of bills of review, and writs of coram nobis, coram vobis, and audita querela.

Rule 61. Harmless Error

Unless justice requires otherwise, no error in admitting or excluding evidence—or any other error by the court or a party—is ground for granting a new trial, for setting aside a verdict, or for vacating, modifying, or otherwise disturbing a judgment or order. At every stage of the proceeding, the court must disregard all errors and defects that do not affect any party's substantial rights.

Rule 62. Stay of Proceedings to Enforce a Judgment

(a) AUTOMATIC STAY; EXCEPTIONS FOR INJUNCTIONS, RECEIVERSHIPS, AND PATENT ACCOUNTINGS. Except as stated in this rule, no execution may issue on a judgment, nor may proceedings be taken to enforce it, until 14 days have passed after its entry. But unless the court orders otherwise, the following are not stayed after being entered, even if an appeal is taken:

(1) an interlocutory or final judgment in an action for an injunction or a receivership; or

(2) a judgment or order that directs an accounting in an action for patent infringement.

(b) STAY PENDING THE DISPOSITION OF A MOTION. On appropriate terms for the opposing party's security, the court may stay the execution of a judgment—or any proceedings to enforce it— pending disposition of any of the following motions:

(1) under Rule 50, for judgment as a matter of law;

(2) under Rule 52(b), to amend the findings or for additional findings;

(3) under Rule 59, for a new trial or to alter or amend a judgment; or

(4) under Rule 60, for relief from a judgment or order.

(c) INJUNCTION PENDING AN APPEAL. While an appeal is pending from an interlocutory order or final judgment that grants, dissolves, or denies an injunction, the court may suspend, modify, restore, or grant an injunction on terms for bond or other terms that secure the opposing party's rights. If the judgment appealed from is rendered by a statutory three-judge district court, the order must be made either:

(1) by that court sitting in open session; or

(2) by the assent of all its judges, as evidenced by their signatures.

(d) STAY WITH BOND ON APPEAL. If an appeal is taken, the appellant may obtain a stay by supersedeas bond, except in an action described in Rule 62(a)(1) or (2). The bond may be given upon or after filing the notice of appeal or after obtaining the order allowing the appeal. The stay takes effect when the court approves the bond.

(e) STAY WITHOUT BOND ON AN APPEAL BY THE UNITED STATES, ITS OFFICERS, OR ITS AGENCIES. The court must not require a bond, obligation, or other security from the appellant when granting a stay on an appeal by the United States, its officers, or its agencies or on an appeal directed by a department of the federal government.

(f) STAY IN FAVOR OF A JUDGMENT DEBTOR UNDER STATE LAW. If a judgment is a lien on the judgment debtor's property under the law of the state where the court is located, the judgment debtor is entitled to the same stay of execution the state court would give.

(g) APPELLATE COURT'S POWER NOT LIMITED. This rule does not limit the power of the appellate court or one of its judges or justices:

(1) to stay proceedings—or suspend, modify, restore, or grant an injunction—while an appeal is pending; or

(2) to issue an order to preserve the status quo or the effectiveness of the judgment to be entered.

(h) STAY WITH MULTIPLE CLAIMS OR PARTIES. A court may stay the enforcement of a final judgment entered under Rule 54(b) until it enters a later judgment or judgments, and may prescribe terms necessary to secure the benefit of the stayed judgment for the party in whose favor it was entered.

Rule 62.1. Indicative Ruling on a Motion for Relief That is Barred by a Pending Appeal

(a) RELIEF PENDING APPEAL. If a timely motion is made for relief that the court lacks authority to grant because of an appeal that has been docketed and is pending, the court may:

(1) defer considering the motion;

(2) deny the motion; or

(3) state either that it would grant the motion if the court of appeals remands for that purpose or that the motion raises a substantial issue.

(b) NOTICE TO THE COURT OF APPEALS. The movant must promptly notify the circuit clerk under Federal Rule of Appellate Procedure 12.1 if the district court states that it would grant the motion or that the motion raises a substantial issue.

(c) REMAND. The district court may decide the motion if the court of appeals remands for that purpose.

Rule 63. Judge's Inability to Proceed

If a judge conducting a hearing or trial is unable to proceed, any other judge may proceed upon certifying familiarity with the record and determining that the case may be completed without prejudice to the parties. In a hearing or a nonjury trial, the successor judge must, at a party's request, recall any witness whose testimony is material and disputed and who is available to testify again without undue burden. The successor judge may also recall any other witness.

Title VIII. Provisional and Final Remedies

Rule 64. Seizing a Person or Property

(a) REMEDIES UNDER STATE LAW—IN GENERAL. At the commencement of and throughout an action, every remedy is available that, under the law of the state where the court is located, provides for seizing a person or property to secure satisfaction of the potential judgment. But a federal statute governs to the extent it applies.

(b) SPECIFIC KINDS OF REMEDIES. The remedies available under this rule include the following— however designated and regardless of whether state procedure requires an independent action:
- arrest;
- attachment;
- garnishment;
- replevin;
- sequestration; and
- other corresponding or equivalent remedies.

Rule 65. Injunctions and Restraining Orders

(a) PRELIMINARY INJUNCTION.

(1) *Notice.* The court may issue a preliminary injunction only on notice to the adverse party.
(2) *Consolidating the Hearing with the Trial on the Merits.* Before or after beginning the hearing on a motion for a preliminary injunction, the court may advance the trial on the merits and consolidate it with the hearing. Even when consolidation is not ordered, evidence that is received on the motion and that would be admissible at trial becomes part of the trial record and need not be repeated at trial. But the court must preserve any party's right to a jury trial.

(b) TEMPORARY RESTRAINING ORDER.

(1) *Issuing Without Notice.* The court may issue a temporary restraining order without written or oral notice to the adverse party or its attorney only if:
(A) specific facts in an affidavit or a verified complaint clearly show that immediate and irreparable injury, loss, or damage will result to the movant before the adverse party can be heard in opposition; and
(B) the movant's attorney certifies in writing any efforts made to give notice and the reasons why it should not be required.
(2) *Contents; Expiration.* Every temporary restraining order issued without notice must state the date and hour it was issued; describe the injury and state why it is irreparable; state why the order was issued without notice; and be promptly filed in the clerk's office and entered in the record. The order expires at the time after entry—not to exceed 14 days—that the court sets, unless before that time the court, for good cause, extends it for a like period or the adverse party consents to a longer extension. The reasons for an extension must be entered in the record.
(3) *Expediting the Preliminary-Injunction Hearing.* If the order is issued without notice, the motion for a preliminary injunction must be set for hearing at the earliest possible time, taking

precedence over all other matters except hearings on older matters of the same character. At the hearing, the party who obtained the order must proceed with the motion; if the party does not, the court must dissolve the order.

(4) *Motion to Dissolve.* On 2 days' notice to the party who obtained the order without notice—or on shorter notice set by the court—the adverse party may appear and move to dissolve or modify the order. The court must then hear and decide the motion as promptly as justice requires.

(c) SECURITY. The court may issue a preliminary injunction or a temporary restraining order only if the movant gives security in an amount that the court considers proper to pay the costs and damages sustained by any party found to have been wrongfully enjoined or restrained. The United States, its officers, and its agencies are not required to give security.

(d) CONTENTS AND SCOPE OF EVERY INJUNCTION AND RESTRAINING ORDER.

(1) *Contents.* Every order granting an injunction and every restraining order must:
    (A) state the reasons why it issued;
    (B) state its terms specifically; and
    (C) describe in reasonable detail—and not by referring to the complaint or other document—the act or acts restrained or required.
(2) *Persons Bound.* The order binds only the following who receive actual notice of it by personal service or otherwise:
    (A) the parties;
    (B) the parties' officers, agents, servants, employees, and attorneys; and
    (C) other persons who are in active concert or participation with anyone described in Rule 65(d)(2)(A) or (B).

(e) OTHER LAWS NOT MODIFIED. These rules do not modify the following:

(1) any federal statute relating to temporary restraining orders or preliminary injunctions in actions affecting employer and employee;
(2) 28 U.S.C. § 2361, which relates to preliminary injunctions in actions of interpleader or in the nature of interpleader; or
(3) 28 U.S.C. § 2284, which relates to actions that must be heard and decided by a three-judge district court.

(f) COPYRIGHT IMPOUNDMENT. This rule applies to copyright-impoundment proceedings.

Rule 65.1. Proceedings Against a Surety

Whenever these rules (including the Supplemental Rules for Admiralty or Maritime Claims and Asset Forfeiture Actions) require or allow a party to give security, and security is given through a bond or other undertaking with one or more sureties, each surety submits to the court's jurisdiction and irrevocably appoints the court clerk as its agent for receiving service of any papers that affect its liability on the bond or undertaking. The surety's liability may be enforced on motion without an independent action. The motion and any notice that the court orders may be served on the court clerk, who must promptly mail a copy of each to every surety whose address is known.

Rule 66. Receivers

These rules govern an action in which the appointment of a receiver is sought or a receiver sues or is sued. But the practice in administering an estate by a receiver or a similar court-appointed officer must accord with the historical practice in federal courts or with a local rule. An action in which a receiver has been appointed may be dismissed only by court order.

Rule 67. Deposit into Court

(a) DEPOSITING PROPERTY. If any part of the relief sought is a money judgment or the disposition of a sum of money or some other deliverable thing, a party—on notice to every other party and by leave of court—may deposit with the court all or part of the money or thing, whether or not that party claims any of it. The depositing party must deliver to the clerk a copy of the order permitting deposit.

(b) INVESTING AND WITHDRAWING FUNDS. Money paid into court under this rule must be deposited and withdrawn in accordance with 28 U.S.C. §§ 2041 and 2042 and any like statute. The money must be deposited in an interest-bearing account or invested in a court-approved, interest-bearing instrument.

Rule 68. Offer of Judgment

(a) MAKING AN OFFER; JUDGMENT ON AN ACCEPTED OFFER. At least 14 days before the date set for trial, a party defending against a claim may serve on an opposing party an offer to allow judgment on specified terms, with the costs then accrued. If, within 14 days after being served, the opposing party serves written notice accepting the offer, either party may then file the offer and notice of acceptance, plus proof of service. The clerk must then enter judgment.

(b) UNACCEPTED OFFER. An unaccepted offer is considered withdrawn, but it does not preclude a later offer. Evidence of an unaccepted offer is not admissible except in a proceeding to determine costs.

(c) OFFER AFTER LIABILITY IS DETERMINED. When one party's liability to another has been determined but the extent of liability remains to be determined by further proceedings, the party held liable may make an offer of judgment. It must be served within a reasonable time—but at least 14 days—before the date set for a hearing to determine the extent of liability.

(d) PAYING COSTS AFTER AN UNACCEPTED OFFER. If the judgment that the offeree finally obtains is not more favorable than the unaccepted offer, the offeree must pay the costs incurred after the offer was made.

Rule 69. Execution

(a) IN GENERAL.

(1) *Money Judgment; Applicable Procedure.* A money judgment is enforced by a writ of execution, unless the court directs otherwise. The procedure on execution—and in proceedings supplementary to and in aid of judgment or execution—must accord with the procedure of the state where the court is located, but a federal statute governs to the extent it applies.

(2) *Obtaining Discovery.* In aid of the judgment or execution, the judgment creditor or a successor in interest whose interest appears of record may obtain discovery from any person—

including the judgment debtor—as provided in these rules or by the procedure of the state where the court is located.

(b) AGAINST CERTAIN PUBLIC OFFICERS. When a judgment has been entered against a revenue officer in the circumstances stated in 28 U.S.C. § 2006, or against an officer of Congress in the circumstances stated in 2 U.S.C. § 118, the judgment must be satisfied as those statutes provide.

Rule 70. Enforcing a Judgment for a Specific Act

(a) PARTY'S FAILURE TO ACT; ORDERING ANOTHER TO ACT. If a judgment requires a party to convey land, to deliver a deed or other document, or to perform any other specific act and the party fails to comply within the time specified, the court may order the act to be done—at the disobedient party's expense—by another person appointed by the court. When done, the act has the same effect as if done by the party.

(b) VESTING TITLE. If the real or personal property is within the district, the court—instead of ordering a conveyance—may enter a judgment divesting any party's title and vesting it in others. That judgment has the effect of a legally executed conveyance.

(c) OBTAINING A WRIT OF ATTACHMENT OR SEQUESTRATION. On application by a party entitled to performance of an act, the clerk must issue a writ of attachment or sequestration against the disobedient party's property to compel obedience.

(d) OBTAINING A WRIT OF EXECUTION OR ASSISTANCE. On application by a party who obtains a judgment or order for possession, the clerk must issue a writ of execution or assistance.

(e) HOLDING IN CONTEMPT. The court may also hold the disobedient party in contempt.

Rule 71. Enforcing Relief For or Against a Nonparty

When an order grants relief for a nonparty or may be enforced against a nonparty, the procedure for enforcing the order is the same as for a party.

Title IX. Special Proceedings

Rule 71.1. Condemning Real or Personal Property

(a) APPLICABILITY OF OTHER RULES. These rules govern proceedings to condemn real and personal property by eminent domain, except as this rule provides otherwise.

(b) JOINDER OF PROPERTIES. The plaintiff may join separate pieces of property in a single action, no matter whether they are owned by the same persons or sought for the same use.

(c) COMPLAINT.

> (1) *Caption.* The complaint must contain a caption as provided in Rule 10(a). The plaintiff must, however, name as defendants both the property—designated generally by kind, quantity, and location—and at least one owner of some part of or interest in the property.
> (2) *Contents.* The complaint must contain a short and plain statement of the following:

(A) the authority for the taking;

(B) the uses for which the property is to be taken;

(C) a description sufficient to identify the property;

(D) the interests to be acquired; and

(E) for each piece of property, a designation of each defendant who has been joined as an owner or owner of an interest in it.

(3) *Parties.* When the action commences, the plaintiff need join as defendants only those persons who have or claim an interest in the property and whose names are then known. But before any hearing on compensation, the plaintiff must add as defendants all those persons who have or claim an interest and whose names have become known or can be found by a reasonably diligent search of the records, considering both the property's character and value and the interests to be acquired. All others may be made defendants under the designation ''Unknown Owners.''

(4) *Procedure.* Notice must be served on all defendants as provided in Rule 71.1(d), whether they were named as defendants when the action commenced or were added later. A defendant may answer as provided in Rule 71.1(e). The court, meanwhile, may order any distribution of a deposit that the facts warrant.

(5) *Filing; Additional Copies.* In addition to filing the complaint, the plaintiff must give the clerk at least one copy for the defendants' use and additional copies at the request of the clerk or a defendant.

(d) PROCESS.

(1) *Delivering Notice to the Clerk.* On filing a complaint, the plaintiff must promptly deliver to the clerk joint or several notices directed to the named defendants. When adding defendants, the plaintiff must deliver to the clerk additional notices directed to the new defendants.

(2) *Contents of the Notice.*

(A) *Main Contents.* Each notice must name the court, the title of the action, and the defendant to whom it is directed. It must describe the property sufficiently to identify it, but need not describe any property other than that to be taken from the named defendant. The notice must also state:

(i) that the action is to condemn property;

(ii) the interest to be taken;

(iii) the authority for the taking;

(iv) the uses for which the property is to be taken;

(v) that the defendant may serve an answer on the plaintiff's attorney within 21 days after being served with the notice;

(vi) that the failure to so serve an answer constitutes consent to the taking and to the court's authority to proceed with the action and fix the compensation; and

(vii) that a defendant who does not serve an answer may file a notice of appearance.

(B) *Conclusion.* The notice must conclude with the name, telephone number, and e-mail address of the plaintiff's attorney and an address within the district in which the action is brought where the attorney may be served.

(3) *Serving the Notice.*

(A) *Personal Service.* When a defendant whose address is known resides within the United States or a territory subject to the administrative or judicial jurisdiction of the United States, personal service of the notice (without a copy of the complaint) must be made in accordance with Rule 4.

(B) *Service by Publication.*

(i) A defendant may be served by publication only when the plaintiff's attorney files a certificate stating that the attorney believes the defendant cannot be personally served, because after diligent inquiry within the state where the complaint is filed, the defendant's place of residence is still unknown or, if known, that it is beyond the territorial limits of personal service. Service is then made by publishing the notice—once a week for at least 3 successive weeks—in a newspaper published in the county where the property is located or, if there is no such newspaper, in a newspaper with general circulation where the property is located. Before the last publication, a copy of the notice must also be mailed to every defendant who cannot be personally served but whose place of residence is then known. Unknown owners may be served by publication in the same manner by a notice addressed to "Unknown Owners."

(ii) Service by publication is complete on the date of the last publication. The plaintiff's attorney must prove publication and mailing by a certificate, attach a printed copy of the published notice, and mark on the copy the newspaper's name and the dates of publication.

(4) *Effect of Delivery and Service.* Delivering the notice to the clerk and serving it have the same effect as serving a summons under Rule 4.

(5) *Amending the Notice; Proof of Service and Amending the Proof.* Rule 4(a)(2) governs amending the notice. Rule 4(*l*) governs proof of service and amending it.

(e) APPEARANCE OR ANSWER.

(1) *Notice of Appearance.* A defendant that has no objection or defense to the taking of its property may serve a notice of appearance designating the property in which it claims an interest. The defendant must then be given notice of all later proceedings affecting the defendant.

(2) *Answer.* A defendant that has an objection or defense to the taking must serve an answer within 21 days after being served with the notice. The answer must:

(A) identify the property in which the defendant claims an interest;

(B) state the nature and extent of the interest; and

(C) state all the defendant's objections and defenses to the taking.

(3) *Waiver of Other Objections and Defenses; Evidence on Compensation.* A defendant waives all objections and defenses not stated in its answer. No other pleading or motion asserting an additional objection or defense is allowed. But at the trial on compensation, a defendant— whether or not it has previously appeared or answered—may present evidence on the amount of compensation to be paid and may share in the award.

(f) AMENDING PLEADINGS. Without leave of court, the plaintiff may—as often as it wants—amend the complaint at any time before the trial on compensation. But no amendment may be made if it would result in a dismissal inconsistent with Rule 71.1(i)(1) or (2). The plaintiff need not serve a copy of an amendment, but must serve notice of the filing, as provided in Rule 5(b), on every affected party who has appeared and, as provided in Rule 71.1(d), on every affected party who has not appeared. In addition, the plaintiff must give the clerk at least one copy of each amendment for the defendants' use, and additional copies at the request of the clerk or a defendant. A defendant may appear or answer in the time and manner and with the same effect as provided in Rule 71.1(e).

(g) SUBSTITUTING PARTIES. If a defendant dies, becomes incompetent, or transfers an interest after being joined, the court may, on motion and notice of hearing, order that the proper party be substituted. Service of the motion and notice on a nonparty must be made as provided in Rule 71.1(d)(3).

(h) TRIAL OF THE ISSUES.

(1) *Issues Other Than Compensation; Compensation.* In an action involving eminent domain under federal law, the court tries all issues, including compensation, except when compensation must be determined:

(A) by any tribunal specially constituted by a federal statute to determine compensation; or

(B) if there is no such tribunal, by a jury when a party demands one within the time to answer or within any additional time the court sets, unless the court appoints a commission.

(2) *Appointing a Commission; Commission's Powers and Report.*

(A) *Reasons for Appointing.* If a party has demanded a jury, the court may instead appoint a three-person commission to determine compensation because of the character, location, or quantity of the property to be condemned or for other just reasons.

(B) *Alternate Commissioners.* The court may appoint up to two additional persons to serve as alternate commissioners to hear the case and replace commissioners who, before a decision is filed, the court finds unable or disqualified to perform their duties. Once the commission renders its final decision, the court must discharge any alternate who has not replaced a commissioner.

(C) *Examining the Prospective Commissioners.* Before making its appointments, the court must advise the parties of the identity and qualifications of each prospective commissioner and alternate, and may permit the parties to examine them. The parties may not suggest appointees, but for good cause may object to a prospective commissioner or alternate.

(D) *Commission's Powers and Report.* A commission has the powers of a master under Rule 53(c). Its action and report are determined by a majority. Rule 53(d), (e), and (f) apply to its action and report.

(i) DISMISSAL OF THE ACTION OR A DEFENDANT.

(1) *Dismissing the Action.*

(A) *By the Plaintiff.* If no compensation hearing on a piece of property has begun, and if the plaintiff has not acquired title or a lesser interest or taken possession, the plaintiff may, without a court order, dismiss the action as to that property by filing a notice of dismissal briefly describing the property.

(B) *By Stipulation.* Before a judgment is entered vesting the plaintiff with title or a lesser interest in or possession of property, the plaintiff and affected defendants may, without a court order, dismiss the action in whole or in part by filing a stipulation of dismissal. And if the parties so stipulate, the court may vacate a judgment already entered.

(C) *By Court Order.* At any time before compensation has been determined and paid, the court may, after a motion and hearing, dismiss the action as to a piece of property. But if the plaintiff has already taken title, a lesser interest, or possession as to any part of it, the court must award compensation for the title, lesser interest, or possession taken.

(2) *Dismissing a Defendant.* The court may at any time dismiss a defendant who was unnecessarily or improperly joined.

(3) *Effect.* A dismissal is without prejudice unless otherwise stated in the notice, stipulation, or court order.

(j) DEPOSIT AND ITS DISTRIBUTION.

(1) *Deposit.* The plaintiff must deposit with the court any money required by law as a condition to the exercise of eminent domain and may make a deposit when allowed by statute.

(2) *Distribution; Adjusting Distribution.* After a deposit, the court and attorneys must expedite the proceedings so as to distribute the deposit and to determine and pay compensation. If the compensation finally awarded to a defendant exceeds the amount distributed to that defendant, the court must enter judgment against the plaintiff for the deficiency. If the compensation awarded to a defendant is less than the amount distributed to that defendant, the court must enter judgment against that defendant for the overpayment.

(k) CONDEMNATION UNDER A STATE'S POWER OF EMINENT DOMAIN. This rule governs an action involving eminent domain under state law. But if state law provides for trying an issue by jury—or for trying the issue of compensation by jury or commission or both—that law governs.

(*l*) COSTS. Costs are not subject to Rule 54(d).

Rule 72. Magistrate Judges: Pretrial Order

(a) NONDISPOSITIVE MATTERS. When a pretrial matter not dispositive of a party's claim or defense is referred to a magistrate judge to hear and decide, the magistrate judge must promptly conduct the required proceedings and, when appropriate, issue a written order stating the decision. A party may serve and file objections to the order within 14 days after being served with a copy. A party may not assign as error a defect in the order not timely objected to. The district judge in the case must consider timely objections and modify or set aside any part of the order that is clearly erroneous or is contrary to law.

(b) DISPOSITIVE MOTIONS AND PRISONER PETITIONS.

(1) *Findings and Recommendations.* A magistrate judge must promptly conduct the required proceedings when assigned, without the parties' consent, to hear a pretrial matter dispositive of a claim or defense or a prisoner petition challenging the conditions of confinement. A record must be made of all evidentiary proceedings and may, at the magistrate judge's discretion, be made of any other proceedings. The magistrate judge must enter a recommended disposition, including, if appropriate, proposed findings of fact. The clerk must promptly mail a copy to each party.

(2) *Objections.* Within 14 days after being served with a copy of the recommended disposition, a party may serve and file specific written objections to the proposed findings and recommendations. A party may respond to another party's objections within 14 days after being served with a copy. Unless the district judge orders otherwise, the objecting party must promptly arrange for transcribing the record, or whatever portions of it the parties agree to or the magistrate judge considers sufficient.

(3) *Resolving Objections.* The district judge must determine de novo any part of the magistrate judge's disposition that has been properly objected to. The district judge may accept, reject, or modify the recommended disposition; receive further evidence; or return the matter to the magistrate judge with instructions.

Rule 73. Magistrate Judges: Trial by Consent; Appeal

(a) TRIAL BY CONSENT. When authorized under 28 U.S.C. § 636(c), a magistrate judge may, if all parties consent, conduct a civil action or proceeding, including a jury or nonjury trial. A record must be made in accordance with 28 U.S.C. § 636(c)(5).

(b) CONSENT PROCEDURE.

(1) *In General.* When a magistrate judge has been designated to conduct civil actions or proceedings, the clerk must give the parties written notice of their opportunity to consent under 28 U.S.C. § 636(c). To signify their consent, the parties must jointly or separately file a statement consenting to the referral. A district judge or magistrate judge may be informed of a party's response to the clerk's notice only if all parties have consented to the referral.

(2) *Reminding the Parties About Consenting.* A district judge, magistrate judge, or other court official may remind the parties of the magistrate judge's availability, but must also advise them that they are free to withhold consent without adverse substantive consequences.

(3) *Vacating a Referral.* On its own for good cause—or when a party shows extraordinary circumstances—the district judge may vacate a referral to a magistrate judge under this rule.

(c) APPEALING A JUDGMENT. In accordance with 28 U.S.C. § 636(c)(3), an appeal from a judgment entered at a magistrate judge's direction may be taken to the court of appeals as would any other appeal from a district-court judgment.

Rules 74-76. [Abrogated]

Title X. District Courts and Clerks; Conducting Business; Issuing Orders

Rule 77. Conducting Business; Clerk's Authority; Notice of an Order or Judgment

(a) WHEN COURT IS OPEN. Every district court is considered always open for filing any paper, issuing and returning process, making a motion, or entering an order.

(b) PLACE FOR TRIAL AND OTHER PROCEEDINGS. Every trial on the merits must be conducted in open court and, so far as convenient, in a regular courtroom. Any other act or proceeding may be done or conducted by a judge in chambers, without the attendance of the clerk or other court official, and anywhere inside or outside the district. But no hearing—other than one ex parte—may be conducted outside the district unless all the affected parties consent.

(c) CLERK'S OFFICE HOURS; CLERK'S ORDERS.

(1) *Hours.* The clerk's office—with a clerk or deputy on duty—must be open during business hours every day except Saturdays, Sundays, and legal holidays. But a court may, by local rule or order, require that the office be open for specified hours on Saturday or a particular legal holiday other than one listed in Rule 6(a)(4)(A).

(2) *Orders.* Subject to the court's power to suspend, alter, or rescind the clerk's action for good cause, the clerk may:
    (A) issue process;
    (B) enter a default;
    (C) enter a default judgment under Rule 55(b)(1); and
    (D) act on any other matter that does not require the court's action.

(d) SERVING NOTICE OF AN ORDER OR JUDGMENT.

(1) *Service.* Immediately after entering an order or judgment, the clerk must serve notice of the entry, as provided in Rule 5(b), on each party who is not in default for failing to appear. The clerk must record the service on the docket. A party also may serve notice of the entry as provided in Rule 5(b).

(2) *Time to Appeal Not Affected by Lack of Notice.* Lack of notice of the entry does not affect the time for appeal or relieve—or authorize the court to relieve—a party for failing to appeal within the time allowed, except as allowed by Federal Rule of Appellate Procedure (4)(a).

Rule 78. Hearing Motions; Submission on Briefs

(a) PROVIDING A REGULAR SCHEDULE FOR ORAL HEARINGS. A court may establish regular times and places for oral hearings on motions.

(b) PROVIDING FOR SUBMISSION ON BRIEFS. By rule or order, the court may provide for submitting and determining motions on briefs, without oral hearings.

Rule 79. Records Kept by the Clerk

(a) CIVIL DOCKET.

(1) *In General.* The clerk must keep a record known as the "civil docket" in the form and manner prescribed by the Director of the Administrative Office of the United States Courts with the approval of the Judicial Conference of the United States. The clerk must enter each civil action in the docket. Actions must be assigned consecutive file numbers, which must be noted in the docket where the first entry of the action is made.

(2) *Items to be Entered.* The following items must be marked with the file number and entered chronologically in the docket:

    (A) papers filed with the clerk;

    (B) process issued, and proofs of service or other returns showing execution; and (C) appearances, orders, verdicts, and judgments.

(3) *Contents of Entries; Jury Trial Demanded.* Each entry must briefly show the nature of the paper filed or writ issued, the substance of each proof of service or other return, and the substance and date of entry of each order and judgment. When a jury trial has been properly demanded or ordered, the clerk must enter the word "jury" in the docket.

(b) CIVIL JUDGMENTS AND ORDERS. The clerk must keep a copy of every final judgment and appealable order; of every order affecting title to or a lien on real or personal property; and of any other order that the court directs to be kept. The clerk must keep these in the form and manner prescribed by the Director of the Administrative Office of the United States Courts with the approval of the Judicial Conference of the United States.

(c) INDEXES; CALENDARS. Under the court's direction, the clerk must:

(1) keep indexes of the docket and of the judgments and orders described in Rule 79(b); and

(2) prepare calendars of all actions ready for trial, distinguishing jury trials from nonjury trials.

(d) OTHER RECORDS. The clerk must keep any other records required by the Director of the Administrative Office of the United States Courts with the approval of the Judicial Conference of the United States.

Rule 80. Stenographic Transcript as Evidence

If stenographically reported testimony at a hearing or trial is admissible in evidence at a later trial, the testimony may be proved by a transcript certified by the person who reported it.

Title XI. General Provisions

Rule 81. Applicability of the Rules in General; Removed Actions

(a) APPLICABILITY TO PARTICULAR PROCEEDINGS.

(1) *Prize Proceedings.* These rules do not apply to prize proceedings in admiralty governed by 10 U.S.C. §§ 7651–7681.

(2) *Bankruptcy.* These rules apply to bankruptcy proceedings to the extent provided by the Federal Rules of Bankruptcy Procedure.

(3) *Citizenship.* These rules apply to proceedings for admission to citizenship to the extent that the practice in those proceedings is not specified in federal statutes and has previously conformed to the practice in civil actions. The provisions of 8 U.S.C. § 1451 for service by publication and for answer apply in proceedings to cancel citizenship certificates.

(4) *Special Writs.* These rules apply to proceedings for habeas corpus and for quo warranto to the extent that the practice in those proceedings:

(A) is not specified in a federal statute, the Rules Governing Section 2254 Cases, or the Rules Governing Section 2255 Cases; and

(B) has previously conformed to the practice in civil actions.

(5) *Proceedings Involving a Subpoena.* These rules apply to proceedings to compel testimony or the production of documents through a subpoena issued by a United States officer or agency under a federal statute, except as otherwise provided by statute, by local rule, or by court order in the proceedings.

(6) *Other Proceedings.* These rules, to the extent applicable, govern proceedings under the following laws, except as these laws provide other procedures:

(A) 7 U.S.C. §§ 292, 499g(c), for reviewing an order of the Secretary of Agriculture;

(B) 9 U.S.C., relating to arbitration;

(C) 15 U.S.C. § 522, for reviewing an order of the Secretary of the Interior;

(D) 15 U.S.C. § 715d(c), for reviewing an order denying a certificate of clearance;

(E) 29 U.S.C. §§ 159, 160, for enforcing an order of the National Labor Relations Board;

(F) 33 U.S.C. §§ 918, 921, for enforcing or reviewing a compensation order under the Longshore and Harbor Workers' Compensation Act; and

(G) 45 U.S.C. § 159, for reviewing an arbitration award in a railway-labor dispute.

(b) SCIRE FACIAS AND MANDAMUS. The writs of scire facias and mandamus are abolished. Relief previously available through them may be obtained by appropriate action or motion under these rules.

(c) REMOVED ACTIONS.

> (1) *Applicability.* These rules apply to a civil action after it is removed from a state court.
> (2) *Further Pleading.* After removal, repleading is unnecessary unless the court orders it. A defendant who did not answer before removal must answer or present other defenses or objections under these rules within the longest of these periods:
>> (A) 21 days after receiving—through service or otherwise—a copy of the initial pleading stating the claim for relief;
>> (B) 21 days after being served with the summons for an initial pleading on file at the time of service; or
>> (C) 7 days after the notice of removal is filed.
> (3) *Demand for a Jury Trial.*
>> (A) *As Affected by State Law.* A party who, before removal, expressly demanded a jury trial in accordance with state law need not renew the demand after removal. If the state law did not require an express demand for a jury trial, a party need not make one after removal unless the court orders the parties to do so within a specified time. The court must so order at a party's request and may so order on its own. A party who fails to make a demand when so ordered waives a jury trial.
>> (B) *Under Rule 38.* If all necessary pleadings have been served at the time of removal, a party entitled to a jury trial under Rule 38 must be given one if the party serves a demand within 14 days after:
>>> (i) it files a notice of removal; or
>>> (ii) it is served with a notice of removal filed by another party.

(d) LAW APPLICABLE.

> (1) *"State Law" Defined.* When these rules refer to state law, the term "law" includes the state's statutes and the state's judicial decisions.
> (2) *"State" Defined.* The term "state" includes, where appropriate, the District of Columbia and any United States commonwealth or territory.
> (3) *"Federal Statute" Defined in the District of Columbia.* In the United States District Court for the District of Columbia, the term "federal statute" includes any Act of Congress that applies locally to the District.

Rule 82. Jurisdiction and Venue Unaffected

These rules do not extend or limit the jurisdiction of the district courts or the venue of actions in those courts. An admiralty or maritime claim under Rule 9(h) is not a civil action for purposes of 28 U.S.C. §§ 1391–1392.

Rule 83. Rules by District Courts; Judge's Directives

(a) LOCAL RULES.

> (1) *In General.* After giving public notice and an opportunity for comment, a district court, acting by a majority of its district judges, may adopt and amend rules governing its practice. A local rule must be consistent with—but not duplicate—federal statutes and rules adopted under 28 U.S.C. §§ 2072 and 2075, and must conform to any uniform numbering system prescribed by the Judicial Conference of the United States. A local rule takes effect on the date specified by the district court and remains in effect unless amended by the court or abrogated by the judicial council of

the circuit. Copies of rules and amendments must, on their adoption, be furnished to the judicial council and the Administrative Office of the United States Courts and be made available to the public.

(2) *Requirement of Form.* A local rule imposing a requirement of form must not be enforced in a way that causes a party to lose any right because of a nonwillful failure to comply.

(b) PROCEDURE WHEN THERE IS NO CONTROLLING LAW. A judge may regulate practice in any manner consistent with federal law, rules adopted under 28 U.S.C. §§ 2072 and 2075, and the district's local rules. No sanction or other disadvantage may be imposed for noncompliance with any requirement not in federal law, federal rules, or the local rules unless the alleged violator has been furnished in the particular case with actual notice of the requirement.

Rule 84. Forms

The forms in the Appendix suffice under these rules and illustrate the simplicity and brevity that these rules contemplate.

Rule 85. Title

These rules may be cited as the Federal Rules of Civil Procedure.

Rule 86. Effective Dates

(a) IN GENERAL. These rules and any amendments take effect at the time specified by the Supreme Court, subject to 28 U.S.C. § 2074. They govern:

> (1) proceedings in an action commenced after their effective date; and
> (2) proceedings after that date in an action then pending unless:
> > (A) the Supreme Court specifies otherwise; or
> > (B) the court determines that applying them in a particular action would be infeasible or work an injustice.

(b) DECEMBER 1, 2007 AMENDMENTS. If any provision in Rules 1–5.1, 6–73, or 77–86 conflicts with another law, priority in time for the purpose of 28 U.S.C. § 2072(b) is not affected by the amendments taking effect on December 1, 2007.

XIII. INDEX OF CIVIL PROCEDURE LOGIC MAPS

XIII. INDEX OF CIVIL PROCEDURE LOGIC MAPS